WINNIPEG
JAN 29 2019
PUBLIC LIBRARY

D0849819

THE OXFORD ILLUSTRATED HISTORY OF THE
HOLY LAND

The 15 historians who contributed to *The Oxford Illustrated History of the Holy Land* are all distinguished authorities in their field. They are:

JOHN J. COLLINS, Yale Divinity School

AVRAHAM FAUST, Bar-Ilan University

ROBERT FISK, writer and journalist

LESTER L. GRABBE, University of Hull

RICHARD S. HESS, Denver Seminary

CAROLE HILLENBRAND, University of Edinburgh

ROBERT G. HOYLAND, New York University

KONSTANTIN KLEIN, University of Bamberg

ANDRÉ LEMAIRE, École Pratique des Hautes Études

MILKA LEVY-RUBIN, Hebrew University of Jerusalem

NIMROD LUZ, Western Galilee College

DENYS PRINGLE, Cardiff University

ADAM SILVERSTEIN, Bar-Ilan University

PETER WALKER, Trinity School for Ministry

H. G. M. WILLIAMSON, University of Oxford

THE OXFORD ILLUSTRATED HISTORY OF THE
HOLY LAND

Edited by

ROBERT G. HOYLAND
H. G. M. WILLIAMSON

UNIVERSITY PRESS

OXFORD
UNIVERSITY PRESS

Great Clarendon Street, Oxford, OX2 6DP,
United Kingdom

Oxford University Press is a department of the University of Oxford.
It furthers the University's objective of excellence in research, scholarship,
and education by publishing worldwide. Oxford is a registered trade mark of
Oxford University Press in the UK and in certain other countries

First Edition published in 2018
Impression: 1

Published in the United States of America by Oxford University Press
198 Madison Avenue, New York, NY 10016, United States of America

British Library Cataloguing in Publication Data
Data available

Library of Congress Control Number: 2017962196

ISBN 978–0–19–872439–1

Printed in Italy by
L.E.G.O. S.p.A.—Lavis TN

CONTENTS

LIST OF MAPS

Introduction

In an aide-memoire following the First World War, the British Prime Minister David Lloyd George wrote to his French opposite number Georges Clémenceau that Palestine was to be 'defined in accordance with its ancient boundaries of Dan to Beersheba'. Lloyd George had been steeped in the Bible from his childhood, so that it is understandable, if politically astonishing, that he should have allowed his instinctive memory to influence his approach to modern political realities.

Different names and geographical definitions bedevil the history of this part of the world and none can do justice to the sweep of what we have set out to describe in the present volume. Precisely for that reason we have deliberately chosen the title *Holy Land*, a familiar name which has never featured on any map worth its salt. It serves to indicate that our intention here is far from political—and that is one good reason why we have called a halt in our historical survey at just the point where Lloyd George was clarifying his thoughts on the post-war settlement. But just as we have stopped short of the modern era, so we have not included anything about the thousands of years of occupation which preceded the biblical period. The Carmel Caves, for instance, have yielded evidence of some of the earliest human occupation known worldwide, a testimony to the geographical centrality of the region as a link between Africa and Europe. Jericho has often been called the word's first city, and archaeology has revealed much about human occupation throughout the millennia since then.

The Holy Land, however, conjures up an approach to territory which is more cultural, and specifically religious, than political, however closely intertwined the two were until relatively recently. This modest strip of land saw the birth of two world religions, Judaism and Christianity, and was of central significance to a third from its earliest days, Islam. It is sobering to recall that Jerusalem has been taken by military force by adherents of each of these three religions; no other city anywhere is of such central religious importance to each. It was therefore inevitable that we should begin our history with Abraham, whom each religion reveres. It is worth reflecting that according to our texts he owned no property in this land apart from a tomb, however, and that he had only limited engagement with the resident population.

The expression 'Holy Land' itself occurs first, and then only once, in the Hebrew Bible, at Zechariah 2:12: 'The Lord will inherit Judah as his portion in the holy land, and will again choose Jerusalem'. These words were written quite late in the Old Testament/

Hebrew Bible period, after the return of the Judeans from their exile in Babylon from 538 BCE onwards. The area was no longer independent at this time but divided between several provinces in the mighty Persian Empire. Neither here nor elsewhere are precise geographical divisions supplied. We are used to referring to the Holy Land in the much earlier period as Canaan, but that too did not exist as a single entity; it comprised a number of minor independent city-states under the overarching hegemony of Egypt. Then came the Israelites, and we eventually have two kingdoms during the first half of the first millennium BCE—Israel in the northern part and Judah (including Jerusalem) in the south. But to the west, along part of the Mediterranean coast, there were the Philistines, so that even then the territory was not united. And in that period the nearest we come to the expression 'Holy Land' refers initially to an area outside the land of Israel altogether, namely God's 'holy abode' on Mount Sinai in Exodus 15:13, echoing the 'holy ground' where Moses encountered God in the burning bush at Exodus 3:5. From there we approach our more familiar usage when Psalm 78:54 reminds the worshippers in the Jerusalem temple that God 'brought them to his holy border, the mountain that his right hand had won'.

Still, this is thin pickings for what became so influential a name in later centuries. It occurs a few times in early apocryphal Jewish writings after the close of the Old Testament period and then more frequently in the later rabbinic sources. It is completely absent, however, from the foundation documents of the Christian faith in the New Testament, and it did not become common Christian parlance (as *Terra Sancta*) until the Middle Ages, no doubt reflecting the attitude of European Crusaders and pilgrims. Accordingly, its use for maps has tended to be restricted to those included in Bibles, where the name is used anachronistically and without proper regard for either ancient or modern political realities. Medieval Muslims took some interest in the term because it appears in the Qur'an, where Moses is recorded as instructing the Israelites to 'enter the holy land, which God has ordained for you', though scholars were at odds over the definition of this term. The legal scholar Muhammad al-Tabari (d. 923), for example, says he knows of four main possibilities: 'Mount Sinai and its environs', 'Jericho', 'al-Sham' (which corresponds roughly to our term 'The Levant'), and 'Palestine and part of Jordan'. Yet the term did not enjoy circulation outside academic circles; rather, attention was paid to specific cities and sites, especially Jerusalem (simply called al-Quds, 'holiness', or Bayt al-Maqdis, 'house of sanctity') and the Temple Mount.

It fits with this spasmodic witness from antiquity that the region is not carefully defined; in the biblical reference cited above it seems to be restricted to Judah, a tiny part of what we usually mean by the term. In subsequent centuries its implicit definition will have varied according to the prevailing political and administrative circumstances. As with the varying definitions of the extent of the land in the Hebrew Bible, so subsequently the various regions within the southern Levant may be included or excluded as appropriate. While a basic working definition could be the land between the Jordan river on the east and the Mediterranean on the west, and between the Sinai desert in the south and the Hermon range in the north, the territory to the east of the

Jordan was sometimes an integral part of the land as well, while at other times areas in the north or the west were effectively excluded. As editors we have deliberately allowed our contributors freedom to concentrate on the natural geographical and national borders that suit their period of study most appropriately (see Map 1). Equally, it should be added, attention to some regions quite apart from the Holy Land itself has sometimes been imperative in order to understand what was going on there (Babylon in the biblical period, Europe at the time of the Crusades, and Turkey during the Ottoman period, for instance); to exclude such material could not be justified.

Two special features mark this *Illustrated History* from some others and so deserve comment. First, in addition to the expected historical survey (which, incidentally, covers some 3000 years, so that it cannot always enter into great detail), we have included three chapters on themes which transcend specific periods of history but which, in their different ways, are important to each of the three major religions and which, furthermore, contribute to the notion of a Holy Land: pilgrimage, sacred space, and Scripture. These are huge topics, of course, and so can effectively only be introduced here, but without including them we should not be able to do justice to some of the major underlying motives and values which drove the significant political actors.

Second, it is likely that, for the early period at least, most readers' knowledge will derive from the Bible, and for many this remains an inspired source for religious belief and practice. Our greatly increased knowledge of the ancient world both from archaeological discoveries and from newly discovered texts of ancient Israel's neighbours shows that we have to tread carefully when assessing the Bible from a purely historical point of view. It is far from our intention to cause any offence or deliberately to challenge personal beliefs, so we have asked all our authors to write with consideration towards those for whom a strictly historical approach may be unfamiliar. The fact remains, however, that these ancient texts were not written according to the methods or standards of modern historians and their purpose was religious, moral, or didactic, using at the same time all the stylistic skills they could bring to their task. We do not believe that the results of modern historical research are in any way incompatible with the continuing use of the Bible as scripture. Nevertheless, it seems only right to warn readers in advance that the 'story' of ancient history may not always coincide with inherited preconceptions. Our hope is that all may nevertheless learn from, as well as enjoy, this summary of current understanding, and that through such understanding appreciation of what each of the faiths had to offer may be deepened without the hostile fragmentation which has characterized much of the history we trace here and which still, sadly, is prevalent in the modern world.

CHAPTER 1
The Birth of Israel

AVRAHAM FAUST

The beginning of Israel: the biblical narrative

THE well-known biblical story of Israel's birth and emergence is the story of a family, and how it became a people. Abraham left his home in Mesopotamia and emigrated to Canaan. This is where he lived with his wife, Sarah, and his children Isaac and Ishmael. His grandchild (Isaac's son)—Jacob—and his great-grandchildren went down to Egypt, as an extended family or a lineage (*hamulah*). They stayed there for a few generations, multiplied, were then enslaved, and eventually left in the epic story of the Exodus, led by Moses. After forty years of wandering in the Sinai desert, they finally entered Canaan under the leadership of Joshua, and conquered it. Joshua's campaign began with the conquest of Jericho, where the Israelites, through the help of a local harlot by the name of Rahab, conquered the city after encircling it for seven days, blowing rams' horns until the city walls miraculously crumbled. This was followed by the eventual conquest of the city of 'Ai, and Joshua's campaigns against coalitions of kings in the southern and northern parts of Canaan. Following the conquest, the land was divided between the various tribes, named after Jacob's descendants. Despite a few side-stories that interrupt its flow (like the story of Judah and Tamar in Genesis 38), the story is very clear, and the narrative flows quite smoothly.

Problems with the narrative

Still, the story is not completely uniform, and it includes some intriguing features. Thus, although Abraham continued to live for fifteen years after Jacob's birth, the story never mentions them meeting, and while Isaac, Abraham's son and Jacob's father, is mentioned in connection with both figures, Abraham and Jacob never interact. Another feature that raises some eyebrows lies in the apparent contradiction between the account of the conquest in the book of Joshua, and the description of the land that was not conquered (in both the books of Joshua and Judges). Thus, cities like Gezer, Megiddo, and Ta'anach, are explicitly mentioned as being conquered by Joshua (Josh. 12:12, 21), but also appear in the description of the remaining land that was not

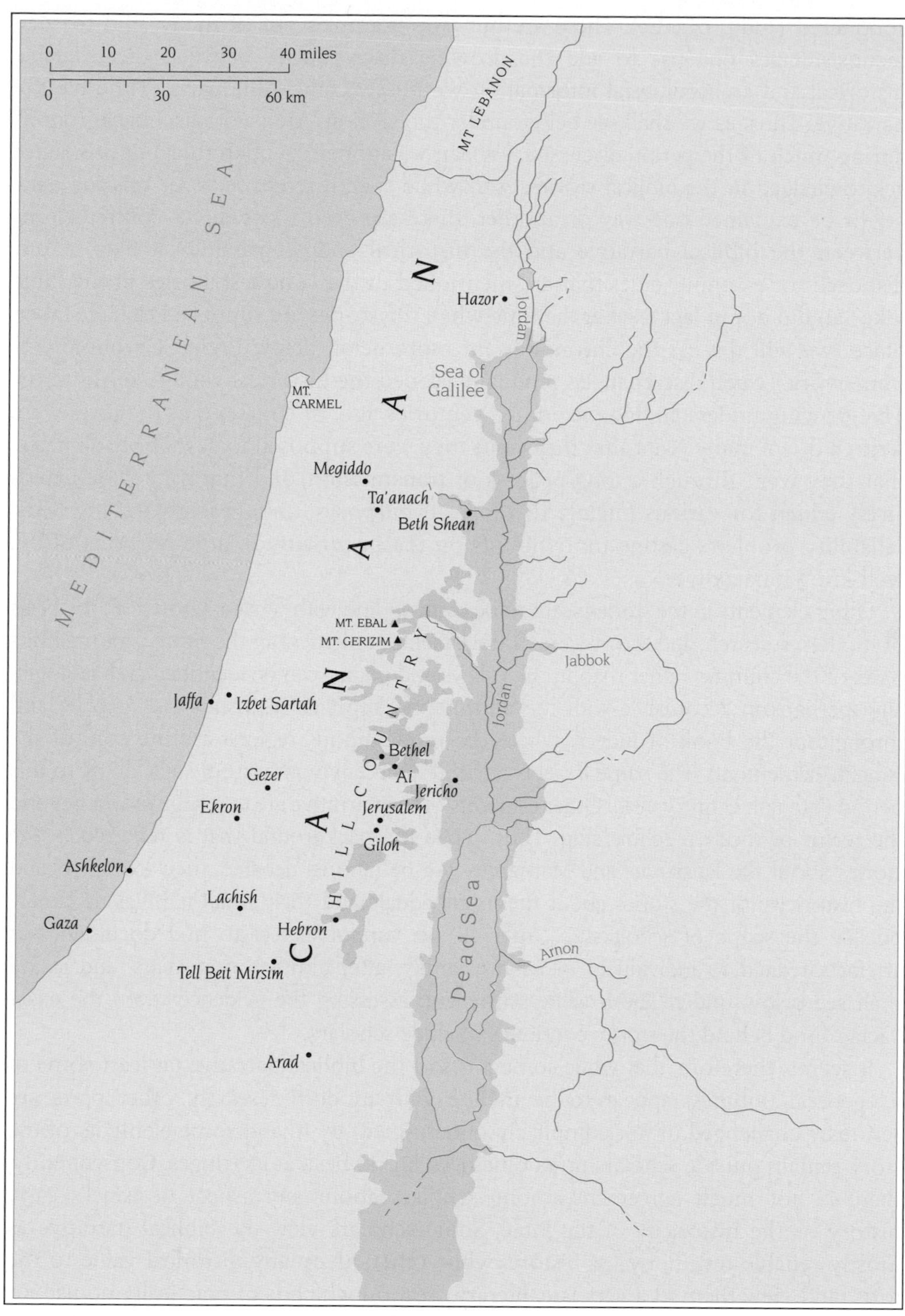

1. Map of the Holy Land in the earliest Israelite period conquered (Judg. 1:27, 29). These are but two examples out of many, and to such inconsistencies one has to add the growing discrepancies between the available historical and archaeological information we possess and some parts of the biblical narrative. Thus, as we shall see below under the section 'Archaeological background', during much of the period discussed, Canaan was under Egyptian rule, but this is not acknowledged in the biblical stories. And while such discrepancies, or missing data, might be explained one way or another, there are even more direct contradictions between the biblical narrative and the historical and archaeological data at our disposal; for example, cities that are mentioned in the conquest stories in the Bible (like 'Ai) did not in fact exist at the time when the stories are supposed to have taken place (we will discuss the chronology in more detail below under 'Chronological framework'). Such discrepancies gradually eroded the historical validity of the texts. The growing understanding (beginning centuries ago, of course) that the texts were written down many years after the events they were supposed to describe took place, that they went through a long process of transmission, and that they were extensively edited for various (mainly theological) purposes, only exacerbated the texts' reliability problem, casting more doubts on the historicity of large portions of the well-known narratives.

Other elements in the stories seem to be more in line with what is known on the basis of modern research, and the process of the Israelite settlement in the more mountainous parts of the country, rather than in the valleys and plains, can be identified archaeologically (perhaps in accordance with the information supplied in Joshua 13:1–7; 17:18; and throughout the book of Judges, where the mountainous regions are the core of the Israelite settlement). The name Israel is attested in an Egyptian victory stela, dated to this period (late 13th century BCE). Other elements of the narrative are to a large extent beyond the realm of modern scholarship. Thus, while the background that is reflected in the stories about the Patriarchs and Matriarchs can be (and is) debated, their existence, and the historicity of the stories about these individuals and their small families, is largely outside the scope of scholarship. After all, we cannot expect to find documents or artefacts related to individuals, or even a family, after almost 4000 years, and as we shall see below under 'The Israelite settlement: assessing the evidence', even the exact background behind the stories continues to elude scholars.

It seems, therefore, that while some parts of the biblical narrative (at least some of its general outlines) appear to be in line with modern research, other parts are seriously challenged (if not completely undermined) by it, and some elements of the story remain outside scholarship's domain, or are, at best, at its fringes. Consequently, there is not much agreement among scholars about any aspect of Israel's early history or the historicity of the Bible. Some scholars view the biblical narrative as mostly reliable testimony for history, while others deny any historical value to the texts, and view them as a very late, literary creation which is of practically no use for the study of the periods it purportedly describes. Most scholars are located somewhere along a broad spectrum between these two extreme views.

So how can we proceed and reconstruct the story of Israel's emergence in Canaan? It appears that a combination of the vast archaeological data we possess and the (more limited) historical information at our disposal, through a very careful and critical reference to the biblical narratives, can allow us to reconstruct Israel's development. While very little can be viewed as a consensus among scholars, this chapter aims to present a plausible middle ground between the two more extreme approaches. We will begin our journey by presenting the chronological framework, and since the biblical story, briefly summarized above, is probably familiar, we will proceed by describing the situation in Canaan in the second millennium BCE, in the periods which are usually known by the names Middle Bronze Age (roughly 2000/1900–1550 BCE), Late Bronze Age (roughly 1550–1200 BCE), and Iron Age I (roughly 1200–970 BCE). We will then summarize the debate regarding the Israelite settlement, and proceed to offer a broad reconstruction of the processes through which Israel emerged in Canaan: we will review the group's early developments, until the formation of the monarchy in the Iron Age II (in the 10th century, according to most scholars; see Chapter 2), and will suggest some possible insights into the way the biblical story—as we know it today—evolved.

Chronological framework

Attempting to synchronize the archaeological periods with the biblical events and stories is not always a straightforward enterprise. The dating of archaeological periods addressed in this chapter, while relying on synchronisms with adjacent regions, was developed largely independently of the biblical narratives, and stands on its own. This statement might seem somewhat surprising, given how much biblical archaeology developed in the shadow of the biblical texts. Still, although nobody would deny that biblical texts influenced the archaeological inquiry in the Holy Land, scholars were usually critical (at least, by the standards of their time) and did not simplistically accept the biblical framework. The dating of the Israelite settlement in Canaan is a good example of this. The Israelite settlement is dated by most scholars, from all schools of thought, including those who accepted the historicity of the conquest narratives in the book of Joshua, to (roughly) 1200–1000 BCE, and its beginning is dated to the late 13th century at the earliest. As we shall presently see, chronologies that are based on the Bible alone date the conquest to about 1400 BCE. This 200-year gap suggests that archaeologists followed the archaeological data, and rejected the biblical chronology when they found that the two did not match (although this does not negate the significance of the biblical chronology in influencing the general landscape of historical reconstruction). Nowadays, many of the dates are decided on the basis of scientific methods, mainly carbon 14 dating, which somewhat changes the traditional dating of some periods.

Biblical chronology, of course, relies first and foremost on the dates supplied in the Bible. One can create a chronological sequence that incorporates the period of the Patriarchs, and even the descent to Egypt and the slavery there, and a biblical chronology of the period of the monarchy in Israel and Judah can also clearly be compiled. The first part—that of the Patriarchs and the slavery in Egypt—is of course much more problematic and relies on a few sketchy and sometimes contradictory pieces of information, while the chronology of the period of the monarchy is more reliable. The most problematic feature, however, is the attempt to connect the two parts—the period of the Patriarchs and the sojourn in Egypt on the one hand and that of the monarchy on the other—something which relies on just one verse. 1 Kings 6:1 states that the construction of the Temple by Solomon was completed 480 years after the Exodus. Since the construction of the Temple was dated by many to around 960 BCE (though it might well have been somewhat later), then the Exodus, which ended the period of slavery in Egypt, should have occurred in about 1440 BCE, and the conquest of Canaan (after forty years in the desert) at about 1400 BCE. And the Patriarchs lived a few hundred years earlier (the exact time of the Patriarchs depends on which biblical verses one uses to create the chronology).

The biblical chronology, however, is not only sketchy, but even the available data are problematic on a number of counts. First of all, many of the numbers that are mentioned in the texts seem typological. Forty years, for example, is used quite often, and seems to designate a lengthy period of time—perhaps a generation—rather than an exact duration of time. Additionally, did the Patriarchs (and other biblical figures) really live for so many years—175 years for Abraham, for example? Or are the numbers exaggerated? Even the 480 years that supposedly separated the Exodus from the completion of the temple in Jerusalem—the only figure that connects the more reliable dates of the later monarchy with those of Israel's prehistory—seems typological, and a number of scholars have pointed out that it might have been a result of a schematized counting of twelve generations (of forty years each). Thus, a more realistic figure for twelve generations would be 240–300 years, and would date the Exodus, and by extension the settlement in Canaan, to the 13th, even the late 13th century (we shall return to this issue below under 'Israel's emergence').

The problematic nature of the biblical chronology is exemplified by the debate over the date of the patriarchal narratives. Even scholars who consider the stories to reflect a specific historical background vary greatly in dating them, and the dates supplied cover approximately a millennium. This great variation is partly the result of some scholars not accepting the biblical sequence of events as such. Still, many of those who accept the biblical sequence of events as broadly historical simply use its very unclear nature to support the period in which they find more cultural and social parallels to the background which is reflected in the stories. Most of the latter, however, place them somewhere between 2000–1500 BCE.

When discussing the Exodus and the settlement, the situation is somewhat clearer. As noted, a literal reading of I Kings 6:1 would place the Exodus in the 15th century BCE, and the conquest of Canaan at the beginning of the 14th, but we have seen that a more critical reading of the verse will direct us to the 13th century BCE, and this seems to be more in line with the external evidence at our disposal (see the following section).

We will now begin our archaeological survey, which supplies the background for Israel's emergence, at the beginning of the 2nd millennium BCE—in the Middle Bronze Age.

Archaeological background

During the Middle Bronze Age (roughly 2000/1900–1550 BCE) Canaan experienced intensive urbanization, especially in the low-lying parts of the country, and to a more limited extent also in the highlands. Many cities were surrounded by massive earthworks, which gave the mounds their present form and to a large extent even created the Levantine landscape of today, which is dotted by mounds. The political structure of the era is not completely clear, but it is likely that the country was divided between many independent or semi-independent city-states. The period is regarded as representing a demographic peak in the area more generally, and some scholars estimate the population as about 140,000 (west of the Jordan). Although the figure is far from certain, and is questioned on many grounds, it does suggest, when compared with the demographic estimates of other periods, the prosperity of the period, something also reflected in the settlement remains uncovered by archaeologists. The relations with Egypt during the time of the Middle Kingdom are not clear. The Execration Texts are groups of texts, uncovered in Egypt, in which names of local rulers in Canaan were inscribed on bowls or figurines and were apparently used for voodoo-like purposes, probably to secure their rulers' loyalty to Egypt. The existence of these texts might suggest that the Egyptians felt some authority over the region but this is not certain. In the later part of the Middle Bronze Age (known in Egyptian history as the Second Intermediate Period) Asian/Canaanite dynasties (known as the Hyksos) ruled over much of lower (northern) Egypt (the Nile delta), and the region was extensively settled by Canaanites who maintained close connections with Canaan itself.

During the 16th century BCE the Hyksos were ousted and were replaced by the 18th dynasty (often referred to as the 'Hyksos expulsion')—an episode that also marks the beginning of the New Kingdom of Egypt. This triggered many campaigns into Canaan, and many cities were devastated in the course of the century. Many archaeologists consider this as the beginning of the Late Bronze Age (roughly 1550–1200 BCE). Although there is much continuity in culture between the two periods, the settlement and demography were greatly affected by the campaigns, and despite gradual recovery during the Late Bronze Age the country did not recover its Middle Bronze Age demographic peak until some point in the Iron Age. Population estimates for the end of the Late Bronze Age (i.e. after the recovery from the nadir of the 16th century) are between 46,000–70,000, and although the figures are uncertain, the comparison with the Middle Bronze Age estimate is quite telling. Settlements were concentrated in the lower parts of the country, and the highlands were only sparsely settled. From at least the 15th century, the country was apparently nominally subjugated to Egypt, and this situation prevailed through the 19th dynasty (roughly the 13th century BCE) and well into the time of the 20th dynasty (until the middle of the 12th century or slightly later). As part of their rule over Canaan, the Egyptians built garrisons in a few places (e.g. Gaza, Jaffa, Beth Shean), and the rest of the country was divided between many city-states, which were vassals of Egypt. Egyptian sources, and especially the Amarna letters (14th century BCE), supply a wealth of information on the political and social organization in Canaan at the time, and we know of the existence of many marginal groups which were active outside the settlements, and whose activity led to severe unrest. Most notable among these groups are the notorious *Habiru*, composed of outcasts or exiled people from various backgrounds, who seem to have caused much unrest throughout the country (such groups were already known in earlier periods). It is a common accusation made by vassal Canaanite princes that their opponents are collaborating with the *Habiru*. Another group (or groups) mentioned in the Egyptian sources is that of the *Shasu*—tribal groups of pastoral nomads that were active outside the settled areas or on their fringes in both Cisjordan (i.e. west of the river Jordan) and Transjordan (i.e. east of it). Towards the end of the period—during the 13th and early 12th centuries—the Egyptians apparently strengthened their hold over Canaan. Archaeologically, this is expressed, for example, by the construction of the so-called Egyptian governors' residencies.

The material culture of the period reflects the existence of many social groups and social classes. Imported pottery is abundant, and some scholars refer to a period of internationalism. Decoration on local pottery is common and was probably used to convey differences between classes and groups. While not many dwellings have been excavated in their entirety, many public buildings, including palaces and temples, are known to archaeologists, reflecting the social distinctions and hierarchy that characterized this period. This is also reflected in burials: hundreds of burials of various types are known from this period, and the differences between them were probably also used to convey social differences between groups, families, and even individuals.

A series of events, beginning in the late 13th century and ending around the middle of the 12th century, marks the end of the Late Bronze Age and the transition to the Iron Age in the region. These include the fall of the Mycenean civilization, the demise of the Hittite empire, the destruction of various major cities like Ugarit, and eventually Egypt's withdrawal from Canaan and its political decline. As far as Canaan is concerned, these large-scale changes (marking the beginning of the Iron Age) were accompanied by a decline in many of the urban centres that existed in Canaan—mainly in the lower parts of the country—as well as by the emergence of two

An ivory knife handle from Megiddo, depicting Canaanite palace court scenes and reflecting the highly hierarchical social structure of the Canaanite cities.

A ceramic assemblage from Shiloh, showing typical forms of the earliest Israelite settlement.

additional phenomena: the Sea People, most notably the Philistines, who came from somewhere in the Aegean world or its fringes and settled in the southern coastal plain, and the Israelite settlement in the highlands.

The term 'Israelite settlement' refers to hundreds of small sites that were established during Iron Age I—beginning at some point in the second half of the 13th century—in the highlands of Canaan in both Cisjordan and Transjordan, and mainly in the area north of Jerusalem, in the region of Samaria. Most of the settlements were quite small, less than one hectare in size, and were not densely settled. Many of the houses were long houses, of the type that later crystallized into the well-known four-room house which dominated the urban landscape of the kingdoms of Israel and Judah in the Iron Age II (10th–6th centuries BCE), and the economy was based on a mixture of grazing, growing grains, and the cultivation of olives and vines. The material culture uncovered in these sites was quite rudimentary, and included a very limited ceramic repertoire that was composed mainly of large pithoi (mainly of the type known as the collared rim jar), cooking pots, and bowls.

A bronze bull figurine discovered near an open, cultic site in northern Samaria, subsequently known as the 'Bull Site'. The simple nature of the site reflects the nature of the local society, which probably lacked a specialized class of priests.

The pottery was simple and undecorated and did not include imported pottery, not even the highly decorated Philistine pottery that was produced in the nearby southern coastal plain, and which constituted nearly 50 per cent of the assemblage in many 11th-century sites there. Hardly any burials are known from these villages, probably because the population buried their dead in simple inhumations in the ground.

The association of these sites with the Israelites was based not only on the (rough) temporal and (more exact) spatial correspondence with the biblical testimony regarding the areas in which the Israelites settled, but also on the clear connections between the culture unearthed in these settlements and the culture of the kingdoms of Israel and Judah of Iron Age II, as well as the reference in an Egyptian stela by a Pharaoh called Merneptah to an ethnic group that he called Israel. The stela is dated to the late 13th century, and although the exact location of this group is not stated, most scholars view it as referring to the settlement phenomenon described above, or part of it.

The stele of the late 13th-century Egyptian Pharaoh Merneptah which contains the earliest reference to Israel outside the Bible.

The Israelite settlement: the growing debate

While the Israelite identity of the settlers was not questioned until recently, there was a major debate on the process through which the settlements came to be. Albrecht Alt, a German biblical scholar, noted as long ago as 1925 that there is a discrepancy between the description of a military conquest of the *entire* country, as depicted in the main narratives in the book of Joshua, and the situation on the ground following the conquest as described in the narratives in the books of Judges, 1–2 Samuel, and the descriptions of the remaining land in Joshua 13:1–7; Judges 1:27–35, in which the Israelites settled only parts of the country, mainly in the highlands. Moreover, from the Egyptian sources that relate to Late Bronze Age Canaan prior to the appearance of the Israelites, it appears that the Canaanite centres of settlement were concentrated in the valleys, the Shephelah (the low-lying region between the Judean hill country and the coastal plain), and the coast, whereas the highlands were only sparsely settled prior to the Israelite settlement. Comparing the Late Bronze Age Canaanite settlement distribution with that of the later Israelite settlement made it clear, argued Alt, that the Israelites settled in less hospitable regions that were largely devoid of Canaanite settlement anyway. This picture, of settlement in sparsely populated and inhospitable regions, does not correspond with a military conquest in which the conquerors annihilate the entire country and can settle wherever they choose, but rather with a more peaceful, and mostly non-confrontational process in which the Israelites occupied the sparsely settled regions of the country simply because they were not populated and so were available for settlement. Alt, therefore, concluded that the Israelite settlement was a long, gradual, and mainly peaceful process, in which pastoral groups crossed the Jordan in search of pastoral lands, and gradually settled in the relatively empty parts of the country.

While the process was mainly peaceful, it was accompanied by occasional confrontations and wars. Towards the end of the Iron Age, when Israel's national history was composed in Jerusalem (by the so-called Deuteronomistic school, that was probably active from the 7th century BCE onward), the various traditions that commemorated the warring episodes (some historical, some clearly more mythical in origin) were combined into the monumental history of Israel. This period of Israel's history was situated between the Exodus and the period of the Judges, and attributed to a local hero of the tribe of Ephraim: Joshua. According to Alt, therefore, the conquest that is described in the book of Joshua never actually happened. Due to the way it reconstructs the settlement process, this school of thought is often called the peaceful infiltration school (or theory).

William F. Albright, sometimes regarded as the doyen of biblical archaeology in its golden age between the two World Wars, strongly opposed this view. He claimed that the story in Joshua is historical, at least in its general outlines, and that the Israelite tribes did conquer Canaan by force. Albright introduced archaeology into the debate, and argued that archaeological inquiry can prove the historicity of the conquest.

A landscape in the hill country of Samaria, typical of the kind of territory in which the new material culture of the earliest Israelites developed.

He suggested that scholars should excavate Canaanite cities (mainly those mentioned in the conquest narratives), and should the Late Bronze Age occupation be devastated towards the end of this period, it would suggest that the conquest traditions are historical. Albright went on to excavate the mound of Tell Beit Mirsim in the south-eastern (inner) Shephelah, and was involved in additional projects, where evidence for violent destruction of the Canaanite cities of the Late Bronze Age was indeed unearthed. In light of its acceptance of the historicity of the main narratives in the book of Joshua, this school came to be known as the unified conquest school (or theory).

The debate between these two schools continued throughout most of the twentieth century, more and more scholars joining in, with figures like the German biblical scholar Martin Noth and the Israeli archaeologist Yohanan Aharoni taking the leading role in the peaceful infiltration school, and the American biblical scholar and archaeologist George E. Wright, the American biblical scholar John Bright, and the Israeli archaeologist Yigael Yadin taking the leading role in the unified conquest school. Members of the latter school stressed the sites in which the Canaanite cities were devastated and destroyed around the end of the Late Bronze Age (e.g. Tell Beit Mirsim, Hazor, Lachish, Bethel, and many others), while their opponents emphasized the sites

Tel 'Eton, a Canaanite site in the foothills west of Hebron, as excavated by the author.

which did not even exist at the time (e.g. Arad, 'Ai, Jericho), and the large gap between the destruction of some of the sites that were destroyed—about a century separates the destruction of Hazor and Lachish—which does not allow these destructions to be attributed to a single campaign.

Notably, while these two schools were the dominant ones during most of the twentieth century, additional theories developed over the years. In the 1960s, and mainly in the 1970s and 1980s, a new approach was developed (mainly by George Mendenhall and Norman Gottwald), which viewed the settlers as being mainly of Canaanite descent, and as local peasants who rebelled against their overlords, and fled to the highlands, where they met a small group of people who did come from Egypt, and together they formed 'liberated Israel'. Although this view—called the peasants' revolt or social revolution—was not directly supported by many scholars, it greatly influenced research and, indirectly at least, altered the academic discourse.

In the late 1980s and early 1990s an even newer approach was developed (separately, and with some differences) by the Israeli scholars Israel Finkelstein and Shlomo Bunimovitz, who noted that when viewed in the long term the settlement process of Iron Age I was only part of a larger cyclic process of settlement and abandonment in the highlands. This approach, which resulted from the systematic study of the discoveries made in the many archaeological surveys conducted in the highlands, noted that during the Early Bronze Age (3rd millennium BCE) the highlands were densely settled, but that settlement declined drastically in the Intermediate Bronze Age (late 3rd millennium). Large-scale settlement was resumed in the early 2nd millennium (Middle Bronze Age), but the new settlement phase persisted for only a relatively short period of time, and during the Late Bronze Age, as we have seen, settlement in the highlands was again very sparse. Then, in Iron Age I, large-scale settlement in the highlands was resumed. Identifying this pattern, it was argued, put the settlement wave of Iron Age I in general, and Israel's emergence in particular, within a broader perspective, so that it should not be viewed as a unique event, but rather as part of the cyclic process of settlement and abandonment in the highlands. Moreover, Finkelstein argued that settlement abandonment and decline (as between the Middle Bronze and the Late Bronze Ages) does not mean that the inhabitants died or left the region, but rather that they abandoned their settled way of life, and became semi-nomads within the very same region. Movement along the settlement–nomadic spectrum is a well-known phenomenon in the Middle East. Nomadism occurs when settlers change their main economic mode, increase their herds, leave the permanent settlement and come to rely mainly on their herds for subsistence. When the populations' livelihood is based on nomadic pastoralism, argued Finkelstein, they do not leave many material remains—hence the rarity of finds attributed to this era in the highlands. Such phenomena are known in the Middle East in various periods, even for reasons as mundane as over-taxation and recruitment to the army. The reason the Middle Bronze Age settlers in the highlands might have reverted to a more nomadic way of life does not concern us here, but according to the new theory the population remained as nomads in the highlands during the following centuries, only to resettle in the late 13th and 12th centuries BCE. Thus, according to this view, the settlers were not outsiders, but rather local pastoral-nomads who settled down after a few hundred years of a pastoral livelihood that did not leave much by way of remains in the archaeological record of the highlands. Due to its reference to long-term processes, and following its explicit reference to the French *Annales* School, this approach is sometimes called the 'longue durée' approach, or the 'cyclic process'.

The last two schools of thought (the 'social revolution' and the 'longue durée' perspectives) viewed the settlers, or most of them at least, as 'local' people (whether semi-nomads or settled population) who lived in the region for many generations, and who for various reasons settled down in the highlands (or moved there from the lowlands, but not from outside Cisjordan). This new trend towards viewing the settlers as 'locals', and not as a new population coming from the outside, eventually led to the development of a new school ('approach' would probably be a more accurate term), which viewed the highland settlers as Canaanites, who for some reason simply moved into the highlands and established new villages there. According to this latter view the settlers were not revolting peasants nor settling nomads, but rather agriculturalists from the lowlands. This last approach is best described as evolutionary.

As for the best name to call the settlers, views differed greatly. Many called them Israelites, as the Merneptah stela clearly indicates that Israel was in existence at the time. Others challenged the 'Israeliteness' of the settlers, suggesting that we cannot distinguish Israelites from other groups that according to the Bible settled in the highlands, viewing the settlers simply as Canaanites. Alternatively, a large number of scholars followed the lead of the American scholar William G. Dever in calling the settlers Proto-Israelites, acknowledging that their later descendants were indeed Israelites, but leaving the settlers' identity in Iron Age I, and that of the Israel that was mentioned in the Egyptian inscription, as an open question.

The Israelite settlement: assessing the evidence

Notably, while strongly supporting their own preferred 'theory', many scholars in the 1980s and 1990s came to view the settlement process as a very complex development, accepting that it was not monolithic. In other words, the debate became more concentrated on the question as to which was the *main* mechanism through which the settlers settled in the highlands, and many scholars agree that all schools of thought are probably right to some extent, and that not all the settlers came from the same background, nor that they all settled down following a similar process.

Still, in the course of the extensive study of the settlement process that evolved in the late 1980s and early 1990s it became apparent that two schools of thought were gradually abandoned and were left with hardly any supporters: the unified conquest theory, and the social revolution. As for the former, there are simply too many sites which either did not exist at the time of the supposed conquest, or where Canaanite life continued as usual in Iron Age I. Moreover, as already noted, the destruction of some of the sites that were destroyed around the Late Bronze Age—Iron Age 1 transition (and which were used by supporters of the unified conquest theory to support their view) are separated by a hundred years; Hazor, for example, was destroyed by fire (which actually fits the detailed biblical description) at around 1250 BCE, whereas Lachish was destroyed around the middle of the 12th century, hence ruling out the possibility that they were destroyed in one military campaign, opening up the question as to who actually was responsible for their destruction, and even whether this can be attributed to the Israelites at all. As for the social revolution theory, although it was very influential, especially by (indirectly) influencing scholars to develop additional scenarios in which Israel was no longer viewed as an outsider, the entirety of the evidence weighs heavily against it. Not only is there no supportive evidence for this scenario, but many finds seem to make it very unlikely. Thus, for example, if Canaanites from the lower strata of society were to rebel and flee to the highlands, and since the Shephelah and the southern coastal plain were a major hub of population during the later part of the Late Bronze Age, we would expect to find a major concentration of settlement in the nearby Hebron highlands. However, this region was relatively sparsely settled in Iron Age I, and the main centres of population in the highlands were further away from Canaanite settlements. Supporters of this school also failed to explain the emergence of a new identity group—Israel—as a result of a social revolution which might be expected to replace the rulers or regime, but not to create new ethnicities. Finally, supporters of this school failed to explain the new material culture that evolved in the highlands.

The debate between the remaining theories regarding the main source of population for the settlement process can be divided into two aspects: (1) did the settlers come from within the population of Cisjordan (as maintained by both the cyclic process and the evolution theories) or from outside it (the peaceful infiltration model)? (2) Did the settlers come from a semi-nomadic background (peaceful infiltration and cyclic process) or did they come from the sedentary population (evolution theory)? Obviously, those who believe that the Israelites were sedentary also claim that they were indigenous to Cisjordan.

Evaluating the Cyclic Process and the Local Nomads School: The idea that all the nomads were local is unlikely. First, the end of the Late Bronze Age was a period of decisive population movements, which seem to have impacted the entire region. It is, therefore, extremely unlikely that the highlands west of the Jordan were alone left untouched by the social upheavals and migrations of the time. Moreover, identifying the central hill-country of Cisjordan as the 'pool' from which the settling population was drawn ignores the fact that the Iron Age I settlement process was not unique to Cisjordan, but took place also across large segments of the highlands east of the Jordan River. Thus, even those who do not believe that a 'foreign intrusion' of population is responsible for the settlement should not exclude Transjordan as the possible place of origin of the settlers. This means that a 'local nomads' theory, which limits the potential origin of the settlers to Cisjordan, is unlikely, and does not fit the historical and geographical contexts.

This leaves us with two possible theories: sedentary Canaanites (the evolution theory) and the peaceful infiltration model.

Evaluating the Sedentary Canaanite Origin School: The rationale in arguing for the Canaanite origins of the highlands population was based, first and foremost, on a total rejection of their nomadic origins. There are also some more positive arguments in favour of a Canaanite origin as well. The negative argument is that the idea of the nomadic origins of the Israelites was based on only a simplistic reading of the biblical material and on some old-fashioned, romantic notions of the desert and desert life, which have nothing to do with reality. The positive argument is that the Iron Age I villages show evidence of sophisticated agriculture; hence the settlers were experienced farmers, and could not have been nomads.

Both arguments, however, are very problematic. While nobody would deny that romantic notions of desert life influenced previous research, modern and sophisticated studies of Bedouin societies illuminate the processes by which they settle down, and show that there is nothing improbable about such processes. As for the sophisticated agriculture argument, this is problematic on a number of grounds. First of all, even if one accepts that pastoral nomads are not expected to be familiar with sophisticated agriculture, there is no reason to attribute the archaeological evidence of such agriculture to the beginning of the settlement process. In fact, the finds are more likely to date to the later phase. After all, even if the settlers were of semi-nomadic origin, they could still be expected to master agriculture after a few generations of settling down and practising it! Even more disturbing is the fact that evidence of the very same advanced agriculture is usually missing from Late Bronze Age Canaanite settlements, from which supporters of this theory suggest the settlers came. It is quite clear, therefore, that the attempts to claim that the settlers could not have originated from pastoral nomads are not substantiated by the available data, and the attempt to connect them with the Late Bronze Age sedentary population does not stand scrutiny. The dissociation of the Iron Age I villages from the Late Bronze Age sedentary population is supported also by the clear differences between the material culture of the highland settlements and that of the Late Bronze Age in most respects.

Although there is similarity in the form of the vessels unearthed in Iron Age I villages and the Late Bronze Age pottery forms (for example of cooking pots and bowls), other forms are different (for example those of the collared rim jars), and major

The discovery of a row of large collared rim jars from Shiloh. These jars, frequently found in early Israelite settlements, differ from the previous local repertoire.

differences can be seen in the repertoire of ceramic vessels of the two different periods. The Late Bronze Age ceramic assemblages were very rich and diverse, while thc ones of Iron Age I were very poor and limited. The lack of decoration on Iron Age I pottery is another major break between the two ceramic traditions. It must be stressed that the 'poor' nature of the Iron Age I assemblages cannot be attributed to its rural nature, as most villages in other periods, and even Iron Age I villages elsewhere, exhibit more varied and elaborate assemblages.

Moving to other types of material culture, the differences are even more striking. The architecture in highland villages includes the prototype of a building that developed into the famous four-room house, which is a new form of long house, greatly deviating from the Bronze Age tradition of courtyard houses and row houses. Additionally, hardly any burials were found in the highland villages, where the population apparently buried its dead in simple inhumations in the ground. This greatly differed from the Late Bronze Age tradition, in which hundreds of burials are known, of dozens of different types, representing various different classes and groups. It is quite clear that the material culture of the highland settlers greatly differed from what is known about the earlier sedentary population of the Late Bronze Age.

A four-room house from 'Izbet Sartah. This design became standard for Israelite domestic architecture.

Finally, supporters of the evolution theory did not provide an explanation as to why a new ethnic identity was created. After all, the movement of Canaanite farmers from one site to another cannot be expected on its own to have created new ethnicities or identity groups.

The Peaceful Infiltration School: The unlikelihood of both the 'longue durée' and the evolution schools of thought leads us back to the peaceful infiltration model as a central process in the emergence of Israel, even if in a more sophisticated manner. Notably, some scholars have suggested that various aspects of the archaeological evidence might actually positively support the pastoral origin of the settlers, for example the big courtyards that were reported in a number of the early settlement sites (like Izbet Sartah and Giloh) which probably served as corrals (the significance of sheep and goats can also be seen in the animal remains in the settlement villages). Many material traits, common in the highland villages, like the poor and limited ceramic repertoire, the lack of decoration, and the use of simple inhumations in the ground, and probably also the ethos that lies behind them (of which more below under 'The Shasu and an all Israelite identity in the late 13th and early 12th centuries BCE'), also correspond with the settlers' supposed pastoral background and are, conversely, not in line with a supposed sedentary background. All these traits are in line with the suggestion that the core group of the settlers came from a pastoral background, like the *Shasu*—tribal groups of pastoral nomads that were active outside the settled areas—who are mentioned in the Egyptian sources of the second millennium BCE.

Israel's emergence

The settlement process was, then, a complex one, and it involved peoples from various origins who settled in the highlands over a long period of time, and as a result of various differing processes. Opinions about the emergence of Israel vary greatly. Some scholars believe that the biblical narratives preserve much history while others reject it outright. In the following, I will try to present a more nuanced reconstruction of the settlement process, reconstructing how Israel first appeared on the scene, and discussing how it gradually evolved as various additional groups were assimilated into it.

The Shasu and an all Israelite identity in the late 13th and early 12th centuries BCE

As noted above, the evidence seems to suggest that the first group of settlers was indeed an outsider group—probably of *Shasu*, as we shall see later in this section, coming from somewhere in the east or south. This group most likely crossed the Jordan peacefully, over a period of time, while interacting with the local sedentary Canaanite population, exchanging their herd product surpluses with grains produced by the sedentary population, and supplementing their own seasonal agriculture. This involved limited hostility, but only rarely full-scale clashes. After some time, however, the pastoral groups faced a very strong opposition from the Egyptian-Canaanite city-state system in the region. The Egyptian empire strengthened its hold over the region at this time, and consequently prevented these pastoral groups from interacting with the city-states of the lowlands. The pastoralist *Shasu*, therefore, had to settle down in the relatively vacant areas of the highlands, and to grow their own grains, since they could not exchange it anymore with the settled population of the lowlands. The *Shasu*, however, were not alone. Additional groups of outcasts and displaced Canaanites were also shunned, and most likely joined them in the process. Identities are always created in contrast to other identities, and the highland settlers formed their identity vis-à-vis the Egyptian-Canaanite system of the lowlands. They took customs that they already practised, and which sharply contrasted with the practices of the lowlanders, and made them into symbols or 'flags' around which they could gather and strengthen their difference from their 'enemies' or their 'other'. Thus, while the Late Bronze Age Canaanite societies made extensive use of decoration on pottery and of imported ceramics for delivering messages related to status and identity, it was no great inconvenience for the pastoral population, who as far as we know did not use decorated and imported pottery anyway (or, at least, used it only sparsely) to make this avoidance into a binding type of behaviour that could be used to mark the contrast between themselves and the population of Egyptian-ruled Canaan. The very traits chosen by the highlanders to mark their boundaries with the lowlanders are in line with them being *Shasu*, and they clearly reflect non-Canaanite habits (Canaanite groups did not completely avoid decoration, but used differentiated styles of decoration to mark themselves as different from other groups). A similar phenomenon can be seen in the poor ceramic assemblage used by the settlers. It is likely that the pastoral population used a very limited repertoire prior to their settlement, and it is likely that this habit was now used to demarcate the differences between the settlers in the highlands and the Canaanite population. Similarly, various lines of evidence (including what was apparently a *Shasu* cemetery that was unearthed in Transjordan) suggest that the semi-nomadic *Shasu* buried their dead in simple inhumations in the ground. This contrasts with the elaborated and varied burials of Late Bronze Age Canaan, and this difference was no doubt also used to demarcate the boundaries between the groups.

An interesting common denominator to all the above traits is that they appear to reflect an ethos, or an ideology, of simplicity or egalitarianism. Such an ideology sharply contrasted with the ethos of the Canaanite society of the Late Bronze Age and the hierarchical Egyptian ruling system, as reflected in both the period's material culture as well as the Egyptian sources. This contrast served the settlers well, as it stressed the differences between themselves and the Egypto-Canaanite system that pushed them to the highlands. Under such circumstances, in which the highlands were settled and isolated from the lowland settlement, the core *Shasu* group could easily have adopted some other groups that were similarly shunned by the lowland system, with all these groups united 'against' their common enemy or 'other', the Egypto-Canaanite system of the lowlands. The *Shasu* and those who joined them are most likely the group which Merneptah mentioned in his famous late 13th century stela: Israel.

The main structure in the Mount Ebal site. Although the interpretation of the structure as an altar is challenged by the majority of scholars, the cultic nature of this simple, isolated site is accepted by most.

Over time the group grew in size as a result of both natural growth and the joining of additional members. Still, although composed of many sub-groups, with different histories and practices, until the middle of the 12th century BCE the group as a whole (Israel) maintained very definite boundaries (as reflected in the archaeological record and in the distribution of the above-mentioned traits), in order to assert its unified identity and mark itself off from the Egypto-Canaanite system that dominated the lowlands. The Egypto-Canaanite system was, therefore, the anvil on which Israel crystallized and defined itself, and which helped the various groups that gradually came to compose Israel to attain their common identity.

The (re)emergence of local identities in the late 12th century BCE

In the mid 12th century (or slightly afterwards) Egypt withdrew from Canaan. The highland group continued to grow, but did not have much interaction with the weakened Canaanite centres of the lowlands. While the common Israelite identity—shared by many sub-groups—probably continued to exist, the settlers now tended to stress local, regional, or tribal identities (sometimes also called totemic identities), probably related to both the former, pre-Israelite identities of the settlers and also to local development in the highlands, at the expense of the more inclusive Israelite one. The process continued over the course of the late 12th and 11th centuries BCE, with the local identities becoming ever more pronounced and more important than the larger Israelite one. At this stage these groups included not only the *Shasu* and some fringe, *Habiru*-like groups, but also individuals and groups that came from within Canaanite society, but which due to various political circumstances made alliances with the highlanders. Those probably included groups like Asher, which is both the name of one of Jacob's sons (and therefore one of Israel's tribes) and a local tribe in Canaan. It is perfectly possible that Asher was just a single local group that at some point became part of Israel (and was later viewed as part of the 'family', and added to the family tree, as reflected in the biblical stories).

Stressing 'Israel' again: the 11th and early 10th centuries BCE

In the late 11th and early 10th centuries, a new powerful 'other' became significant. The Philistines were newcomers from outside the region, probably from somewhere (perhaps from more than one place) within the Aegean world or its fringes. The

An Egyptian depiction of the sea battle against the invading Philistines and other 'Sea Peoples'.

Egyptian sources mentioned the Philistines' foreign origins, and the Bible locates their origins in the Island of Crete (e.g. Amos 9:7; Jer. 47:4). Their foreign origin is clearly expressed also in their material culture, which included many foreign traits such as their locally produced Mycenean IIIC1 pottery (also known as Philistine monochrome) which later evolved into the bichrome Philistine pottery. In addition, one could cite the use of hearths in their structures, the use of cooking jugs, the high proportion of pork in their diet, and the list could go on.

The Philistines settled in the southern coastal plain as early as the first half of the 12th century BCE, but they were probably confined to the coastal plain because of their hostile relations with the Egypto-Canaanite system. Gradually, especially toward the end of the 12th and in the 11th century BCE (after Egypt withdrew from Canaan), they began to expand, and at some point started to encroach on the highlands. The Philistines were the most powerful group in Canaan in the 11th century BCE, with large and elaborate cities—Ashkelon might have covered up to 60 hectares and Ekron covered around 20 hectares, compared with Canaanite towns of only a few hectares, and Israelite villages of about one hectare or less. The size of the Philistine centres, and the finds unearthed in them, reflect a very hierarchical and complex society, with public buildings and an elaborate material culture. This powerful group's encroachment into the highlands resulted in a very asymmetrical type of interaction between the complex, highly urbanized Philistines and the simple villagers of the highlands.

Decorated Philistine pottery; it can be easily distinguished from early Israelite pottery.

Under such circumstances, however, the highlanders de-emphasized the importance of their local identities, and re-stressed their more inclusive one—that of 'Israel'—in order to face the common enemy. Thus, the highlanders used existing features, like their egalitarian ethos, and their use of simple and undecorated pottery, which were also very suitable for defining themselves in contra-distinction to the highly hierarchical Philistines with their decorated pottery, and invested new meaning in them.

In addition, other traits, which had not hitherto served to mark identity, were invested with new meanings, which could now serve to highlight and stress the differences between themselves and the non-local Philistines. These traits include, for example, the taboo on pork, and circumcision. Pork was very popular among the Philistines, probably a habit that they brought with them from outside the region. One impact of this habit was that other groups, which did not consume much pork to start with, completely avoided this meat in order to differentiate themselves from the Philistines (and the latter, interestingly enough, increased the percentage of pork in their diet during the 12th and 11th centuries BCE, probably for the same reason, i.e. to demarcate boundaries). Pork avoidance was not a good trait to demarcate Israelites from Canaanites (who also consumed small quantities of pork), but it was a very good way to demarcate the Israelites from the Philistines, and pork was therefore strictly avoided in this context. As for circumcision, the Iron Age I Philistines were probably uncircumcised (this is not only evidenced by the biblical testimony, but can also be seen in Egyptian sources). Many of the local groups in Canaan, however, were circumcised, so this trait, just like pork avoidance, became important only once the Israelites interacted with the uncircumcised Philistines.

Thus the Philistines became another anvil on which Israelite identity was forged and renegotiated.

Israel's development

It should be noted that throughout its history, additional groups joined Israel. It is even possible that in the long run the number of people who were of settled Canaanite origin exceeded those who were of *Shasu* origin. What is important, however, is not the total number of peoples who gradually joined in, or their relative proportions within the Israel group, but the process by which the new group was created, and how it defined itself. The first group was, following the above reconstruction, composed of *Shasu*. Israel's ethos and self-identity were therefore based on that of this core group. This might explain the importance of the nomadic ideals that were memorialized in some parts of the Bible. As more groups joined in, they too influenced Israel's self-definition and added their own stories and traditions, and in so doing gradually transformed Israel. What is important for the present discussion, however, is that the various new groups joined an existing one, and rather quickly assimilated into it, i.e. they adopted its basic or core ethos and history, while only slowly and gradually changing it.

A colourful faience tile depicting one of the Shasu people, who may have formed the core group of the earliest Israelite settlers.

A good comparison might be society in the USA today. This is an English speaking society. Still, if one examines the ancestors of present-day Americans it becomes clear that most of them did not speak English before arriving in North America (or before the Europeans arrived in the case of Native Americans). So how come that all their descendants speak English, and not any other language? This is because the original group spoke English. All the other groups which gradually assimilated into this group, while constantly changing it, accepted its core traits. English was one such trait, and hence every 'new-comer' adopted it. The same is true for ancient Israel. Although most Israelites in the period of the monarchy were perhaps of different origins, and not descendants of *Shasu*, they nevertheless accepted the core values and history of the original Israel as they merged into it, while gradually modifying it and expanding its history, as we will see below under 'The history of Israel'. The Exodus story, to be discussed next, was one such story and one which also became the story of all Israel.

The Exodus group and the Exodus story

While some scholars view the Exodus story as, generally speaking, reliable historically, and others see it as a late invention with no historical value whatsoever, most believe that the narrative has a certain historical core, even if things did not take place in the manner described in the Bible. According to this view, some of the highland settlers (probably a small minority) came, one way or the other, from Egypt. Though the size of this group is debated, most scholars agree that it was in the range of a few thousands, or even perhaps only hundreds. Still, despite the limited size of this group, it appears that during the process of Israel's ethno-genesis its story became part of the common history of all the Israelites.

When and how did the Exodus story become a national epic? Was the Exodus group part of Merneptah's Israel? Most of those who accept some historical core for the story of the Exodus from Egypt date it to the 13th century, at the time of Ramesses II, while others date it to the 12th century, during the time of Ramesses III. Clearly, if there was an Exodus in the 13th century this group of people could have been part of Merneptah's Israel. However, despite the assumed significance of this group, it is likely that it was incorporated at a later stage, only after Merneptah's time, or at least that it was not identical to Merneptah's Israel. The way divine names were used in antiquity was important as a means to mark identity. Isra*el* uses the theophoric component 'El', whereas the Exodus group, which clearly brought with it some of what became the history of Israel, was apparently devoted to the God YHWH, who shows up in the many biblical names which end with *-iah* or which begin with *Je-* or *Jo-*. Thus, it is likely that Isra*el* preceded the arrival of the Exodus group, or was at least initially separate from it, and it is possible that the Exodus group was not Israel's 'core' group, or at least was only part of it.

The process by which all of Israel came to share this Exodus history, which was really the history of only some of them, is illustrated by the American archaeologist, William G. Dever:

> The 'Exodus–Conquest' story is perhaps really about a small group…A simple analogy may help us to understand this phenomenon. In mainstream American tradition, we all celebrate Thanksgiving as though we ourselves had come to these shores on the Mayflower. That is the myth; yet in fact, most of us got here some other way…

While Dever's words seem to give a general idea of how an important story of one group can become that of a much larger one, we still need to ask why the story of a possibly late-coming group (or at least not the main group) was accepted by the other components of Israel, and turned into a 'national epic', shared by all. We have seen that Merneptah's Israel defined itself against the Egyptian empire (which in a sense indirectly forced them to settle) and its subordinated Canaanite city states, and this in itself made the Exodus story easy to accept by the original 'core' group. The Egyptian oppression of Canaan, which lasted until about 1140 BCE, made the Canaanite groups also prone to accept the story. Memories of oppression in Egypt, or by Egypt, were therefore shared by all components of the emerging Israel (and to this one can also add the memory of the so-called Hyksos expulsion), and this made the reception of the Exodus story quite easy (regardless of the question of what exactly constituted the story in its early stages).

The history of Israel

More stories and traditions were probably incorporated and evolved in a similar fashion, and in a long drawn out process were combined and edited so as to create the common history of *all* Israel, which (in the final form known to us from the Bible) was written down only centuries later.

While the core traditions were always integral parts of the group's history and values, new elements were being added all the time, and gradually merging with the core traditions. Some new traditions probably remained 'local' and did not ever become the tradition of all Israel, while some others, probably those that better suited the needs of the group at crucial junctions of its history, became more widespread.

Thus, while some scholars raise strong points in support of the historicity of the narratives about the Patriarchs, claiming that even some details (like the price of slaves) are accurate, others have pointed out that the stories about Abraham focus on the southern part of the land of Israel, especially concentrating on sites that were located in Iron Age II within the kingdom of Judah. The Jacob stories, on the other hand, focus on the north, and mainly on sites that were within the Kingdom of Israel in Iron Age II. Abraham, who also figures more in the stories which use YHWH (Yahweh) as God's name, was therefore interpreted by many as the original ancestor in the traditions of southern groups. Jacob, who figures prominently in the stories which use Elohim as God's name, was interpreted as a major figure in the history of northern groups. While clearly the patriarchal figures cannot be associated directly with the Iron Age II political entities (i.e. Jacob with the kingdom of Israel, and Abraham with the kingdom of Judah), if one follows the above interpretation then it is possible that the different stories were woven together in a similar fashion to the process suggested above for the reception of the Exodus story, in which different stories became central as time went by and as needs changed, gradually incorporating more traditions and stories into what became a (usually) coherent all-embracing narrative.

This explanation can also help explain the intriguing fact that the stories never mention any meeting between Abraham and Jacob. If the story as we know it is composed of the amalgamation of different local 'ancestors' into a single, chronologically evolving story, no such meeting is to be expected. Another possibility is that stories which took place over centuries were telescoped into the life of just three figures. At an even later stage, the narrative of the conquest most probably crystallized, incorporating many separate memories and stories, some historical and some of which were regarded as historical by the editor, but which were probably not (e.g. the story of the conquest of 'Ai).

While the process is shrouded in mystery, and we cannot be positive regarding the truth of this reconstruction in general, or even of its separate details, the above is a possible, indeed plausible, reconstruction of the process by which the biblical story developed into its current form, serving the evolving needs of Israel.

Is the story historical? As noted above, this is very difficult to answer. Some parts clearly are, others are probably not, and scholars still debate many issues. The scenario presented above is also not certain, and only presents one possible way, plausible at best, in which the story could have evolved.

This might be a good place to refer to the concepts of 'archaeological truth' and 'historical truth', as developed by the Jewish thinker usually known as Ahad Ha'am (Asher Zvi Hirsch Ginsberg, 1856–1927). In 1904 he published an article called 'Moses', in which he addressed the controversy over whether Moses was a historical figure or not. Ahad Ha'am contributed to this debate by making the distinction between 'archeological' truth, which for him was the absolute, scientific truth (which we would call today 'historical truth', and which had nothing to do with the modern discipline of archaeology), and 'historical' truth, which for him described the way in which people *understood* and *perceived* history. Ahad Ha'am claimed that even if, in terms of archaeological truth, Moses never existed, this only matters to a few scholars. As a concept, even as a literary figure, Moses changed history, serving as a very powerful motif that led people to embark on campaigns and demand freedom. In his words:

> Historical truth is that, and that alone, which reveals the forces that go to mould the social life of mankind. Every man who leaves a perceptible mark on that life, though he may be a purely imaginary figure, is a real historical force; his existence is an historical truth.

Thus, a few scholars can debate whether Moses actually existed as a person, and perhaps 'will erase or alter a paragraph of a chapter in the book of archaeology; but it will not make history erase the name of its hero'. Ahad Ha'am adds that:

> real history has no concern with so-and-so who is dead, and who was never seen in that form by the nation at large, but only by antiquarians; its concern is only with the living

> hero, whose image is graven in the hearts of men, who has become a force in human life. And what cares history whether this force was at one time a walking and talking biped, or whether it was never anything but a creature of the imagination, labelled with the name of some concrete man? In either case history is certain about his existence, because history feels his effects.

As antiquated as Ahad Ha'am's view of history is, the distinction he made should be borne in mind when one asks about the historicity of an event or a figure. We may conclude that something did not actually happen, but this will not necessarily deny its importance or force.

By way of conclusion

The 'real' story, of Israel—the one that can be identified on the ground, and more concretely discussed and debated—begins in the second half of the 13th century BCE. As for earlier epochs, the evidence is fragmentary and problematic, and no real consensus can be identified. The earlier elements in the history of Israel are likely to include some memories, but we cannot go any further than that. The late 13th century BCE is when the real, 'archaeological' Israel begins, in tandem with Merneptah's Israel inscription. In the above we have attempted to reconstruct the very complex, real, or 'archaeological', history of this Israel, how it evolved and interacted with more groups, and how it defined and redefined itself through time.

'Historical' Israel (in the sense used by Ahad Ha'am) also probably evolved at the same time, but its development was an even more complex story, advancing not only 'forwards', but also 'backwards' in time, developing the earlier history of Israel and its ancestry (whether 'real' or not), and also 'sideways' (in partial correspondence with the archaeological history of Israel), as more and more groups were incorporated into it, and their stories were sometimes (if they fitted with the conditions and circumstances) embedded within the main history of Israel.

Each group that joined Israel, through whatever process, had its own stories, traditions, and practices. Many of these histories remained local, and were not shared by all Israel, nor did they usually find their way into the Bible (though, perhaps, this is the background to some of the more obscure stories, traditions, and verses in the Bible). Still, when some aspects and motifs of the 'local' stories were deemed appropriate—especially when Israel confronted new groups, and some traditions were now fitting and could serve Israel in its self-definition against those groups—more and more stories were incorporated into the 'national' history of Israel, until it received the form in which it is known to us today.

CHAPTER 2

Iron Age

Tribes to Monarchy

LESTER L. GRABBE

THE books of Joshua and Judges, 1 and 2 Samuel, and 1 Kings 1–11 impart the biblical picture of how Israel became a state. A grand narrative about the founding of the Israelite kingship begins in 1 Samuel 1 and continues to the end of 2 Kings. This is a gripping story that cannot fail to engage all sorts of readers, whether looking at it as theology or literature or entertainment. For many these chapters are history: they describe the foundation of the kingdom of Israel and, later, the kingdoms of Israel and Judah. The question of history is an issue that we shall address. Yet the story that emerges in Judges, 1 and 2 Samuel, and the first few chapters of 1 Kings is a vivid and coherent one that excites the imagination and creates an image of a nation emerging with much trauma from a tribal collective.

When viewed as a grand drama, the books of Judges, 1 and 2 Samuel, and the first chapters of 1 Kings have several main acts and actors: the tribal origins of Israel, the judges, the prophet Samuel, the Philistines, King Saul, King David, and King Solomon. We shall take up each of these in turn and discuss what we know about them from the variety of sources at our disposal, meaning the biblical text, contemporary sources (including inscriptions), and archaeology. First, however, let us examine briefly what we mean by 'history' and 'historical' as the terms are used by modern historians.

Writing the history of ancient Israel

For many believers, if we want to know the history of ancient Israel, we only need to read the Bible. Were it that simple! We can begin discussing this question by noting—as most readers will accept—that the Bible is not a history book. That is not why it was written, and that is not primarily why we read it. The Bible is a religious book: it tells us about theology, ethics, examples of good and bad choices, how to live, and so on. It is also a great work of literature, at least in parts, as is becoming better recognized by literary scholars. A book like Job could take its place in a collection of the world's greatest literature. And of course the Bible contains historical material, but the conveying of accurate history, as discerned by modern historical scholars, is not its main purpose.

The Hebrew Bible—whether Jewish or Christian, or as read by Muslims—did not reach its present form until the Middle Ages. That is, the standard Hebrew text referred to as the *Masoretic text* was written down in complete form in only about the tenth century of the Common Era, with both the consonants and the vowel and accent marks in the text. Earlier than about 700 we find merely the consonantal text, while the correct vocalization was preserved only by oral tradition. Yet we have some evidence that even the consonantal text was not put in its present form until the first century; before that a variety of textual variants are attested as being known and used by Jewish readers and writers. If we go several centuries further back, to the second or third century BCE, we find that some books had widely divergent forms. For example, the book of Jeremiah was known in one form quite similar to the present-day Masoretic consonantal text, but alongside that version was a much shorter version which also differed in the arrangement of some of its contents. Many scholars think the shorter version (known in Hebrew from fragments found among the Dead Sea Scrolls and in the Greek translation of the Septuagint from perhaps the third century BCE) is more original and closer to the form of the book that was compiled near to the lifetime of the prophet Jeremiah.

As for the books of Samuel, which are of major concern for us in the present chapter, we have evidence of at least three different versions. There is the Hebrew Masoretic text that we are familiar with in many modern translations. Yet there is also a somewhat different version known from the Greek Septuagint translation, but some Greek manuscripts are closer to the Masoretic text than others, perhaps because of later Jewish and Christian revisions. Finally, we have evidence that there was a third version because fragments of such a version (which has material not found in either the Hebrew Masoretic text or the Greek) have been found among the Dead Sea scrolls. If we are trying to write the history of ancient Israel, which one of these three versions should we use? The three versions do not differ greatly in overall outline of events, but there are many differences in detail.

What the existence of the various versions illustrates is that the biblical text grew up over a long period of time. Most scholars think that many of the traditions we now find in the Bible were mainly preserved by oral tradition; that is, they were remembered and handed down the generations by word of mouth but not written down. Although we find evidence of writing in Israel from about 1000 BCE, very few examples are preserved. We have some inscriptions in the centuries after this time, but very few. Evidence of writing becomes more abundant from about the seventh century BCE, though many think that little of the Bible was written down before this time. Thus, the history of the early centuries of Israel may have been edited and written down only at the end of the kingdom of Judah in the sixth century BCE or even later. As we shall see, the historical picture in the text often conforms to the time of the later editors rather than the reality of the original event centuries earlier as accessible to us from archaeology and early inscriptions.

Origins of Israel

As was described in Chapter 1, Israel arose sometime in the Late Bronze Age but developed through the next archaeological period, which is Iron Age I (usually dated about 1200–1000 BCE). The core of Israel was the highlands of central Palestine and the hills of Judah. Archaeological studies show that settlement in these areas was sparse in the last part of the Late Bronze Age, but it began to expand during Iron Age I. Over the next two centuries the population increased considerably, though the inhabitants mainly lived in villages and farmsteads rather than cities. This fits the general picture of the book of Judges.

It has long been noticed that the Israelite judges fall into two categories. There are the deliverer figures, who come to the rescue at a time of crisis, and are often larger-than-life figures (e.g. Samson). Then there is the list of 'minor judges' in Judges 10:1–5 and 12:8–15. These look more like local rulers who led a tribe or small collection of tribes. In Hebrew, the word *shophet* can mean a 'judge' in our sense of a legal figure who makes decisions according to law. But also in Hebrew (and related Semitic languages, such as Phoenician) the word can mean 'leader, ruler'. Thus, many of the 'judges' (*shophtim*) in the book of Judges were actually local leaders who did more than just

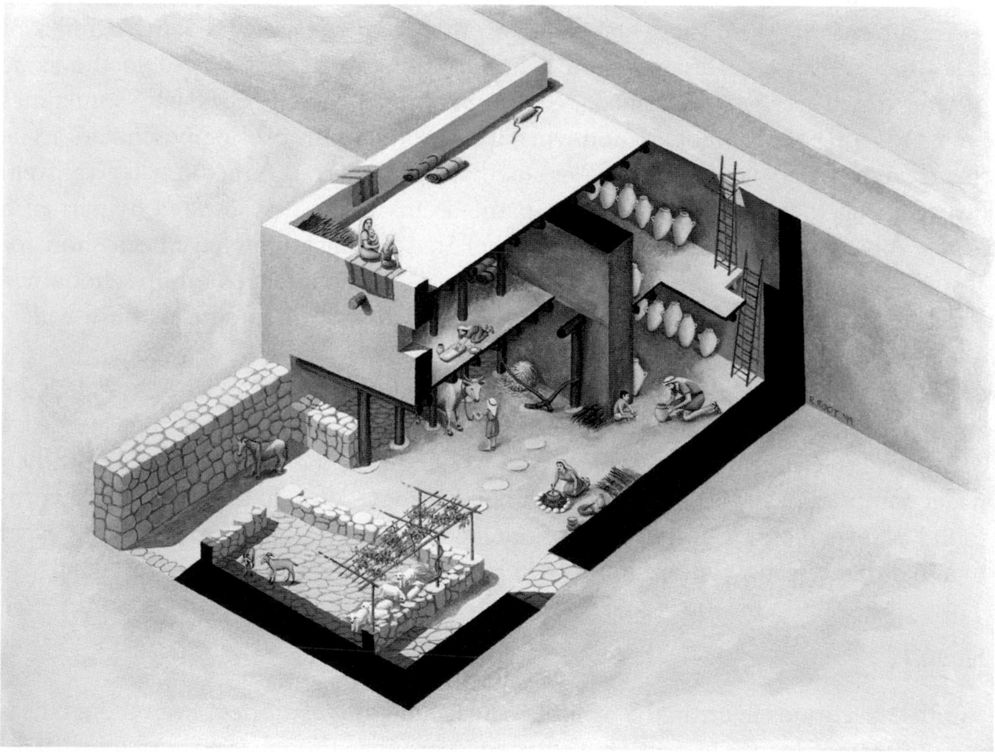

A reconstruction of a four-room house—typical domestic architecture of the early Israelite period.

judge but also provided broader leadership. The various stories about individual judges cannot be confirmed, since we have no information apart from the biblical text. Some of them look quite credible, but others (such as Samson) can only be fantasies in their present form, though they may be based on a real person.

We now come to the problem of the relationship of Judah to Israel. In much of the Bible, the textual emphasis is on Israel as a whole, with Judah just one of the tribes. Yet it is obvious historically that Judah had its own national identity and was separate from and a rival of Israel from an early period. Notice why this is a likely conclusion. Judges 5, 'the Song of Deborah', is regarded as one of the earliest sections of the Hebrew Bible, written in an archaic Hebrew dialect. It is thought to give insight into an early stage in the development of Israel. First, the 'Song of Deborah' gives a list of tribes that differs from the later lists we are so familiar with. It also shows that the call for the tribes to band together against Sisera was rejected by several tribes (5:16–18). Finally, Judah is completely absent, as it is in most of Judges. Most important, Saul's kingdom clearly excluded Judah (see especially 2 Sam. 2:8–9); on the other hand, David ruled first over Judah alone for seven years (2 Sam. 2:11). Thus, Judah was originally separate and later joined Israel under David. Then, after the reigns of David and Solomon, Israel and Judah separated into two kingdoms. Was this the splitting of a unity, or was it not a simple reversion to their original situation? The indication is that they reverted to two entities as they had been for much of their history, Israel and Judah.

To summarize, then: Israel first came together in the Judean and Samarian hills of Palestine, probably coalescing from a number of groups that settled in the same general area. These people formed a collection of independent tribes, who sometimes joined together for collective action when it suited their purpose. Many scholars argue that common worship of the God *Yhwh* (perhaps pronounced something like Yahweh) helped bring the tribes together. The name seems to be first attested as part of a topographical name, '*yhw* of (the land of the) Shasu', which may have been short for *bt-yhw* 'house of Yahwe'. Some think a group of Shasu or a related group who joined Israel at this time brought the worship of Yhwh, which then spread more widely through the tribes.

This brings us to the book of Samuel and the figure of Samuel, who looks like the last of the judges. At this point, these tribes began to realize that they needed a collective leader to prevent some of the horrible things that had taken place in their wider community and also to succeed in their collective aims. In the memorable words found at several points in Judges, 'In those days there was no king in Israel, but every man did that which was right in his own eyes' (17:6; 21:25). It was time for a king.

Samuel

Samuel is a curious figure in the biblical text. He functions as a priest, even though he is not of the priestly tribe of Levi. He also acts as a prophet, though it was not unusual for prophets to come from among the priests and Levites. But he also looks very much like

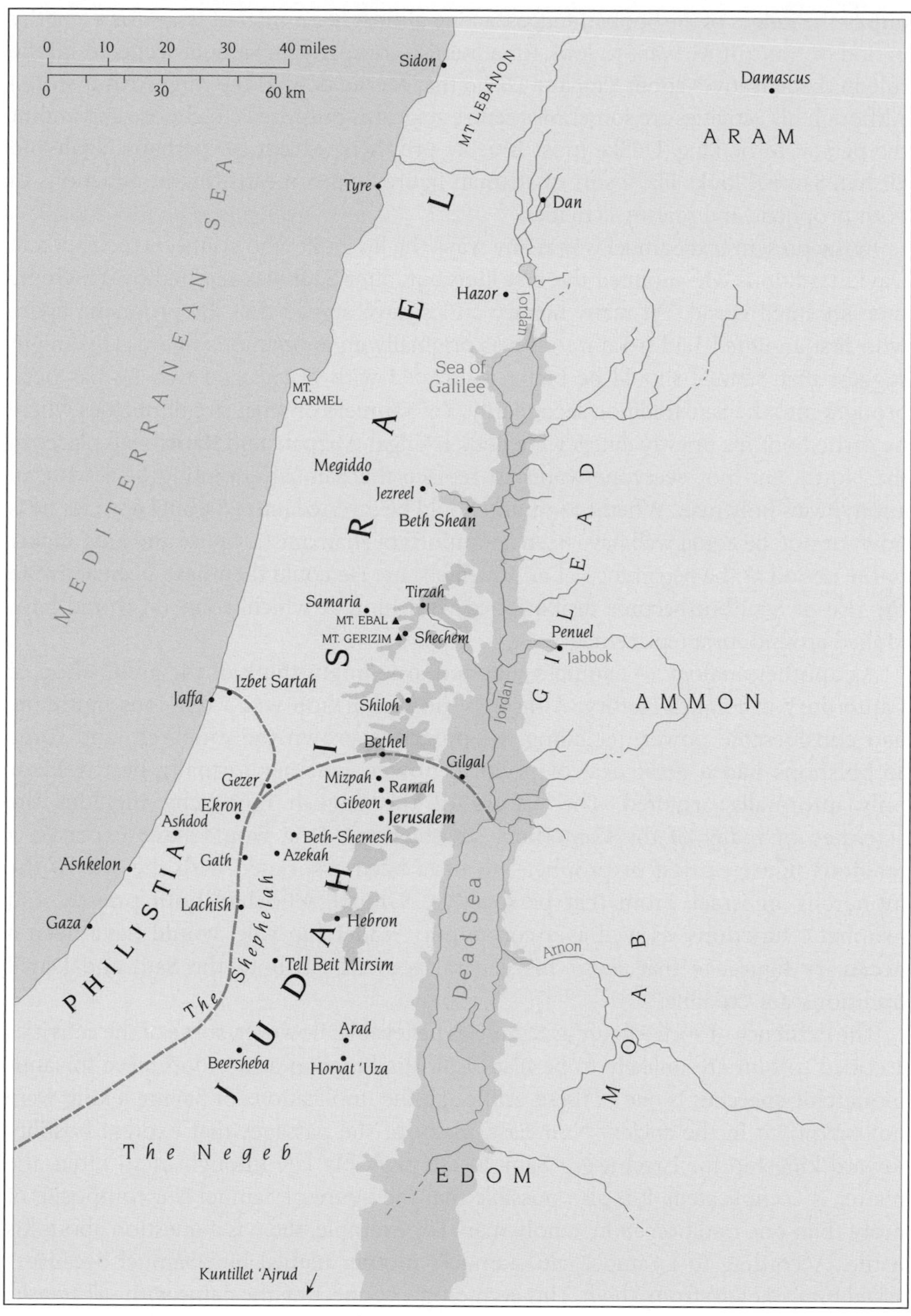

2. The Holy Land in the period of the Israelite monarchies one of the judges of the book of Judges, acting almost like a ruler of Israel for a lengthy period of time. (If we want to look for a literary comparison, Samuel seems to fill the role in the narratives about Saul and David that Merlin does in the King Arthur story.) Although his activities are sometimes centre stage, his purpose is to choose and anoint the person to be king. Unlike most Israelite prophets (except for perhaps Elijah and Elisha), Samuel looks like a sort of shaman figure, which means that he functions in both prophetic and priestly activities.

In the present text Samuel is in many ways the linchpin who connects the Saul and David traditions. He anointed the first king but, after Saul was rejected by Yhwh, he then anointed David. Yet many literary critics have argued that the prophetic figure who first anointed Saul (1 Sam. 10:1) was originally an anonymous figure. This might suggest that Samuel should be better associated with David, and that he has been brought into the Saul tradition secondarily. Yet Samuel's original circuit of cities where he carried out his priestly duties were Bethel, Gilgal, Mizpah, and Ramah, all places in the North, and not everyone wants to replace the Samuel anointing Saul with an anonymous holy man. Whether Samuel should be inserted into 1 Samuel 9–10 (as he is now) or not, he could well have been an important shamanistic figure and king maker in the period at the beginnings of an Israelite state. He could then have been active in the rise of Saul but become disillusioned with him, at which point he would have looked around for a replacement.

As another analogy to Samuel's function, one might think of the archbishop of Canterbury in English history. Although the archbishop was a religious figure, he had considerable power, including the power to crown the monarch, and some archbishops had a great deal of political power, whether formally bestowed or only informally acquired. The history of the English monarchy includes the activities of many of the Canterbury archbishops. One would have expected a religious figure—priest or prophet—to have been associated with the rise of the monarchy in Israel. From that perspective, Samuel, who had both priestly and prophetic functions, as well as a community leadership role, would have been a necessary figure. In that sense, his general activities in both the Saul and David traditions are credible.

The existence of such a figure as Samuel is believable; however, some of the activities ascribed to him are unlikely to be historical. His function as a mouthpiece for anti-monarchic speeches is one of these. Although the implications of having a king were not unknown in the ancient Near East, many of the passages that express hostility toward kingship for Israel (e.g. 1 Sam. 8) are probably late (though as so often, the matter is complicated). It is also possible that the figure of Samuel is a composite of more than one tradition about a holy man. For example, there is a question about his name. According to 1 Samuel 1:20, Samuel's mother named him Samuel because 'I asked him' (*she'iltiv*) from Yhwh. This etymology, connecting the name with *sh'l* 'to ask', does not fit Samuel but Saul whose name means 'asked (of God)'. This illustrates how complex the Samuel tradition was.

The Philistines

The Philistines are notorious as an ancient, cruel, barbaric warrior people, in the image commonly conjured up by their name, especially among those who have a knowledge of the Bible. Yet we have gained a good deal of information about the Philistines in recent years, primarily through archaeology, and we have a considerable understanding of how they came to settle in the coastal plain of Palestine and how they lived in this new homeland. We know they were a part of the 'Sea Peoples' who came from Cyprus, the Aegean, and elsewhere north and west in the Mediterranean. Various of the Sea Peoples were fought and subdued by the Egyptians, and some were even settled in Egypt and incorporated into the Egyptian army. Egyptian inscriptions not only talk about them but even depict them in battle and migrating with their families.

Surprisingly, the Philistines first appear in Genesis where they are alleged to be active during the so-called 'Patriarchal Period', which is variously dated to the early or middle second millennium BCE. At this time, no historical Philistines existed, because the movement of the Sea Peoples and their encounter with Egypt had not taken place. We can only assume that this is an anachronistic feature of Genesis, written at a time when the Philistines had long been associated with the coastal plain to the west of Judah. The author was apparently not aware that they were not a part of the original inhabitants of Canaan. The Philistines surface again in the book of Judges, especially in the story of Samson, where they more directly relate to history. The reason is that the Philistines seem to have settled in the southern coastal plain of Palestine in the 12th century BCE, or the early part of Iron Age I.

The main biblical account of the Philistines is in the books of Samuel. Because of the amount of work being done in the ancient area of Philistia (the southern coastal plain of Palestine between Gaza and the hills that lead up to Jerusalem), there has been

A relief of the sea battle in which the Egyptian Pharaoh Ramesses III repulsed the Sea People. Some of them, including the Philistines, settled in the coastal regions of the Holy Land.

Samson, by Solomon J. Solomon.

much archaeological comment on the history of the Philistines as presented in the Bible. Here there is potential engagement between biblical text and archaeology. Unfortunately, many of the welcome archaeological finds do not impinge directly on the Bible. For example, the pebbled hearth which has recently been noted as characteristic of the Philistine area for many centuries seems to have no analogue in the biblical text.

At this point, we shall consider some biblical examples from 1 Samuel that relate to the Philistines and ask, when might these episodes have been written down? These examples are (1) the Ark Narrative, (2) the list of Philistine cities, (3) the architecture of Philistine temples, (4) Achish, king of Gath, (5) the question of metal workers in 1 Samuel 13:19–21, and (6) some details of military matters.

Our first example is the so-called 'Ark Narrative' (1 Sam. 4–6). This is the story of how the Ark of the Covenant was taken into battle by Israel against the Philistines, assuming that God would aid them. Instead, it was captured by the Philistines, who put it in the temple of Dagon in Ashdod. The next day the statue of Dagon was found on the ground. The Philistines set it back upright, but the following day it was not only lying on the ground but its hands and feet were cut off and lying on the threshold. The text notes that this is why those entering the temple of Dagon do not step on the threshold

A figurine of Ashdoda, a Philistine goddess not mentioned in the Bible.

(1 Sam. 5:5). Furthermore, the people of Ashdod were struck with a physical affliction. Exactly what it was is unclear, but it seems to have affected an intimate region of the anatomy. The Ark was moved to other Philistine cities, but the inhabitants also suffered the same physical affliction. According to the Greek version (and implied in the Hebrew of 1 Samuel 6:4–5, 18) they were also infested with a plague of mice. Finally,

they put the Ark in a cart hitched to two cows, and allowed it to return across the border to Israel by itself.

Some see evidence of earlier memory here. One scholar argued that at the core of 1 Samuel 1 to 1 Kings 1 is a 'Prophetic Record' that goes back as early as the 9th century. This optimism for early narratives in 1 and 2 Samuel has not been widely matched, however, since many other scholars have found what they see as evidence of late composition, editing, and insertion, and prefer the more conventional date in the 7th century. For example, it has been noted that the Ark Narrative does not contain language that we know of from Deuteronomy, which suggests that it might well be written after the time of Deuteronomy (which is usually dated to the 7th century BCE). Above all, though, we must observe the intent of the story, which is not to record the history of Israel. Rather, the story seems to have two aims. The first is obvious: to show the power of the God of Israel, Yhwh, and that he is mightier than the god of the Philistines. A secondary theme related to this also draws attention to the fact that the Israelites were not respectful of Yhwh when they took the Ark into battle with the presumption that its presence would protect them. On the contrary, the important thing was to be right with God, not simply to rely on a talisman to aid them.

The other aim of the story is to ridicule the Philistines, especially their worship. Their affliction with an embarrassing disease, not to mention a plague of mice, makes them a laughing stock, while their god Dagon lies broken in pieces on the temple floor. We have no confirmation about a Philistine custom of not treading on the threshold of their temples, though such a custom may have been known to ancient Israelites. Needless to say, nothing in the Philistine mythical tradition would have explained it as arising from a defeat of Dagon or the destruction of his image by Yhwh. Yet for the Israelites this tradition-honoured custom was caused by Yhwh's humiliation of Dagon in his own temple. The Israelites must have roared with laughter when this story was told around the campfire! As to the origin of the story it could be early or late. Yet the indication is that it reflects a period long ago, when Israel first got the better of the Philistines. This suggests that it was first written down (as opposed to just being told orally) at a later time. That would fit the 7th century better than the 9th.

Our second example considers the list of Philistine cities. Several such lists are found (Josh. 11:22; 19:43; Judg. 1:18; 1 Sam. 6:17; Jer. 25:20; 2 Chron. 26:6). 1 Samuel 6:17 lists five cities that have become known as the Philistine Pentapolis: Ashdod, Gaza, Ashkelon, Gath, and Ekron. Gath was destroyed by the Aramean king Hazael about 830 BCE and ceased to be a major Philistine site (2 Kgs 2:18). The biblical text seems to remember the original importance of Gath, which suggests an early memory. Whether the cities were united into some sort of Pentapolis, with a council of *seranim* (apparently the Philistine word equivalent to 'lords, nobles') making decisions for it as pictured in the text (e.g. 1 Sam. 5:8, 11), is a separate question. With Gath and Ekron both roughly the same size but also much larger than the other three cities in Iron Age I (*c.*1200–1000 BCE) and Iron Age IIA (*c.*10th century BCE), would they have been content to share power and authority equally with the smaller cities? Would they not have been rivals, at least in certain ways? These data do not seem to be reflected in the text in any way. As one prominent scholar notes, 'The treatment of the five Philistine main sites as a unified block was not historical: it was an element of "theological historical writing" projected back.' We also have the statement in 1 Samuel 7:14 that the cities of Gath to Ekron were returned to Israel after the Ark incident. This is clearly unhistorical in the light of archaeology: we have no evidence of Israelite/Judahite occupation at this time. Indeed, 1 Samuel 17:52 evidently has Ekron in Philistine hands during the time when David was young, not too many years afterward (Gath will be further discussed below under 'David').

The next consideration relates to the architecture of Philistine temples. The main example of this is not in Samuel but Judges. The placement of the pillars supporting the roof in the Philistine temple in Judges 16:25–30 looks like a match to those found in archaeological excavations, where pillars placed closely side by side support the roof. Yet we must qualify this positive statement with two more negative ones. First, the statement that there were people on the roof who could observe events on the ground floor of the temple (as if overlooking an unroofed courtyard) is not confirmed by anything so far found. Secondly, this description of a Philistine temple could be quite late, since temples existed in Philistine towns until very late (note 1 Macc. 10:84; 11:4). Thus, this does not suggest textual data earlier than the conventional 7th century date mentioned earlier.

For the fourth example, a number of biblical passages refer to Achish, king of Gath (1 Samuel 21:11, 13; 27:2–4, 11; 1 Kgs 2:39). We have an inscription from the 7th century, showing there was an Achish who was ruler of Ekron. It has been suggested that the author of the narrative wrote in the 7th century but made use of the name of a contemporary ruler in the area of Philistia. Because Gath was already a strong element in the David tradition, however, he made Achish a ruler of Gath. This is a reasonable argument, but it seems to me that those who see Achish as a ruler of Gath in an early tradition about David also present a reasonable picture. At the moment, I see no way of demonstrating for certain whether Achish is a late introduction into the narrative or an early element in the tradition.

A fifth example concerns 1 Samuel 13:19–21, a passage that is often mentioned but seldom discussed in proper depth. This passage essentially says that the Philistines control the working of metal, and that for repair or sharpening of farming implements Israelites had to travel to the Philistines and pay them. The passage is somewhat difficult, partly because it may be corrupt and partly because the instruments listed are not all clearly identified, though their status as metal farm tools seems obvious from the context. What is done to them by the Philistine metal workers is also not certain. Does the word indicate 'repair' or does it mean simply 'sharpen'? To renew a ploughshare that had been blunted or even damaged by stones would probably cost two-thirds of a sheqel (the value of the Hebrew word *pim* in the passage), but this would seem extremely expensive as a price simply to sharpen a sickle. Moreover, the Israelite farmer could easily have found appropriate whet stones in the environment to use to sharpen a sickle or mattock. On the other hand, repair of a ploughshare damaged by stones would require the skill of a specialist and would have been worth the price of a *pim*.

Gath has provided the first physical evidence on the state of metallurgy technology in Philistia in the early Iron Age. Both bronze and iron working are attested for Iron Age IIA, once again indicating the importance of both metals at this time. But what we do not find is any indication that the Philistines controlled metal technology. As the archaeologist who excavated Gath notes, 'one cannot speak of a Philistine monopoly on metal production in the late Iron Age I and Iron Age IIA (the available evidence from the ancient Levant does not support this supposition)'. It seems to me an absurd notion that Israelites had to go to Philistia just to sharpen their farm implements, not only paying a very high price but also taking the time and trouble to travel there and back. What we find in 1 Samuel 13:19–22 is a statement of theology, not contemporary metal technology.

Finally, for our last example we want to consider some issues relating to the military. Only a couple of instances can be looked at, but they are helpful in the question of dating. First, we have the question of Goliath's armour. Although there are a few who argue that it reflects Iron Age I, many have followed the German specialist Kurt Galling in maintaining that 'the narrator... has put together the wholly singular weaponry of Goliath from diverse elements of military equipment known to him' at a

The Valley of Elah, the traditional site of David's slaying of Goliath.

rather later time. An archaeologist has argued that Goliath's armoury represents a Greek hoplite soldier of the 7th century, though he also recognizes that some parts of the description fit Assyrian equipage. This last point complicates matters: is an actual soldier with his weaponry being described, or is the image of Goliath simply made up eclectically (as Galling seems to be saying)? In either case, though, a later time than Iron Age I or Iron Age IIA (12th to 9th century BCE) is being represented.

Saul

Although the story of Saul starts out well, the overall picture of Saul in the biblical narrative is negative. If we read the account carefully, King Saul was a problem for the narrator of 1–2 Samuel without a doubt. But to the historian, this is an excellent reason for believing he was a historical personage. It seems clear that the narrator wanted to tell the story of David but had to deal with Saul as well, even though he would rather have ignored or forgotten about him. According to narrative logic, the rulership and dynasty should have begun with David. The whole story of the monarchy is of the legitimacy of the Davidic dynasty and the illegitimacy of the northern kingship. The Northern Kingdom should not have existed, and the northern kings were presented as usurpers.

How is this to be explained, if David was also a usurper—not part of the dynasty originally chosen by God? The narrator of 1 Samuel has to present it that Saul's dynasty was not just wiped out, but that his descendants were null and void as far as kingship was concerned—a rather strange concept, if it was the king and dynasty originally chosen and anointed by Yhwh. If Saul's rulership and dynasty could be overturned, why not that of David? Yet the narrative insists on treating them quite differently. Thus, it seems that the narrator was stuck with Saul and his family. He had a strong tradition about the Saulides, and he had to deal with it. He could not ignore them and simply write about his beloved David. We can only conclude that Saul was a historical character, however much the text might have distorted his memory. But what else can we say with more or less confidence about this figure?

As has long been observed, 2 Samuel 2:9 describes Saul's son Ishbaal (or Ishbosheth) as ruling over 'Gilead, the Ashurites, Jezreel, Ephraim, and Benjamin'. This is reasonably the territory ascribed to Saul. It is especially important because it does not include Judah, for reasons which will be discussed below under David. Apart from some territory on the other side of the Jordan, the core of the fiefdom is the central hill country, which archaeology suggests is the centre of the Iron Age I settlement area. Many of Saul's activities could have been accomplished in two years (cf. 1 Sam. 13:1, which most scholars think is a damaged text), though many scholars feel that is too short a time for his reign. Apart from this corrupted text, there is no reason why Saul could not have ruled for a longer period of time.

Saul was supposed to have originally made his name by fighting the Amalekites (1 Sam. 15). On the surface, this appears unlikely, since the territory of the Amalekites was presumed to have been in the Negev (Num. 13:29), whereas Saul was fighting in the north. That is a valid objection, since Saul's territory does not appear to have included Judah, much less the areas to the south of it. It has been argued, however, that Saul attacked Amalekites who were living in the region of Samaria. This is much more credible as a historical event.

Much of the Saul tradition involves fighting against the Philistines. It is plausible that Saul fought the Philistines, but the biblical picture that the Philistines were expanding into Israelite territory in the hill country is not very plausible. On the contrary, *it is more likely that the Israelites first attacked the Philistines than the other way round.* Philistines had lived happily in the coastal region for well over a century. They were far from exhausting its 'carrying capacity', i.e. its ability to maintain their population at a reasonably high level. The Shephelah (foothill region) acted as a transition zone, and also provided opportunity for the Philistines to expand if they had wanted to do so, without moving into the highlands.

It was probably the case that the highlanders made periodic raids into the prosperous lowlands, to carry off livestock and stored grain and perhaps take a few captives for slaves or for ransom. This is a regular story through history, known from many examples (such as Scottish raids into the English border country during medieval times). Such raids would have forced the Philistines to send troops occasionally on retaliatory incursions into the highlands. But the idea that the Philistines were wanting to expand their territory into the highlands at this time looks unlikely. On the other hand, occasional raids may not have been sufficient as the population of the highlands grew, as it was during the Iron Age I period (1200–1000 BCE). It is most likely that the ones aiming to expand their territory at this time would have been the Israelites, though the Philistines would most likely have eventually reacted to developments in the hill country.

In summary, we can note some salient points about the tradition concerning Saul and his family. First of all, Saul looks like a chieftain, with a court that meets under a tree (1 Sam. 22:6). We have two versions of how he became king, each of which is plausible but are to some extent mutually exclusive. One is that he was anointed by Samuel (1 Sam. 9:1–10:16 (23) + 13:2–14:52), which looks like a biased account from a prophetic source that wants to make Saul subordinate to Samuel. Contrary to the text, prophets were not the dominant leaders in Israel at any time, much less at this time. The other account—more likely to be reliable—is that he arose as a deliverer or military leader (1 Sam. 11:1–15). Israel would have been in need of a military leader at this time, especially if they wanted to move out of their highland home into more amenable territory that was controlled by the Philistines.

If the population in the central highlands was already moving toward a new socio-economic situation characterized by a developing centralization, this would have been a good background for the rise of the monarchy. Saul was a successful leader, the first to develop a standing army, who had the support of the people. Saul was not only able to unite the Israelite tribes (though keep in mind that this did not include Judah) but also to incorporate Canaanites and other minority groups into the emerging state.

Loyalty to Saul continued after his death, creating rebellions and other problems for David; indeed, David almost wrecked the monarchy by his sabotage of Saul's rule in order to gain the throne for himself. One scholar sees the historical Saul as the petty king of Gibeon with Benjaminite roots who expanded into surrounding territory to create a state called 'Israel'. Attempts to control local trade routes and find markets brought him into conflict with the Philistines and other independent states. He died trying to expand into the Jezreel-Beth She'an corridor.

David

The focus of 1 and 2 Samuel is on David. He appears already in 1 Samuel 16 and takes up the rest of 1 Samuel and all of 2 Samuel. The importance of David to the 'Bible story' becomes clear already in these two books and is reinforced by many references in the books of Kings and the prophetic and psalmic literature. It is David who becomes the ideal king and the model for those kings of Israel and Judah who followed him (even if they did not necessarily live up to that ideal). Yet surprisingly, David did not necessarily live up to his own ideal. The David narrative in Samuel shows many personal flaws and actions that are censured in the text. The first thing to notice about David is that he is inextricably associated with Judah. As mentioned above, for most of their history, Israel and Judah were two separate entities.

The path of David to the throne is an important part of the story. The text shows that it was complicated, but it also seeks to legitimate David by a variety of means. Note the many ways that the text points to him as the rightful king over Israel. First, he comes as an apprentice to Saul's court, where he can be educated and trained as a courtier (1 Sam. 16:14–23). While a young man in the Israelite court, he performs individual duties for Saul's health, having a personal—even intimate—relationship with the king (1 Sam. 16:14–23). He fights as a champion against Israel's enemies, personally getting rid of the Philistine champion who was terrifying all the Israelite warriors (1 Sam. 17). David then wins the hand of the king's daughter by virtue of his martial deeds and marries her (1 Sam. 18:17–27). A very important step is his anointing by the prophet-priest Samuel (1 Sam. 16:1–13). Finally, even the king's son and heir recognizes David's right to rule (1 Sam. 18:1; 20:12–17; 23:16–18). The writer has thus made every effort to legitimate David. Why? Was it because many people in his own time and also later considered him a usurper?

From the outset David was a warrior. This is one of the best attested pieces of data about David in the text. He first fought as a commander under Saul, but had to flee when Saul was determined to eliminate this competitor (1 Sam. 17–19). After this, David went over to the enemies of Israel, the Philistines. He raised a personal army and fought as a mercenary for Achish, the Philistine king of Gath, but mainly he fought for his own gain and also to escape from Saul's pursuits (1 Sam. 20–31). He supposedly even mustered his men to fight with the Philistines against Israel in Saul's final battle, but the Philistines were too suspicious and dismissed him (1 Sam. 29).

After Saul's death Israel was ruled for several years by his son Eshbaal (or Ishbaal, his real name [1 Chron. 8:33], though the text of Samuel calls him Ishbosheth, 'man of shame'!). David, however, was crowned king over Judah, with his capital city being Hebron (2 Sam. 2). As discussed above, Judah seems to have maintained its independence from Israel for most of its history. David was not content with this state of affairs, however, but schemed with members of Saul's family (like Abner) to take the throne over Israel as well, which indeed happened after a few years (2 Sam. 3–5). David now ruled over a kingdom which consisted of Judah and Israel, though it was only a small kingdom, taking up only the southern part of Palestine that was not ruled by the Philistines.

David continued Saul's fight with the Philistines, especially according to the text of 2 Samuel in 5:17–25 and 8:1. Yet several scholars have argued that the reality of the situation was different, and that David may not have fought with the Philistines but arranged a truce that allowed a peaceful coexistence throughout his reign. There are a number of arguments in support of this. First, David's wars with the Philistines in 2 Samuel 5:17–25 seem only a passing episode, with little consequence; indeed, taking little space to describe. The motive for the Philistines to attack him also looks rather trumped up. These campaigns (and the statement in 2 Sam. 5:25) fit Saul better and were probably borrowed from the Saulide tradition. Secondly, David does not defeat the Philistines (only the tacked on summary statement in 2 Sam. 5:25 claims this), yet the Philistine threat simply disappears from the text. Thirdly, we also have the reference to the 600 warriors from Gath, under the command of Itai, who assist David at the time of Absalom's rebellion (2 Sam. 15:18–22): where do these loyal warriors come from if the Philistines from Gath and elsewhere were enemies of David? Fourthly, Achish king of Gath is clearly at peace with Solomon after the time of David (1 Kgs 2:39–40). Finally, Judah seems to have expanded into the Shephelah in the first half of the 9th century, yet there is no evidence of conflict with Gath which would have dominated the area as a large city at this time. This indicates that an earlier agreement (presumably one made in the time of David) was still in effect. Thus, David (as well as Solomon) was not troubled by the deadly enemy that Saul faced, which left him free to undertake other interests.

The idea that David did not fight with the Philistines takes some getting used to. But if this interpretation is correct, was he still seeking an essential expansion of his territory? According to 2 Samuel, David fought a variety of the surrounding peoples. Essentially, he expanded his territory to the north and east and south, into Moab, Ammon, Edom, and the region of Aramean rule (2 Sam. 8; 10:1–11:1; 12:26–31). The extension of control into Edom and Transjordan is credible. These were smaller, weaker territories and also close at hand. It would not have been difficult for David to take some measure of control in these areas to the east if he did not have to worry about the Philistines on his western flank. However, to defeat the Arameans—even placing a garrison in Damascus (2 Sam. 8:6)—would have been an entirely different matter. The statement that David defeated and took control of the Arameans looks completely contrived. It would have taken large resources, which David's kingdom probably did not have, and would have required a considerable feat of logistics not only to march north and defeat the Arameans but—more important—maintain their submission under David's rule.

A compelling case has now been presented that David's defeat of Hadadezer of Zobah is a literary creation, based on the Aramean king Hazael in the 9th century. This thesis looks compelling, with David's actions against the Arameans being a duplication of events from a much later time. The Arameans are unlikely to have engaged in any confrontation with Israel during David's lifetime. However, David may well have expanded into Transjordan. Moab probably did not develop into a state until a century later, and an Edomite kingdom probably first appeared in the 7th century. But this would have made it easier for David to take control of these areas.

In general, we can say that the story of David's conquests contains only a few genuine historical elements. It certainly looks as if the driving of the Philistines from the central hill country is no more than a literary creation. The same also applies to the conquest of the Arameans, though some expansion of territory at the expense of the Moabites and Ammonites is a possibility. But the one event that seems to have the greatest support from history is the conquest of Jerusalem.

What the various traditions suggest is that there was a collective folk memory of a time when Jerusalem was not Israelite, and even that it came into Israelite hands much later than some of the surrounding territory. This is a remarkable memory, especially if we keep in mind that it would have been more convenient to believe that Jerusalem was conquered with the rest of the territory and divided up by the Israelites without any complications.

Woodcut of Ottoman Jerusalem.

Yet the text acknowledges complications: Jerusalem is sometimes the property of Judah (Josh. 15:63; cf. Judg. 1:8) and sometimes within the territory of Benjamin (Josh. 18:28; Judg. 1:21). In both cases, it recognizes that some of the original inhabitants, the Jebusites, continued to live in the city, alongside the Judahites (Josh. 15:63; Judg. 1:21) or Benjaminites (Judg. 1:21). In spite of this tradition, 2 Samuel 5:6–9 requires David to conquer the city from the Jebusites again. What sort of entity Jerusalem was is not clear. The story suggests a type of fortress, though this does not mean a large or grand settlement, as is confirmed by the image of the Jebusite king of Jerusalem (as 2 Sam. 24:23 seems to label him) who does his own physical threshing of grain at his threshing floor which occupies a central point on the eastern ridge (2 Sam. 24:20–3). David's sons acted as priests at this time, possibly even before he took Jerusalem (2 Sam. 8:17). In any case, David made the Jebusite priest Zadok one of his two chief priests. It was long ago recognized that Zadok was formerly a priest from the pre-Israelite Jerusalem cult, though the evidence for this is rather convoluted.

At this point, we should consider the matter of archaeology, especially as it relates to Jerusalem. The Iron Age begins about 1200 BCE, which is approximately the time that we first find Israel mentioned by name in historical sources. Iron Age I is conventionally dated to about 1200–1000 BCE. According to the text, we should find a Jebusite city for Iron Age I, which was then replaced in Iron Age IIA–B by an expanding city that functioned as an administrative centre and a capital of a considerable kingdom, under David and Solomon. The monumental architecture in the Middle Bronze Age, on one side, and in the 8th to 7th centuries BCE, on the other, are sometimes referred to as two 'bookends', marking off the history of the city. The lack of other finds relating to fortification suggests that Jerusalem was unwalled and unfortified between the Late Bronze Age and Iron Age IIB (16th to mid-8th centuries BCE), and thus Jerusalem was modest at best.

Excavations on the Ophel (the area between the City of David and the temple area) show that the earliest buildings there date only from the ninth century or, more likely, between the eighth and the early sixth centuries BCE. Recent studies have drawn attention to two major contradictions between the biblical account and the Jerusalem of the tenth century BCE as derived from archaeology. Rather than being a great city, the capital of a far-flung empire, as one archaeologist has commented the 'paucity of remains from this time slot in the City of David does not allow one to assume that the population of the city exceeded 2,000'. This agrees with the assessment that Jerusalem of the 10th and 9th centuries was a small town occupied mainly by public buildings, not exceeding 12 hectares and approximately 2000 inhabitants.

This of course differs from the picture given in the biblical text. Yet it is supported by recent excavations, such as the one at the Givati parking lot south of the Temple Mount, which has shown that there were no Iron IIA fortifications on the southeast

---

Right: A modern view of the site of the original City of David; it occupied the raised spur of land stretching south from (but not including) the temple site, seen at the top of the photograph.

ridge ('City of David' settlement); rather, it appears that all fortification remains in Jerusalem from the Iron Age are the outcome of one comprehensive building operation, and this operation took place toward the close of the 8th century BCE, several centuries after the time of David.

In sum, the view that Jerusalem of the tenth and ninth centuries was a small town occupied mainly by public buildings, not exceeding 12 hectares and approximately 2000 inhabitants, seems to be prevailing among archaeologists. The city exhibited the characteristics of a regional administrative centre or the capital of a small, newly established state (the towns of Megiddo, Hazor, Gezer, and Lachish showing similar characteristics at the same time). For the Jerusalem settlement to be little more than a village at the time of David is not a problem. This was probably all that was needed for David's state, considering its small size and complexity. It was certainly an advance on Saul's open-air court under a large tree (1 Sam. 22:6)!

What we find in 1–2 Samuel is the story of a young Judahite warrior made good. He seems to have grown up in a society that was not heavily stratified; nevertheless, there was no doubt tribal leadership, with Judahite elders and perhaps even a tribal chieftain or chieftains. Was David the heir of one of these tribal leaders? There are also some hints that his family was not so humble. After all, he was brought into Saul's court, unlikely to happen to a complete nobody. In any case, David became some sort of mercenary leader: surprisingly, this image appears to be agreed on by two archaeologists who otherwise take somewhat different views on the 'United Monarchy'.

In the biblical story, David fits the image of the hero figure; there are many folkloristic elements and a variety of traditions; yet there are also traditions with some interesting twists, such as the willingness to acknowledge some of David's weaknesses, the need to legitimate David from a variety of angles—suggesting that he was not seen as legitimate by everyone—and the admission that David did not do certain things that we might have expected. One of the interesting points about the Davidic tradition is how 'lumpy' it is. That is, it often disagrees with what we would expect from the biblical text as a whole.

Relationship of Saul and David

It seems clear that there is a historical core to both the Saulide and Davidide traditions. The question now is whether they were simply independent traditions that did not intersect (i.e. that the individuals Saul and David actually had nothing to do with each other), or whether there was a historical connection between them, as the text suggests. In other words, was there a tradition about Saul, who was in some way the first northern king, and then separately a tradition about the first king of Judah, but at the core of the tradition these two were completely separate and had nothing to do with each other? Such an interpretation is quite believable in itself and has the merit of being simple. Why must we complicate the story more than is necessary, even though the biblical redactors certainly did?

Saul and David, by Rembrandt.

Yet in the present narrative the David traditions are in part bound up with the Saul tradition. Therefore, the present redacted text has the traditions heavily intertwined, but was that the case in the beginning? A closer examination exposes greater complexity. Note the following: There is first of all the saying, 'Saul has slain his thousands, but David his tens of thousands' (1 Sam. 18:7; 21:12; 29:5). Not a major datum but nevertheless one worth noting, and one likely to be early according to some commentators. If this is an early saying, where did it come from if the David and Saul traditions were originally separate? Secondly, one of the major characteristics of the David tradition (as we already noted above) is the extent to which his reign is legitimated, strongly suggesting that David was a usurper. Why go to all this trouble to make David's rule legitimate if he had been accepted as the first king of Judah by the tradition from the beginning? This suggests that the present picture of the text (that he actually effected a change of dynasty with regard to all Israel) was not a secondary creation but one already there in the tradition when the text was redacted.

Thirdly, one could take the example of Saul's daughter (and David's first wife) Michal. She could have been added to the tradition simply to give a further negative picture of Saul, since her story is ultimately a negative one in which she is rejected and childless, though remaining David's wife. But her story is more complicated and interesting than this. For example, she helps David escape from her father by a clever deception (1 Sam. 19:11–17). After she was married to another man, David expended some effort to get her back (2 Sam. 3:12–16).

Finally, we have to ask: if the Saul tradition was simply about the first king of Israel, separate from Judah, what happened to his dynasty? We know that at a later time, kings well attested in historical sources ruled over Israel. But if the Saul tradition was completely independent of the David one, what happened to the Israelite monarchy that had begun with Saul? Did it simply peter out? If so, what filled the vacuum, and how did it get started up again? It is such questions that make us turn to the David tradition and ask whether the present text is right that David in some way was the successor on the throne of the inchoate state of Israel begun by Saul.

An Aramaic inscription from Dan containing the earliest certain reference outside the Bible to 'the House of David'; it probably dates about 150 years after David's time.

It is as if the Davidic tradition (and we might add, the Solomonic tradition) is *necessary* to fill the gap between Saul and the history of the two kingdoms or monarchies of Israel and Judah. If so, then the much-debated concept of the 'united monarchy' under David and Saul is correct, after all—but only in a particular sense. That is, the first king Saul ruled over a portion of the central highlands, though apparently not Judah. The Judahite David—possibly a tribal leader of Judah or perhaps a 'king' (in some sense) of Judah—took over from Saul (or Saul's son), establishing some sort of rule over both the northern highlands and the Judean highlands.

Solomon

Solomon is an anomalous figure in the Bible. He is David's son and heir. Although he is faced with internal opposition to his kingship, he deals with this quickly and efficiently. But beyond this he fights no wars, makes no conquests, builds no empire. No battle for land is recorded for Solomon nor the conquest of a single square foot of soil. Yet surprisingly he controls a territory far bigger than anything left to him by David. We are not talking about the region between Dan and Beersheba, or even the whole of Palestine and southern Syria. No, Solomon allegedly controls the entire region between

An aerial view of Tel Beersheba, the traditional southern extremity of the Holy Land in the Israelite period.

Egypt and Asia Minor (1 Kgs 5:1), including the trade and economy between the Hittites and Egypt (1 Kgs 10:26–9). It is a veritable Israelite empire. David did not have such power or territory, so where did Solomon get it?

What we see in the case of Solomon is a *Königsnovelle*, a royal Oriental tale. This is a well-known literary type, of which we have a number of examples in antiquity. In such a story, the hero has great wealth, honour, power, and is extremely wise and clever. Once past Solomon's violent consolidation of his throne, the narrative about the whole of Solomon's reign (1 Kgs 2–11) seems to be rather different from those about Saul and David. One is immediately struck by how uniform it is. Although the text shows signs of editing (for there are some repetitions and signs of unevenness), it is essentially a folktale about an Oriental potentate—it is a royal legend.

This is partly shown by Solomon's great wealth. The quantity of gold that Solomon receives each year is 666 talents plus the revenue from trade, etc. (1 Kgs 10:14–15). Only a great empire, such as that of the later Persians, could collect so much wealth: according to Herodotus (3.91) the Persians collected 14,560 talents of silver in tribute annually—the equivalent of 1120 talents of gold. The idea that Solomon could raise 666 talents of gold plus much additional wealth each year is a gross flight of fancy on the part of the writer. In this story, though, the height of marvels is Solomon's great wisdom (1 Kgs 10:3, 6-8, 23–4), though we are given little in the way of examples of how this is demonstrated.

The episode relating to the queen of Sheba illustrates the historical problem (1 Kgs 10:1–13). Although I have characterized the Solomon story on the whole as an 'Oriental tale', the Sheba story is one of the most stereotypical: it has all the marks of a folk tale. The main figure has no name: she is simply 'the queen of Sheba'. She herself is a representative of wealth, wisdom, and power. Yet her function in the story is to marvel at all that Solomon and Jerusalem have to show her: in spite of all her own wealth and wisdom, Solomon's are much greater. He leaves her speechless. The queen of Sheba story has sometimes been defended by explaining it as a journey to establish trade relations between southern Arabia and Israel, yet the biblical text says not a word about such a purpose. On the contrary, according to 1 Kgs 10:1, the queen of Sheba came to Solomon 'to test him with riddles', another element in the *Königsnovelle*. As one ancient Near Eastern specialist expressed it, 'the story of the Queen of Sheba's visit is too much like a fairy-tale in style and in use of narrative themes to be regarded as anything other than a romance from the Persian era'.

This becomes even clearer when we consider the archaeology. What kind of a settlement was Jerusalem in Iron Age IIA (often equated with the age of Solomon)? Was it a minor settlement, perhaps a large village or possibly a citadel but not a city, or was it the capital of a flourishing—or at least an emerging—state? The comments made above about the city in the time of David essentially apply to the city of Solomon, as well—that it was a small settlement.

Solomon's main achievement was building the temple to Yhwh. This might seem just a part of the stereotype, but there are reasons for thinking it was a historical fact.

We would have expected the building to be ascribed to David as the founder of a new dynasty, yet even though according to the text of 1 Chronicles 22 and 29 David did all the work of preparation, it is made very clear that he did not build the temple. Furthermore, it is difficult to find an event during the history of the later kings that might indicate such a temple founding. However, we need to keep in mind that Israelite and Judahite society was not monotheistic at this time. Although Yhwh seems to have been the national God (and there is no evidence that he was worshipped by other peoples elsewhere in the ancient Near East), other deities were also worshipped. Solomon was named after the old god of Jerusalem, Shalem/Shalim. Saul had sons with Baal as a part of their names. We find in some documents not more than a century after David and Solomon people with Baal names. Yhwh was by no means the only God among the Israelites at this time, even if he was very important.

The story of Solomon is a colourful and exciting one, as well as being a theological cautionary tale of how wealth and intellectual gifts can lead you astray if not moderated by piety and humility. But what can we say about the historicity of the Solomonic kingdom? Solomon's alleged building programme of cities and monumental buildings cannot be confirmed archaeologically. On the contrary, Jerusalem was a small settlement—the capital of a small tribal state or something similar. We find evidence of a series of representatives (often relatives) who were sent to the northern areas as the first attempt to build a network of loyalty in an area that had not yet declared for Solomon's rule. Thus, Solomon was historical but he differed considerably from the biblical picture. The king's name shows that he was non-Judean in origin (the name Solomon comes from Shalim/Shalem, the old god of the pre-Israelite inhabitants of Jerusalem). According to some, the Bathsheba story was not suppressed because there was a worse story: Solomon was not David's son! Solomon was born of a Jerusalem mother but not necessarily of a Judean father.

Most biblical historians accept the existence of Solomon but reject the biblical image of a great empire or a powerful ruler over a major state. Solomon simply consolidated what David had conquered and apparently managed to rule peaceably (at least most of his reign) over a small polity in central Palestine. The reality had little to do with the later legend. Thus, here and there might be a verse that reflects the historical Solomon, but to many the Solomon story is the most problematic of the kings in 1 and 2 Kings, providing the thickest cloud of obscurity over the history that lies behind it.

Conclusions

Although this chapter presents only an all-too-brief overview of the relevant texts and their historicity, there are a number of important conclusions, which we can summarize as follows:

1. A religious figure—a shaman-like personage, combining both cultic and prophetic elements in his activities—was probably prominent in the first steps toward a

monarchy. He was remembered in the biblical text under the name Samuel, though whether there was only one figure or perhaps several whom the tradition brought together as a composite is a matter of debate (note that the etymology of his name offered in 1 Samuel 1:20 is actually that of Saul [the Hebrew name 'Shaul' looks as if it is derived from the Hebrew word *sha'ul* 'asked']). It is obvious that the Samuel tradition is complicated, and some sections of it are unlikely to be historical.

2. The narrative about the Philistines is difficult, partly because a good deal of the new knowledge from recent excavations does not directly confirm statements in the text. There are certainly some early elements in the text, especially the recognition that Gath was an important city in the Iron Age I and early Iron Age IIA period, a rival to Ekron and even replacing it later. Yet it also seems clear that some elements in the text reflect a much later period (e.g. Israelite possession of Gath and Ekron), while other elements could be early or late (e.g. the architecture of Philistine temples).

3. An individual named Saul seems to have been an important figure in the origin of the Israelite polity. He came to the throne probably as a military leader by popular acclaim (1 Sam. 11:1–15), whereas the prophetic tradition that the king was subject to Samuel's choice and censure is unrealistic (1 Sam. 9:1–10:16, 23; 13:2–14:52). He fought the Philistines with some success, and set the highland clans on the course of a national state, though it began as a tribal union that Saul brought together and perhaps turned into a tribal state. The apparent boundaries of Saul's kingdom (2 Sam. 2:9) are reasonably in line with the natural and demographic resources in Cisjordan. This union did not originally contain Judah. The text itself does not suggest an extensive administrative apparatus in the case of Saul. However, the tradition also recognizes that David was not the first king, which is likely to be correct.

4. David arose from Judah, probably from a prominent family, not the humble origins that some texts seem to suggest. In spite of not being from the Israelite area, he seems to have found a place at Saul's court where his military exploits and perhaps his intrigues made him a rival, and thus an enemy, of Saul. The text makes both Saul and David mainly military leaders. David left Saul's service and established himself as head of a band of mercenaries fighting for the Philistines and living by raiding, probably including some areas of Israel and even Judah. When Saul was killed, David was eventually able to unite the inchoate state of Israel with Judah under his rule, making Jerusalem his residence and capital. A strong link is made between David's rise and Saul's court, but much of this looks like a deliberate attempt to legitimate David as king from a variety of angles: anointing by Samuel (1 Sam. 16:1–13); armour-bearer in Saul's court and who plays the lyre for Saul personally (1 Sam. 16:14–23); slaying of Goliath (1 Sam. 17); marriage to Saul's daughter (1 Sam. 18:17–27).

5. As ruler, one of David's main achievements was to make an agreement with the Philistines so that his energies were not wasted in fighting them; to what extent he expanded Saul's territory is a moot point, though he probably extended his control into Transjordan. The hill country of Israel and Judah still seems to be the core of his kingdom. Thus, David in a sense ruled a united monarchy, but it was not the great

'United Monarchy' pictured by the biblical text, especially under Solomon. As with Saul, the text does not suggest an extensive administrative apparatus. Contrary to expectations David does not build a temple (though in 1 Chronicles a strenuous effort is made for him to do everything short of the actual building).

6. Solomon succeeded David. He was possibly not even David's son, and he bore the name of the old deity of Jerusalem. He did not expand David's realm in that he was not a great military leader, but he consolidated David's conquests into Transjordan and peripheral areas. However, the truce with the Philistines seems to have been maintained, since nothing is said about them during Solomon's reign. He expanded Jerusalem, though it was still small by later standards, but, most important, he built the temple. This and other factors led later to a legend of an Oriental potentate of fantastic power, wealth, and wisdom, which we find in 1 Kings 1–11 but which had little in the way of historical reality behind it. The original tale seems to have spared no achievement or tale of wealth and magnificence for Solomon; however, a later Deuteronomist, whose concern was theological, tempered the story with criticisms of Solomon's being led astray by his wealth and especially his excessive harem. Apart

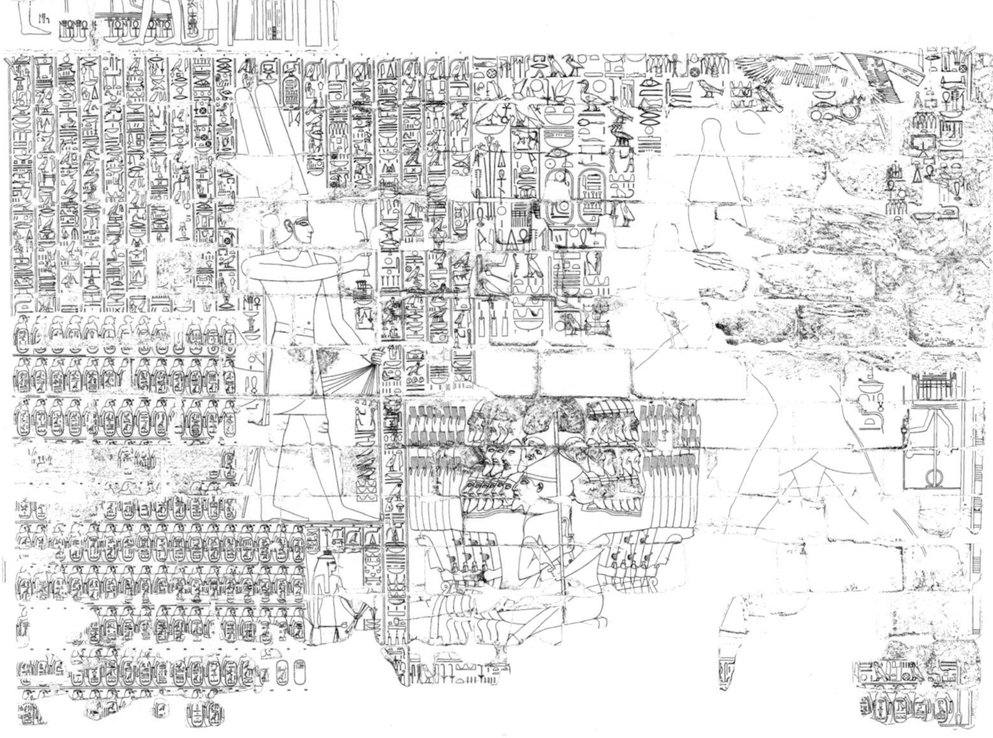

Pharaoh Shoshenq (Shishak) I's conquest inscription, including an account of his invasion of the Holy Land.

from building the temple, Solomon's main achievement was holding together the realm he inherited from David.

7. Not a part of our texts, but to complete the story: after Solomon's death, the rivalries, and perhaps external events such as the invasion of the Egyptian Pharaoh Shoshenq (1 Kgs 14:25–6), split the kingdom shortly before 900 BCE. At this point, leadership passed to the northern territory which had the greater concentration of natural resources and wealth potential. After only a few decades, the rise of the Omri dynasty established the kingdom of Israel as the dominant power in the region and led to a true Israelite state (David and Solomon still presided over what were probably tribal states). Whether Judah was its vassal, as some have suggested, or just its junior partner, as others have argued, probably makes little difference.

CHAPTER 3

Israel and Judah

(c.931–587 BCE)

ANDRÉ LEMAIRE

FOR the kingdoms of Israel and Judah, the historian has to take into account three different kinds of sources:

1. Contemporary epigraphy: Hebrew inscriptions are becoming more numerous, especially from the 8th century BCE on. From *c.*800 BCE on, we now have many ostraca (inscriptions on shards), inscriptions on vessels or on weights, seals, seal-impressions, bullae (small stamped pieces of clay originally tied to a papyrus), as well as one papyrus. They mainly give us a glimpse into the contemporary royal administration. Unfortunately we have only very few fragments of royal monumental inscriptions. Yet this kind of inscription is attested for the Philistine, Moabite, Ammonite, and Aramaic kingdoms neighbouring Israel and Judah, and some of them (for instance, the Mesha and Tel Dan inscriptions) explicitly mention kings of Israel and Judah. Furthermore, if Egyptian epigraphy is mainly useful for the very beginning of this period, later on Mesopotamian cuneiform inscriptions are more illuminating, mentioning several kings of Israel and Judah, along with suggestions of their political role in the Levant. Both kingdoms had to face the power of the Neo-Assyrian and Neo-Babylonian empires that finally absorbed them.
2. Contemporary archaeology: Many ancient towns of the kingdoms of Israel and Judah have been partly excavated: for instance, Gezer, Samaria, Dor, Megiddo, Hazor, and Dan, for the kingdom of Israel and Jerusalem, Lachish, Beersheba, and Arad for the kingdom of Judah. Although the dating of the various strata is sometimes discussed and still approximate for the 10th and 9th centuries, it is generally clearer for the 8th, 7th, and beginning of the 6th centuries. Furthermore several surveys of parts of the country throw light on the agricultural and pastoral economy and its evolution during this period. These archaeological data allow us to better understand the economical and demographical situation of both kingdoms.
3. A synchronistic historiographical tradition about this period is contained in several biblical books: the books of Kings, the books of Chronicles, and several historical references or allusions in the prophetic, legal, and wisdom books. This

historiographical tradition needs to be critically appreciated, taking into account the results of textual and literary criticism. While the present form of the books of Kings was apparently fixed during the 6th century BCE, the books of Chronicles present us a revised historiographical tradition probably written in the second half of the 4th century BCE. This revision apparently used the books of Kings as a source but it is not clear whether their author(s) had other independent historical sources concerning the First Temple period as well. The books of Kings themselves contain genuine historical information, often written in the 'annalistic style'. The names of several kings that they mention are also attested in the Syro-Palestinian and Mesopotamian sources, though of course it needs to be remembered that these themselves should also be critically evaluated, with allowance made for their character quite often as propaganda. Yet, the biblical historical tradition, the earliest writing of which probably dates from the 10th century, was apparently updated and revised several times. In particular, in the second half of the 7th century, the ideology most clearly expressed in the book of Deuteronomy clearly influenced the editing of the books of Kings, and this Deuteronomistic ideology, including especially the Torah as an ideal constitution and its cult centralized in Jerusalem, has to be taken into consideration for a historical appreciation.

The chronology of the synchronistic historiography of the books of Kings is detailed and seems generally well informed. Yet there are several detailed problems with some variants in the textual tradition contained in the early Greek translation of the Old Testament known as the Septuagint, and sometimes there are discrepancies of a few years when comparing this chronology with the mention of Israelite and Judean kings in the Mesopotamian historiographical tradition. Actually one of the difficulties seems to be that the synchronistic tradition of the books of Kings does not always specify the length of co-regencies. Thus the proposed chronology remains approximate, generally by one or two years but sometimes by as much as about ten years.

To understand the history of the kingdoms of Israel and Judah, it is also necessary to appreciate the main geographical features of each kingdom. The kingdom of Israel was larger, wealthier, and more populated than the kingdom of Judah. The kings of Israel dominated the central Cisjordan territory from about ten kilometres north of Jerusalem to lower Galilee, generally including Gezer and the Sharon plain as well as the higher valley of Jordan (Hazor, Dan). Yet this last part of the territory together with northern Transjordan (Gilead) was also sometimes occupied by the Aramaic kingdom of Damascus, while central Transjordan, east of the Dead Sea and north of the river Arnon, was disputed by the Moabite kingdom. Actually the kingdom of Israel revealed itself as in many ways unstable: its capital moved several times (Shechem, Penuel, Tirzah) before being fixed in Samaria by Omri king of Israel towards 880 BCE. The royal succession was often fixed by a military *coup d'état* and the kingdom knew several dynasties, the longest one, the Jehu dynasty, lasting less than one century. Finally, due to its geographical position, it was more exposed to the expansion of the Neo-Assyrian Empire.

The kingdom of Judah occupied the southern central Cisjordan, mainly the mountains of Judah and the territory of Benjamin with most of the Shephelah (the lowlands to the west of the Judean hills) and of the Negev in the south as far as Beersheba. On the western side, the kingdom was limited by the Philistine kingdoms of Ekron and mainly of Gath before the latter was destroyed by Hazael of Damascus about 810 BCE. The territory of Judah was less fertile than Israel but its capital was always Jerusalem, famous for containing the temple and the royal palace built by Solomon. Though there were two assassinations of kings, they always belonged to the same dynasty, the 'House of David' (mentioned in the Tel Dan and Mesha stelae), for more than four centuries. Comparatively isolated in the mountains of Judah, this kingdom suffered less from the interest and ambition of the Neo-Assyrian Empire but was subject to Edomite pressure in the south at the end of the period.

Since the kingdom of Israel was more powerful than Judah and sometimes dominated it politically, we may distinguish the different early periods according to the dynasties of the northern kingdom.

War between Israel and Judah (c.931–881 BCE)

The secession of Israel from David's House was not accepted by the new king of Jerusalem, Rehoboam son of Solomon: for half a century there was war to fix the precise border between the two kingdoms. Jeroboam was chosen as king of Israel by an assembly of Israel, apparently with Egyptian support (1 Kgs 12:20). He claimed that his legitimacy came from his designation by the prophet Ahijah from Shiloh (1 Kgs 11:29–39) and established his kingdom's capital first at Shechem, then at Penuel and later on at Tirzah (northern Tell el-Far'ah, about 10 km north-east of modern Nablus). He also established two royal sanctuaries near the northern and southern border of its kingdom, at Dan and Bethel (1 Kgs 12:26–33).

The separation of Israel from Jerusalem apparently had the support of pharaoh Shishak/Shoshenq I, the founder of the 22nd dynasty: 'In the fifth year of Rehoboam's reign, Shishak king of Egypt attacked Jerusalem. He removed the treasures of the house of Yahweh and of the royal palace, and seized everything' (1 Kgs 14:25–6). This looting of the treasures of Jerusalem by Shishak/Shoshenk I apparently fits in with a campaign to Palestine undertaken by this pharaoh which is indicated in a list of Judean and Israelite towns to be found on a wall of the Karnak temple and also by a fragment of Shoshenk I's stele found at Megiddo. In its present state, the fragmentary Karnak list does not contain the name 'Jerusalem' but it does include the names of several places in the Negev as well as those of towns from the northern kingdom of Israel. The detailed interpretation of this list is still discussed: it does not seem necessary to think of a list of destroyed towns but rather of towns which had to pay homage to pharaoh. Since Rehoboam seems to have opposed this invasion, several Judean towns were apparently destroyed while, in Israel, Jeroboam I may have spontaneously paid homage to his earlier protector so that there was no reason to destroy them.

Shoshenq I apparently died not long after this campaign. The war between Israel and Judah to fix the border between them was to start again and raged during the reigns of the Jerusalem kings Rehoboam and Abijah/Abijam (*c.*914–912), as well as part of Asa's reign (*c.*912–871: 1 Kgs 14:30; 15:8, 16).

During this period, the kingdom of Israel revealed itself as unstable. According to the Bible, the prophet Ahijah from Shiloh criticized Jeroboam I (1 Kgs 14:9–11), perhaps because Shiloh did not become a royal sanctuary and had to suffer from the competition of those of Bethel and Dan. Jeroboam's son Nadab was soon assassinated by Baasha of the house of Issachar while he was besieging 'Gibbethon, a Philistine city' (1 Kgs 15:27).

Baasha became king of Israel at Tirzah (1 Kgs 15:33: *c.*909–886). He went on with the war against Judah and fortified Ramah, about 8 km north of Jerusalem, threatening the northern access to the Judean capital. King Asa of Jerusalem (*c.*912–871) replied by sending important presents to 'Ben-hadad son of Tabrimmon, son of Hezion', king of Damascus, so that he should break his treaty with Baasha and make an alliance with him. The Aramean army 'attacked Iyyon, Dan, Abel Beth-Maacah, and that part of Kinneret which belongs to the land of Nephtali' (1 Kgs 15:18–20). We do not know how long the Aramean occupation of the Northern Jordan valley lasted but Baasha had to stop fortifying Ramah and king Asa used the stones of Ramah to fortify his own cities of Geba (in Benjamin) and Mizpah (1 Kgs 15:17–22); according to 1 Kgs 15:12, he also undertook a cultic reform expelling 'the male prostitutes attached to the shrines'.

This Israelite withdrawal reinforced internal opposition, the leader of which seems to have been the prophet Jehu son of Hanani (1 Kgs 16:1). The reign of the son and successor of Baasha, Elah, was very short (*c.*886–885). He was assassinated by Zimri 'chief of half the chariots' but he was not accepted by the Israelite army besieging the city of Gibbeton who proclaimed their commander Omri as king. The latter attacked Tirzah and burnt the royal palace (*c.*885). After eliminating another rival, Tibni, Omri remained alone as king of Israel (*c.*881).

The dynasty of Omri/Ahab (c.881–841)

The dynasty of Omri and his son Ahab is very negatively judged in the books of Kings (1 Kgs 16:25–6) but Omri and Ahab were powerful kings in the political context of the Levant in the first half of the 9th century. Actually Omri is mentioned in the Mesha stele (often known also as the Moabite Stone, lines 4–5) as a king who dominated Moab, and Ahab is mentioned, with the king of Hamath and the king of Damascus, at the head of a contingent of 10,000 foot soldiers and 2000 chariots as one of the leaders of the anti-Assyrian coalition at the battle of Karkar against Shalmaneser III. The archaeological excavations of Samaria, Hazor, Megiddo, and Jezreel seem to indicate

---

Left: Pharaoh Shoshenq (Shishak) I's conquest inscription at Karnak (for a line drawing, see p. 59).

The Mesha stele (also known as the Moabite Stone), which records how Omri, the king of Israel, subdued Moab and how Moab later regained its independence.

The Kurkh stele of the Assyrian king Shalmaneser III, including a description of his battle against a coalition including king Ahab of Israel.

the importance of the fortifications and constructions during this period, which seems to have been a thriving one for Judah as well as for Israel.

The revival of Israel was marked by the building of a new capital, at Samaria, and by a very active foreign policy. Omri submitted Moab to the tribute, and allied himself with the king of Tyre, Ittobaal, marrying his son Ahab with the daughter of Ittobaal, Jezebel (1 Kgs 16:31). Furthermore he reconciled himself with the king of Jerusalem, Asa. The son of Omri, Ahab (*c.*874–853), continued with the same foreign policy in relation to the kingdoms of Moab (2 Kgs 3:4; Mesha stele, line 6), Tyre, and Damascus, as well as in relation to Judah, where the reconciliation was sealed by the marriage of his daughter Athaliah with Joram, the son of the Jerusalem king Jehoshaphat (2 Kgs 8:18.26). By this marriage, Judah more or less accepted being in Israel's sphere of influence. This active foreign policy of alliances with the neighbouring kingdoms was aimed at preventing the Assyrian threat. In 853, the Assyrian annals report that Shalmaneser III attacked the united kingdoms of the Levant with their three leaders Irhuleni, king of Hamath, Adadidri, king of Damascus, and Ahab the Israelite. This battle temporarily stopped the advance of the Assyrian army.

While recognizing some of the achievements of Ahab (1 Kgs 16:34; 22:39), the biblical tradition was probably influenced by the propaganda of the following Jehu dynasty and stressed the negative aspects of his reign, especially the development of the cult of one of the main Canaanite gods, Baal, and the misuse of royal power severely condemned by the prophet Elijah (1 Kgs 18; 21). For the deuteronomistic redactor, Ahab 'did more that was wrong in the eyes of Yahweh than all his predecessors' (1 Kgs 16:30), and became the archetypical bad king; he could only have a violent death and the story of 1 Kgs 22:29–38 tells how he died at the battle of Ramoth-Gilead. This battle, however, originally concerned his son Joram (see later in this section) and we do not actually know how Ahab died, although it was apparently not long after the battle of Karkar.

The fact is that his successors were not so successful as Ahab had been. His son Ahaziah (*c.*853–852) soon died after 'falling through a latticed window in his roof-chamber in Samaria' (2 Kgs 1:2) and Mesha, king of Moab, seized this opportunity 'to rebel against the king of Israel' and stopped paying his tribute of wool, lambs, and rams (2 Kgs 3:5). Later on, the brother of Ahaziah, Jehoram, became king (852–841) and tried to master this revolt by organizing a military expedition against Moab with the help of his allied king, Jehoshaphat of Judah. After some successes, the siege of Kir-Hareseth (probably today's Kerak in Jordan) finally failed (2 Kgs 3:27) and Moab remained independent. Finally, with the help of the new king of Jerusalem Ahaziah, Jehoram tried to retake Ramoth-Gilead from the army of the new Aramean king Hazael. Jehoram was wounded during this battle. He retired to Jezreel to recover from his wounds but was then assassinated by his general, Jehu, with all his family, alongside the king of Judah, Ahaziah, and the mother of king Jehoram, Jezebel. The Ramoth-Gilead battle and the *coup d'état* of Jehu in 841 BCE are mentioned not only in the historiographical tradition of the Bible (1 Kgs 22, where originally the king of Israel was Jehoram son of Ahab; 2 Kgs 8:25–9; 9–10; see also Hos. 1:4–5) but also in the fragmentary stele of Tel Dan where king Hazael of Damascus claimed responsibility for killing 'two powerful kings who harnessed two thousand chariots and two thousand horsemen': Jehoram the king of Israel and Ahaziah 'the king of the House of David' (lines 6–9). These tragic events marked the end of the Omri/Ahab dynasty in Israel.

During this period, the kingdom of Judah was living somehow in the shadow of the kingdom of Israel: king Jehoshaphat (*c.*871–846) 'made peace with the king of Israel' (1 Kgs 22:44) and married his son Joram (*c.*848–846–841) to Ahab's daughter Athaliah. Actually the Judean army participated in the battles of the Israelite army but neither army succeeded in mastering the revolt of Mesha (see earlier in this section) and Joram also failed to master the revolt of Edom, which became an independent kingdom (2 Kgs 8:20–3). The son of Joram, Ahaziah, reigned only a few months. He was killed during Jehu's *coup d'état* and his mother Athaliah took upon herself the regency in the name of her grandson Jehoash. He was brought up in the royal temple by Ahaziah's sister, Jehosheba. When Jehoash was seven years old, a *coup d'état* organized by Jehoiada, the priest of the royal Jerusalem temple and husband of Jehosheba, killed Athaliah, the daughter of Ahab and Jezebel, and put Jehoash, Athalia's grandson, on the throne (*c.*835).

The dynasty of Jehu (c.841–749)

The *coup d'état* of Jehu (*c.*841-814) represented a major political change in the history of the kingdom of Israel, a kind of revolution. With the support of traditionalist leaders, Elisha and Jehonadab son of Rechab, 'Jehu suppressed Baal from Israel' (2 Kgs 10:28), destroying the Samarian temple of Baal and its priests (2 Kgs 10:15–27). The killing of Jezebel cut political relations with Tyre as well as with Jerusalem, where Athaliah became regent. The kingdom was politically isolated and had to submit to Shalmaneser III king of Assyria (submission and payment of tribute are represented on the so-called Black Obelisk of Shalmaneser from Nimrud, now in the British Museum). Meanwhile, Hazael, king of Damascus, resisted the Assyrian army. When the Assyrian king stopped his campaigns to the West (after 833), Hazael could take his revenge: he occupied all the northern Transjordan territory of Israel while Mesha, his probable ally, occupied the southern part: the territories of Gad and Reuben (2 Kgs 10:32–3 and also the Mesha stele, lines 7–21). Later on, during the reign of Jehoahaz son of Jehu (2 Kgs 13:1; *c.*819–814–803*), the situation worsened: 'Hazael left Jehoahaz no armed force except fifty horsemen, ten chariots, and ten thousand infantry; all the rest the king of Aram had destroyed and made like dust under foot' (2 Kgs 13:7). Israel had to submit completely to Damascus, becoming its vassal. This is the period of several stories told about the prophet Elisha and it was marked by Aramean and Moabite raids in Cisjordan (2 Kgs 5–6; 13:21) and 'a seven years famine' (2 Kgs 8:1). 'All through the reign of Jehoahaz, Hazael king of Aram oppressed Israel' (2 Kgs 13:22).

* Note that when dates are provided in this triple format, the first two dates indicate the length of the co-regency while the final one refers to the king's death.

A detail of the Black Obelisk of Shalmaneser III showing the submission of the Israelite king Jehu.

The situation was not much better in Judah. After the *coup d'état* of the priest Jehoiada, Judah was also isolated and Jehoash (*c*.841–835–802) probably lost the Judean territories south-east of the Dead Sea, especially Horonayim as indicated in the Mesha stele, lines 31–3. Hazael himself wanted to subdue the whole Levant. After subduing Israel he 'attacked Gath and took it' (2 Kgs 12:17). The archaeological excavations of Tell es-Safi/Gath in Philistia, which lay along the Mediterranean coast, throw light on the way the Aramean army conducted the siege, digging a trench around the city. Later on, this Aramean army 'moved on against Jerusalem' and Jehoash had no other choice than to pay a heavy tribute so that Hazael would withdraw from Jerusalem (2 Kgs 12:17–18). These failures strengthened the internal opposition to the king who, apparently around 819, had put aside the priest Jehoiada and took upon himself the direction of the administration. Finally his servants conspired against him and two of them killed him (2 Kgs 12:21–2).

The Aramean domination of the whole Levant stopped when the Assyrian army of Adadnirari III started new campaigns to the west from 805. This is probably the reason why the Aramean army of Barhadad son of Hazael had to stop the siege of Samaria (2 Kgs 6:24–7:19). In 802, Adadnirari's campaign reached the Mediterranean Sea.

Damascus had to pay a heavy tribute, apparently heavier than the one of king Joash of Samaria, who probably submitted voluntarily. The Aramean army was weakened by the Assyrian campaigns so that the king of Israel, Joash, could defeat it at Apheq, probably in the Jezreel valley (2 Kgs 13:14–25). The Aramean leader Barhadad had to recognize the independence of Israel and the extent of its territory as far as the Jordan as well as the establishment of an Israelite trading quarter in Damascus (1 Kgs 20:31–4). That was the beginning of half a century of prosperity and success for Israel.

For his part, the king of Jerusalem, Amaziah son of Jehoash of Judah, seized the opportunity of the weakening of Damascus to subdue the Edomite kingdom, which he defeated in the valley of Salt (2 Kgs 14:7). After this victory, he felt himself strong enough to provoke the king of Israel (Joash) but he was defeated and captured at Beth-shemesh in the Shephelah. Jerusalem was looted by the Israelite army and part of her city wall broken down. For half a century the kingdom of Judah became practically a vassal of Israel.

When Joash of Samaria died, he was succeeded by his son Jeroboam II (*c.*790–750). The choice of this throne name in imitation of that of the first king of the northern kingdom of Israel expresses the renewal of the kingdom of Israel. Actually Jeroboam II was king for about forty years of prosperity and success in the cultural, economic, and political fields. From *c.*800 BCE, Hebrew inscriptions seem to become more and more numerous, especially those connected with the royal administration such as the Samaria ostraca, the Kuntillet-'Ajrud inscriptions, several seals and seal-impressions (among them the famous seal of 'Shema' servant of Jeroboam' found in Megiddo). This development of the use of writing probably explains the setting down in writing of the Elisha stories (cf. 2 Kgs 8:5) as well as oracles from the prophets such as Amos and Hosea. These prophetic writings may have been stimulated by the existence of an early Aramaic literary tradition about 'the seer Bala'am son of Be'or' as attested on the plaster inscriptions from Tell Deir 'Alla in the Jordan valley (cf. also Num. 22–4).

With peace, the economic situation became better: archaeology and epigraphy seem to attest the development of the use of oil-presses, and the Samaria ostraca as well as several prophetic oracles allude to the quality and abundance of oil (probably

Seal of Shema', servant of Jeroboam II (found at Megiddo).

exported to Phoenicia and Egypt) and of wine. The inscriptions and drawings from Kuntillet-'Ajrud, a royal Israelite road station about fifty kilometres northwest of Eilat (at the northern tip of the Red Sea, on the Gulf of Aqaba), founded at this time (2 Kgs 14:22 and archaeology), also reveal the importance of the international trade of Israelites and Phoenicians between Gaza and the Red Sea.

Jeroboam II was also successful in his relations with his neighbours. As shown by the Kuntillet 'Ajrud inscriptions in Phoenician as well as the Samarian Phoenician inscription mentioning Milkiram, king of Tyre, the Israelite king had very good relations with the kingdom of Tyre. Towards the end of his reign, he seized the opportunity provided by the weakening of the Damascus kingdom by the Assyrian campaign. With Moab as an ally, he regained northern Transjordan (Gilead) as indicated in Amos 6:13 and a fragmentary royal Moabite inscription.

During this period Judah was a vassal of Israel. The peaceful situation brought economic and demographic development. King Amaziah was probably liberated at the coronation of Jeroboam II. He soon left the administration of the kingdom to his son Uzziah/Azariah, this co-regency terminating with the assassination of Amaziah in the Lachish fortress (2 Kgs 14:19–20; Lachish is about 30 miles south-west of Jerusalem). The long and peaceful regency and reign of Uzziah/Azariah (*c.*790–776–739) seems to have been prosperous for the development of agriculture and breeding, especially in the Shephelah where the disappearance of the kingdom of Gath permitted an expansion of the Judean territory. At this period, Jerusalem also started to expand on to the Western Hill and Judah collaborated with Israel and Phoenicia at this time in building up the international trade through Eilat.

Thus, at the end of his reign, Jeroboam II succeeded in re-establishing 'the frontiers of Israel from Lebo-Hamath to the Sea of the Aravah' (2 Kgs 14:25).

These last successes, however, were very ephemeral and were denounced by the prophet Amos (6:13–14). There was apparently a big earthquake with the destruction of houses and cities in about 760 (Amos 1:1 and archaeology) but the damage wrought by this natural catastrophe was apparently soon repaired. More serious for the prophet Amos were the abuse and misuse of the social elite who were living opulently without any interest for the poor and, at the opposite extreme, took unfair advantage of their work and production. At the same time, according to the prophet, this elite class was short-sighted, and was not aware of the danger coming from the Assyrian Empire (Amos 6:1–7).

The success of the Jehu dynasty was short-lived: after Jeroboam II's death, his son Zechariah only reigned six months before being murdered at Ibleam by Shallum son of Yabesh (2 Kgs 15:8).

The last kings of Israel (c.750–722)

The murder of the son of Jeroboam II marks the beginning of the end for the Israelite kingdom. In a period of less than thirty years, there were four assassinations of kings and violent changes at the head of the kingdom. This instability at a dangerous time when the kingdom had to face the expansion of the Neo-Assyrian empire was to lead to its disappearance, as emphasized by the prophet Hosea (8:4; 10:3–4.7).

After the murder of Zechariah, Shallum was king for only one month (2 Kgs 15:13). He was himself killed by Menahem whose reign was ten years long (2 Kgs 15:17: *c.*750–740). Menahem had to face Assyrian campaigns to the west (743ff.) from Tiglath-Pileser III (745–728) and he appears in Neo-Assyrian lists of vassal kings paying tribute as *Minihimme Samarinaia* (i.e. Menahem of Samaria). The amount of the tribute indicated in the Bible was very high: 'a thousand talents of silver', and Menahem had to lay 'a levy on all the men of wealth in Israel, and each had to give the king of Assyria fifty silver shekels' (i.e. 570 g). Such a capitation on apparently 60,000 leading citizens was, we can imagine, probably very unpopular and, when Menahem died, his son Pekahiah (*c.*741–740) was soon assassinated by one of his officers, Pekah son of Remaliah, who became king (*c.*740–732).

Pekah apparently counted his reign years from the assassination of Zechariah son of Jeroboam II (750), probably because he considered the kings who came after as usurpers. With Rezin king of Damascus, he tried to organize resistance to Assyria by forming a coalition of all the Levantine kingdoms. The king of Judah, Jotham son of Uzziah/ Azariah (*c.*749–739–735/4), refused to join this coalition, probably because he was aware

The Astartu relief of Tiglath-Pileser III.

that it could not be successful against Tiglath-Pileser III's Assyrian army. Pekah and Rezin attacked Jerusalem to replace Jotham with another prince, 'the son of Tabeel' (Isa. 7:6). This war between Israel and Damascus, on the one hand, and Judah, on the other hand, is generally called the 'Syro-Ephraimite' war. Apparently Edom joined the anti-Assyrian coalition in attacking Eilat, which became Edomite from now on (2 Kgs 16:6). The situation was very critical in Jerusalem since king Jotham died just as the invasion was getting under way and when his son Ahaz (*c.*735/4–719) was only twenty years old. The prophet Isaiah advised him to keep quiet (Isa. 7) but, thinking that the situation was desperate, Ahaz preferred to send a large gift to Tiglath-Pileser III so that the Assyrian army intervened to the rear of Pekah and Rezin (2 Kgs 16:7–8). The Assyrian army first invaded Philistia (734), probably stopping the siege of Jerusalem, and then attacked the kingdoms of Damascus and Samaria (733–732). Finally Damascus was taken and Rezin killed in 732 (Assyrian annals and 2 Kgs 16:9). Damascus, Gilead, Galilee, and the Sharon plain now became Assyrian provinces. All the kings of the Southern Levant submitted and sent tribute to Tiglath-Pileser III. At the instigation of the Assyrian king, Pekah of Samaria was assassinated and replaced by a new king, Hosea (*c.*731–722), who had to pay a heavy tribute (Assyrian annals and 2 Kgs 15:30). The kingdom of Israel was now limited to central Cisjordan, called 'Ephraim' (Hos. 4:17; 5:3.5.9, etc.).

Hosea paid tribute to Tiglath-Pileser III but ceased to do so on the death of the Assyrian king (727). After reinforcing his power at home, Tiglath's successor Shalmaneser V besieged Samaria (724–722) and finally captured it in his last year which is also the accession year of his successor Sargon II (722). According to the Assyrian annals, 27,280 Israelites were deported as prisoners to Assyria. Among them, 200 charioteers were joined to the Assyrian army and the others were settled in Assyrian provinces, 'in Halah and on the Habur, the river of Guzan, and in the cities of Media' (2 Kgs 17:6). Ephraim became the Assyrian province of Samaria with a governor nominated by Sargon II and some people from other parts of the Assyrian empire were settled there (2 Kgs 17:24), especially after the revolt of Iaubidi of Hamath (720).

Aside from a few cuneiform tablets from Samaria and Gezer, and some seals and a few other fragments, our textual documentation about the territory of the ancient kingdom of Israel practically ceases with the downfall of Samaria. Furthermore, besides a few Israelite names here and there in Assyrian documents (Nineveh, Nimrud, Dur-Katlimmu), we have also almost no documentation about the deportees who were dispersed in the Assyrian empire. Yet, during the Assyrian war, especially during the siege of Samaria, it is quite probable that many Israelites sought refuge in Judah, especially in Jerusalem, which became more populated at about this time, with the occupation of the Western Hill. It is even possible that some of these refugees were later integrated in the Judean administration. This might have been the case, for instance, with Shebna, who is mentioned as a prominent character in 2 Kgs 18:18.26, 19:2, and Isa. 22:15, and this may explain why several Israelite literary traditions could later on be assimilated to the Judean traditions in Jerusalem (on which more below under 'The kingdom of Judah alone').

The coexistence of the two Hebrew kingdoms, Israel and Judah, lasted only a little more than two centuries (*c.*931–722). Israel was clearly the stronger kingdom and often played a leading role in relation to the small kingdom of Judah. Yet Israel was the first to disappear. Why? One of the reasons is probably its instability with its numerous *coups d'état*, military conspiracies, and murders of kings. The king seems to have been essentially a military chief, soon replaced after a defeat. There was also some difficulty fixing the capital and organizing an efficient administration since the kingdom was born from a revolt against a heavy administration (forced labour and taxes: 1 Kgs 12). The capital was not fixed for some fifty years, when Samaria was eventually built by Omri, and there was never a central sanctuary but only local royal sanctuaries in Bethel, Dan, Gilgal, and Samaria. Part of the population evidently kept its Canaanite traditions, partly similar to the ones of the kingdom of Tyre, including the cult of Baal, so that there was a confrontation between both cults as underscored by the story of Elijah on Mount Carmel (1 Kgs 18). Although Jehu destroyed the Baal temple and massacred its servants (841), there were still many Baalist names in the Samaria ostraca (first half of the 8th century). At the head of the royal government, there seem to have been several officials titled 'servants' in the 8th century, who are known from their seals and bullae ('Shema servant of Jeroboam', 'Abdi servant of Hosea', 'Commander of the army, servant of Hosea'). 1 Kgs 18:3 indicates that there was probably a 'chief of the (royal) house' at the head of the royal administration of king Ahab. From the Samaria ostraca, local fields of olive trees and vineyards seem to belong to royal servants staying at the royal palace in Samaria where they received their choice products (see 1 Sam. 8:11–14). Although 'elders' are sometimes mentioned (1 Kgs 12:6.8.13; 20:8; 21:8; 21:11; 2 Kgs 6:32; 10:1.5), their political role is not very clear. It seems that the royal power was eventually influenced by the role of the prophets as royal advisers, as in other countries of the ancient Near East. Actually prophets seem to have played an important role by criticizing royal policy and administration or intervening in successions, or legitimating *coups d'état* by a divine oracle in favour of the new king.

The kingdom of Judah alone (c.722–587)

Confronted with the power of the Assyrians, the kings of Judah adopted a different policy to that of the erstwhile Israelite kingdom: they submitted and accepted being vassals, paying tribute to the king of Assyria. This policy permitted Judah to keep a king from David's House for about 135 years longer.

As we have just seen, this submission to Assyria was connected with the death of king Jotham and the accession of Ahaz (*c.*735/4–719) in a dramatic context. Ahaz voluntarily appealed to Tiglath-Pileser III for Assyrian military intervention against Hosea of Israel and Rezin of Damascus and reinforced this appeal with a generous 'gift' of silver and gold (2 Kgs 16:7–8). Later on, when Tiglath-Pileser III captured the Aramean capital (Assyrian annals) king Ahaz went to meet him personally at

Damascus (2 Kgs 16:10; 732), probably to thank him for his intervention and confirm that he wanted to be a faithful vassal.

In the context of this meeting, the biblical historiography tells how Ahaz made a number of changes in the royal temple of Jerusalem, replacing the small bronze altar with a big altar with steps (2 Kgs 16:10–18). His father, king Jotham, had already made his own changes to the temple, opening a fortified gate in the northern wall surrounding the temple to give people access to the royal temple (2 Kgs 15:35b). The work of Jotham and Ahaz meant that the temple was now not only a royal temple but a temple open to 'all the people' (2 Kgs 16:15). It officially became the central temple of all Judah under Ahaz's son, Hezekiah.

Hezekiah (*c.*727–719–699) was probably designated as the royal successor of Ahaz on the death of Tiglath-Pileser III. He was contemporary with the downfall of the kingdom of Israel and likely originally influenced by the prophet Isaiah. He took drastic measures for cultic and administrative reform.

According to 2 Kgs 18:4, 'he suppressed the hill-sanctuaries, smashed the sacred pillars, cut down every sacred tree and broke up the bronze serpent that Moses had made' and which 'they called Nehushtan'. This was really a drastic reform because Hezekiah not only attacked provincial sanctuaries but also traditional sanctuaries and customs that were assigned to the Patriarchs (Gen. 12:6–8; 13:4; 18:1; 21:23; 26:25; 28:16–22; 33:20; 35:1–8.14–15) and to Moses (Num. 21:6–9). From now on, the Yahwistic cult should be practised only in the Jerusalem temple which, following the architectural modifications made earlier, became the only 'national' temple where Judean people went on pilgrimage for the great feasts. This biblical historiographical tradition of the centralization of the cult in Jerusalem by Hezekiah has sometimes been put in doubt by commentators but the archaeological excavations of Beersheba and Arad seem to confirm its historicity with an approximate date in the second half of the 8th century for the destruction of the Arad sanctuary and of the Beersheba altar.

At the same time, taking into account the probable presence of Israelite refugees in Jerusalem, Hezekiah tried to collect the literary traditions from the kingdom of Israel and to unify them with the Judean literary traditions. This integration of literary traditions at the time of Hezekiah is explicitly mentioned in Proverbs 25:1. The earliest redaction level of Deuteronomy and of the overall history in the books of Kings probably also dates from this period.

This cultic and cultural reform was connected with an administrative one in collecting the tithe in the temple and the royal storehouses. The calculation of the tithe is mentioned in an ostracon from the part of Jerusalem known as the Ophel, and several yearly dated 'fiscal bullae' probably date from Hezekiah's reign. They are apparently contemporary with the numerous royal seal-impressions on jars (LMLK ['for the king'] + name of a town) found especially in the excavated remains of the city of Lachish at the time when it was destroyed by King Sennacherib (see later in this section). In addition, there are several surviving bullae with the name of 'Hezekiah son of Ahaz, king of Judah' (Jerusalem excavations and unprovenanced), although these

The altar of Beersheba. The stones, here reassembled, were found separated and in secondary use, probably as a result of Hezekiah's religious reform.

were unfortunately found without the papyrus (contract or letter?) which they would have been used to tie up. The centralization of the collection of tithe produced important reserves of wheat, wine, and oil in royal storerooms, either to be exported to Phoenicia and Egypt or to be kept in storerooms for the needs of the army.

With the influx of Israelite refugees and the centralization of the cult in Jerusalem, the capital became more heavily populated. Archaeological excavations have revealed that a new city-wall was built along the Kidron valley while, protected by a northern 'broad wall' 8 m thick, the Western Hill developed quickly into a new quarter, the *Mishneh* (2 Kgs 22:14). It was of course necessary to provide water for the inhabitants of this new quarter. Hezekiah 'made the pool and the conduit and brought water into the city' (2 Kgs 20:20). This is the famous Hezekiah tunnel cut into the rock, more than 500 metres long, from the Gihon spring to a pool in the Tyropoeon valley, and still visible today. This tunnelling, a considerable technical achievement, was celebrated by the masons in an inscription engraved in the wall of the tunnel, discovered in 1880.

The Siloam inscription, celebrating the accomplishment of the work on Hezekiah's Tunnel.

During the whole reign of the Assyrian king Sargon II (721–705), Hezekiah was a faithful vassal, paying tribute. He did not join the failed anti-Assyrian revolt of Ashdod (712/711: Assyrian annals, Isa. 20:1). Yet, when Sargon died on the battlefield in 705, Hezekiah thought that it was time to become independent again and so organized an anti-Assyrian coalition with Ashdod, Gaza, Tyre, and Edom. He was apparently supported by pharaoh Shabako and received an embassy from Merodach-baladan/*Marduk-apla-iddina*, the king of Babylon who was fighting against Assyria (2 Kgs 20:12–19). Furthermore, since Padi, the Philistine king of Ekron, refused to join this coalition, he took him as a prisoner in Jerusalem (Assyrian annals) and prepared for war against Assyria.

After mastering the Babylonian revolt at the battle of Qish (704), the new Assyrian king Sennacherib (704–681) decided also to master the revolt of the Southern Levant kingdoms whose leader was Hezekiah. This was achieved by his third campaign (701) which is reported in the Assyrian annals, in the reliefs of the capture of Lachish in the Nineveh palace, and in several parallel stories in the Bible (2 Kgs 18:17–19:36; Isa. 36–7) and is probably alluded to in an Egyptian tradition transmitted by Herodotus (*Histories* II, 143). Furthermore, archaeological excavations have discovered traces of the widespread destruction caused by this campaign. This war between Assyria and Judah is a classic case of the advantages and problems that can be raised for the historian when we compare the biblical sources, Near Eastern historiographical traditions, and archaeology.

Sennacherib first subdued the Phoenician cities, replacing Lulli king of Sidon by Ittobaal. Mitinti king of Ashdod, Puduilu king of Ammon, Kammusunadbi king of

The so-called Taylor Prism, which records in detail the Assyrian king Sennacherib's campaigns including that in the west in 701 BCE.

Moab, and Aiarammu king of Edom soon also submitted and paid tribute. Sennacherib entered Philistia, deported the king of Ashkelon, Sidqa, and defeated an Egyptian/Ethiopian army near the city of Eltekeh. He captured Ekron, slew the governors and nobles who had rebelled, and took some of the inhabitants as prisoners. He put Padi back on the royal throne of Ekron. He could then attack the leader of the coalition, Hezekiah, and the kingdom of Judah. He besieged the main fortress of the Judean kingdom in the Shephelah, Lachish, and finally captured it using a siege-ramp and battering-rams. Meanwhile he sent his *turtanu*/general-in-chief with a military detachment to ask Hezekiah for his unconditional surrender (2 Kgs 18:17–19:36). Having probably already liberated Padi, Hezekiah refused, at the instigation of the prophet Isaiah. The *turtanu* brought this news back to Sennacherib who was then besieging Libnah (a town in Judah whose precise location is uncertain). For some reason (plague in his army and/or approach of a new Egyptian/Ethiopian army?), Sennacherib retired to Nineveh and Hezekiah hurried to send his messengers to Nineveh to submit and pay a heavy tribute of '30 talents of gold and 800 talents of silver' (Assyrian annals, cf. 2 Kgs 18:14).

Though Jerusalem was not captured, Hezekiah's revolt had failed totally, and the Assyrian campaign had terrible consequences for the kingdom of Judah. A great part of the Shephelah territory was given to the Philistine kings (Ashdod, Ekron, Gaza) and many cities and villages were destroyed. Hezekiah's reign that started so well ended in a catastrophe because of his revolt against Assyria.

Part of the Assyrian relief depicting the siege and capture of Lachish, showing here some captives submitting before Sennacherib.

His son and successor Manasseh understood the warning, all the more so because his long reign (*c*.699–645) corresponded with the height of the Assyrian empire under its kings Esarhaddon (680–669) and Ashurbanipal (668–627). Manasseh was apparently a faithful vassal to Assyria and is mentioned among lists of kings paying tribute (676? 673?), as well as among the vassal kings who helped Ashurbanipal's campaign in Egypt (667). At least some of the Judean detachment sent to Egypt probably stayed on as mercenaries of the pro-Assyrian pharaoh Psammetichus I (664–610): this was probably the origin of the Elephantine community of Judean mercenaries that lasted at least till *c*.400 BCE.

Unfortunately, we have little certain information about Manasseh's long reign of more than half a century. The king probably thought that the country first and foremost needed peace with urgent rebuilding and he may have stopped Hezekiah's reform of worship, while being open to Assyro-Aramean cultural influence, especially to the worship of 'all the host of heaven' (2 Kgs 21:5). Yet, the Assyrian dependence apparently also had positive aspects, especially the possibility of developing regional trade, and this peaceful period allowed the Judean economy and population to recover. His successor Amon (*c*.645?–640), apparently followed the same pro-Assyrian line but he was assassinated by his servants (2 Kgs 21:23). The 'land assembly' (probably an assembly of the Judean nobility), which seems to have played an important political role in the kingdom of Judah, especially when there was a problematic succession, punished the conspirators with death and made Amon's young son Josiah king in his place (2 Kgs 21:24).

During the first part of Josiah's reign (640–609), the young king probably went on with the pro-Assyrian policy of his immediate predecessors. Yet Assyrian power quickly declined after the death of Assurbanipal (727) so that in 622 Josiah felt free to take up again the reforms of his forefather Hezekiah and organize the renewal of the Judean kingdom with reference to an early form of Deuteronomy (2 Kgs 22–3). He suppressed the sanctuaries other than Jerusalem, especially the Bethel sanctuary (2 Kgs 23:15–20), and got rid of the traces of astral worship developed during the period of Assyro-Aramean domination. He also organized a pilgrimage to celebrate Passover in Jerusalem (2 Kgs 23:21–3). Seizing the opportunity of the disappearance of Assyrian power, he annexed to Judah not only Bethel but also probably part of the Mediterranean coast, as implied by the discovery of a late 7th-century Hebrew ostracon at Mezad Hashavyahu near the Mediterranean coast between Joppa and Ashdod. He also apparently built fortresses in the Shephelah (Lachish, Azekah) and in the Negev (Tel 'Ira, Arad, Aroer, Horvat 'Uza, Horvat Radum). These Negev fortresses reinforced the frontier of Judah with the Edomite kingdom. Like pharaoh Psammetichus I, Josiah probably also used Greek mercenaries (*Kittim*) in his army (Arad ostraca) to defend this frontier.

The archaeological excavations of these Negev fortresses has revealed that they were well administered and that military officers could read and write, as shown by the Lachish, Arad, and Horvat 'Uza ostraca. Towards the end of the Judean kingdom, the diffusion of writing is also attested by numerous Hebrew seals, seal-impressions, and

Fifty bullae from the City of David excavations, dating to the final years of the kingdom of Judah.

bullae, especially in Jerusalem and the Judean Shephelah. Unfortunately, except for a palimpsest papyrus found in a cave in the Judean desert (in Wadi Murrabba'at), the Judean documents on papyrus and leather were not preserved because of the climate. Yet this development of the use of writing fits with the hypothesis that several biblical books were probably written or revised at this time.

The international context changed very quickly and pharaoh Necho II (610–595) wanted to support the last Assyrian king Assur-uballit II who was resisting the Babylonians under their king Nabopolassar at Harran. Josiah apparently opposed this help because he did not want any Assyrian or Egyptian control over the Southern Levant. When he met Necho at Megiddo in an unspecified context, 'pharaoh Necho slew him' (2 Kgs 23:29).

This tragic death in May–June 609 was the beginning of the end for the Judean kingdom. It now became unstable, often swinging out of time between the two great powers: Babylonia and Egypt.

At the death of Josiah, the land assembly chose his younger son Jehoahaz as his successor, probably because his first son was pro-Egyptian. He was king for only three months: 'Pharaoh Necho removed him from the throne . . . and imposed on the land a fine of a hundred talents of silver and ten(?) talents of gold. Pharaoh Necho made Josiah's son Eliakim king in place of his father and changed his name to Jehoiakim. He took Jehoahaz and brought him to Egypt, where he died. Jehoiakim paid the silver and gold to Pharaoh, taxing the country to meet Pharaoh's demands; he exacted it from the

A silver amulet found in a burial cave at Ketef Hinnom on the edge of Jerusalem. Written near the time of the fall of Jerusalem, it has a version of the priestly blessing (Num. 6:24–6), making it the earliest known surviving piece of the biblical text.

people of the land, from every man according to his assessment...' (2 Kgs 23:33–5). Hebrew ostraca recently published with amounts of assessment could well be connected with the payment of this exceptional tax.

Nominated king by the pharaoh, Jehoiakim soon had to change tack: in May/June 605, the Babylonian crown prince Nebuchadnezzar defeated the Egyptian garrison of Carchemish (Babylonian chronicle) and the whole of Syria–Palestine fell into the

Babylonian sphere of influence. When Nebuchadnezzar became king of Babylon (604–562), he campaigned against Philistia, captured Ashkelon, and received the submission of all the kings of the Levant (604: Babylonian chronicle and Saqqara papyrus), including king Jehoiakim, but three years later, probably because of a Babylonian defeat by the Egyptian army (Babylonian chronicle), Jehoiakim 'broke with him and revolted' (2 Kgs 24:1). For the first time, Nebuchadnezzar now let his vassals harass the king of Judah: 'he launched against him raiding-parties of Chaldeans, Edomites, Moabites and Ammonites' (2 Kgs 24:2). In December 598, Nebuchadnezzar mustered his army against Judah while the Edomites attacked Ramath-Negev and occupied the whole Negev (Arad ostraca). King Jehoiakim died in Jerusalem, perhaps assassinated, and his young son Jehoiachin became king for three months. The Babylonian army laid siege to the city but when Nebuchadnezzar arrived, 'Jehoiachin, king of Judah, his mother, his courtiers, his officers and his eunuchs, all surrendered to the king of Babylon' (2 Kgs 24:12). This surrender is well dated by the Babylonian chronicle: 2 *Adar* (16 March 597). Nebuchadnezzar took Jehoiachin and his family as prisoners into Babylon where they were well treated. Like other western kings and leaders, they received official rations from the royal palace, as illustrated by Babylonian administration cuneiform tablets. At the same time, Nebuchadnezzar deported 'all the men of substance, seven thousand in number, and a thousand craftsmen and smiths' (2 Kgs 24:16). Though the number of deportees is different in 2 Kgs 24:14 (10,000) and Jeremiah 52:28 (3023), the number and selection of the deportees apparently aimed at the managerial staff of the Judean kingdom in order to prevent another revolt.

Nebuchadnezzar chose another son of king Josiah, Mattaniah, as king of Judah, and gave him the throne name Zedekiah. His kingdom had not only lost much of its elite but also part of its territory, the Negev having been annexed to the Edomite kingdom. Furthermore, the preceding king was still alive and probably considered by part of the population as the legitimate king. In these conditions, Zedekiah had some difficulty asserting himself in front of his servants and officers.

Following the accession of Psammetichus II in Egypt (*c.*595–589), in 594 there was a tentative move to coordinate a Southern Levant revolt against Babylonia with the participation of the Phoenicians, Edom, Moab, and Ammon, but this move was denounced by the prophet Jeremiah (Jer. 27–8), and it finally failed: Zedekiah then went to Babylon (Jer. 51:59), probably to assure Nebuchadnezzar of his fidelity. Yet Egypt was still active, as shown by the visit of Psammetichus II to the Southern Levant (*c.*592), and, after the accession of a new Pharaoh, Hophra (*c.*589–570), probably with the support of the Ammonites, 'Zedekiah rebelled against the king of Babylon' (2 Kgs 24:20).

The reaction of Nebuchadnezzar was quick: he 'advanced with all his army against Jerusalem, invested it and erected watch-towers against it on every side' (2 Kgs 25:1, probably January 588). During the siege, the fortresses of Lachish and Azekah in the Shephelah still tried to resist (Jer. 34:7). The book of Jeremiah and the Lachish ostraca reveal that Judean opinion was divided in face of the Babylonian invasion. One party, with Jeremiah as its leader, wanted to surrender, but a military faction insisted on resisting to the very end, hoping for some help from Egypt. At the beginning of 587, an Egyptian army advanced into Philistia and the anti-Babylonian party seemed to triumph: the siege was provisionally stopped, the freeing of slaves postponed, and Jeremiah imprisoned. Yet the Egyptian army was defeated and the siege against Jerusalem started again, provoking severe famine in the city. On *Tammuz* 9 (probably 29 July 587), there was a breach in the city-wall, Zedekiah and his military escort fled by night towards the southern end of the Jordan valley known as the Aravah, probably to seek refuge in the Ammonite kingdom, but the Babylonian army overtook them near Jericho.

The repression was terrible: at Riblah, Zedekiah saw the slaying of his sons and then had his eyes put out before being brought to Babylon in fetters. We do not hear of any further news about him. Jerusalem, the rebellious city, was looted and totally burnt down (temple, royal palace, houses) by Nebuzaradan, captain of the king's bodyguard. The city-wall was pulled down. The inhabitants of Jerusalem (according to Jer. 52:28, 832 in number) were deported to Babylonia. Actually, recently published cuneiform tablets indicate that they were mainly deported to two places in Babylonia: *Al-Yahudu* (approximately: 'New Jerusalem') and *Bît-Abiram*. Only the farmers (vine-dressers and labourers), who had previously taken refuge in the city during the war, remained in the country.

'Nebuchadnezzar . . . appointed Gedaliah son of Ahikam, son of Shaphan, governor over the few people left in Judah' (2 Kgs 25:22). This Gedaliah belonged to the great family of Shaphan, close to Jeremiah. He was apparently one of the leaders of the pro-Babylonian party and may have been previously some kind of prime minister (*asher 'al habbayit*) according to a bulla found in Lachish. He moved the capital of Judah to Mizpah, about 10 km north of Jerusalem, since Jerusalem was in ruins while the territory of Benjamin had apparently not been destroyed during the Babylonian invasion. Later on, Gedaliah was assassinated by 'Ishmael son of Nethaniah son of Elishama who was a member of the royal house' (2 Kgs 25:25) and who then escaped to Ammon (Jer. 41). Expecting reprisals from the Babylonians, surviving members of Gedaliah's staff, among them Jeremiah, sought refuge in Egypt. According to Jer. 52:30, in 582 the Babylonians deported a further 745 Judeans and suppressed the kingdoms of Ammon and Moab (Josephus, *Jewish Antiquities* X, 181–2). Either in 582 or already in 587, the southern part of the Shephelah (Lachish, Mareshah) and of the Mountain of Judah (Hebron) was then annexed to the Edomite kingdom.

From now on, the eventual future of the Judean culture and religion would depend on the deportees in Babylonia at least as much as on the people inhabiting the small Babylonian province of Judah.

CHAPTER 4

Babylonian Exile and Restoration

(587–325 BCE)

H. G. M. WILLIAMSON

WHEN Nebuchadnezzar, king of Babylon, captured Jerusalem for a second time after persistent rebellion in 587 BCE he made a comprehensive job of destroying the city. The temple, which had stood since Solomon's reign some 400 years before, together with the adjacent royal palace, was completely demolished after the confiscation of any remaining valuables. The rest of the city was rendered more or less uninhabitable, and excavations in recent decades, though limited in extent because of continuing occupation, reveal that much of it was burned down.

The destruction was not just physical, however. Zedekiah, the last of the kings in the line of David, is said to have witnessed the execution of his sons before himself being blinded and led away into exile. Although other members of the family also survived, none was ever to rule again over Judah as an independent state. The northern kingdom of Israel had been obliterated 150 years previously at the hands of the Assyrians, as we saw in Chapter 3, so that the whole land was now subsumed into the provincial system of the mighty Babylonian empire.

Along with the royal dynasty, therefore, all the institutions of statehood also came to an end at this time. Of particular significance for later history down to our own day, of course, was the religion of the people, which up until that point had been what we might call a state religion. As we know from the Old Testament, this religion was varied in its forms of expression and could even tolerate a degree of independent critical comment. Nevertheless, to the extent that it presupposed the organs of statehood in many aspects the religion as it had hitherto existed could not survive unchanged. The law, which became such a fundamental part of later Judaism (and in varying degrees also of Christianity and Islam), could no longer be administered by the king and his subordinate officials and judges. The focus of royal and national aspirations on the temple (as we know from many of the Psalms) could not continue, and Zion—a religious way of looking at Jerusalem as the city of God—had been overthrown, taking down with it many of the secure beliefs of the people about its special place in God's affections.

The 'House of Ahiel', part of Jerusalem as completely destroyed by the Babylonians in 587/586 BCE.

Previously any nation that had undergone such trauma had effectively come to an end. The other small nation-states in the wider region are now just names in the history books—Moab, Edom, and so on. But somehow enough of Israel and Judah survived in a transformed state to become the fountainhead of the three great monotheistic religions of the world today. Our task in this chapter, therefore, is not just to trace the political history of the Holy Land during these centuries, but through that to uncover the intellectual and spiritual developments which accompanied it.

Judah under Babylonian rule

So far as the territory of Judah itself is concerned for the brief fifty years or so that the Neo-Babylonian Empire lasted, the story can be rapidly told, not least because we have very few sources on which to base our reconstruction. The southern part of the territory had already been severed from Judah ten years before on Nebuchadnezzar's first invasion; it was annexed by Edom (later, Idumea), and later sources suggest that, to whatever extent parts of the population may still have identified with the traditions of Judah, it became a quite separate administrative and formal religious entity.

The small part of Judah which lay to the north of Jerusalem, namely the tribal territory of Benjamin, escaped most lightly from the effects of the Babylonian campaign. Archaeology attests that the main towns in the region enjoyed continued occupation, and indeed it looks as though the main Babylonian administrator had his official residence in one of them, namely biblical Mizpah (Tel en-Nasbeh). Probably there or at the nearby Bethel a sanctuary was built or refurbished to replace the ruined site of the Jerusalem temple. It is likely that this favoured treatment was the result of the inhabitants of this region not opposing the incoming Babylonians but urging acquiescence in their imperialistic demands. Among the circumstantial evidence which leads to this suggestion is the teaching of the prophet Jeremiah, who came from this region and whose message brought him into great trouble when it was delivered in the far more nationalistically minded court circles in Jerusalem.

As for the heartland of Judah, Jerusalem was effectively deserted and was certainly not the provincial capital. We may speculate that the temple site continued as some sort of focus for lamentation and commemoration, but firm evidence is lacking. A few miles to the south a site known now as Ramat Rachel, whose identification with a biblical town is uncertain, seems to have taken over as the centre of local administration if the recently excavated remains of relatively sumptuous buildings and

Tel en-Nasbeh (biblical Mizpah) as being excavated already in the 1920s.

of many official seal impressions are anything to go by. Elsewhere we can only suppose that a simple form of subsistence agriculture following widespread destruction continued among the remaining peasant population.

It is probable that, after a few abortive attempts at governance through prominent local individuals, Judah became a directly administered province within the Babylonian empire, just as the region of Samaria to the north of Judah certainly did. It may well have been exploited for imperial purposes for its olive production especially, but more than that cannot be said. The narrative thread of its history is only picked up again (and then only sporadically) once the Babylonian empire had been succeeded by the Persians under Cyrus the Great, who was king of Persia from 559 until his death in 530 BCE (the date of his birth is unknown).

The Babylonian exile

In many ways, the future of the Holy Land was shaped more during these decades by what happened elsewhere than in the land itself, so that we have to give some attention to the community of Judean exiles in Babylon.

Remains of one of the gateways into Babylon.

It is difficult to overemphasize the importance of the different policy that the Babylonians implemented with regard to exiled peoples from all who preceded them. When earlier on some of the population of Israel were taken away by the Assyrians, for instance, they were settled in various different locations far to the east and were gradually assimilated into their new surroundings. Despite many later exotic fables and myths, the 'lost ten tribes' of Israel were precisely that. No cultural or religious life survived outside the land of Israel itself.

With the Babylonians, however, it was all different. Following both their successful campaigns in Judah, they took many of the elite population to Babylonia. Among the first wave of exiles, for instance, were Ezekiel the prophet and, indeed, Jehoiachin the king. We know from both the Bible and from a clay Babylonian tablet that Jehoiachin and his family were kept for many years under house arrest and that subsequently he was granted a limited but relatively privileged form of freedom. Even more important, what we already supposed from the writings of Ezekiel has now been dramatically confirmed by the recent publication of an important collection of nearly 100 texts that the community was kept together in new settlements where they could maintain a good deal of their identity and internal social structures. Some of these texts come from a previously unknown but apparently rural place in Babylonia called Al-Yahudu, 'The City of Judah' (or 'Judahville', as some have dubbed it). While the texts themselves are banal enough, the interesting thing about them from our point of view is that a good proportion of the names are undoubtedly Yahwistic, that is to say, self-consciously belonging to the religion or culture of Yahweh, the name of the Israelite God. Of course, others mentioned may also have been part of the same community even if their name does not betray them. Some of these texts are dated to the Neo-Babylonian period (605–539 BCE), so that they bring us much closer to the immediate realities of the Babylonian community than anything that was available to us before.

Now, the importance of this Babylonian policy is that it enables us to piece together some of the strategies whereby this community was able to maintain its identity despite the need to adapt itself quite radically in order to survive. Several of the features that still to this day we identify as distinctive of Judaism probably gained especial importance during those years. The extent to which they were already practised before is disputed, but either way it was now that they gained particular significance. It is not unlike ex-pat communities in the modern world, who stress certain features of their homeland culture far more than do those who have never journeyed abroad. Sabbath observance, particular food laws, religious practice that was no longer tied to the temple cult with its sacrifices and offerings but focused more on prayer, and the recital of sacred texts and psalms in a manner that prefigured the later development of synagogues—these all served to mark out this community as distinctive in its foreign environment. Beyond that, we read in Ezekiel of social leadership by elders, suggestive of a move towards a form of lay governance in distinction from that of either royalty or priesthood. To be sure, the orders of priests and Levites continued to develop in their complicated structures and inter-relationships, and Jehoiachin's generous treatment by the Babylonians may well have encouraged the maintenance of a hope that one day the monarchy would be restored, but in practical terms the national faith of Judah and Israel rapidly adapted itself to a form of religion that was no longer dependent on either. Without the exile, there would have been no later Judaism.

In addition we can well understand that opinion would have been divided over the question of return and restoration. For some the exilic experience was painful and their hopes for a return to Judah would be realized quicker than they might ever have imagined. Many others, however, took Jeremiah's advice to settle down in their new homes. The later fifth-century BCE archives of the Murashu banking family in Nippur (about 100 miles south-east of modern Baghdad in Iraq) testify to the integration of people with Jewish names into the economic life of the local region. Many chose not to return to Judah when the opportunity arose, and thus began (as simultaneously and separately in Egypt) the life of diaspora Judaism. After all, some of the greatest Jewish texts of later times, such as the authoritative version of the Talmud, were brought to completion precisely in Babylonia. Our present story, however, demands that we trace the route of those who returned to the Holy Land in the late sixth century and later.

The start of Persian rule

In 539 BCE the face of the whole ancient Near East was transformed when the Achaemenid Persian king Cyrus entered Babylon. The last king of Babylon, Nabonidus (555–539 BCE), had made himself very unpopular in Babylon by his particular devotion to the moon-god Sin and by taking himself off for long periods of time to the sanctuary in the Arabian oasis of Tema (modern Tayma), thus neglecting his religious duties in Babylon. According to the account written under Cyrus's direction in the famous Cyrus Cylinder, the Persian monarch, whose origins and rapid rise to power were already becoming the stuff of legend, was therefore welcomed into Babylon as a liberator and as one who would more scrupulously observe the royal duties associated with that city's god Marduk. How much of all this should be ascribed to both negative and positive propaganda by the eventual victor may, of course, be debated, but the dramatic change in imperial rule is not in question.

The Cylinder also talks of Cyrus restoring certain sanctuaries which had long lain deserted or ruined and this, together with all its talk about military peace and political harmony, has sometimes led to claims that the Cylinder amounted to the first declaration of human rights. It has also been mistakenly claimed that it directly supports the Bible's account of Cyrus's permission to any Judeans in Babylon who wished to return home and to rebuild the temple. This attractive position is unfortunately exaggerated, however. What Cyrus wrote concerned only the locality of Babylon itself, and the whole text is designed to bolster his image and to win him the support of the local population, including especially its elite. In other respects he and his successors could be as autocratic and indeed ruthless as any other ancient Near Eastern ruler.

The Cyrus Cylinder, recording Cyrus's welcome into Babylon and his restoration of certain sanctuaries in the region in order to bolster his claim to local legitimacy.

This lithographic depiction of Jerusalem from the South by David Roberts catches something of the romance with which the return from exile is often popularly associated.

That does not mean, however, that the biblical account should therefore be dismissed. There is some slight evidence from elsewhere round the Fertile Crescent that peoples were restored to their original homeland, and we may deduce from this and other complementary evidence that the Persians decided that their policy of domination could best be served by having where possible loyal and hence compliant subjects. Indeed, it is worth noting that all the leaders in Jerusalem of whom we know for the next century or more came from Babylon (Zerubbabel, Ezra, Nehemiah, and so on). For the most part the biblical sources are well disposed towards the Persians, and the degree of freedom with which the Judeans were allowed to administer their own affairs is an important stepping stone on the way from the religion of ancient Israel and Judah to the Judaism with which we are familiar later on.

It is likely that the return of some to Judah during the reign of Cyrus and his immediate successors was at first welcomed on all sides. The period of exile had lasted only fifty years and we know that some contact between the communities was maintained. Families that had been divided were now reunited and we can imagine how initial hopes for full restoration would have been high. Sources contemporary with those early years, such as the prophets Haggai and Zechariah, make no reference whatsoever to differences or disagreements between the two main parts of the population back in Judah. After some initial delay the temple was finally rebuilt during the first part of the reign of the Persian king Darius I—a king who, after securing the throne in the teeth of much rebellion over an initial two-year period, successfully undertook significant administrative reforms throughout the empire.

Constitutional arrangements

What were the constitutional arrangements in the Holy Land as taken over by Cyrus from the Babylonians and then re-ordered administratively by Darius? The evidence on which to base an answer is somewhat piecemeal and not always clear, so that there has been a good deal of dispute about this. Something of a consensus position has emerged, however.

At the highest level, as we know from Herodotus, the Persian empire was divided into large divisions known as satrapies. At first the Holy Land was part of a very large satrapy which also included Babylon, and we know from the names of subordinate officials over the main regions that (contrary to what Herodotus implies) this lasted longer than the main administrative reforms of Darius. Probably during the reign of his successor Xerxes (486–465 BCE) this satrapy was divided into two, with the Holy Land falling into the one called 'Beyond the River' (basically everything to the west of the Euphrates excluding Egypt). These were financial as much as political divisions, and the satraps themselves were answerable to the king. Given the principle of devolution that the Persians favoured, as we have already noted, the satraps wielded considerable power as well as enjoying great authority, and there were occasions when one or another could take the lead (always ultimately unsuccessfully) in revolt against the king. Not surprisingly, therefore, the court also made use of loyal independent monitors and observers ('the king's eyes') to report back directly to the centre. This dual form of control was no doubt aided by the famous Persian system of roads, with official stations conveniently located along the way, that enabled swift communication between the centre and the periphery, all directly accountable to the central treasury (of whose records in the official bureaucratic language of Elamite we have several thousands of examples).

Within the satrapy there were smaller regions known as provinces, usually with a governor, who might well be a local dignitary. At this point, however, the Persians exercised what we may well think was a wise policy of flexibility. Within the Holy Land, we know from archaeological research that the land's culture (pottery types, architectural style, and so on) was increasingly differentiated. On the one hand the coastal plain was ever more strongly influenced by Greek culture, and from the great sea ports there was an openness to the wider Mediterranean world to the west. The central hill country, which had been the heartland of the older kingdoms of Israel and Judah, by contrast, was more conservative and maintained a certain broad similarity in these respects even though politically the two separate entities had long been divided one from the other. Finally the scrub and desert regions to the south, the Negev, were in any case always more difficult to control directly. It is true that built settlements gradually increased in number (and of course there were a few that were of great antiquity) but the region's geographical remoteness at the very borders of the empire favoured its semi-autonomous nature.

In response to these differences, the Persians exercised their rule with discrimination. The Phoenician city-states (Tyre, Sidon, and others) were broadly supportive of Cyrus and his successors (e.g. Cyrus's son Cambyses in his invasion of Egypt; support also in the later Graeco-Persian wars), in return for which they were allowed to keep their hereditary monarchs, were able later to mint their own coinage, and were able to continue their commercial enterprises with considerable freedom. It would therefore be wrong to lump them together as a 'province' in the usual sense of the term; the region was granted considerable autonomy to maintain a traditional way of government in return for which the Persians profited by both political support and the benefits of the much-needed Phoenician maritime skills.

In relation to the remoter southern region the Persians initially adopted an equally pragmatic approach. In his advance against Egypt Cambyses deliberately did not seek to subdue the region but rather, according to Herodotus, welcomed Arabian help and thus established 'friendly relations' with them. This light touch continued for some while, the Arabs agreeing to make annual 'gifts' rather than having to make any sort of formal revenue payments. It is possible that these 'gifts' were in reality a form of tribute made in exchange for the delegation to them of the control of the lucrative spice trade through their territory from Arabia to the Mediterranean coast. At any event, such a friendly cooperation was probably as much as the Persians could hope realistically to achieve in that area, especially as the local kings held sway over a very considerable territory, according to one or two relevant inscriptions. This picture seems to change in the later part of the Persian period, however, perhaps after the Egyptian revolt at the

A coin inscribed with 'Yehud', the Aramaic name of the province of Judah. This is one of the few small pieces of evidence relating to continuity of the province's status during the fourth century BCE.

end of the fifth century. By then, the northern part of the Negev, at any rate, was becoming more densely settled, so that a more direct form of rule would have become fiscally rewarding. Aramaic ostraca from Beersheba and Arad dating to this period, at least, are suggestive of closer Persian administration.

So far as the central hill country is concerned, we know little enough in detail about the northern province of Samaria, though from the Bible, the Aramaic papyri from the 'Jewish' colony of mercenaries at Elephantine in Egypt, and also from some slightly later papyri found in a cave a little to the north of Jericho, we know the names of a number of the governors, most famous among them Nehemiah's arch-foe Sanballat. This standard form of rule—a province with a local governor—was probably mirrored in Judah as well throughout the Persian period, and again the names of a number of the governors are known to us from biblical and epigraphic sources. It should be noted, however, that the province of Judah was very small in size by comparison with the previous kingdom and that its population was equally modest, perhaps 20,000 rising over time to 30,000 people only.

An aerial view of Ramat Rachel, just south of Jerusalem, which has been shown by recent excavations to have been a major administrative centre for the province of Judah even though it is not mentioned in the Bible.

Although the temple was rebuilt during the early years of the Persian empire, being rededicated in 515 BCE, Jerusalem took much longer to recover as a significant political centre. Even during Nehemiah's governorship (445–433 BCE, with a second term probably following after a gap of three years) he had to take strong measures to encourage more people to move back to it. We have thus to envisage a three-way division of administration: the Satrap, who had some sort of residence still at Mizpah, a little north of Jerusalem, the main local administration based still at Ramat Rachel, and religious affiliation traditionally bound to Jerusalem with its temple but only gradual transference thither of any more practical form of rule. We, of course, are programmed by the Bible to think of Jerusalem as the eternal capital, but in practice this relates more to the development of the evolving religion of Judaism during those centuries than to the bureaucracy; that shifted to Jerusalem only gradually, albeit steadily.

Judah under the Persians

The Persian empire endured from 539 until it was swept away by Alexander the Great in 331 BCE. For that two-hundred year period it is not possible to write a continuous historical narrative for Judah—still less for Samaria. The sources available to us shine brilliant shafts of light on a few specific incidents but it is not possible to join them up together according to the usual basic historical canons of cause and effect. They are rather like the gems of a precious necklace that have lost the silver chain which keeps them all in order.

The sources we do have seem to get us very close to the heart of the events that they relate. They include some letters in Aramaic (rather than Hebrew) in the book of Ezra which seem certainly to be based on original documents (albeit edited for their present use) relating to both the building of the second temple and to the mission of Ezra. Equally, the first year or so of Nehemiah's term as governor is related in lively first-hand detail. And the much later Jewish historian Josephus seems to have had access to a reliable source which tells the unedifying tale of a high priest murdering his brother in the temple, for which reason the Persian official Bagoses suspended the sacrificial cult for seven years (*Antiquities* 11 §§297–301).

Some of the dates of the events these sources relate are disputed. While the rebuilding of the temple is agreed by nearly everyone to be 520–515 BCE, based on the stated years of King Darius, and while equally certainly the first year of Nehemiah's work was 438 BCE, there is disagreement over whether Ezra came to Jerusalem in the seventh year of Artaxerxes I (458 BCE) or of Artaxerxes II (398 BCE). Equally, the incident retold by Josephus might be during the reign of Artaxerxes II or III. On one possible reconstruction, then, we should know nothing whatsoever about the whole of the fourth century BCE, and even if we favour the alternative dates there is little enough to fill up our knowledge of those decades. It is somewhat ironic, therefore, that one historian has been able with some justice to say that we know less of the history of Judah during that century than of any since it became part of Israel in whatever shape or form.

The best we can hope to achieve, therefore, is to attempt a 'before and after' comparison, to see how the society and its related institutions (not least religious, of course) had developed during those centuries. It is clear that the individual sources which have survived were preserved because of their contribution to that end and not for reasons of a consecutive political history. So we do best to analyse them in that light.

Temple building

The account of the first returns from Babylon and the building of the temple seem primarily concerned to stress two or three important facts about the institution even while masking some factors relevant to the precise course of events. The main narrative is driven by a concern to emphasize that the temple was built on the orders of, and to some extent with the protective support of, the Persians at the highest level. Although, as I have already said, genuinely contemporary sources give no indication of any serious divisions within the Judean community itself, this narrative in Ezra 1–6, which was probably only put together much later and with the advantage of hindsight, indicates that opposition came from rival groups in the northern territory of Samaria. While this was cleared up by an exchange of letters between the local Persian 'sub-satrap' Tattenai and the imperial court, it is clear that there were very real tensions on the ground between neighbouring small provinces for reasons that one may only speculate about. The previously more dominant province of Samaria may have felt threatened by the revival of the previously insignificant Judah to its south. Equally, the arrival of returnees from Babylon, however much to be welcomed at one level, may well have led to disputes about land ownership in specific areas, and this will have been exacerbated by the several indications we have in a variety of texts that the economy of Judah through much of this period was extremely precarious, so that the pressures on resources at any given time could easily have been a flashpoint for tensions. After all, these were not just immigrants in the way we mostly think of them nowadays. Rather, they were 'return migrants' who came with high ideals and who may have had difficulty in coming to terms with developments in Judah during the previous fifty years. Finally, as we shall see directly, there developed sharp differences of opinion over who could be full members of this nascent community, and this may well have included both economic and social relationships with those from the neighbouring provinces. Thus we can well understand that within a relatively short period of time the idealism of the returnees and the initial welcome by those who had remained in the land could become fractured. Given that the temple was a project of particular importance to those who returned, the desire to establish its full imperial legality against any who might see it as an expression of rebellious independence was obviously important.

Second, the narratives go to great lengths to stress that from an internal Judean standpoint as well this temple was the direct and legitimate successor (one might almost say continuation) of the previous temple of Solomon. It was built on exactly the same spot, we are assured several times, and to the same general design. The way by which the materials were collected is based on the previous account of that for the first temple, and even the vessels which had furnished the first temple and which had been removed by Nebuchadnezzar to Babylon were returned by Cyrus. Obviously, therefore, anyone who wanted to claim continuity with the earlier days of Judean independence would need to gather faithfully at this new temple.

Third, the chief movers in the building (albeit under prophetic goading) were the high priest Joshua and a descendant of the family of David named Zerubbabel. It is probable that he did not come with the earliest group of returnees (whose leader was the even more shadowy figure Sheshbazzar) but in a subsequent migration a few years later. It has sometimes been suggested that this was indicative of a move to reassert Judean royal authority and that he was removed by the Persians in consequence. As a matter of fact there is no evidence for this speculation whatsoever, but at the same time we can hardly suppose that the involvement of a Davidic figure in the building of the temple that stood in succession to that of Solomon was not regarded as highly significant. It is true that we know little of what happened to the family after Zerubbabel. A seal whose authenticity some now challenge suggests that his daughter Shelomith may have married the next governor of Judah, but that does not really get us very far, and after that we have only the testimony of lists to indicate that the family identity was known in later generations (which is not at all surprising). So the importance of Zerubbabel working alongside the high priest may be seen as a further item of propaganda to legitimize the new temple.

However precisely all this corresponds with exact history, we are presented here with a clear statement that the true Judean community is the authorized heir to its pre-exilic predecessors but that it is not left unchallenged by some who lived around it and possibly also by some closer to home within the territory itself (presumably for the most part among those who had never been in exile). As we have already noted, those who returned had come to adopt more pronounced identity markers than those who remained because in exile that had been necessary in order to preserve themselves from cultural assimilation. How the resulting potential for social dispute was worked out was a significant element in the next episodes that have been recorded.

Ezra

Assuming for the moment an early date for Ezra, his journey to Jerusalem will have been in 458 BCE, well over fifty years after the temple had been completed. While he is presented in our texts with his priestly and scholarly credentials, it is not difficult to read between the lines that he also had some form of official standing in the Achaemenid (Persian) court. Whether we can go so far as some have claimed in titling him 'Secretary of State for Jewish Affairs' may be questioned, but it is likely that he had some position of bureaucratic importance and that the framing of his commission could well have been in response to a request from himself for precisely some such mission. The way that the Persians worked with local authorities was, as we have seen, varied and pragmatic, so the idea that he should be sent with some authority to determine the proper boundaries between the extent of religious and civil imperial law is not unreasonable. There are some analogies for this sort of thing elsewhere and it may have been felt necessary after the debacle which is recorded in the second half of Ezra 4, resulting in suspicion resting (probably unfairly) on Judah's loyalty to the crown. The chapter records an exchange of letters between some local officials and King Artaxerxes about building work that was being undertaken in Jerusalem and suggesting that the Judeans were planning to rebel. Artaxerxes replies that the work is to be forcibly stopped. Because the exchange is completely out of chronological sequence where it now stands in the text (the context is the much earlier reign of Darius) it is difficult to know quite what to make of this. However, it is interesting that in Artaxerxes' twentieth year Nehemiah requests permission to travel to Jerusalem to restore the city. Had it recently suffered as described in Ezra 4, and was Ezra himself somehow involved in the work that was destroyed, given that Ezra probably went to Jerusalem earlier during the reign of the same Artaxerxes? There is no direct evidence to support this conjecture, but it at least explains the various texts quite attractively.

Be that as it may, Ezra is presented in the narratives about his mission (Ezra 7–10 + Neh. 8) as one who acted as far as he could in line with the specific demands of Artaxerxes' written edict but with a very different emphasis from what we might have expected. Far from the general administration of the law, the real key to his work, the enduring impact of which cannot be exaggerated, is that he effectively devised means to make the older laws of Israel applicable in new circumstances long after the social and political circumstances for which they were originally drafted had passed into history. In most cases of this kind the old law becomes a dead letter, an object of venerated antiquity, and new laws have to be drafted. It is true that the Mosaic law, the Torah (or Pentateuch—the first five books of the Bible), probably includes some legislation, especially in the cultic sphere, which was only finalized in its present form at about this same time (during or after the exile at the earliest), but that does not apply to the bulk of what we now have. The law's presupposition of Israel dwelling in its own land in an independent state where the law could be administered by local judges who were not in any way answerable to foreign powers is far removed from the circumstances of the tiny province of Judah within the mighty Persian empire. What we find for the first time with Ezra both in his own narrative and in other closely related passages (such as Neh. 10) is that these old 'dead' laws are revived by a method of interpretation that (not always very convincingly) combines this element with that, one law with another, so as to extend their life in fresh directions. This is hermeneutics at its liveliest!

A particular problem with which Ezra is confronted is, famously, that some men have married 'foreign' wives. Now, we might well suppose on a straightforward reading of earlier narratives that this was not a problem provided the wives did not draw their husbands away from faithful worship. After all, Moses himself had a foreign wife, as did many others of the early heroes of the faith. In treating this subject in his own later and very different circumstances, Ezra succeeds in appealing to laws that referred to many foreign peoples who no longer existed in his day, to the concept of

Ezra, depicted in the eighth-century Codex Amiatinus of the Latin Vulgate from Jarrow as a diligent scribe and student of the Torah.

the 'holy seed' that had been differently used in the stories about Abraham, and to the laws which forbad the mixing of types of seed or material in such a way as to suggest that the laws that spoke of the dangers of being enticed away from faithful worship by a foreign partner could now be applied to questions of social solidarity if not ethnicity. We might say that he was trying to get away from the letter of the law in favour of its 'spirit', the only trouble with that observation being that this is normally a process of which we strongly approve whereas in Ezra's hands it became one with extremely harsh consequences, namely the expulsion of the wives with their children. And of course this is made even worse by the probability that these wives for the most part were not really 'foreign' at all but simply members of such alternative communities as those who had remained in the land and never been in Babylon or who lived in Samaria even while adhering to fundamentally the same religion as Judah.

Now, even if some of this makes us feel uneasy we can at least sympathize with Ezra's dilemma that his small and embattled community might have been in danger of a total loss of identity if strong measures for its preservation had not been taken. Even more importantly, however, we see that for the first time the Law of Moses is beginning to be treated as something that was fixed and unalterable and which at the same time was meant to be the source of regulation for the community. There is a notion of Scripture developing here, something which requires as its corollary the requirement of endless reinterpretation in order to keep it relevant to ever changing circumstances. Judaism effectively began here, so that, if our reconstruction of the history is correct, the old adage that 'Ezra was the father of Judaism' has something to be said for it. Of course, his way had been prepared by many before him, some of whom we have already met, and his methods were to be developed and refined by many after him, but equally I do not find any other candidate for this essential breakthrough in textual interpretation that he initiated.

Nehemiah

So far as our extant sources are concerned, Ezra's immediate successor is Nehemiah, though in truth it is difficult to think of anyone more different in personality, style, ambition, or ministry.

Nehemiah was a lay person who had risen to a position of considerable trust within the court as one of the king's cupbearers. Without official administrative status he will nevertheless have been something of a personal confidant of the king and his immediate entourage and therefore capable of exercising far more influence than many others with more exalted stations. On receiving disturbing news from Jerusalem (was this the debacle suggested by the ending of Ezra 4, which is out of its proper chronological order?), he tells us that he was seized of the concern to journey there in order to lead the restoration work on the city. After securing the king's blessing for this venture he relates at length and in lively fashion how he travelled, inspected, secured the people's support, and rebuilt the destroyed walls in the teeth of opposition from neighbouring provinces. Following this he also took steps to increase the city's very depleted population. It seems, therefore, as though it was with Nehemiah that Jerusalem at last regained its political and administrative dominance of the region which had been lost under the Babylonians and had been replaced by alternative centres at Ramat Rachel and Mizpah. The wall-building was less a genuinely defensive measure (hardly necessary anyway in the tightly controlled empire) than a prestige project designed to recapture and reinforce Jerusalem's pre-eminent position.

Nehemiah's account included in the biblical book that bears his name clearly falls into two parts, and this may give us a clue as to developments behind the text that he does not make explicit. On the one hand, the bulk of the material is made up of a detailed first-person narrative focused exclusively on the building of the wall. That all took less than a year, however, and of what came later we are told nothing. In this material Nehemiah is not called the governor and he leads by virtue of his force of personality and the support of some loyal personal gang. Elsewhere, a number of short paragraphs are found interspersed into this account or added to its conclusion which tell us that Nehemiah was governor for twelve years, that he then returned to Babylon for some extended period and then came back to Jerusalem for a second term as governor, requiring the rectification of a number of abuses that he found had developed during his absence. It is these later deeds that each time he asks God to remember for his good, and interestingly the building of the wall is never mentioned in this connection.

It seems probable that we should interpret this to mean that he was not appointed as governor when he first journeyed to Jerusalem but came more in the way of a personal envoy with royal support. His success (recorded in the longer account) may then have led the king subsequently to appoint him as governor, and it is this that he wants to be remembered, not least because for each act that he makes in that capacity there is a parallel elsewhere in the book based on alternative accounts which suggest that the same things were done under priestly leadership.

If broadly along the right lines, this reconstruction suggests that he faced opposition not only from external opponents but also from those within the Judean community itself. How should we explain that, and what might be its consequences in the longer term?

If we look first at those who opposed him from outside, we find that they were led in particular by one Sanballat. We hear of him from several sources from outside the Bible as well, not least the Aramaic papyri from Elephantine. There, in 408 BCE, he is referred to as the Governor of Samaria (Nehemiah never actually graces him with that title!) but his sons are now acting for him, so that we may presume that by then he was quite elderly; this suits his active period in Nehemiah's time some thirty years earlier very well. We hear elsewhere of at least one more Sanballat in the same office a little later on, so that it seems clear that he was the founder of something like a family dynasty of governors during the second half of the Persian period.

Beside Sanballat is usually mentioned his henchman Tobiah the Ammonite (this latter probably being little more than a derogatory slur). It looks from a number of hints

A silver bowl from Tell el-Maskhuta in Egypt. Round the side is a votive inscription naming the donor as 'Qainu son of Gashmu [Geshem] king of Kedar', the latter being one of the named opponents of Nehemiah.

in the text that Tobiah had been resident previously in Jerusalem and that he had a number of supporters and family ties there (see Neh. 6:17–19; 13:4–9). At the least, therefore, he was probably a leading member of those circles which favoured a far more open stance towards the people in Samaria (and perhaps elsewhere) than the rigorous policies of Ezra allowed, and it is even possible that during the hiatus after Ezra's work and the arrival of Nehemiah he had been put in a position of temporary authority there. If so, we can well understand why he resented Nehemiah's arrival and teamed up with Sanballat, who equally would have been dismayed on both social and economic grounds by the increasing isolation of Jerusalem that seemed to be transpiring.

What is presented to us in narrative terms as a series of personal vendettas may thus well be only a cover for more deep-seated divisions of opinion about how the

---

Left: Nehemiah as depicted by Gustave Doré inspecting the ruined walls of Jerusalem by night.

evolving province of Judah should position itself. It appears that there was one party of the elite in particular, including both the leading priestly families and those of greater wealth, who favoured an open attitude to their opposite numbers in other regions. On the other hand, led especially by those who came from Babylon, where the struggle for community identity was no doubt more immediately pressing, there were those who saw Judah's future as bound up with a purer or more isolationist stance, and this, of course, was expressed as much in religious as in social terms. It may be too early to speak of specific 'parties' or sects, but we can see how already the outlines of the later Jewish groups were beginning to take shape (see Chapter 5 for fuller detail).

The fourth century

We really know nothing of the course of events in Judah during the fourth century BCE. Such hints as we have suggest that it was basically a question of 'more of the same', and our survey below (see 'Samaria and the Samaritans') of the situation in Samaria would support that. One factor is of great enduring significance, however, even though it is not possible to trace the detail with any great confidence.

It is universally agreed that many parts of what we call the Old Testament reached something like their present shape during this period. Of course, some parts are certainly even later (like the final form of the book of Daniel). Equally, other parts had been written earlier, but that does not rule out the likelihood that they were not only preserved but also given their final shape at this time. The book of Psalms, for instance, on its own account includes psalms from all periods of Israel's history, and informed analysis concludes that much the same could be said of many of the other biblical books. In some cases we may well suppose that they were written precisely in order to give expression to points of view in the ongoing debates that have already been mentioned. The book of Ruth, for instance, is quite remarkable in tracing how one of the ancestors of no lesser a figure than David himself was a woman from Moab, one of the most despised of the neighbouring people, while the story of the prophet Jonah is equally startling in its demonstration (to Jonah's own chagrin) that God cares for and can have mercy on such an archetypical enemy as Assyria. The books of Chronicles, which seem also to have been written during the fourth century BCE, take a far more open stance than the books of Samuel and Kings upon which they are partly based towards the inhabitants of the territory of what used to be the Northern Kingdom of Israel. Set alongside the books of Ezra and Nehemiah and other passages which advocate an equally exclusive stance, we can thus see how the Jerusalem community remarkably preserved texts that represented varying points of view in what was undoubtedly a long-standing and perhaps sometimes bitter source of disagreement about how the community should understand and represent itself. The religions which have shared in their inheritance of this material as scripture would do well to attend to the variety of its many voices.

Samaria and the Samaritans

The history of Samaria during the Persian period is even less well illuminated than Judah. Most references in written sources come from elsewhere, not least the Bible itself as well as, for instance, the Elephantine papyri already mentioned. In addition to some contemporary coins, a collection of mostly fragmentary papyri come to us from a find in a cave at Wadi Daliyeh, seven miles north-west of Jericho. Although they seem to have been deposited by refugees from Alexander the Great's soldiers following early resistance to Greek rule at the start of the Hellenistic period, they include a number of legal documents from the Persian period from which tatters of historical information can be dredged, such as the names of some in authority.

Samaria was a province within the satrapy of Beyond the River, just like Judah. It is certainly curious that Sanballat seems to have been the first of several generations of the same family to hold the office of governor. This may simply be coincidence, but we need also always to consider the position of each province within the wider policies of the empire as a whole. The invasion of Greece under the earlier king Xerxes was not a success, as we know, but it may well have left a seriously deleterious state of affairs in the western regions of the empire, requiring time to recover and simmering resentment against Persian rule. The start of the reign of Xerxes' son Artaxerxes was marked by a good deal of unrest and even revolt, not least along the Mediterranean seaboard and Egypt. The need to secure the region as a whole and to counter the constant Greek naval threat might well have led Artaxerxes to reform his nature of rule in the region by the appointment of governors on whom he was sure he could rely. While this is purely speculative, it becomes attractive in these circumstances to ask whether Sanballat's appointment a little before Nehemiah might not be related to this concern as well as the agreement with which Artaxerxes responded to his confidant Nehemiah's request to restore Jerusalem as a token of imperial favour.

Relations between Jerusalem and Samaria were not only fraught at the political level but also the religious, and that in ways that are often confused in people's thinking. It is easy to think that the group we know of later as the Samaritans should be identified with the residents of Samaria under the leadership of Sanballat and his associates. And indeed, much later Jewish propaganda points precisely in this direction. Other indications, however, hint at quite a different story which is certainly much closer to the historical reality.

Known facts from which to start include: not all the inhabitants of the Northern Kingdom were taken away by the Assyrians following the fall of Samaria in 721 BCE, so that many who worshipped the God of Israel must have continued to live in the region. The Samaritans whom we know of later had their temple and religious centre of gravity at Shechem (beside which stands Mount Gerizim, which they revere), not Samaria. The Samaritans have the Law of Moses (the Pentateuch) as their scripture.

There are two or three places where there seems to have been some modification in favour of their own form of religion, but they are very limited and for the most part the

A copy of the Samaritan Bible, comprising the first five books of the Hebrew Bible—the Pentateuch or Torah.

text is identical with the Jewish version. (Of course, one should not ignore the possibility that the Jewish version has done the same.) As this was not completed until the Persian period, some close contact with Jerusalem at least until that time has to be presupposed. Excavations in relatively recent times have now unearthed the Samaritan Temple on Gerizim, showing that it was built sometime in the fifth century rather than the later Hellenistic period, as had formerly been supposed on the basis of Josephus's account. Despite many earlier claims, there is no evidence in the language of any of the other Samaritan texts that their authors were descendants of the foreigners brought into the land by the Assyrians. Despite some translations, 2 Kings 17:29, on which much of the later polemic about the 'foreignness' of the Samaritans is based, refers not to *Samaritans* but to *Samarians*, i.e. residents of Samaria (whether the city or the wider region).

In addition to these facts, there is a short account in Nehemiah 13:28 about how one of the grandsons of the high priest was a son-in-law of Sanballat and that Nehemiah

The recently excavated Samaritan Temple site; most of what is visible comes from a period later than the original temple, but the latter is now known to date to the fifth century BCE.

therefore 'chased him away'. This implies at the least that, as was suggested earlier, there was close contact between some of the priestly families in Jerusalem and some of the inhabitants of the north.

On the basis of all this material, it may, with all due caution, be suggested that during the Persian period, and perhaps partly in reaction to the rigorous policies of Ezra and of Nehemiah, there were those in Jerusalem who found the direction of travel too restrictive for their liking and moved north to the old venerable site of Shechem (which had certainly been abandoned in the recent past) and that they established a viable alternative form of Israelite religion there. Many of its adherents will have been perfectly legitimate lay members of 'Israel' who had continued to live in that region for many generations past; they call themselves appropriately 'the sons of Joseph'. They would have been joined by priests from Jerusalem with their own recently completed form of the Law of Moses. At that time, while there will obviously have been some tension between Jerusalem and Shechem, there was no reason for either group categorically to denounce the other. Rather like with other communities later, such as those to whom we owe the Dead Sea Scrolls, they were initially simply a variant form of adherents to the same religion as that practised in Jerusalem. They built a temple on Gerizim (which can claim some sort of Pentateuchal legitimacy, of course, in a way that Jerusalem cannot; see Deuteronomy 27, where Ebal may well once have read Gerizim, the mount of blessing according to 11:29 and 27:12) and practised a full form of cultic and sacrificial worship there. It was not until much later, as Chapter 5 will show, that relations came to serious enmity when the Jewish leader John Hyrcanus destroyed the Samaritan temple in 128 BCE. Thereafter relationships could no longer be healed, and much that we consider typical of Samaritanism comes from that later date. But we need to be careful not to read those hardened attitudes anachronistically into the much earlier period with which we are here concerned.

Conclusions

Only a minority of the total population of the Holy Land experienced the Babylonian exile for themselves, though its impact on the history of world religion has been incalculable. Aided by the new Babylonian policy of keeping national groups together, it obliged the exiled community to develop new ways of expressing their religion as a major part of their cultural identity without the support of the traditional pillars of a temple or a sovereign monarch. In the land too, the continuing communities that had not been exiled had similar challenges to face, though perhaps not in so drastic a fashion.

The 'restoration' when it came, therefore, was not really a restoration at all in many senses. The monarchy was not revived, the territory became an imperial province rather than a national state, and even the territory itself was much reduced in size by comparison with what had been the case before.

The remarkable fact remains, however, that the presentation of all this in the scriptural texts is very much to stress the elements of continuity with what preceded even though, as we have seen, what actually emerged at the end of the period under review was a variety of closely related religious groups whom we may by now call Jews, of whom the Samaritans were initially a part, albeit with some radical distinctive features. Elsewhere in the Holy Land (i.e. to the south and the west as well as in parts of the northern area) loyalties, cultural expression, and religious identity were different, though not so enduring, while equally Babylon continued as a major centre for developing Judaism for many centuries to come, along with the growing diaspora initially in Egypt but increasingly throughout the Mediterranean world.

The history of the Persian period in the Holy Land is in many ways poorly known, and certainly it is not possible for us now to write anything like a consecutive narrative account. History is more than just political events, however, and the religious developments during those centuries, fraught and disputed as they may have been, claim our attention as the foundation stones of much that has succeeded not only in the land itself but worldwide. And perhaps the greatest legacy of all has been the concept of a Scripture which can be endlessly reinterpreted to meet shifting challenges through time even while at the same time providing an unchanging anchor for personal and communal identity. Chapter 5 will show how, from this root, the religions of Judaism and Christianity developed and spread.

CHAPTER 5

The Hellenistic and Roman Era

JOHN J. COLLINS

The Hellenistic era

IN 332 BCE Alexander the Great entered Palestine on his way from Tyre to Egypt. He placed a garrison at Gaza, but left the conquest of the region to his commanders. The classical accounts of Alexander's campaign make no mention of Judea or Samaria. Only Josephus, the Jewish historian from the late first century CE, claims that Alexander went to Jerusalem (*Ant* 11. 325–39). Alexander supposedly prostrated himself before the High Priest, and attributed the success of his campaign to the God of the Jews. He then offered sacrifice in the temple, under the direction of the High Priest, granted a request that the people observe their traditional laws, and be exempt from tribute in the seventh year. Alexander also supposedly authorized the building of the Samaritan temple on Mt Gerizim. The whole story is a transparent fabrication, but it is indeed likely that Alexander or his deputy confirmed the right to live by the ancestral laws, as the Persians had also allowed.

Judea was a very small country at the time of Alexander's conquest. The sea coast was controlled by the Syrian and Phoenician cities. The neighbours with whom the Judeans traditionally had most interaction were the Samaritans, to the north, who worshipped the same God and had essentially the same scriptures, with some distinctive modifications, but who also had their own temple on Mt Gerizim. There is a long history of antagonism between Samaria and Judea, attested in the Persian period in the books of Ezra and Nehemiah, but relations were complex, and we also read of intermarriage between the high priestly families. Josephus even claims that Sanballat, governor of Samaria, built the temple on Mt Gerizim at the time of Alexander's conquest to accommodate a priestly son-in-law from Jerusalem (*Ant* 11. 322), although that story too is unlikely to be historical. Archaeological evidence suggests that the temple had been built somewhat earlier. Alexander settled Macedonians in Samaria, as punishment for an uprising in which they had burned alive the Macedonian governor of Syria. From that point on, the Samaritans were centred in Shechem and around Mt Gerizim. Relations with Judea eventually deteriorated into open conflict at the end of the second century BCE.

The Ptolemaic era

Alexander's death was followed by a period of conflict between his generals (the Diadochi), which led to the division of the territory he had conquered and the establishment of Hellenistic kingdoms. Two of these would have far-reaching impact on Judea, the Ptolemaic kingdom in Egypt and the Seleucid kingdom in Syria. Ptolemy I captured Jerusalem in 312 BCE. The *Letter of Aristeas* claims that he enslaved more than 100,000 people, relocated others to Egypt and absorbed some of them into his army. While the numbers are not reliable, it is likely that Ptolemy deported people, and that this was one of the sources of the later Judean community in Egypt. Some Jews also served in the army of Seleucus.

Ptolemaic control over Judea was consolidated after the battle of Ipsus in 301, and lasted just over a century, until the Seleucid conquest in 198 BCE. We are poorly informed about the history of this period. The only narrative is that of Josephus, who tells the colourful but folkloristic 'tale of the Tobiads' (*Ant* 12. 160–234). Much of the narrative centres on the custom of tax-farming—selling the right to collect taxes to the highest bidder, who then collected as much as he could. The High Priest appears to be the dominant person in Jerusalem, although the Tobiad family vied with him for influence. The Zenon papyri, a dossier relating to the activities of the chief finance minister for Ptolemy II in the area of Palestine, suggest that the fiscal operations of the Ptolemies were centrally controlled, and do not refer to the High Priest or to the Tobiads at all. The papyri show that there was an active slave trade in the region in this period.

One development in this period that had important, if indirect, ramifications for life in Judea was the rise of Hellenistic cities in the region. There were two main clusters of Greek cities, one along the coast, from the Egyptian border up to Tyre, and one across the Jordan in the area around the Sea of Galilee. There were also isolated Greek cities in Galilee, Samaria, and Idumea. We know of some thirty cities in Palestine which were either founded or were given new Hellenistic identities in this period. (For example, Beth Shean, south of the Sea of Galilee became Scythopolis.) These cities were Greek-speaking and lived a Greek way of life. They were busy centres of commercial activity. Needless to say, Judea could not remain isolated from its surroundings. While our evidence about Jerusalem in this period is very limited, the city is mentioned several times in the Zenon papyri. Moreover, about a thousand stamped amphorae handles from the island of Rhodes have been found in Jerusalem. These presumably contained imported wine, and the quantity is far greater than would have been required by the Ptolemaic garrison.

It is difficult to ascribe any literature to Judea in the third century BCE. One plausible candidate is the world-weary book of Qohelet (Ecclesiastes), which complains that there is no profit to be had in life because of the inevitability of death. His concern for 'profit' may reflect an enhanced commercial context in Jerusalem, but both the date of composition and the implications for the cultural context are disputed. Some of the Aramaic writings found in the Dead Sea Scrolls, such as the *Genesis Apocryphon*, *Aramaic*

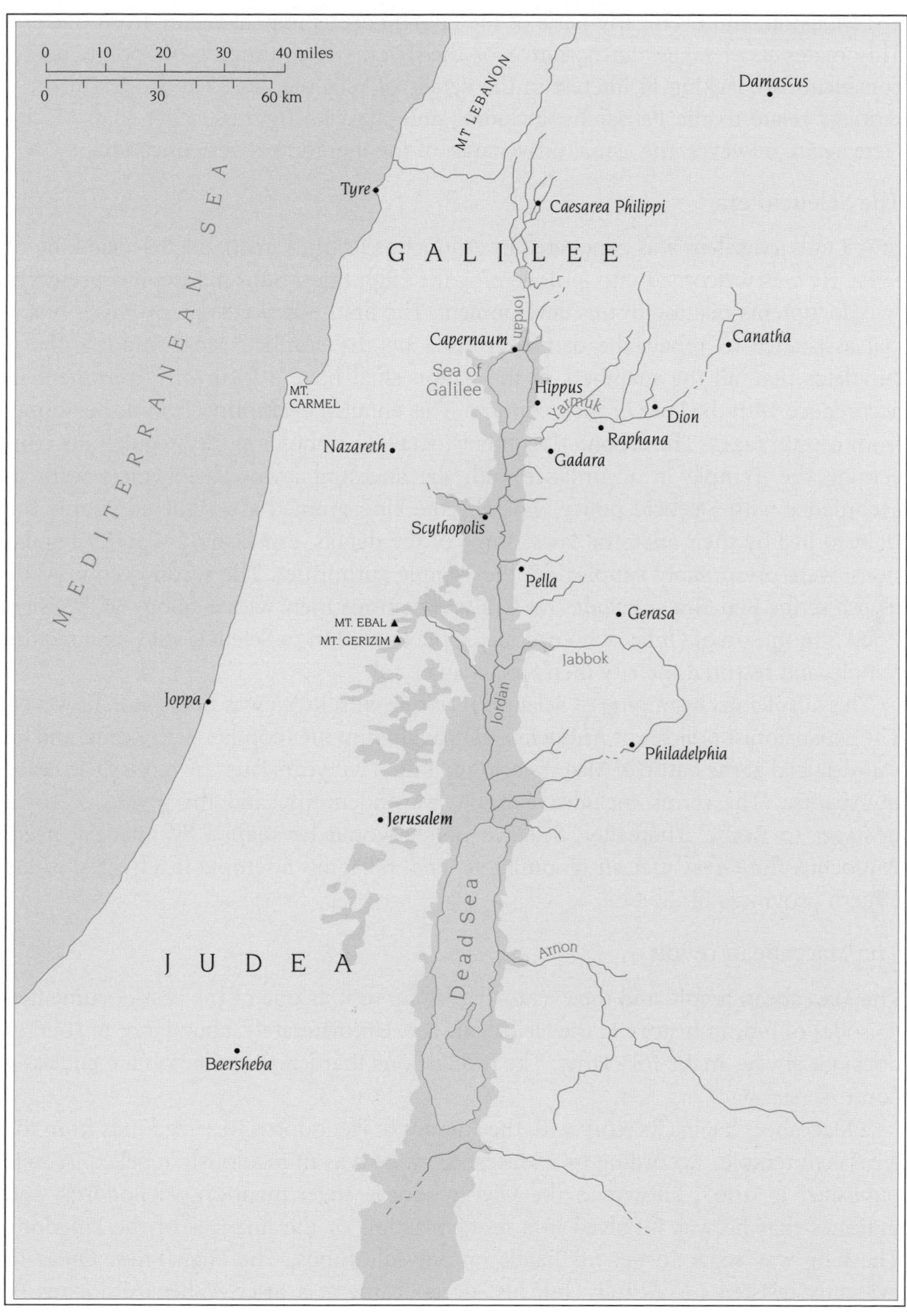

3. The cities of the Decapolis

Levi Document, and even early parts of the Enoch corpus may also date from this era. This material all takes the narrative of the Torah as a jumping-off point, but is conspicuously lacking in interest in the details of religious law. The stories in these writings relate to the Patriarchs, including ante-diluvian figures, rather than Moses. Here again, however, the actual provenance of the literature is very uncertain.

The Seleucid era

In 198 BCE Jerusalem was conquered by Antiochus III (the Great), the Seleucid king of Syria. He was welcomed into Jerusalem by the High Priest Simon. Josephus preserves two documents relating to this development. The first, *Ant* 12.138–44, promises financial assistance to repair the damage caused by the conflict. Most importantly, it stipulates that 'all the members of the nation shall have a form of government in accordance with the laws of their country'. This entailed exempting Temple personnel from certain taxes. The second document (12.145–6) upholds purity regulations concerning the Temple in accordance with the ancestral laws. These edicts were in accordance with Seleucid policy, whereby the king granted a conquered people the right to live by their ancestral laws. Some of the details, especially the purity regulations, were presumably supplied by the Temple authorities. The second-century BCE Jewish scribe Ben Sira concludes his 'praise of famous men' with a eulogy of the High Priest Simon, son of Onias, who negotiated the transition to Seleucid rule, repaired the temple, and restored the city (Ben Sira, chapter 50).

This auspicious beginning of Seleucid relations with Judea was not to last, however. The expansionist policies of Antiochus III brought him into conflict with Rome, and he was defeated at the battle of Magnesia, in 190 BCE. Two years later, he ratified the Peace of Apamea. The terms included a heavy war-indemnity, and the giving of royal hostages to Rome. Thereafter, Seleucid policy would be shaped by financial need. Antiochus the Great met an ignominious end, pillaging a temple in Elymais, in his eastern provinces in 187 BCE.

The Maccabean revolt

The Maccabean revolt, and the events that led up to it, is one of the best-documented episodes of Judean history in the Hellenistic age. Unfortunately, abundance of sources does not always make for clarity. The motivations that led to the revolt are endlessly controversial.

2 Maccabees begins its story with the attempt of Heliodorus to seize funds from the Jerusalem temple. According to 2 Maccabees 3, he was miraculously repelled. A stele published in 2007, known as the Olympiodoros stele, mentions Heliodorus, and indicates that he was involved in a reorganization of the finances of the kingdom. The king was eager to get his hands on any idle funds. The High Priest Onias III evidently resisted successfully, but his success came at a price. When Antiochus IV Epiphanes succeeded to the throne in 175 BCE, he replaced Onias as High Priest, and appointed his brother Jason instead.

Coin of Antiochus IV Epiphanes ('God Manifest').

As 2 Maccabees tells the story, the initiative came from Jason. He offered to increase the tribute if he could build a gymnasium and enroll the people of Jerusalem as citizens of Antioch-at-Jerusalem. Wherever the initiative lay, it is clear that the king was motivated by the possibility of higher revenues. Jason, too, was probably motivated by the prospect of gain. He aimed to improve relations, and presumably commerce, with the neighbouring Greek cities. The people of Jerusalem who wished to be citizens of Antioch-at-Jerusalem would presumably pay for the privilege, thus making possible the increase in tribute. It is not clear whether Antioch-at-Jerusalem was a new foundation, adjacent to Jerusalem, or was rather Jerusalem itself under a new name. The latter seems more likely; there was only one High Priest and one Temple. 2 Maccabees expresses outrage at the idea of young priests competing in the gymnasium and adopting Greek fashions. But Jason's 'reform' provoked no resistance. It was not the cause of the revolt. Three years later, Jason found himself outbid by Menelaus. Again, while some people may have disapproved, the change provoked no resistance.

What triggered fighting in Jerusalem was not resistance to Hellenizing innovations, but rivalry between Jason and Menelaus. Antiochus had invaded Egypt in the winter of 170/69 BCE, and had gained control of most of Egypt, even while his young nephew, Ptolemy VI Philometor, remained on the throne. A second invasion in 168 BCE was less successful. Antiochus was confronted by the Roman legate Popilius Laenas on 'the day of Eleusis', and ordered peremptorily to withdraw. A rumour spread in Judea that the king had been killed, and Jason took the opportunity to launch a coup against Menelaus, shutting him up in the citadel. When the king heard this, he took it that Judea was in revolt, and sent in his troops to sack the city and pillage the temple. The repression of the revolt was all the more severe because the king had been humiliated in Egypt.

Thus far, the sequence of events is quite intelligible. What followed next has exercised scholars since antiquity. According to 2 Maccabees 6:1, 'not long after this the king sent an Athenian senator (or: Geron the Athenian) to compel the Jews to forsake the laws of their ancestors and no longer to live by the laws of God; also to pollute the temple in Jerusalem and to call it the temple of Olympian Zeus'. People, we are told, could neither keep the Sabbath, nor observe the festivals of their ancestors, nor so much confess themselves to be Judeans (2 Macc. 6:6). According to 1 Maccabees, they were forbidden to circumcise their sons or even to have copies of the Law. 2 Maccabees adds that they were required to celebrate the king's birthday and march in procession honouring Dionysus.

These measures have usually been taken to constitute a religious persecution. Such measures were very rare in antiquity. Pagans were tolerant of diversity. For attempts to suppress a traditional cult we must go back to Josiah in the late seventh-century BCE, or even to Akhenaten in the second millennium.

1 Maccabees construes these measures as an attempt by the king to unify his empire: 'The king wrote to his whole kingdom that all should be one people, and that all should give up their particular customs. All the Gentiles accepted the command of the king' (1 Macc. 1:41–2). But this is patently untrue. In 166 BCE the king held a celebration at Daphne in honour of his 'great victories' in Egypt. Each of the peoples in his kingdom was supposed to bring statues of its gods, to celebrate the diversity.

The great historian of ancient Judaism, Elias Bickerman, could not believe that an enlightened king would have taken such measures of his own volition. So he supposed that the repressive measures and suppression of the traditional Jewish law were the work of Menelaus, who wanted to stamp out resistance to the Hellenizing 'reforms' such as the introduction of the gymnasium. Bickerman won the support of another great historian, Martin Hengel, but the theory fails for want of evidence. Conversely, some scholars have supposed that the revolt must have come first, and posit an initial uprising that went unnoticed in the sources.

The latter theory is on the right track, insofar as it recognizes that Antiochus IV Epiphanes was not engaging in religious persecution but in suppressing a revolt. The revolt in question, however, was nothing more than Jason's coup against Menelaus, which directly disputed the authority of the king. As noted already, a king who conquered a city had the right to abrogate the ancestral laws, but normally restored them in an act of graciousness, designed to win the support of the people. Conversely, when a people revolted, the king had the right to suspend the ancestral law, and this is what happened in the case of Jerusalem. What was at issue was the identity of the people and their right to exist as a distinct entity, even if they were subject to overlords. Antiochus singled out those features of the laws that had high symbolic value as markers of Judean identity—Sabbath, circumcision, the festivals. These things were religious, to be sure, as they were concerned with the cult of the divine, but they were also markers of Judean identity, and that is what Epiphanes wanted to erase.

Epiphanes did not succeed in this endeavour. 2 Maccabees 11:24–5 preserves a letter attributed to his son, Antiochus V:

> We have heard that the Jews do not consent to our father's change to Greek customs, but prefer their own way of living and ask that their own customs be allowed to them. Accordingly, since we choose that this nation also should be free from disturbance, our decision is that their temple be restored to them and that they shall live according to the customs of their ancestors.

(Some scholars think that this decision was already taken by Antiochus IV.) The Jews' lack of consent had to be forcefully expressed, by the force of the Maccabees' arms. It does not appear, however, that the Maccabees had aspired to independence. The rallying cry of Mattathias in 1 Maccabees was zeal for the Law. The great achievement of Judas Maccabee was that he purified and rededicated the temple. There were truces between the combatants at various points in the struggle. After the death of Judas, his brothers proved adroit at exploiting rivalries between Seleucid pretenders. Jonathan Maccabee was installed as High Priest by the Syrian king, Alexander Balas (1 Macc. 10:1–20). Syrian authority began to fade after Jonathan was succeeded by his brother Simon in 143 BCE. Simon finally conquered the Akra—the Syrian garrison in Jerusalem that had been a thorn in the side of the Maccabees. Yet, the first recognition of Simon as leader came from Demetrius II of Syria. A stele set up to honour Simon in 140 BCE notably fails to claim that he achieved independence. The eventual independence of the Hasmoneans (the descendants of the Maccabees) was due as much to Seleucid decline as to their own aspirations. After the death of Antiochus Sidetes in 129 BCE, Judea, under John Hyrcanus I, was completely independent.

The success of the Maccabees was due in part to their willingness to compromise on the Law and fight on the Sabbath. They correctly realized that they would be wiped out if they did not. Not all Judeans thought likewise. The decision of the Maccabees to fight on the Sabbath came in reaction to the death of a group of pious Jews, called *Hasidim*, who chose to die rather than violate the Sabbath. Some light may be thrown on the thinking of the Hasidim by the apocalyptic writings of the time. The *Testament* or *Assumption of Moses* tells the story of a man named Taxo, who in a time of persecution took his seven sons and went into a cave to purify themselves and die, reasoning that if they did so, their blood would be avenged by the Lord, as promised in Deuteronomy 32. The Book of Daniel, which appears to have been written during the very years of the Maccabean campaign, explains that the conflict is really between the heavenly 'princes' of the nations (or patron angels) and that the conflict will be resolved when the archangel Michael, prince of Israel, arises in victory. The role of the pious is to persevere, trust in their heavenly deliverer, and stay pure, even letting themselves be killed. If they do this they will be rewarded in eternal life with the angels in heaven. Daniel famously says that when the pious fall, they will receive little help. Since the time of St Jerome, this has been taken as a slighting reference to the Maccabees. Whether this is correct or not, it is clear that Daniel's reaction to the persecution is very different from that of the Maccabees.

Some of the apocalypses now collected in 1 Enoch were also written around the time of the Maccabean revolt (*the Animal Apocalypse, the Apocalypse of Weeks*). The *Animal Apocalypse* (1 *Enoch* 85–90) has a much more positive attitude to the Maccabees than does Daniel, and appears to endorse the use of the sword. The apocalyptic genre first appears in Judaism in the books of Enoch and Daniel. It is characterized by a strong interest in the heavenly world, and hope for eternal life with the angels, a belief that first appears in Judaism at this time. Parts of 1 *Enoch* were written before the Maccabean revolt (the *Book of the Watchers*, the *Astronomical Book*). The hope for afterlife with the angels, then, does not appear to have arisen in response to the deaths of righteous Judeans in the Maccabean era. There can be no doubt, however, that the experience of persecution, where people were killed for observing the Law, instead of being rewarded with long life as promised in the Law, greatly contributed to the hope for resurrection and a heavenly afterlife.

It should be emphasized that the Maccabean revolt was not a revolt against Hellenistic culture. The Maccabees were not isolationists. Judas even sent an embassy to Rome to establish an alliance, in 161 BCE. For this delegation he selected Eupolemus, son of John, son of Accos, a member of a prominent priestly family. Eupolemus is credited with a history of the Judean people, written in admittedly poor Greek. He was probably selected for the delegation because of his knowledge of Greek. His father had negotiated with Antiochus III at the time of the Syrian conquest of Jerusalem. The alliance with Rome did not have immediate significance in the Maccabean era, but Rome would become all too active in Judean affairs a century later.

The Hasmoneans

In the early part of the Maccabean rebellion, Judas and his brothers gathered Judeans who were living in Galilee and Gilead, in Gentile environments, and brought them to Judea for their protection (1 Macc. 5). The next generation sought rather to expand the borders of Judea. John Hyrcanus I (135–104 BCE) extended Judean control over Idumea and Samaria. His son Aristobulus pushed farther north, into the territory of the Itureans. Josephus tells us that when John Hyrcanus conquered the Idumeans, about 128 BCE, he

> permitted them to remain in their country so long as they had themselves circumcised and were willing to observe the laws of the Jews. And so, out of attachment to their ancestral land, they submitted to circumcision and to having their manner of life in all other respects made the same as that of the Judeans. And from that time on they have continued to be Judeans. (*Ant* 13. 257–8)

Similarly, when Aristobulus conquered some of the territory of the Itureans in 104–103 BCE, he 'compelled the inhabitants, if they wished to remain in their country, to be circumcised and to live in accordance with the laws of the Judeans' (*Ant* 13. 318). Later, when the inhabitants of Pella refused to accept the laws of the Judeans, Alexander Jannaeus destroyed the city. He also launched attacks against the Hellenistic cities of the coastal plain and Transjordan. While the Hasmoneans are not remembered for their piety, they insisted on the observance of the distinctive Jewish laws, precisely those that had been outlawed by Antiochus Epiphanes. Even at the beginning of the revolt, according to 1 Maccabees, Mattathias and his friends went around and tore down the pagan altars that had been set up at the king's command, and forcibly circumcised all the boys who had been left uncircumcised because of the king's decree (1 Macc. 2:45–6). John Hyrcanus destroyed the Samaritan temple on Mt Gerizim and conquered Shechem and Samaria.

Hyrcanus's son Aristobulus I (104–103 BCE) was the first of the line to assume the title of king. From this point onward, the Hasmoneans acted like Hellenistic kings and their reigns were marked by dynastic struggles. Aristobulus had his mother imprisoned, and then starved to death. He imprisoned three of his four brothers, and while he initially trusted the other, Antigonus, he eventually had him murdered. He favoured Greek culture, and styled himself *philellen*, lover of the Greeks. Nonetheless, he imposed Jewish law, including the requirement of circumcision, on a segment of the Itureans in the north.

The highpoint of Hasmonean expansion came under Alexander Jannaeus (103–176 BCE), who was involved continually in foreign and internal wars. He conquered Gadara, east of the Jordan, and the Philistine cities on the Mediterranean coast, including Gaza. It is unclear just when Galilee was Judaized. There is little archaeological evidence for Hasmonean conquest, but it clear that Galilee was under Hasmonean control by the end of Jannaeus's reign, as can be seen especially from the spread of Hasmonean coins. Some sites went out of use, others received new populations and new settlements appeared. The Jewish character of Galilee in the Roman period had its roots in Hasmonean colonization. Stepped pools for ritual baths (often called *miqvaoth*) first appear in the archaeological record in the Hasmonean period. Hellenistic amphorae, which were very common in Jerusalem in the period between 180 and 150 BCE are virtually absent in Hasmonean Jerusalem, and are unattested in the Hasmonean palaces.

Jannaeus also faced insurrection at home, led by the Pharisees, one of the Jewish parties that first arose in the Hasmonean period.

The Jewish sects

According to the historian Josephus, there were three main parties (*haireseis*) in Judea, the Pharisees, the Sadducees, and the Essenes. In the *Jewish Antiquities*, Josephus first introduces them in the time of Jonathan Maccabee, in the middle of the second century BCE (*Ant* 13. 171–3). In the Jewish War, however, he introduces them in the period after the death of Herod, around the turn of the era (*JW* 2. 119–66). The Pharisees, in any case, were active already from the time of John Hyrcanus onwards.

The parties described by Josephus are usually referred to as sects. The terminology of sectarianism derives from the history of Christianity. A sect is defined over against a church, or mainline religious institution. Not all the Jewish parties were sects in this sense.

In the Hasmonean and early Roman periods sects and parties must be understood against the background of what may be described as 'common Judaism'. All branches of Judaism accepted the Torah of Moses as their ancestral Law, and observed basic practices prescribed therein, such as circumcision and the Sabbath. They also observed the major festivals prescribed in Leviticus 23, from Passover to the Day of Atonement. For all, the Jerusalem temple was a focal point, which they supported by tithes and taxes, and was also periodically a place of pilgrimage. Differences arose, however, in the interpretation of the Torah, and this had implications for the correct practice of the temple cult.

Of the parties described by Josephus, the Sadducees were the most traditional. They seem to have been aristocratic priests, and had their following among the wealthy. At least two High Priests, Caiaphas and Ananus, are said to have been Sadducees. They accepted only the written law and did not believe in the resurrection of the dead or in angels (Acts 23:8). They affirmed free will.

The Pharisees differed from the Sadducees insofar as they attached great importance to the traditions handed down by previous generations. They were popular among the masses. According to Josephus, they were already an influential group in the reign of John Hyrcanus, and they were already at odds with the Sadducees. Hyrcanus himself was a disciple of the Pharisees, but parted ways with them. A Pharisee named Eleazar called on him to give up the High Priesthood, on the ground that his mother had been a captive (*Ant* 13. 288–92). The Sadducees seized the opportunity to get the king to join their party and suppress the regulations of the Pharisees. Essentially the same story is told in the Talmud (b. Qidd 66a), but there the king is identified as Alexander Jannaeus. Consequently, there is some doubt as to whether the Pharisees had already risen to prominence as early as the second century BCE.

Josephus does not mention the Pharisees explicitly in the reign of Alexander Jannaeus (103–176 BCE), until the scene of his death, but most scholars believe that they led the popular opposition during his rule. On one occasion he was pelted with citrons during the Feast of Booths (*Ant* 13.372–3). He responded by having 6000 of his opponents killed. Subsequently there was open revolt against him. The rebels invited the Syrian king Demetrius Eukairos ('well-timed', alternatively known as Akairos, 'the untimely one') to intervene, but the intervention backfired as the people rallied to the native Judean king. Jannaeus had 800 of the rebels crucified, and killed their wives and children before their eyes (*Ant* 13.380). On his death-bed, however, suffering from quartan fever, brought on by heavy drinking, Jannaeus advised his widow to yield a certain amount of power to the Pharisees, with a view to winning over the masses (*Ant* 13. 401). She had two sons, Hyrcanus and Aristobulus, but Jannaeus left the royal power to the queen Salome Alexandra. She appointed Hyrcanus as High Priest 'because of his greater age, but more especially because of his lack of energy' (*Ant* 13. 408), and she followed the advice of Jannaeus with regard to the Pharisees:

> she permitted the Pharisees to do as they liked in all matters, and also commanded the people to obey them; and whatever regulations, introduced by the Pharisees in accordance with the tradition of their fathers, had been abolished by her father-in-law Hyrcanus, these she again restored. And so, while she had the title of sovereign, the Pharisees had the power. (*Ant* 13.408)

The Pharisees, then, were committed to the accurate interpretation of the Law, in light of their traditions, and were influential with the masses, but they also aspired to political power. The highpoint of their political influence was in the later part of the Hasmonean era (75–63 BCE).

The third 'sect' mentioned by Josephus, the Essenes, are not mentioned at all in the New Testament, at least by that name. They are described in much greater detail than the other parties in the *Jewish War* 2. 119–61, a fact that would seem to be due to the sources at the historian's disposal. They are also described by Philo of Alexandria, and by Pliny the Elder. While Josephus says that they are not confined to any one city, the lifestyle he describes is reminiscent of later Christian monasticism. It involves a multi-year process of admission, and common possessions. Josephus, Philo, and Pliny all say that the Essenes were celibate, although Josephus concedes that a second order of Essenes married. Their lifestyle was characterized by study, work, and worship. They believed in the immortality of the soul, and reward and punishment in the hereafter, but not in the resurrection of the body.

The Essenes have attracted much attention in modern scholarship because of the discovery of the Dead Sea Scrolls, which were found in caves near Qumran, on the shore of the Dead Sea, south of Jericho, between 1947 and 1955. The Scrolls include two rule-books. One, the so-called Damascus Document, describes a new covenant, at least some of whose members marry and have children, although they also contribute to a common fund. The other, the Community Rule (*Serek ha-Yahad*), is strikingly similar to the account of the Essenes in Josephus's *Jewish War*. This too describes an association with a multi-year process of admission and common possessions. It makes no mention whatever of women and children. It clearly envisions reward and punishment after death, but does not clearly refer to the resurrection of the body. The Community Rule was identified as an Essene document almost immediately after its discovery. The identification was suggested by the fact that the Roman writer Pliny describes an Essene settlement south of Jericho, near the Dead Sea, in the general area where the Scrolls were found, but ultimately it rests on the correspondences between the Community Rule and the account of Josephus. (Qumran was evidently the site of an Essene settlement, whose ruins have been excavated, but it was by no means the only residence of the sect.) While the identification continues to be disputed, most scholars find it compelling.

The site of Qumran beside the Dead Sea. The Scrolls were found in caves in the mountain ridge along the right-hand side of the picture.

The correspondence between the Scrolls and the accounts of the Essenes is not complete. The accounts by Josephus and Pliny, and also the philosopher Philo, make no mention of messianic expectation, or of a coming war between sons of light and sons of darkness. But then again Josephus generally gives short shrift to such ideas: these were not aspects of Judaism that were generally presented to the gentile world. There are some correspondences in beliefs. The Scrolls do not speak clearly of the resurrection of the dead, although they certainly envision reward and punishment after death. The main correspondences, however, concern structural aspects of the community, such as the multi-year process of admission and the sharing of possessions. The Scrolls never explicitly require celibacy, but the absence of women and children from the Community Rule is remarkable. The movement described in the Scrolls was evidently extensive. Fragments of nearly a thousand writings were found in the caves. It would be remarkable if such an extensive movement had escaped the notice of Josephus. It seems more economical to assume that the sect described in the Scrolls

Part of the War Scroll, one of the Dead Sea Scrolls which describes the coming war between the sons of light and the sons of darkness.

was in fact the Essenes, while granting that the Greek and Latin accounts may not give an entirely accurate picture of the movement.

Both the classical accounts of the Essenes and the Rule of the Community warrant the epithet 'sectarian'. They describe a distinct association, with its own provision for admission and expulsion. It is clear from the Scrolls that this movement was also at odds with the Hasmonean rulers.

The Scrolls include a distinctive kind of commentary on prophetic texts, called *pesharim*, which typically interpret the prophecies as predictions of events in their own history. These commentaries often refer to a figure called the Teacher of Righteousness, or Righteous Teacher, who was a revered authority figure within the sectarian movement. He is said to have clashed with other figures, called the Wicked Priest, and the Man of the Lie. The Wicked Priest was apparently a High Priest, and there have been many attempts to identify him.

In the early phase of scholarship on the Scrolls, it was often assumed that the sect arose because of a dispute about the High Priesthood. The sectarians often refer to themselves as 'sons of Zadok'. Zadok was the High Priest in Solomon's temple. His descendants were thought to have been High Priests down to the Maccabean era, when the line was disrupted by Antiochus Epiphanes. The Hasmoneans had taken over the High Priesthood, but they were not legitimate heirs of the office. Accordingly, many scholars reasoned that Jonathan Maccabee, who assumed the High Priesthood in 152 BCE, must have been the Wicked Priest. The Scrolls, however, never object to the legitimacy of the ruling priests. Rather, they object to their interpretation and practice of the Law. This point became clear when a text called 4QMMT (*Miqsat Maᶜase Ha-Torah = Some of the Works of the Law*; 4Q means that it was found in Cave 4 at Qumran), came to light in the mid-1980s. This text was addressed to a leader of Israel, presumably a High Priest. It gave a list of some twenty-two instances in which the writer's interpretation of the Law differed from that of his opponents, and appealed to the ruler to recognize that the writer's interpretation was correct. Many of the points at issue concerned purity, and seem arcane to the modern reader. (One, for example, concerns the purity of liquid streams: if a liquid is poured from one vessel into another, and the second one is unclean, does the purity travel upstream?) The text also included a long exposition of the calendar, arguing that it should have 364 days, not 354 as was usual in Jewish tradition. It indicates that it was because of these differences that the author's movement had separated itself from the rest of the people. Several of the issues discussed are also attested in rabbinic literature. In those cases, 4QMMT agrees with the Sadducean interpretation and disagrees with that of the Pharisees.

We do not know when this text was composed, but a plausible setting can be found in the reign of Salome Alexandra, when the Hasmonean house switched its allegiance from the Sadducees to the Pharisees. While the Pharisees are not mentioned by that name in the Scrolls, many scholars believe that they are referred to as the 'seekers after smooth things', people whose interpretation of the Law was too lenient. The 'Man of the Lie' is often thought to have been a Pharisaic leader. We need not conclude that 4QMMT is a Sadducean document, but rather that the Essenes agreed with the legal interpretation of the Sadducees, against that of the Pharisees. 4QMMT would then have been addressed, most probably to the High Priest Hyrcanus II, as an appeal not to follow the interpretation of the Pharisees. If so, the appeal was rejected, and Hyrcanus may well have come to be viewed as the Wicked Priest. This dispute, however, was not what caused the sect to break away. It had already separated itself from the majority of the people because of differences in legal interpretation.

It is apparent both from the Scrolls and from Josephus that the Essenes did not participate in the Temple cult while it was administered by the Hasmoneans, because they regarded it as impure. The fact that they followed a different calendar would have intensified their differences with the Temple. It is clear from a commentary on Habakkuk that the Wicked Priest and the Teacher of Righteousness observed the Day of Atonement on different days. The Essenes did not reject the Temple in principle. They hoped to return to it in the messianic age, but they found Hasmonean practice unacceptable.

The end of Hasmonean rule

After the death of Alexandra, war broke out between the brothers Hyrcanus and Aristobulus. Aristobulus prevailed, and Hyrcanus renounced his claim to the throne. At this point, the Idumean Antipater, father of the future King Herod, began to interfere. He formed an alliance with the Nabatean prince Aretas, and persuaded Hyrcanus to flee from Jerusalem to Petra. Aretas then marched against Aristobulus and defeated him in battle. At this time the Roman general Pompey was campaigning in Asia. He defeated Mithridates, king of Pontus, in 66 BCE, and dispatched his lieutenant Scaurus to Syria. When Scaurus heard of the conflict between the Hasmonean brothers, he proceeded to Judea. Both brothers offered him tribute. Scaurus decided to back Aristobulus, and ordered Aretas to withdraw.

Pompey now came to Damascus. Three Judean parties appeared before him—Hyrcanus, Aristobulus, and the Judean people who wished to be rid of both of them. Pompey deferred his decision, but when Aristobulus withdrew abruptly he became suspicious and marched to Judea. Aristobulus promised to surrender the city to Pompey, but the people barred the gates. Pompey then took Aristobulus prisoner and marched on the city. The partisans of Hyrcanus opened the gates, but those of Aristobulus mobilized to resist on the Temple Mount. Pompey laid siege to the Temple Mount for three months, but eventually breached the wall. A bloodbath ensued, in which as many as 12,000 were said to have died. Pompey insisted on entering the Holy of Holies, where only the High Priest was allowed. He took Aristobulus and his sons captive. When he celebrated his triumph in Rome in 61 BCE, Aristobulus had to walk before his chariot. Pompey greatly reduced the territory of Judea, but allowed Hyrcanus to remain as High Priest without the title of king.

The Roman era

The capture of Jerusalem by Pompey ushered in the Roman era in Palestine. Some commentary on these events has survived in the *Psalms of Solomon*, written in the self-styled 'conventicles of the pious', sometimes suspected to be Pharisees. On the one hand, they celebrate the downfall of the Hasmoneans, who are described as sinners, who usurped the throne of David, although God had made no promise to them. On the other hand, Pompey is a lawless one, who acted arrogantly and whose heart was alien to God. The Psalmist prays to God to raise up a son of David as king to rule over Israel, in effect a messiah (*Pss Sol* 17:21). We also find the hope for a messiah about this time in the Dead Sea Scrolls, where the typical hope is for two messiahs, a kingly messiah of Israel and a priestly messiah of Aaron. Messianic expectation had been dormant in Judaism for much of the Second Temple period. It revived in the middle of the first century BCE, partly because of disillusionment with the Hasmoneans and partly in response to the loss of sovereignty through the Roman conquest. It would become a significant factor in the history of Judea in the following centuries.

Herod

The decades that followed Pompey's conquest of Jerusalem were a time of transition both in Rome and in Judea. The turmoil in Judea involved several abortive attempts to restore the Hasmonean line. Hyrcanus II and Antipater the Idumean threw in their lot with Caesar in the Roman civil war. Consequently Hyrcanus was restored to political status as ethnarch (which translates roughly as 'tribal/ethnic leader'), and Antipater was named procurator. Antipater installed his two sons, Phasael and Herod as governors in Jerusalem and Galilee. Herod proceeded to make his name by capturing and executing a bandit chief named Ezekias. After Julius Caesar's death, Antipater and his sons aligned themselves with Cassius, one of the leading instigators in the plot to assassinate Caesar.

Antipater was poisoned by a certain Malichus in 43 BCE. Herod quickly avenged his death by having Malichus assassinated. The upheavals of the Roman civil wars, however, created an opportunity for Antigonus, the surviving son of Aristobulus. He persuaded the Parthians to install him as king in Jerusalem. Hyrcanus's ears were cut off to disqualify him from the High Priesthood. Phasael committed suicide to evade capture, but his brother Herod and his family escaped to Rome, where he was declared king of Judea by the Senate. With Roman assistance, he captured Jerusalem in 37 BCE, and married Mariamme, a granddaughter of Hyrcanus II.

Herod's reign (37–4 BCE) may be divided into three periods. The first, approximately 37–25 BCE, saw the consolidation of his rule. The second, 25–13 BCE was the peak of his prosperity and influence with Rome, and was marked by his great building projects. The final period, 13–4 BCE, was marred by conflict with his own family.

Herod had various enemies to contend with when he came to power. The people were suspicious of an Idumean 'half-Jew', who owed his position to the Romans. The nobility was hostile. Herod dealt with the opposition by having forty-five of the most eminent and wealthy nobles executed and confiscating their property, thereby laying the basis for his own wealth. His Hasmonean mother-in-law, Alexandra, agitated to have her son Aristobulus installed as High Priest. She succeeded for a while, until Herod had the young man murdered. Eventually, after the death of Antony and Cleopatra, he had his wife Mariamme executed, on suspicion of infidelity, and finally he had his mother-in-law Alexandra executed too. Hyrcanus II, the deposed High Priest, lived in harmony with Herod for a time after his return from Parthia, but he too was executed after the battle of Actium in 31 BCE, lest he pose any threat to Herod's claim to the throne.

A greater challenge to Herod was presented by Cleopatra, who coveted his territories. Herod could not easily oppose her because of his dependence on Mark Antony. Antony granted her the Phoenician and Philistine coast except for Tyre and Sidon, and also the plain of Jericho. Herod had to lease his own territory from the Egyptian queen, but he managed to maintain a good relationship with Antony. When Antony and

---

Right: Caesarea, one of Herod's great building projects.

Cleopatra were defeated at the battle of Actium, Herod adroitly switched his loyalty to Augustus, who returned to him the region of Jericho and much of the coastal plain.

Herod prospered as a Roman client king. His reign was distinguished especially by his building projects. He built a theatre in Jerusalem, an amphitheatre in the plain nearby, and a palace for himself adorned with marble and gold. Samaria was reconstructed and renamed Sebaste. He built a splendid city on the coast, on the site of Straton's Tower, and named it Caesarea, which had a great harbour and a temple to Caesar that was visible far out to sea.

He built a fortress at Herodium south-east of Jerusalem, and refortified the old Hasmonean fortresses of Hyrcania, Machaerus, and Masada. He also engaged in building far beyond the borders of Judea. He built a temple on the island of Rhodes and contributed handsomely to many other cities, including Athens, Antioch, and Nicopolis (which was founded by Augustus near the site of Actium). He sponsored games at Caesarea, and even in Jerusalem, and gave generous support to the Olympic games. To create an impression of culture, he surrounded himself with people trained in Greek rhetoric, of whom the most eminent, Nicolaus of Damascus, served as his court historian. In all of this, he played the role of the Hellenistic king, noted for his benefactions, and strengthened ties with neighbouring principalities. Much of his wealth seems to have come from trade and from the resources that he controlled. He courted popular support by cutting taxes, in 20 BCE by a third and in 14 BCE by a quarter. He tried hard to relieve a great famine in 25 BCE, but the fact that there was a famine shows that the prosperity of his reign did not extend to the common people.

Herod's most famous building project was the reconstruction of the Jerusalem temple, which he made into the largest sanctuary in the ancient world. The work on the temple provided steady employment for many long after Herod's death. (The temple was only completed in 64 CE, on the eve of the Jewish war with Rome.) The fame of the temple added to the attraction of Jerusalem as a place of pilgrimage for the religious festivals. While Herod claimed that the rebuilding of the temple was an act of piety, it is generally agreed that his attachment to Judaism was superficial. He erected pagan temples in cities that were predominantly Gentile, but not in Jerusalem. His coins bear no human likeness. No images were placed in public buildings in Jerusalem. When people objected to imperial trophies in the theatre in Jerusalem, thinking they were statues, Herod had them taken down to show that they were simply wooden frames. He demanded that a Nabatean who wished to marry his (Herod's) sister adopt Jewish customs, and when he refused the marriage was called off. The famous quip of Augustus, that he would rather be Herod's pig than his son (Macrobius, *Saturnalia* 2.4.1) may even suggest that he kept some of the food laws. He did, however, offend the populace by placing a golden eagle over one of the temple gates, and this became a source of conflict when he was seriously ill at the end of his life. Two teachers and their students knocked it down and cut it to pieces. Herod sentenced them to death by burning.

The last phase of Herod's reign was marred by feuds within his own family. He had ten wives in all. Herod's main conflicts were with the sons of the Hasmonean princess Mariamme, Alexander and Aristobulus, whom he sent to Rome to be educated for five years or so (approximately 23–18/17 BCE). There was rivalry between these sons of Mariamme and Herod's son by his first wife, Antipater. Eventually Herod had Alexander and Aristobulus strangled. Antipater was imprisoned for plotting against the king, and was executed just before Herod's death. Herod was buried in the fortress he had built at Herodium. (The tomb has only recently been discovered by an archaeological excavation.) He had had a brilliant reign, but he was hated as a despot and his family life was tragic.

After Herod's death

Herod's death was followed by an uprising, which was put down harshly by Varus, the governor of Syria. His kingdom was divided among three sons named in his will. Archelaus received Judea, Samaria, and Idumea, but was given the title of ethnarch rather than king. Herod Antipas received Galilee and Perea, with the title of tetrarch (provincial governor). Herod Philip received the regions of Batanea, Trachonitis, and Auranitis, also as tetrarch.

Archelaus was deeply unpopular, and was removed and exiled after two years. Judea then became a province governed by a procurator. The procurators oversaw the province from their residence in Caesarea, but the High Priests, who now served at the pleasure of the Roman governor, were entrusted with the leadership. They also presided over the Sanhedrin, an assembly which had already existed in Hasmonean times, which exercised wide legislative and executive powers.

Herod Philip ruled for thirty-eight years, apparently with success. More information has survived about Antipas, who ruled for more than forty years. Like his father, he engaged in some notable building projects. He rebuilt Sepphoris in Galilee and constructed a new capital city, Tiberias, on the sea of Galilee, in honour of the emperor Tiberius. He prospered until the reign of Caligula, when he was urged by his wife Herodias to ask for the title 'king', which had been granted to his nephew Agrippa in the territory of Philip. Caligula decided that Antipas was a traitor and exiled him to Gaul.

Of the governors in Judea in the period 6–42 CE, the most notable was Pontius Pilate, infamous as the one who passed sentence on Jesus of Nazareth. Philo (*Legatio* 38) cites a letter of Agrippa, which describes Pilate as 'a man of inflexible disposition, harsh and obdurate'. He caused a crisis by having the Jerusalem garrison enter the city with their standards, and had to have the images removed in face of popular protest. He took funds from the temple treasury to pay for an aqueduct. He was eventually recalled because of the harshness with which he suppressed a gathering of Samaritans led by a prophet at Mt Gerizim.

When Claudius became emperor in 41 CE, he restored the kingdom of Herod, with Agrippa as king. Agrippa was careful to observe Mosaic law. He died suddenly after three years. Thereafter the territory was governed by procurators, under the governor of Syria. Eventually, in 53 CE, Agrippa II was given the territory that had been ruled by Philip, and later parts of Galilee were added to that.

Turbulent times

The first century CE was a turbulent time in Judea. The wars in the previous century had usually been fought by rival claimants to the throne. After the death of Herod, most of the unrest took the form of popular movements.

According to Josephus, after the death of Herod a Galilean named Judas 'incited his countrymen to revolt, upbraiding them as cowards for consenting to pay tribute to the Romans and tolerating mortal masters, after having God for their lord' (*JW* 2.118). Josephus describes this man as a sophist, who founded a new 'sect' or 'philosophy'. (It is not clear whether he should be identified with Judas the son of Hezekiah, the 'brigand', who led a revolt after the death of Herod, in *JW* 2.56; the father, Hezekiah, had earlier been defeated by Herod.) He describes this 'philosophy' further in the *Jewish Antiquities*, 18.4–10, where he associates Judas with a Pharisee named Zadok. Josephus claims that they started a fourth philosophy, in addition to those of the Sadducees, Pharisees, and Essenes. This school agreed with the Pharisees in most respects, but was distinguished by a passion for liberty, and a refusal to acknowledge any master but God (*Ant* 18. 23). Josephus blames this 'philosophy' for the whole development that led to the revolt against Rome in 66 CE. For much of the twentieth century, scholarship accepted the view that there was a continuous resistance movement in Judea, associated with the family of Judas, and subsumed the various groups to which Josephus refers under the name of 'Zealots'. More recent scholarship, however, notes that Josephus reserves the name of 'Zealots' for a group that came into existence during the revolt against Rome, and is sceptical of the claim that there was any unifying ideology. The fourth philosophy was most probably a construct of Josephus, to facilitate his claim that most Judeans were not responsible for the revolt.

Popular resistance movements were of different kinds. Josephus refers to 'bandits' as a constant presence in the years leading up to the revolt. It is likely, however, that the figures in question had an agenda that went beyond mere banditry. Josephus claims that Judas, the son of Hezekiah, caused fear 'by plundering those he encountered in his craving for greater power and in zealous pursuit of royal rank' (*Ant* 17.271–2; *JW* 2.56). A servant of King Herod named Simon was distinguished by his size and proclaimed king by his followers. He was captured and beheaded by the Romans. Another figure around the same time, named Athronges, had no royal connections, but because of his size aspired to the kingship. He carried out guerrilla warfare for a time, but was eventually captured. Josephus is unsympathetic to these 'bandits': 'whenever seditious bands came across someone suitable, that person could be set up as king, eager for the ruin of the commonwealth, doing little damage to the Romans, but causing extensive bloodshed among their countrymen' (*Ant* 17. 285).

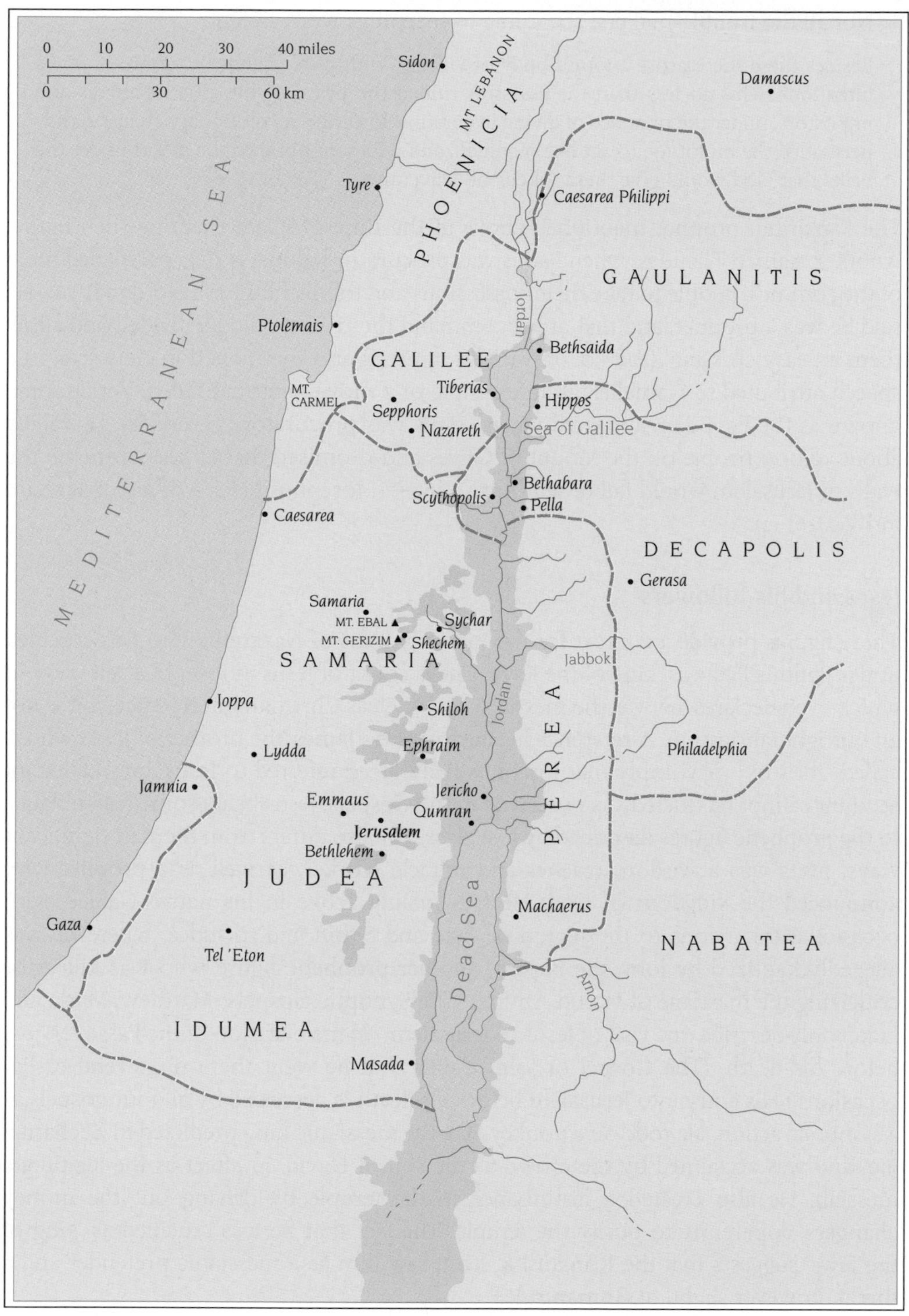

4. Map of the Holy Land under Roman occupation in the first century

Not all the trouble-makers, according to Josephus, were violent:

> Besides these there arose another body of villains, with purer hands but more impious intentions, who no less than the assassins ruined the peace of the city. Deceivers and impostors, under the pretence of divine inspiration fostering revolutionary changes, they persuaded the multitude to act like madmen, and led them out into the desert under the belief that God would give them tokens of deliverance. (*JW* 2.258–60)

The Samaritan prophet mentioned above in the time of Pilate was one such figure. Another, named Theudas, when Fadus was procurator (about 45 CE), 'persuaded most of the common people to take their possessions and follow him to the Jordan River. He said he was a prophet, and that at his command the river would be divided and allow them an easy crossing' (*Ant* 30. 97–8). This figure is also mentioned in Acts 5:36, in a speech attributed to Gamaliel, as an example of a movement that failed. Yet another, known as the Egyptian, appeared when Festus was procurator (52–60 CE). He rallied about 30,000 people on the Mount of Olives and promised that at his command the walls of Jerusalem would fall down (*Ant* 20.169–71; Josephus gives a different account in *JW* 2.261–2).

Jesus and his followers

These figures provide a context for the career of Jesus of Nazareth, who was crucified under Pontius Pilate as 'king of the Jews'. The account of Jesus in Josephus *Ant* 18.63–4, which even declares 'he was the messiah', shows clear Christian interference, if it is not an outright fabrication. A reference in *Ant* 20.200 to James 'the brother of Jesus who is called Christos', may imply that Josephus had indeed referred to Jesus, but the extant account cannot be trusted. As portrayed in the Gospels, Jesus bears some resemblance to the prophetic figures described by Josephus, but also differs from them in significant ways. Jesus was a wisdom teacher and miracle worker, as well as a prophet who announced the kingdom of God. He was mainly active in his native Galilee, with occasional excursions to the region of Tyre and Sidon and to Judea, where he was allegedly baptized by John the Baptist, another prophetic figure who was killed for criticizing the marriage of Herod Antipas. The Synoptic Gospels (Matthew, Mark, and Luke) only describe one visit of Jesus to Jerusalem, on the occasion of the Passover, just before his death. (The Gospel of John claims that he went there on several earlier occasions.) His entry into Jerusalem before his death is described by all four gospels as a symbolic action. He rode on a donkey, like the messianic king predicted in Zechariah 9:9, and was acclaimed by the crowd as the son of David, in effect as the legitimate messiah. He also created a disturbance in the temple by driving out the money changers, apparently to purify the temple. The fact that he was crucified as 'king of the Jews' suggests that the Romans, at least, saw him as a messianic pretender and a threat, however slight, to Roman rule.

Jesus is the only Jewish figure of this era who retained a following after his death, due to the belief in his resurrection. According to the Acts of the Apostles (1:4), the risen Jesus ordered his disciples to wait in Jerusalem for the gift of the Spirit, and then to become his witnesses in all Judea and Samaria, and to the ends of the earth. Acts describes a community in Jerusalem that shared its possessions. The members sold what they had and gave the proceeds to the apostles for those in need. We do not know how long this community survived. A little later we find the apostle Paul taking up a collection for the brethren in Jerusalem, who were evidently in need. The initial ideal of communal life was predicated on the assumption that Jesus would come again to usher in the kingdom of God, and this did not happen.

The followers of Jesus became a source of contention in Jerusalem in the following decades. Stephen was stoned to death for his outspoken criticism of the Temple. According to Acts 8:1, a severe persecution ensued, and all except the apostles were scattered throughout the countryside of Judea and Samaria. Yet Jerusalem remained the hub of the early Christian movement, as can be seen from the Acts of the Apostles and from Paul's comments in the Epistle to the Galatians (1:17–18). Herod Agrippa had James the brother of John killed, and had Peter arrested (Acts 12:2–3). Later James the brother of Jesus was stoned, on the orders of the High Priest. Paul was arrested in Jerusalem, and eventually conveyed to Rome. The followers of Jesus had their own meetings and were in effect a sect in Judea in the decades after the death of Jesus. Their relationship with other branches of Judaism, however, is unclear. There seems to have been a range of attitudes among the early Christians regarding observance of the Law and the Temple cult. Many scholars believe that the Jesus movement was also strong in Galilee, but the evidence is indirect at best. (At the end of the Gospel of Matthew, Jesus directs his disciples to go to Galilee.)

According to Eusebius (*Hist* 3.5.3), the people of the Church in Jerusalem were commanded in a revelation to leave Jerusalem at the outbreak of the war against Rome, and move to Pella, east of the Jordan. A similar tradition is found in Epiphanius. Modern scholars are divided as to its authenticity. The Jesus movement had already spread far outside the land of Israel long before this, through the efforts of Paul and others. Nonetheless, there was still a Christian presence in the land in the second century, as can be seen from the example of Justin Martyr, who was a native of Neapolis Flavia (biblical Shechem, modern Nablus), who published a fictitious debate with a rabbi, Trypho, dealing with the relation of Christianity to Judaism.

The war against Rome

The tensions in Judea erupted into open warfare in 66 CE. Several factors contributed to the worsening of the situation. Jewish religious sensibilities were undoubtedly a factor. Josephus claims that 'what more than all else incited them to the war was an ambiguous oracle, likewise found in their sacred scriptures, to the effect that at that time one from their country would become ruler of the world' (*JW* 6. 312–13). It is not clear which oracle he had in mind. Roman use of temple funds was a recurring aggravation. But it is unlikely that most Jews burned with the kind of desire for freedom that Josephus attributes to the fourth philosophy. The Jews were by no means the only people to rebel against Roman rule. There were also revolts in Britain, Gaul, Germany, and Pannonia-Dalmatia. The economic situation in Palestine was dire, as can be seen from the prevalence of banditry and even more so from the occurrence of severe famine in the 40s. Scholars disagree as to just how oppressive Roman taxation was, but there can be little doubt that people found it burdensome. There was a general increase in Roman taxation under Nero and an extraordinary levy under the procurator Albinus in the early 60s. The problems were exacerbated by the insensitivity and incompetence of the Roman procurators. The Roman historian Tacitus says that Felix, a freedman who was procurator from 52 to 60 CE, 'practiced every kind of cruelty and lust, wielding the power of a king with all the instincts of a slave' (*Hist* 5.9). His rule saw the rise of assassins (*sicarii*, or 'dagger-men') in Jerusalem, who targeted those who collaborated with Rome, and counted a High Priest, Jonathan, as one of their victims. Josephus and Tacitus (*Hist* 5.10) agree that Gessius Florus (64–66 CE) was the last straw. Florus raided the temple treasury and put down the ensuing protests with great cruelty. Despite the pleas of King Agrippa, the people rebelled. The rebels seized the fortress of Masada, and offerings for the emperor were suspended.

The Jewish war effort was hindered from the beginning by internal division. Class conflict had been a problem in the years leading up to the revolt, as had the lack of effective leadership by the Judean ruling class. The chief priests, Pharisees, and those related to the Herodian house favoured peace, but they were quickly defeated by the rebels, and the High Priest Ananias was murdered. An attempt by Cestius, the governor of Syria, to capture Jerusalem failed, and he was routed in the course of his retreat. At this point enthusiasm for the revolt swept Jerusalem, and the chief priests and Pharisees committed themselves to organizing the resistance. Josephus, the historian, was entrusted with the defence of Galilee.

Josephus's tenure in Galilee did not last long. From the beginning, he was at odds with a more radical rebel, John of Gischala. Nero appointed an experienced general, Vespasian, to conduct the war against the Jews. Josephus made his stand at Jotapata, which fell to the Romans in the summer of 67 CE. He took shelter with forty comrades in a cave. When they were discovered, he wished to surrender, but his companions opted for suicide. Josephus contrived to survive and went over to the Romans. He endeared himself to Vespasian by prophesying that the Roman general was the world ruler predicted in the ambiguous oracle mentioned above. In fact, Vespasian was acclaimed as emperor a year later.

Upheavals in Rome and the elevation of Vespasian delayed the progress of the war for a time. In the meantime, Jerusalem was torn by factions. The Zealots, led by John of Gischala, conducted a reign of terror in Jerusalem. Another radical, Simon bar Giora, led a rival faction. Yet a third party, led by Simon's son, also emerged. Only when the siege of Jerusalem got underway in 70, under Titus, son of Vespasian, did the various factions manage to unite. They resisted heroically, but eventually the walls were breached. Josephus claims that Titus had decided to spare the temple (*JW* 6. 237–43), but in fact it was set on fire. The Romans killed all who came in their way. Both John of Gischala

Masada, built by Herod but reused in the first Jewish revolt against Rome; it was the last holdout to fall, 74 CE.

The Arch of Titus in Rome.

The siege and destruction of Jerusalem, by David Roberts.

and Simon bar Giora were kept to be paraded in the triumphal procession in Rome, where some of the temple treasures were also displayed. (The commemorative arch of Titus still stands in Rome.) Some of the Jewish soldiers were forced to fight in gladiatorial contexts in Caesarea and Antioch. The fortresses of Herodium, Machaerus, and Masada were still in rebel hands. Masada was the last to fall, in spring of 74 CE. Josephus's account of the mass suicide of the defenders, who chose death rather than slavery, became the stuff of Jewish legend, although it has not been corroborated by archaeology.

After the revolt

The destruction of Jerusalem brought a violent end to the Second Temple period. The sacrificial cult, which had been the focus of religious life for centuries, was now no more. Jews throughout the empire still had to pay the temple tax, which now became a 'Jewish tax' for the temple of Jupiter Capitolinus. The Sanhedrin no longer existed, so there was no longer any vestige of Jewish self-rule. Even the population was decimated by death and captivity. Vespasian confiscated and sold off large portions of the land. The anguish of the years after the revolt is well expressed in the great apocalypses of 4 Ezra and 2 Baruch, which find their only consolation in the hope for a future messianic age. For the present, as 2 Baruch concludes plaintively, 'we have nothing now save the Mighty One and his Law' (2 Bar 85:3).

The people of Judea would muster their energies for one more revolt against Rome in 132–135 CE, under the leadership of Simon Bar Kosiba, better known as Bar Kokhba, 'son of the star'. In this case, there was no Josephus to leave us a narrative of the revolt, and we have to rely on passing references in the Roman historian Dio and the *Historia Augusta.* According to the latter, the rebellion was sparked by a prohibition of circumcision. Dio attributes it to the foundation of a new city, Aelia Capitolina, on the site of Jerusalem, and the erection of a temple to Zeus on the site of the Jewish temple. The ban on circumcision may not have been directed specifically at the Jews, as other peoples practised it too. (An exception was later made for the Jews by Antoninus Pius.) Bar Kosiba's nickname, 'Son of the Star', shows that he was thought to be the messiah (the star of Balaam's Oracle in Num. 24:17). There is a tradition that he was so proclaimed by Rabbi Akiba (j. Taanit 4.8). On his coins, he styled himself 'prince of Israel'. The rebels enjoyed some initial success. It is unclear whether they captured Jerusalem. Bar Kosiba minted coins with the legend 'for the freedom of Jerusalem'. His last stand was at Bethar, eleven kilometers south-west of Jerusalem. The siege lasted a long time, before the rebels were reduced by hunger and thirst. According to Dio, 'nearly the whole of Judea was made desolate' (Dio 69.12.1–14.3).

The rise of rabbinic Judaism

Jewish tradition credits the survival of Judaism to a group of sages who assembled at Yavneh (Jamnia), north-west of Jerusalem by the Mediterranean coast after the destruction of Jerusalem. Yohanan Ben Zakkai allegedly received permission from Vespasian to set up a gathering of sages there. The so-called 'council of Jamnia' is variously credited with fixing the canon of Hebrew scriptures and the central prayer of the daily liturgy, the Eighteen Benedictions. The historicity of this development has come under scrutiny in recent years. The evidence for it is late and legendary. Nonetheless, it is likely that there was some gathering of sages at Jamnia (although surely not a 'council') and that they began the process that would lead to the first great work of rabbinic Judaism, the Mishnah about a century later. This was a collection of legal traditions, supposedly based on the oral law that had been handed down for centuries. The Mishnah, together with the later legal compilations called the Jerusalem Talmud and the Babylonian Talmud, and the Midrash, which consists of narrative commentary on the biblical text, constitute the corpus of rabbinic writings, which has remained authoritative in Judaism down to the present. They are called 'rabbinic' because they cite the opinions of scholars and teachers called 'rabbis', a term of respect that means 'my great one'.

The traditional narrative of the origin of rabbinic Judaism supposes that the rabbis were the surviving Pharisees, and that they replaced the priests as religious authorities after the fall of the temple. This view is now widely rejected. The Pharisees were an association with several thousand members. Rabbis, in contrast, were appointed, in Palestine or ordained, in Babylonia, and they never numbered more than a few dozen in Palestine. Rabbinic literature never refers to sages before 70 CE as rabbis, even in the

A first-century stone from the synagogue at Magdala with carvings of characteristic Jewish motifs.

case of prominent figures like Hillel, in the time of King Herod. Only one rabbi, Gamaliel II, is known to come from a Pharisaic family. We do not know to what degree the Mishnah reflects the traditions of the Pharisees, but a simple identification is unwarranted.

The institution of the synagogue provided an important link between the periods before and after 70 CE. The synagogue developed especially in the diaspora, but several synagogues have also been identified in the land of Israel, in places ranging from Gamla, east of the sea of Galilee, to Magdala, on the western shore, to the fortresses of Masada and Herodium, to Qiryat Sefer and Modi'in in the western Judean foothills. There were also synagogues in Jerusalem, which catered to pilgrims, among their other functions. A Greek inscription from Jerusalem in the first century CE describes the purposes of the building:

> Theodotos, son of Vettenos, priest and archisynagogos, son of an archisynagogos and grandson of an archisynagogos, built the synagogue for the reading of the Law and for the teaching of the commandments and the guest-house, and the rooms and the water installations for the lodging of those in need of it from abroad.

The Gospels speak of synagogues at Nazareth and Capernaum, and Josephus mentions synagogues in Tiberias and Caesarea. Synagogues are sometimes referred to as 'houses

The synagogue at Capernaum. The earlier first-century synagogue was built on this same site.

Mosaic of the Zodiac on the floor of a synagogue in Sepphoris, indicative of the more Roman character of the city after the failure of the two great Jewish revolts.

of prayer' (*proseuchai*), but at least in the period before 70 they served a range of community purposes. They were typically square or rectangular buildings, modelled on Hellenistic council halls (*bouleuteria*).

Archaeological evidence for the synagogue in the period between 70 CE and 250 CE is scant, however. There are a few exceptions, not all of them certain, in upper Galilee and in Judea. It is possible that more synagogues from this period will yet come to light, but the evidence at present suggests a significant break in continuity after the revolts. When the synagogue revived as an institution in late antiquity, it took on more of the character of the Temple, and became primarily a place of worship.

The cities of Galilee, most notably Tiberias and Sepphoris, took on a more Roman character after the revolts. Both acquired theatres. Sepphoris built a Roman temple and received a new name, Diocaesarea. Both cities adopted Roman coinage.

While the origin of the rabbinic movement may lie in the assembly at Jamnia, it would be a long time before the rabbis achieved authoritative status. Papyri from the region of the Dead Sea in the Bar Kochba period (132–135 CE) show that Jews there were governed by Roman provincial law, with only occasional features that correspond to later rabbinic rulings. Not until the third century would there be a revival of Jewish life in the land of Israel, under the leadership of the rabbis.

CHAPTER 6

A Christian Holy Land

(284–638 CE)

KONSTANTIN KLEIN

DOMINE IVIMUS—'Lord, we have come'. A group of otherwise unknown pilgrims wrote these few letters, which most likely date to the second quarter of the fourth century. Undoubtedly, they were Christians, since the text was carved on a smooth stone block deep in the basement of Jerusalem's Church of the Holy Sepulchre shortly after its construction, in a chapel that today bears the name of Saint Vartan and the Armenian Martyrs. Next to the Latin words, they skillfully scratched a ship with its bow to the left, the mast unstepped, and two rudders, as if it was entering the harbour. On the one hand, this is a record of the growing influence of pilgrimage to the Holy Land from the fourth century onwards, when pilgrims would disembark at the harbours of Caesarea Maritima, Dor or Gaza, and from there begin their tour of the holy places. On the other hand, the anchoring motif might also suggest a more spiritual interpretation: by coming to Jerusalem, the pilgrims had reached the safe harbouring place they longed for in their mundane lives. Though they might not have been aware of it, they were pioneers in what would soon become a mass movement by Christians bent on seeing with their own eyes the places where Christ had lived out his life.

Looking forward from the destruction of the Temple in 135 CE, such a movement would have seemed all but impossible. The small Christian community that existed at that time did steadily grow in number, it is true, but this made them all the more suspect in the eyes of the Roman authorities. And their refusal to participate in public religious rites and festivals made them vulnerable to charges of disloyalty and exposed them to occasional mob violence. Such incidents of persecution were for a long time rare and isolated, but matters changed in the mid-third century when the emperor Decius (249–251), in January 250, promulgated a universal edict criminalizing those who refused to offer a sacrifice to the gods for the benefit of the emperor. Many Christians would not comply, for which they were executed, an early victim being Pope Fabian (236–250). The edict lapsed after eighteen months, but was renewed by Emperor Diocletian in 303 and continued in force for a decade, though erratically applied. A nadir had been reached. Yet succour came from an unexpected quarter:

The *Domine ivimus* inscription, Church of the Holy Sepulchre, Jerusalem.

Emperor Constantine (306–337) converted to Christianity in 312, allegedly in response to a vision that he saw before the battle of the Milvian Bridge, and the very next year he signed the Edict of Milan (313), which guaranteed to Christians, as well as to followers of other religions, 'the right of open and free observance of their worship for the sake of the peace of our times, that each one may have the free opportunity to worship as he pleases'. In the wake of this, Christians from all over the Roman Empire began to develop a certain patriotism towards the Holy Land, which went from being a heavenly construct to an earthly reality, occupying a well-defined physical space.

Pilgrimage to the Holy Land, however, was not a completely new phenomenon: even after the destruction of the Second Temple, pious Jews from the region were travelling to Jerusalem. While an edict of the emperor Hadrian (r. 117–138 CE) eventually forbade them to enter their holy city, it seems that soon there were exemptions and that in late antique times the ban was less strictly observed. However, there were also early Christian travellers, for example Melito, the bishop of Sardis near Smyrna, who visited the Holy Land in the second half of the second century in order to compile what would become the oldest Christian canon of biblical books. Other theologians would follow, Origen, the early Christian scholar, being the most famous among them. From the fourth century onwards a new literary genre was born: descriptions of the holy sites as well as of the Christian pilgrims' experiences. Two fourth-century accounts by laymen stand at the beginning of this new tradition: Firstly, the so-called Bordeaux

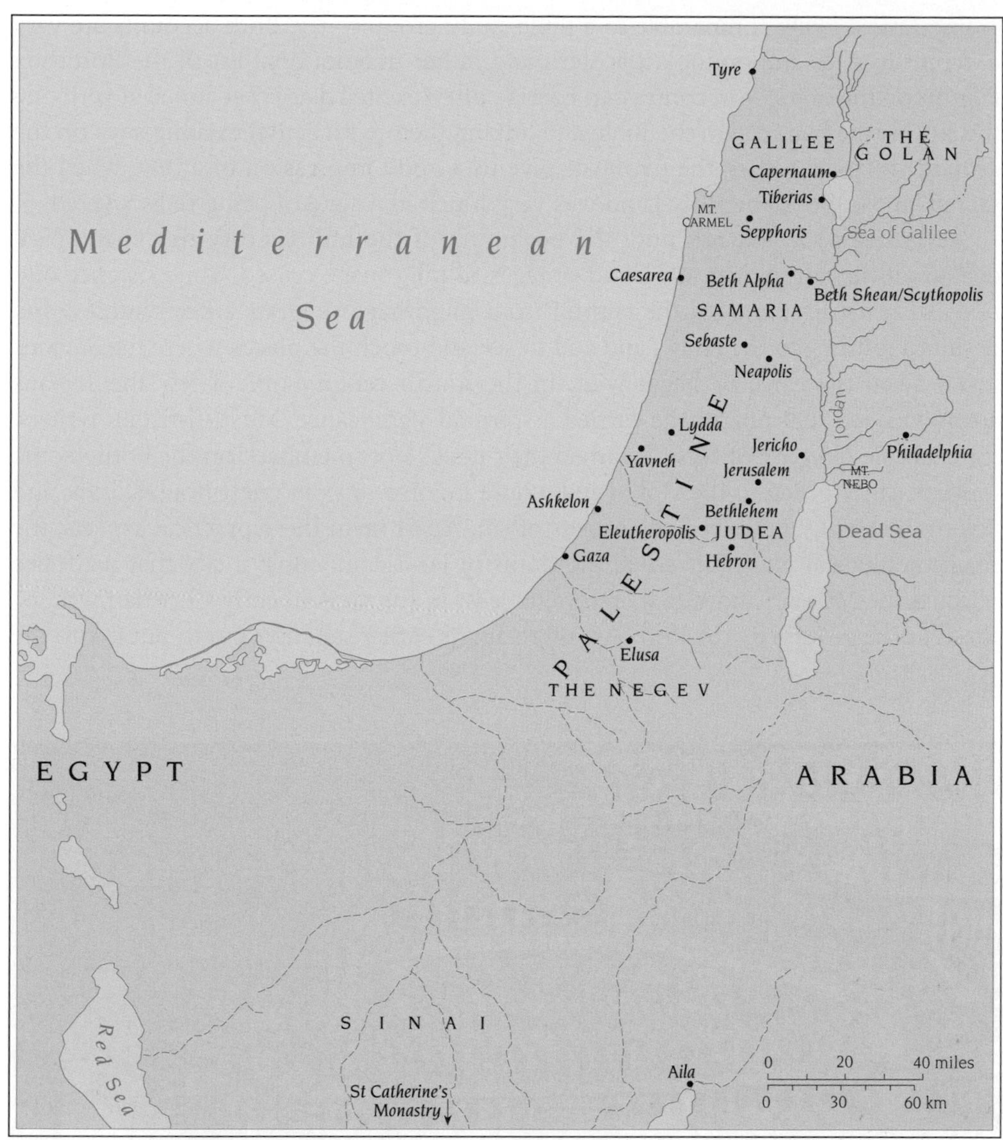

5. Map of the late antique Holy Land and neighbouring regions

Pilgrim who made his way from Gaul to Constantinople in 333 CE from where he embarked on a journey through the Holy Land. He is the first independent witness to the church buildings which had been founded only half a decade earlier by the imperial house of Constantine the Great. Secondly, Egeria, a woman from northern Spain or southern Gaul, whose journey is commonly dated to between 381 and 384 CE, wrote down her impressions in a letter that she sent home to her 'dear sisters', a circle of women most likely comparable to a Bible study group today. Both accounts are very different in style and outlook, the stern and rather unemotional list of the Bordeaux Pilgrim on the one side in contrast to Egeria's often excited diary that aimed at verifying the stories she had read in the Bible and linking them with actual existing sites on the ground. Taken together, the two texts give us a good impression of a time when the sacred landscape of the Holy Land was very much in a state of being rediscovered.

Nevertheless, it was not until the beginning of the fifth century that theological debate on the advantages and disadvantages of pilgrimage ceased. The existence of a body of texts discouraging the faithful from pilgrimage suggests a keen interest and desire to journey to the Holy Land and to see and touch the places where the Saviour had walked the earth to begin with. In the fourth century only a few theologians acknowledged that pilgrimage carried a spiritual significance. Most Christian writers, for example Gregory of Nyssa, warned their flocks not to embark on the bothersome journey, since going to the Holy Land would involve stays in guest houses, inns, and taverns, generally perceived as hotbeds of sin. Apart from these practical aspects, the main theological issue concerned the status of Jerusalem: could a city that had once rejected the Messiah and was therefore (at least in the view of early Christian writers) razed to the ground by the Romans still retain its earlier sanctity? Or, to put it into the

Jerusalem depicted on the Madaba Mosaic Map.

words of R. A. Markus, how on earth could places become holy? Was it not necessary to make a clear distinction between the worldly city and the heavenly one, as described in the Book of Revelation?

And indeed, for the Bordeaux Pilgrim, travelling in 333 CE, Jerusalem might not have looked very different from any other small city of the Roman Empire—were it not for the newly-built Christian *basilica.* A construction with a groundplan adopted from secular court buildings, it was so new to Christian architecture that the writer actually had to explain what he meant when using this term. The Bordeaux Pilgrim paid special attention to the few Christian landmarks that were there to visit in the first half of the fourth century. A contemporary pagan description, however, would have focused on the secular buildings of Jerusalem which were not different from those in any other provincial Roman backwater. The once famous city had been destroyed by the future emperor Titus in 70 CE, and then refounded by Hadrian in 130 CE under the name of Colonia Aelia Capitolina (referring to Hadrian's hereditary surname, Aelius)—even though the building work seems to have started about a decade earlier, as recent excavations on one of the main streets, the *cardo valensis,* suggest. For a long time, life in Jerusalem had to a large extent been shaped by the effects of military presence: the Tenth Legion (*legio X Fretensis*), founded by Octavian during the civil war in 41/40 BCE, had been garrisoned in the city from the 70s of the first to the 80s of the third century. It had played a major part in the crushing of the Jewish rebellion against the Romans including the famous siege of the city, during which the legion had camped on the Mount of Olives, as well as in the abatement of the Bar Kokhba revolt sixty years later following the Hadrianic refoundation. There is, however, considerable debate concerning the exact position of its camp. It cannot be excluded that it was located in the southern half of today's Old City: however, most scholars believe that it was close to what formerly had been Herod's Palace, the citadel of the city, called Tower of David in the sources. The task of the legion was maintaining the peace in the region, and it stood directly under the command of the Roman provincial governor of Judea. The military presence ensured that Jerusalem (or Aelia Capitolina) evolved into a normal provincial town with its typical urban institutions, such as a temple to the Capitoline Jupiter, places for theatrical performances, shops, paved streets, baths, and brothels. Since Roman law required pottery to bear its maker's stamp, and this also included the soldiers' workshops, we are well informed about the Tenth Legion's and its detachments' daily life thanks to bread stamps, amphorae, and building inscriptions (often repair works of already existing infrastructures such as roads, walls, and aqueducts). In the wake of the military reforms of the emperor Diocletian, the Tenth Legion was moved to Aila on the Red Sea around the year 284 CE. Nevertheless, retired veterans stayed behind, settled in and near Jerusalem, for example in Ramat Rachel, and contributed to the overall picture of the city that was largely non-Christian. Quoting from the beginning of the Book of Isaiah, the fifth-century church historian Socrates Scholasticus would describe the city of Aelia of these days as deserted like a booth in a vineyard and a lodge in a cucumber field.

While the Christian historian of the Church, Eusebius, had contrasted this deserted provincial town with the heavenly Jerusalem, Saint Jerome, quoting from Luke 17:21, poignantly concluded that one could enter the Kingdom of Heaven just as well from Britain as from Jerusalem. Nevertheless, more and more pilgrims came to the Holy Land. While they surely had different reasons to do so, one particularly important event would set the tone: the journey to Palestine of Helena, Constantine's mother, in 326 CE. What is often referred to as the first important Holy Land pilgrimage, was at the same time clearly connected to her son's patronage of Christianity and his summoning of the Council of Nicea in the previous year. There is nothing to suggest, however, that Helena's journey should not be seen in the tradition of earlier imperial travels, the so-called *itinera principum*. She entered the cities of the Roman East in the splendour and grandeur of a member of the imperial house, granted amnesty to prisoners, and showered gifts upon widows and orphans, but also, and this was the novelty of her journey, upon the rising Christian communities emerging from the traumatic period of persecution. The only contemporary account we have describing her activities is a text written by Eusebius, bishop of Caesarea Maritima, the provincial capital and hence the metropolitan bishopric for Jerusalem. While the precedence of the Holy City over all Churches had been specifically emphasized already at the Council of Nicea, this was not reflected in the administrative structure: The bishop of Jerusalem was subordinate to the metropolitan bishop of Caesarea. Our main source on Helena is Eusebius' biography of the first Christian emperor, Constantine, a text that both exaggerates and downplays facts around Jerusalem. On the one hand, it is obvious that his *Life of Constantine* is a text full of panegyric praise for the emperor, imbued with the author's joy about Constantine adorning the entire Empire, and especially the Holy Land, with

Reconstruction of the Church of the Holy Sepulchre in the fourth century.

magnificent churches, and over-emphasizing Constantine's anti-pagan acts such as the destruction of heathen temples. However, at the same time, the text can also be read as the manifestation of a considerable level of local rivalry: the promotion of the city of Jerusalem meant a weakening of Eusebius' own episcopal see in Caesarea. This may explain a certain reticence in his account. While Eusebius granted considerable space in his text to Helena's journey, he remains silent on his own role in the events. There is good reason to assume that he did not belong to the close entourage of the pious dowager empress who in all likelihood was accompanied by Macarius, the bishop of Jerusalem. Whether for reasons of ecclesiastical competition or on theological grounds, the subtext of the description is that not too much emphasis should be placed on physical sites in the Holy Land or on physical objects of veneration such as relics—and even on the cross. In the controversy over the status of Jerusalem as a holy city, Eusebius clearly belonged to the faction advocating that the place that had once rejected the Messiah was not more holy than any other place in the Roman Empire.

When he described Constantine's order that a pagan temple in the city was to be razed to the ground, he enigmatically wrote that during the excavations 'at last against all expectation the revered and all-hallowed testimony (*martyrion*) of the Saviour's Resurrection was itself revealed'. The legend of Helena discovering the True Cross of Christ became famous only seventy years after her journey, when a western bishop, Ambrose of Milan, linked her name with the events in his funeral oration on the emperor Theodosius the Great. Therefore, the majority of scholars assumed that Eusebius' wording in the *Life of Constantine* did not refer to the True Cross but to the Tomb of Christ. However, the possibility cannot be excluded that in the wake of Helena's visit a piece of wood was discovered which was identified as the True Cross.

While the exact nature of the discoveries of 326 CE cannot be determined, it is easier to assess the archaeological evidence of the church buildings which were constructed on the site of Christ's Crucifixion and Resurrection. While in pre-Constantinian times, the Christian meeting place was located on Mount Zion, the religious heart of Jerusalem was now moved to the building complex that is known today as the Church of the Holy Sepulchre on the main road, the *cardo maximus*, and near to the *forum*. In late antique times, the compound consisted of two separate churches: the rotunda of the Resurrection (*anastasis*) as well as a five-aisled *basilica* with a gallery which was the only church building in the city facing west. Both churches were connected via an open courtyard which contained the rock of Golgotha or Calvary, the assumed spot of the Crucifixion. The building compound played a major role in the city's processions as attested in early liturgical texts, and within the next two centuries many Old Testament traditions, such as the sacrifice of Abraham or the altar of Zachariah, were transferred from their former localization on the Temple Mount to the Church of the Holy Sepulchre. The annual celebration of the church's dedication, the so-called *encaenia*, was originally a strongly anti-pagan festival that over the decades gained an anti-Jewish symbolism. Similarly, many Christian authors from Jerusalem or elsewhere constantly reminded their readers that Constantine's churches faced the ruins of the Jewish

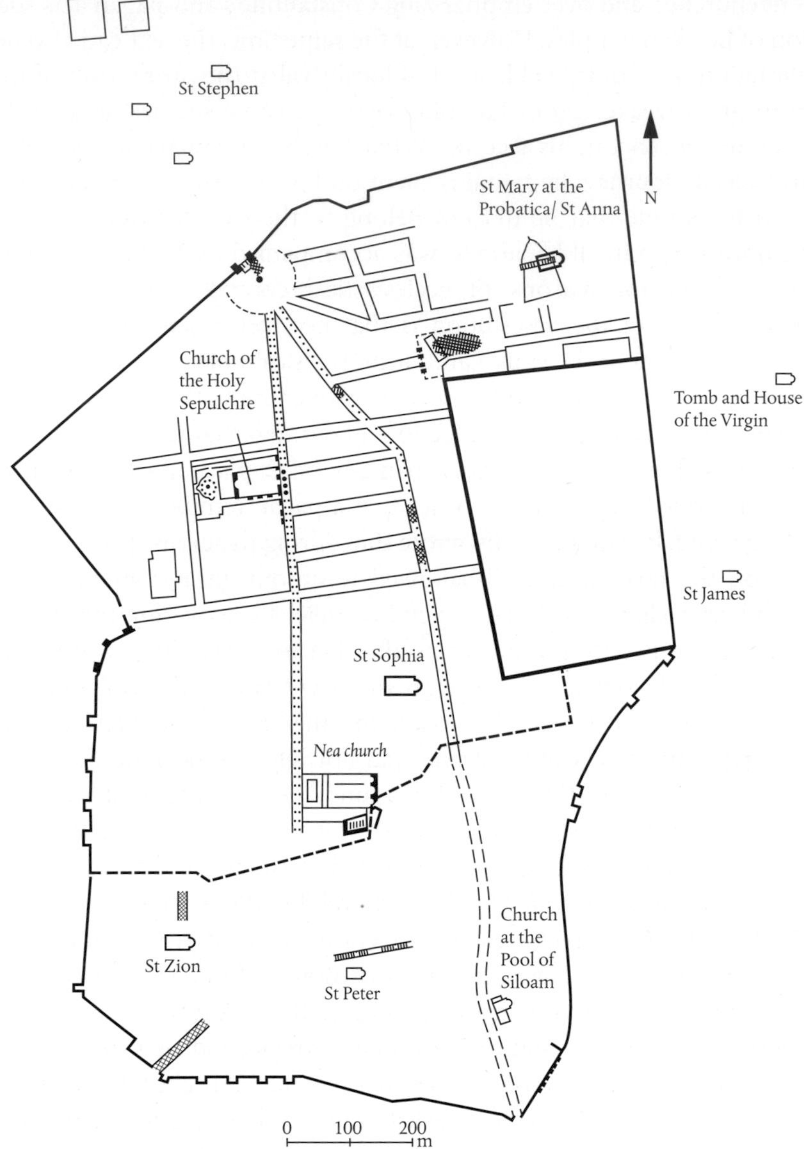

Plan of Jerusalem in Late Antiquity.

Temple that was left empty throughout late antiquity just as Jesus Christ had predicted according to the Gospels. While the Pilgrim of Bordeaux still visited the Temple Mount in 333 CE, later pilgrims excluded this large landmark from their accounts, another sign that the entirety of local tradition concerning this site had been moved elsewhere. The reorganization of Jerusalem's space can be exemplified by the urban layout as depicted on the sixth-century Madaba map, a mosaic giving a birds-eye view of the Holy Land: the vignette of Jerusalem shows the Church of the Holy Sepulchre in the middle of the city (while in fact it is located much more to the west) whereas the Temple Mount, covering more than a fifth of the late antique city remained undepicted.

Constantine's mother Helena also supervised the construction of two other buildings, a three-aisled church close to the top of the Mount of Olives named Eleona ('olive-yard' in Greek) which commemorated Christ's Ascension, as well as the Church of the Nativity in nearby Bethlehem. This *basilica* covered a cave which was considered to be the birthplace of Jesus Christ. It consisted of a double forecourt, a five-aisled nave and an octagonal structure in the east which contained a platform with a 3.9 m wide opening through which pilgrims could behold the grotto of the Nativity. When this building was destroyed in the sixth century, perhaps in the wake of the Samaritan revolts, a new church was constructed during the reign of the emperor Justinian (r. 527–565). Despite its younger date, the new church took up the Constantinian design which was not only emphasized by the ground plan but also by a set of Corinthian capitals for the colonnades and pillars that were newly manufactured but used a by then outdated decoration type. The previously open ceiling of the grotto was closed; two flights of steps, still extant, now made the grotto accessible for pilgrims. Taken together, the three Constantinian church buildings, the Church of the Nativity, the Church of the Holy Sepulchre, and the Eleona, commemorating the Ascension, can be interpreted as turning the statements on Jesus Christ in the Nicean Creed into stone: 'Who for us men, and for our salvation, came down and was incarnate and was made man; He suffered, and the third day he rose again, ascended into heaven.'

While these three churches were commissioned by the imperial house, there is yet another important church building which was erected on the initiative of the local clergy: the church on Mount Zion, the earliest meeting place of the Christian community and assumed episcopal see of Jacob, the brother of the Lord. A previous building on this spot is mentioned by the pilgrim Egeria, then around 390 CE a monumental five-aisled church was built, most likely by Bishop John II, perhaps aided by donations from the Theodosian dynasty. It commemorated the events of the Last Supper as well as of Pentecost and was therefore associated with the Holy Spirit. Again, a connection between the construction of the church and a Church Council can be drawn: the Council of Constantinople in 381 CE confirmed the Creed of Nicea, but also debated and clarified the divinity of the Holy Spirit as the third person of the Trinity. Over the following centuries the Church on Mount Zion also functioned as a storage place for a variety of sacred objects, such as the relics of Saint Stephen, a corner stone from the Temple, the crown of thorns, and the column of flagellation. The construction of this church also marked the beginning of stational liturgy, i.e. the incorporation of various holy places into liturgical processions. This enabled the pilgrims to re-enact the Gospel stories on the respective feast days by visiting sites and reading out the corresponding biblical passages. Most processions centred on the Church of the Holy Sepulchre and the one on Mount Zion, however, on the most important feast days such as Easter or Pentecost, the holy places on the Mount of Olives were equally incorporated into the processions. It was, however, not before the Late Middle Ages that a distinct route of the stations of the Cross was introduced: Franciscan Friars from Italy as well as travelling laymen from Germany and the Low Countries counted the steps from one holy site commemorating Jesus Christ's way of the cross to the next. Upon their return to Europe they recreated processional routes with these stations in their hometowns, with the Franconian cities of Bamberg (1503) and Nuremberg (1506–1508) being the first places to put forward this liturgical novelty. Through the influence of the Franciscan Custody of the Holy Land, a similar Via Dolorosa was reimported to Jerusalem and is still the centre of a procession every Friday. There were also attempts to recreate the sacred topography of Jerusalem in late antique times, for example in the fifth-century church of Santo Stefano in Bologna that contained five chapels commemorating Jerusalemite sites, which is why the church became known by the name of Santa Gerusalemme. At the same time, at the eastern end of the Roman Empire in the Caucasus several churches were constructed in the Georgian royal city of Mtskheta carrying the names of Christian cult places in Jerusalem.

Hagiographical sources mention an increased influx of pilgrims from the eastern parts of the Roman Empire as well as from Christian populations under Sasanian rule from the fifth century onwards. At the same time the travel accounts testify to the gradual geographical broadening of areas conceived as being part of the Holy Land. This can be illustrated by comparing places visited by pilgrims over the centuries: Whereas the Pilgrim of Bordeaux did not pay attention to sites in the Sinai region, Egeria's account abounds in their description. Egypt became a goal of Christian pilgrimage only in the late fourth century, Egeria, Melania the Elder, Jerome, and Paula being among its first visitors whose journeys we find recorded in texts. While the coastal area of the Levant attracted relatively few pilgrims (with the exception of Lydda/Diospolis with its shrine of Saint George), the Judean Desert with Jericho, the Jordan River, and the Dead Sea, as well as Mount Nebo in Transjordan with its churches commemorating Moses, all became destinations that only few would miss. Jerusalem remained a central starting point for further excursions, as can be reckoned from the pilgrim account of the sixth-century pilgrim Theodosius (dating to before 518 CE) who described several tours that proceeded from Jerusalem in a star pattern to the four points of the compass. In Late Antiquity the city was connected via direct roads to Neapolis (modern-day Nablus) via Scythopolis to the North, Philadelphia (modern-day Amman) via Jericho to the East, Elusa via Hebron to the South, as well as with the Mediterranean coast via the towns of Emmaus/Nicopolis, Lydda/Diospolis or Eleutheropolis leading to the provincial capital, Caesarea Maritima.

This city had been founded by Herod on the site of an older settlement (*Turris Stratonis*) and named in honour of the emperor. Caesarea Maritima has been well excavated; however, we are equally well informed about its buildings by several literary sources beginning with the Jewish historian Flavius Josephus who mentioned the city's

The sacrifice of Isaac, synagogue mosaic floor, Beth Alpha, Galilee.

grid plan, its theatre, and many of its temples. The numismatic evidence points to a veneration of a variety of Greco-Roman deities in the provincial capital such as Zeus, Poseidon, Apollo, Heracles, Dionysos, Aphrodite, and Athena—as well as the Egyptian gods Isis and Serapis. A third-century *mithraeum* is attested as well. After Herod's death the royal palace became the seat of the Roman prefect; the nearby residence of the financial procurator of the Roman province of Iudaea/Palaestina became the residence of the governor of the late antique province Palaestina I, when in the fourth century the administration of the Holy Land was rearranged into three separate Palestinian provinces. The city did not differ much from other Roman provincial towns, and few authors fail to mention the Hellenic, i.e. pagan, dominance. However, Caesarea had important Jewish, Samaritan, and Christian minorities. Various literary sources record information on Jewish life in Caesarea, although there is precious little epigraphic or archaeological evidence. From Jewish sources on the interpretation of the Mosaic Law, we know that Rabbi Judah ha-Nasi excluded the Jewish inhabitants of Caesarea (as well as those of Ashkelon 100 km southwards on the coast) from some religious observations. These exemptions may be interpreted as incentives for Jews to settle in places that had been deprived of their Jewish population in the wake of the Jewish War in 66–70 CE, which, after all, had started with a rebellion against Roman rule in Caesarea Maritima. A number of inscriptions which were discovered in one archaeological site points to the existence of a synagogue. However, the textual sources mention several such buildings. All but three of these inscriptions (which may come from a different place) were written in Greek. This agrees with what we learn from Jewish sources on one of the most prominent figures of third-century Caesarea, Rabbi Abbahu. An authority on the Jewish law concerning weights and measurements and rector of the Caesarean Academy, he was well known for his command of Greek, which was uncommon for Rabbis of his time, and he even insisted on having his daughters learn the language.

A passage in the Palestinian Talmud mentions that when Rabbi Abbahu died in 309 CE, the columns of the colonnaded streets of Caesarea started to weep tears, even though the sky was blue and no natural explanation could be found. The miraculous phenomenon, however, is mentioned in a Christian source too. For the exact same year, Eusebius of Caesarea reported in his account *On the martyrs of Palestine* that the columns of the city could no longer bear the sight of innocent Christians slaughtered during the persecutions that took place in his episcopal city. The rivalry between Jews and Christians in Caesarea, which occasionally resulted in outbursts of physical violence, is similarly apparent in competing texts. At the Church Council of Chalcedon (451) Jerusalem was elevated into a Patriarchate equalling those of Rome, Constantinople, Antioch, and Alexandria; Caesarea thus lost its supremacy but nevertheless remained a centre of Christian learning, mainly due to its important library which was used not only by Christian writers such as Eusebius himself or the church father Jerome, but also by secular historians like Procopius, a native of the city. The city enjoyed a period of prosperity in late antiquity when the emperors Anastasius and Justinian carried out important building projects; its population measured over 100,000 people, and its harbour remained an important naval base.

Gaza with its port Maiuma was the main point of arrival for pilgrims coming by boat. Just like Caesarea, it possessed a diverse population consisting of pagans, Jews, and Christians. Close to the city was the shrine of Saint Hilarion, who was assumed to be the first hermit of the region. The epigraphic evidence points to an important role for the shrine in the lives of the Christian inhabitants of the area, not least by making Hilarion a fairly popular given name. Due to the continuous history of settlement and the political situation in the Gaza strip in the last sixty years, we are rather ill-informed on the physical layout of the city. A temple of Zeus Marnas, a typical amalgam of the Greek god combined with an oriental equivalent, is mentioned in the *Life of Porphyrius*, a hagiographical tale allegedly written by a disciple of the saint who is credited with the spectacular demolition of said temple. However, the historicity of the entire text has continuously been doubted, and there is little evidence elsewhere in the sources for a cult of Zeus Marnas. From another piece of hagiography, the *Life of Peter the Iberian*, we learn more about religious conflicts between pagans and Christians in the region. Peter, a Georgian prince who came to the East Roman Empire as a hostage, was ordained bishop of Maiuma in 452 or 453 CE. His bishopric at the seaport of Gaza appears to have been a centre of Christianity, while the mother town of Gaza remained predominantly pagan. It has been shown that Peter's biographer and successor, John Rufus, stylized the princely bishop as a worthy successor of Saint Hilarion by including many episodes in the late-fifth-century text making Peter's deeds resemble those of his famous predecessor. The shrine of Hilarion is mentioned by the so-called Piacenza Pilgrim (*c.*570) who also recorded a shrine of the holy martyr Victor, one of the few Christian sites near Gaza that is also archaeologically attested. Despite the mixed population, the Piacenza Pilgrim labelled the inhabitants of Maiuma and Gaza as 'great lovers of pilgrims' while he did not fail to mention the worldly luxury of other coastal cities of the Levant: he marvelled at the silk and fabric production in Tyre, but was also appalled by the city's brothels. Compared to earlier pilgrimage accounts, the Piacenza Pilgrim seems to have been much more open to spectacular occurrences (like an exceptionally large lemon in Jericho) as well as to non-Christian inhabitants of the area, such as Samaritans on the slopes of Mount Carmel or the hostile atmosphere in Sebaste near Nablus, where the Samaritan inhabitants would sweep over his footprints with straw.

He is also the first to give an elaborate account of the Galilee region in the north of the Holy Land. The whole area, in which—for Christian pilgrims—Jesus grew up and worked the majority of his miracles, appeared to the Piacenza Pilgrim like a vast garden park. Its ample production of grain equalled that of Egypt, the granary of the Roman Empire, and according to this text was renowned for its wine, oil, fruits, and honey. His paradise-like description attests to the region's agricultural boom in late antiquity. Not only do we learn from a variety of texts that oil and in particular wine from the Holy Land was sought after throughout the Empire, but also that image from the literary sources can be corroborated by the growing number of finds from Mediterranean shipwrecks being brought to light over the past decades. The *amphorae* discovered in underwater surveys mainly point to wine destined for general consumption as a luxury good all over the later Roman Empire. However, an unmeasurable number of *amphora*-sherds excavated all over the Holy Land containing Jewish or Samaritan inscriptions stating that the vessel was licit/*kosher* attest to the similarly important role of the local vineyards producing wine for religious consumption.

The Piacenza Pilgrim's description of Galilee is also a good example of personal piety, for example when he confessed in his pilgrim account that he carved the names of his parents into a stone bench in Cana, where the Lord had turned water into wine at the eponymous wedding. While Christian authors in general only rarely reported on Jewish synagogues, the Piancenza Pilgrim visited one in Nazareth where he was shown an ABC that allegedly the Lord himself had carved when learning how to write. His account is also a testimony of Jewish–Christian coexistence. This would be true for the entirety of late antique Palestine, though over the centuries the parameters were shifting. As was made clear in the contesting stories on Caesarea's weeping columns, Judaism and Christianity stood in intense competition. Both religions aimed at excluding one another from being the interpretative authority of the biblical text. Both textual traditions, the Mishnah and the Talmud on the one side, the New Testament and Christian theology on the other, can be seen as texts that only revealed their full meaning when read together with the Old Testament, but the Old Testament would equally only unfold its true meaning through the prism of the younger texts. The rather different focus (ritual praxis in the Mishnah and the Talmud versus prophetical faith in the New Testament) also attests to a structural parting of the ways between the two religions. The Mishnah—collected, organized, and codified around the year 200 CE under the chief redaction of Judah ha-Nasi (d. 217 CE)—marks the beginning of a new phase of Jewish life in the Holy Land. After the destruction of the Temple in 70 CE, Jewish tradition credited the Jewish sage Yohanan ben Zakkai (*c.*30 BCE–90 CE) as the chief figure who helped to pave the way out of total destruction into a new beginning.

The most evident change was the reorganization of the Temple rituals into the synagogal service, including the abolition of blood sacrifice. This most drastic change has often been called a complete reinvention of Judaism. While synagogues existed already before the destruction of the Second Temple, especially in the diaspora (the Greek island of Delos having one of the earliest examples that are archaeologically attested) but also in the Holy Land, their exact function was disputed in Antiquity just as among modern scholars. In a way, synagogues, although existing as a building type before, saw their birth in the days of Yavneh and the reorganization of Judaism at a time when social and legal norms were in upheaval. Yohanan is said to have transformed his school at Yavneh (or Jamnia, the place of the Crusader castle of Ibelin) into a gathering place for survivors from the Great Sanhedrin, the Jewish assembly which exercised the highest religious and political authority before the Jewish War. He insisted that certain aspects referring to the special sacred status of Jerusalem should be transferred to Yavneh, where the Sanhedrin reconvened, albeit with much less authority than compared to before 70 CE. The Romans acknowledged it as the ultimate authority in Jewish religious matters, under a new name as the Palestinian Patriarchate. At the end of the third century, the Sanhedrin eventually dropped its own name, calling itself now *Beth ha-Midrash*, 'house of learning'. Already in the second century, the Patriarchate had moved back and forth between Yavneh and Usha in the western part of Galilee, and after brief interludes in Shefaram, Beit Shearim, and Sepphoris, it finally moved to Tiberias in 193. There as well as in other Galilean towns such as Beth Alpha, Sepphoris, Beth Shean, and Capernaum, large synagogue buildings often decorated with magnificent floor mosaics testify to a time of prosperity in late antique Judaism. While the Patriarchate still wielded power over important matters such as regulating the Jewish calendar and excommunication, it became more of a consistory. The Patriarch—*ha-Nasi* (the prince) in Hebrew—enjoyed almost royal authority, not least because as a rule he came from the house of the Pharisee Rabbi Hillel, who had lived at the turn of the eras and was regarded as a descendant of King David. In the line of Patriarchs, Judah ha-Nasi, the aforementioned redactor of the Mishnah, stands out as the figure under whom the Patriarchate reached its zenith.

The Mishnah is an important work in terms of its theological, legal, and social implications, but it is also a piece of literature which attests to a rich cultural life. The text offers answers to contemporary questions anew in the form of Rabbinic interpretations complementing the biblical canon. In the previous centuries, Judaism had a clear centre in Jerusalem and its Temple to which people went to with legal cases pertaining to religious law. In the new reality without this centre of teaching and study, Rabbinic discourse began to be written down—largely out of fear that the old legal traditions would be forgotten. The Mishnah uses actual cases to exemplify Jewish law, thus connecting everyday realities with the biblical norms. The Rabbis never introduced new laws, but rather showed how biblical laws could be pragmatically exercised. The Mishnah forms the basis for the two Talmudim, the Babylonian and the Palestinian (or Jerusalem) Talmud, the latter compiled in Galilee in the fourth to fifth centuries, thus predating its Babylonian counterpart by roughly 200 years. The Talmud incorporates the Mishnah together with other written discussions from Rabbis of the fourth century (the so-called Gemara). Written largely in Jewish Palestinian Aramaic—and not in Hebrew—it offers a synopsis of exemplifications of the Mishnah since the time of the latter's redaction.

The Palestinian Patriarchate wielded its influence far into late antique times until it was dissolved by the emperor Theodosius II in 427, after the death of the last patriarch, Gamaliel VI. From this time onwards the tax revenue belonging to the Patriarchate was transferred to the imperial treasury, and no successor for Gamaliel was appointed. The same period witnessed the gradual exclusion of Jews from public office. Scholars have often linked the end of the redaction of the Palestinian Talmud with the suppression of the Patriarchate. While this causal link has been questioned in recent years, the relative proximity of the two suggests at least a certain connection. The reign of Theodosius II (r. 408–450 CE) also witnessed a massive increase in the suppression of paganism all over the later Roman Empire. However, not all legislative actions against paganism were automatically directed against temples or statues: the overall image that derives from Roman legislation is that the closing of temples was important, not their destruction. In some cases, the old and august temples carried a notion of identity for the urban populations who cared for their preservation—we may assume this to be the case for the predominantly pagan cities along the Levantine coast. The temples there may not have been used for religious services anymore, but the monuments with their architectural grandeur provided the inhabitants of the late antique world there and elsewhere with an environment that separated them from the barbarian world around them. A law issued in 399 CE has often been interpreted as a safeguarding provision for the temples. In this law, the emperor Arcadius, Theodosius' father, decreed that the ornaments of public works should be preserved. Another decree from the same year proclaimed the marking of temples with the sign of the Cross an easy way to avoid their destruction. The content of this law was reinforced under the reign of Theodosius in 435 CE, where it was stated that all pagan sanctuaries still in use 'shall be destroyed by the command of the magistrates'—but again adding that a purification by the mark of the sign of the venerable Christian religion, i.e. the Cross, was equally sufficient.

When reading the predominantly Christian sources on the late antique Holy Land, one might gain the impression that paganism hardly existed there, as Christian writers rarely mention it. However, the opposite was the case: in his fourth-century *Mystagogical Catecheses*, Bishop Cyril of Jerusalem warned his audience of baptismal candidates not to participate in pagan festivals—in this we may see an allusion to the fact that, despite the growing Christianization of Jerusalem, paganism was still very much alive. According to Eusebius of Caesarea, however, the cleansing of a pagan site in Mamre was ordered as early as the Constantinian construction of the three churches in Jerusalem and Bethlehem. According to the Bible, this was the place where Abraham had built an altar and learned of his wife's pregnancy from the three angels. At the same time that Helena visited the Holy Land, Constantine's mother-in-law, Eutropia, was also in the region. According to Eusebius, it was she who informed Constantine that the place where Abraham had once lived was tainted by pagan worship: 'Idols fit only for absolute destruction have been set up beside it, [. . .] and an altar stands nearby, and foul sacrifices are constantly conducted there.' The emperor immediately decreed the destruction of the sanctuary and explicitly stated that any idols that were found at the place should be consigned to the flames and the altar completely demolished. Constantine commissioned the *comes* Acacius to devote all possible effort and endeavour to clearing the whole area and had a *basilica* built on the spot. Excavations carried out in 1926–1968 unveiled remarkable findings, including deliberately broken fragments of pagan statues and reliefs dating to the times before the destruction: a relief depicting an androgynous Hermes with female breasts and jewellery was hardly recognizable as the figure's face had been chiselled off. A statue of Dionysus did not fare better: the head of the deity had been smashed with one vigorous blow.

Despite this, it seems that Mamre's pagan character was far from being fully extinguished: more than a hundred years later, in the mid-fifth century, the church historian Sozomen, who himself stemmed from the region, reported on an annual pagan fair and an apparently peaceful coexistence of Christians, Jews, and pagans all cherishing this cultic place associated with Abraham. At the same time we see how in the holy city of Jerusalem previously pagan sites were taken over by the Christians and converted into churches: the double pools of Bethesda, north of the Temple Mount, were an important pagan cult site connected with the Greco-Roman god of healing, Asclepius, but also visited by Jews, as can be seen in the Gospel story of Jesus healing the paralytic. Similarly, the pool of Siloam (south of today's Old City) was a pre-Christian sacred site. Two churches were lavishly built during the first half of the fifth century near these pools: One at Bethesda, and one at Siloam at the culmination of a long procession route dating to the Second Temple period. By overbuilding them with churches, these formerly pagan sites were turned into Christian ones.

After the initial imperial commitment in the times of Constantine the Great that manifested itself in the three church foundations already discussed, the Holy Land was much less in the focus of the consequent emperors for over a century, leaving aside the

---

Right: Caesarea Maritima, ruins of the Roman baths.

unsuccessful plans of Julian the Apostate (r. 361–363 CE) to rebuild the Jewish Temple in the last year of his reign. The only pagan emperor after Constantine had started a religious reformation which intended to restore Graeco-Roman polytheism as the state religion. Confiscated temples were restored, while at the same time privileges for Christians were revoked. One of these cases directly concerned a Christian community in the Holy Land, namely the city of Maiuma which had been separated from pagan Gaza by an edict from Constantine that was now reversed. While in practice Julian's short-lived reforms had little impact, because of his sudden death on campaign against the Sasanians, his extravagant plan to rebuild the Jerusalem Temple appeared to many Christians as an outrageous scandal. Just as Constantine had commissioned his confidant Acacius to destroy the pagan shrine at Mamre, Julian commissioned his friend Alypius with the symbolic and expensive task of the construction works. His endeavours came to a sudden end, when, according to the pagan historian Ammianus Marcellinus, frightful balls of fire broke out near the new foundations and attacked the workmen who eventually gave up the attempt. The same supernatural causes that marked the building project a failure were described in a Syriac letter attributed to Bishop Cyril of Jerusalem. Christians interpreted the signs (that can be ascribed to a massive earthquake) as divine intervention.

With Julian's death the imperial house of Constantine died out. After a number of short reigns (Jovian, Valentinian, and Valens), Theodosius I gained the purple in 379 CE and became the founder of the Theodosian dynasty which looked more favourably on the Holy Land, as expressed through donations, mainly via female members of the court. Jerusalem received city walls, in all likelihood initiated by Aelia Eudoxia, the wife of Arcadius. Her daughter-in-law, Aelia Eudocia, travelled to the Holy Land in a pilgrimage much echoing that of Helena a century before her, and eventually took up residence in or nearby Jerusalem from 442/443 CE until her death in 460 CE. Since a Roman empress residing in the Holy Land seemed an extraordinary case, it is not surprising that most contemporary church foundations in the region (among them the aforementioned churches at Bethesda and Siloam) have been attributed to her patronage. However, even though Eudocia is mentioned frequently in the sources, there are relatively few buildings that can be attributed to her with any certainty, among them the restoration of a bathing complex in Hamat Gader, a pilgrims' station on the Jerusalem–Jericho road with a chapel to Saint Peter, a hostel outside Jerusalem with a chapel to Saint George, and the Church of Saint Stephen. This ecclesiastical building was Jerusalem's first church dedicated to a saint (that is, not to an event in Christ's life and passion). It was located outside the northern city gate (modern Damascus Gate) and had a complex architectural plan with a polygonal apse as well as floor mosaics, and was adorned with architectural sculpture echoing Constantinopolitan fashions. A monastery and hospital, possibly a *leprosarium*, were connected with the church and are attested until the ninth century.

During Eudocia's stay in the Holy Land a watershed event took place that had, among others things, a great impact on the status of Jerusalem. Until 451 CE the city was subordinate to Caesarea Maritima. The city's bishops, most notably among them Cyril, had ambitiously tried to further Jerusalem's rank, although it was not until the times of Juvenal (422–458 CE) that Jerusalem was promoted to the rank of a Patriarchate that commanded over the three Palestinian provinces. In 451 CE, another Church Council convened near Constantinople, in the small suburb of Chalcedon on the Asiatic side of the Bosphorus. The dispute that had made the meeting necessary concerned the nature of Jesus Christ, more precisely how his divine and human nature related to each other. One party argued that the human nature in Christ was totally absorbed by his divine nature, which meant that after the union of the divine and the human in the Incarnation, Jesus Christ had only one single nature. Hence, they have been labelled, in particular by their opponents, as Monophysites or Miaphysites. This was the theological position held by the venerable School of Alexandria, and—at least for political reasons—by Palestinian clerics, at least until 451 CE. The other party condemned these views as heresy and affirmed a doctrine of the union of two natures in Jesus Christ, the divine and the human, without separation and without mixture, hence they have been called Dyophysites, i.e. those who believe in two natures. Similar questions had been discussed twenty years earlier at the preceding Council of Ephesus (431 CE), and Bishop Juvenal of Jerusalem had emerged from that meeting as an influential figure, since he had understood that the religious importance of his episcopal see could turn the scales in the constant power struggle between the four existing Patriarchates. In Ephesus, Juvenal had sided with the man who was arguably the most important church leader of these days, Cyril, Patriarch of Alexandria. At another meeting in 449 CE, Juvenal had proved his loyalty to Alexandria, clearly in the hope of separating the provinces of Palestine and Arabia from the Patriarchate of Antioch and of himself becoming patriarch of these regions. At the Council of Chalcedon in 451 CE, however, Juvenal made a volte-face and did not back Cyril's successor (and nephew), Dioscorus. When it became clear that the alliance between Rome, Antioch, and Constantinople was too strong, Juvenal deserted the Alexandrines and signed the Christological formula declared by the winning party. His sudden change of mind was duly rewarded: Juvenal left the Council as first Patriarch of Jerusalem.

However, a large group of Palestinian monks adhering to the Alexandrine dogmatic positions was puzzled by Juvenal's seemingly opportunistic move and his Christological somersault. This party, led by the monk Theodosius, aimed at organizing resistance to Juvenal who eventually was welcomed not by enthusiastic crowds, but by a mob of angry monks which drove him out of the city and elected Theodosius as new patriarch. Juvenal found unexpected support from a fraction of monks in the Judean Desert headed by a certain Euthymius. The latter had founded several monasteries east of Jerusalem after he had arrived in the Holy Land as a pilgrim from his hometown Melitene in Armenia at the beginning of the fifth century. Euthymius' decision to accept the dogmatical decisions of the Council and not to forsake his allegiance to Juvenal at first must have seemed very confusing. Suddenly, the desert monks were isolated. Their anti-Chalcedonian counterparts were guided by Theodosius, but had an equally important monastic leader among them: Peter the Iberian. He was not only about forty years younger than Euthymius, but also had much better connections: Peter was of royal blood, the son of a Georgian king who had sent him as a hostage to the court in Constantinople, where Peter, according to his biographer, John Rufus, was raised at the court of the imperial couple, Theodosius II and Eudocia. Within a very short time, the anti-Chalcedonians won over many laymen, clergymen, and monks, but most importantly, the empress dowager herself. Despite these courtly connections, however, their side did not prevail. The reigning emperor, Marcian, a driving force behind the meeting in Chalcedon backed the council's decisions. He had Juvenal reinstalled by military force about a year and a half after his deposition, and drove most of the anti-Chalcedonians into exile in Egypt, among them Peter the Iberian, while the counter-patriarch Theodosius was thrown into prison.

Over the following decade, most Christians—including the former insurgent monks—accepted the Chalcedonian doctrine so that in 456 CE a union was reached, at least according to the writings of Chalcedonian authors. However, conflicts over dogma remained a recurring theme in the history of the Holy Land for the rest of late antiquity. While today these issues might appear as theological subtleties, the choice between acceptance or rejection of a certain dogma was a vital decision for late antique Christians, since adhering to the wrong side implied risking one's salvation in the afterlife. Peter the Iberian's biographer John Rufus penned another work, called the *Plerophoriae*, a collection of what the author called 'witnesses' and 'revelations'. It contains many episodes narrated from an anti-Chalcedonian perspective demonstrating what could go wrong if adhering to the wrong side. Even being accidentally present during a Chalcedonian service would bring about death, as was the case for a Miaphysite woman in one of these tales.

The monasteries of the winning party, headed by Euthymius, continued to play an eminent role in the politics of the Holy Land: already in the fifth century, almost all important ecclesiastical positions were filled with former monks of the desert monasteries. The next time this group demonstrated its power was in 516 CE. The Patriarch of Jerusalem, John, had called all monks from the desert into the Holy City, since matters were urgent: The miaphysite-leaning emperor Anastasius in Constantinople was attempting to enforce his religious views throughout the Empire. Already in 513 CE, the former patriarch of Jerusalem, Elias, had refused to accept the synodical letters sent by the Patriarch of Antioch which condemned the Council of Chalcedon. For his adherence to this dogma, Elias had been deposed and exiled to Aila on the Red Sea three years later, when the emperor sent a military commander to Jerusalem in order to re-enforce his anti-Chalcedonian theology. The commander appointed John, formerly a deacon of the Church of the Holy Sepulchre, since John had promised to accept the Antiochean theology. His first official act, however, was to break this promise. On learning this, the emperor sent another military commander to Jerusalem in order to force John as well as the monk Sabas, the heir to Euthymius' position, and all the

The monastery of Saint Catherine's, Mount Sinai.

monks of the Holy Land to accept the letters, or to oust John from his patriarchal see, just as had been done with Elias a few months earlier. John was indeed thrown into prison where he again promised to preach against the Chalcedonian dogma in two days, as a result of which he was released. John knew of the considerable influence of the monks in the desert with Sabas as one of their leaders. Unlike the emperor in Constantinople, they were very much present and influential in Jerusalem, one reason for him—beyond all Christological controversies—to adhere to the doctrine of Chalcedon that these monks had strictly maintained from 451 CE onwards. John immediately summoned all the monks to the holy city. Upon hearing of the emperor's plans to imprison and exile John, they came in very large numbers and assembled in the Church of Saint Stephen built by Eudocia. It must have been an impressive gathering, one that also included Hypatius, a nephew of the emperor, who happened to be in the city. While the military commander still expected John and Sabas to anathematize the dogmatical decisions of Chalcedon, they ascended the pulpit and unanimously proclaimed anathema upon the Patriach of Antioch and upon everyone who did not accept Chalcedon's rulings. Certainly impressed by the number of the assembled monks, the commander fled to Caesarea, while Hypatius, the imperial nephew, proclaimed that he honoured the communion of the Palestinian monks. His uncle, however, prepared to condemn to exile both the patriarch as well as the monastic leaders Sabas and Theodosius.

When this plan became known in the Holy Land, Sabas and a fellow-monk, Theodosius, again summoned all the monks of the desert and wrote a petition to the emperor, explaining to him that his rule rested on God's command that he may bestow peace on all churches, and in particular on 'the mother of the churches'—as the Church of Jerusalem was frequently called in late antique times. The petition explained that salvation was manifested and accomplished in the Holy Land. It stressed the importance of the venerable relic of the Holy Cross, and of all the holy places. The senders did not fail to repeat a claim first made by Bishop Cyril of Jerusalem in the fourth century, framed as a question to the emperor: if Jerusalem's inhabitants touched the truth each day with their own hands as they passed through the holy places, how then were they—more than five hundred years after the coming of Christ—to learn the faith anew? Then, the tone of the petition became threatening: if life and death depended on their account of the faith, the monks wrote, it was death that they preferred. If the emperor insisted on their acceptance of the anti-Chalcedonian beliefs, they assured him that their blood would willingly be shed, and that all the holy places be consumed with fire.

What Sabas and Theodosius stated in their letter is nothing less than religious blackmail and their threat achieved its goal: the emperor left them in peace and Patriarch John remained in his see. This act of monastic self-confidence displayed at the beginning of the sixth century was an exceptionally strong one. Compared to the attempts of the fourth- and fifth-century bishops and patriarchs to promote the Holy Land's importance—even to Juvenal's bold change of mind in 451 CE, it becomes clear that the monks and clergymen had only in the last decades come to understand the potential of the empire-wide importance of the Holy Land with its *loca sancta*. If we believe our main source on this era, the monk Cyril of Scythopolis, who penned the biographies of Euthymius and Sabas, it was Sabas himself who managed to propel the status of the Holy Land to new heights. He travelled to the capital in 530 CE, where he was welcomed with highest honours by the reigning emperor Justinian. In Constantinople, Sabas did not shrink from rebuffing the empress Theodora, a well-known supporter of the Miaphysite cause. Nevertheless, he presented her husband with a list of requests which were all granted: apart from tax exemptions and the construction of a hospital in Jerusalem, Sabas urged the emperor to rebuild the churches which were destroyed in the wake of a recent uprising of the Samaritans.

The Samaritan religion was closely connected to Mount Gerizim near Neapolis (modern Nablus) in Samaria. The hill was, according to Samaritan belief, identical with the place where Joshua had set up an altar after the Children of Israel came to the promised land. Rather than the Temple Mount in Jerusalem, God had chosen Mount

Gerizim as the place for his sanctuary. The rival temple was a cause of permanent tension between Samaritans and Jews until it was destroyed in the second century BCE under the reign of the Hasmonean John Hyrcanus I. Later, a temple to Jupiter was constructed on the spot, often ascribed to Hadrian, while it seems more likely according to the archaeological evidence that it was built during the reign of Antoninus Pius (r. 138–161 CE), when other monumental buildings were also constructed in Neapolis. The sources speak about increased tensions between Samaritans and Christians from the reign of Zeno (r. 474–491 CE) onwards. Samaritan sources report that the emperor wanted to transform their sanctuary into a church or a shrine for his deceased son, thus causing an uprising. Christians in Neapolis were killed, and the rebellion spread as far as Caesarea where several buildings were destroyed, prompting the emperor to subdue the insurgence. In the wake of these events a church dedicated to the Virgin Mary was built on top of the mountain, most likely between 484 and 489 CE.

As with the foundation of Aelia Capitolina in the wake of the Bar Kokhba Revolt (132–135 CE), the sources are not entirely clear whether the Samaritan uprising was a result of the construction works or whether the erection of the church was partially meant to be a punishment for the revolt, though the latter seems to be the more likely option. In the following years, a Roman garrison was stationed on the mountain. In 495, under Anastasius, Samaritan sources record that a woman convinced several men to seize the church and massacre the soldiers, a plan that utterly failed and only resulted in a new military intervention. In 529 CE, led by the messianic figure Julian ben Sabar, the Samaritans launched their most violent attacks: the sources speak of the murder of the bishop of Neapolis as well as of massacres of local priests and the destruction of several churches—this is the uprising Sabas was mentioning at the imperial court in 530 CE. Sabas' wish was granted by Justinian, but another Samaritan uprising took place in 556. This time, it seems that they sided with the Jews, perhaps as a reaction to imperial favours granted to the Christian Church by Justinian. Again, there were uprisings in Caesarea, but they seem to have spread to various other places as well. In all likelihood, fights in Bethlehem resulted in the burning down of the Church of the Nativity, which was later rebuilt by the emperor using a Constantinian decorative scheme. Justinian's successor, Justin II (r. 565–574 CE), had to face another uprising in 572 CE, this time on the slopes of Mount Carmel, where around the same time the Piacenza Pilgrim described the hostile atmosphere between Samaritans and Christians. Ultimately, the series of uprisings of the late fifth and sixth centuries resulted in a harsh legislation against the Samaritans whose numbers dwindled dramatically.

The monk Sabas, begging Justinian to reconstruct the churches destroyed in the uprising of 529 CE, would not live to witness the even more devastating destructions of the 550s, since he died two years later. Among the remaining requests on his list, there was the construction of a church to the Virgin Mary in Jerusalem—another wish to which Justinian would respond favourably. After an initial plan to construct a large-scale church of Mary was abandoned during the Patriarchate of Elias due to financial problems, the emperor took it up. The now much larger church was consecrated in November 543 CE, on the feast day of Mary's Presentation in the Temple. It was located at the south end of the *cardo maximus* and became Jerusalem's largest church building. An engineer was sent from Constantinople, and a completely new quarry had to be dug for the construction works. The excavated ashlars corroborate the description of the building works by Procopius of Caesarea: some of them have a weight of more than 8 tons—in terms of dimensions there was only one other building that eclipsed the size of these stones: the foundation walls of Herod's Temple, known today as the Western Wall. It makes sense to compare the size and position of this new church to Eusebius' description of Constantine's plans of his Church of the Holy Sepulchre. As it was positioned opposite the Jewish Temple Mount that was left in ruins, so the new church of Mary was elevated on a hill approximately at the same height as both the Temple and the Constantinian church. At the same time, the church's exceptional size and its position on, as Procopius put it, the highest of hills (a reference to Isa. 2:2) made sure that the building became a major landmark that was visible throughout all processions that traversed the city from the Church of the Holy Sepulchre to the Church on Mount Zion or from any holy site on the Mount of Olives. Procopius' description of Justinian's building activities lists many places in the Holy Land; however, arguably the most important of these building projects, may also go back to one of the requests made by Sabas, who had asked the emperor to construct a fort in the desert against Saracen incursions. Justinian may not exactly have fulfilled this wish, but he gave money to build something else, a fortified monastery at the foot of Mount Sinai, known to today as Saint Catherine's Monastery with its chapel of the Burning Bush and its renowned collection of manuscripts and Byzantine icons.

Justinian's new church of the Virgin Mary—as well as a multitude of other churches in Jerusalem and in other places of the Holy Land—were soon to suffer destruction, not at the hand of Samaritans or Saracens, as Sabas had feared eighty years earlier, but by the Sasanian Persians who under Shah Khosrow II (r. 590–628 CE) conquered large parts of the late antique Near East. Cities such as Antioch and Caesarea were captured, providing the Sasanians access to the Mediterranean. Particularly in the Galilee region, the Jews joined forces with the Persians, and eventually marched with them on Jerusalem in 614 CE. The sources tell us that the patriarch of Jerusalem, Zachariah, fell into Sasanian captivity, and that an abbot called Modestus, who eventually would become Zachariah's successor, gathered an army near Jericho. However, their attempt to retake the city failed since the newly-mustered troops fled upon the sight of the much larger Persian army. According to an Armenian source, the Persian capture of Jerusalem resulted in a death toll of 17,000 Christians. Another source claims that about 4500 prisoners were massacred by the Sasanians and their allies in or near a water reservoir, the Mamilla pool.

The capture of the city was surely the most dramatic event in the history of the Holy Land since the Bar Kokhba revolt, even though the contemporary sources (let alone

The monastery of Saint Euthymius in the Judean desert.

later ones) surely exaggerated when it came to the exact numbers of massacred Christians or to the churches which were destroyed. In several ecclesiastical buildings (among them the Church on Mount Zion and the Church of the Holy Sepulchre, which was restored by Modestus) burnt layers dating to the early seventh century are archaeologically attested. However, some of the churches that were listed in the sources as having been heavily destroyed do not show any traces of destruction or repairs, and the overall evidence for the alleged Persian destruction is meagre. Even though only seven burial sites for victims of mass executions have been discovered, the killing of the Christian inhabitants near the Mamilla Pool described in the sources can be archaeologically corroborated by the discovery of a cave filled with human bones, predominately of young women. The site can best be described as a mass grave, and it is marked by an inscription in the form of a prayer for the salvation and succour of those whose names the Lord knows. The phrase is not uncommon in late antiquity, and, as a rule, refers to the donors, apparently too many to list in the inscription, and not to the victims of the Persian massacre. A similar mass grave was excavated in the 1980s outside Jerusalem close to the monastery of John the Baptist on the Jordan River. Paleopathological research demonstrated that many of the buried men and women suffered from leprosy and tuberculosis. It is likely that they lived in the monastery

Children of Israel: 'O my people, enter the Holy Land which God has assigned to you.' Moreover, the first direction of prayer (*qibla*) set by Muhammad was Jerusalem. This presumably explains the series of monumental building projects and investments undertaken in the Holy Land by the new Muslim rulers. According to contemporary sources one of the first of these projects was the erection of a mosque on the Temple Mount in Jerusalem. A Gallic Christian pilgrim by the name of Arculf who visited the Holy Land around the year 670 reported on his return that 'near the wall on the east, in the famous place where once had stood the magnificent Temple, the Saracens have now built an oblong house of prayer, which they pieced together with upright planks and large beams over some ruined remains. This they attend and it is said that this building can hold three thousand people.' Another local Christian source dated to the same period reports that 'they proceeded in haste to the Capitol (the Roman name for the Temple Mount). They took with them men, some by force, others by their own will, in order to clean that place and to build that cursed thing, intended for their prayer and which they call a mosque.' These descriptions, written during Mu'awiya's rule, are followed by later Muslim traditions recounting how 'Umar himself went up to the Mount immediately following the conquest, prayed there, and personally led the clearing of the garbage that had been purposefully piled up there by the Byzantines, putting the rubbish 'by the handful into the lower part of his mantle'.

Although the exact date of these events is not clear, it is evident that the initial structure built on the Mount was temporary and was based on spolia found *in situ*, as Arculf's account clearly relates. It was towards the end of the century that the caliph 'Abd al-Malik (685–705) embarked upon the building of a permanent structure on the Temple Mount that would be known as the Dome of the Rock (*Qubbat al-Ṣakhra*). According to the early 11th-century Muslim scholar al-Wasiti, who compiled early Islamic sayings on 'The Virtues of Jerusalem', 'Abd al-Malik spent seven years of Egypt's revenues, the richest of the provinces, in order to fund the magnificent building. A freedman who served as the Caliph's right-hand man, Raja' ibn Haywa, was appointed in charge of the project. Raja' gathered craftsmen throughout the caliphate and the result was the glorious structure that still stands today. Gold coins that were left over from the project were melted down and laid upon the domed roof, making it glitter from afar. The impressive concentric structure topped by this dome was supported by pillars and surrounded by an outer arcade. Inside were two arcades flanked by two concentric rows of pillars, and at the centre was located the stone upon which the world rested according to Jewish tradition (*even ha-shtiya*), a tradition adopted by Islam as well. The structure was covered both inside and out by coloured glass mosaics, prevalent in late antiquity, exhibiting aniconic patterns such as vegetative scrolls and motifs, vessels and winged crowns like those worn by Sasanian kings.

Though an Islamic creation, the Dome was made by local craftsmen, probably both Byzantine and Sasanian, and seems to have been inspired by such Byzantine commemorative monuments as the local Holy Sepulchre, the octagonal church of Caesarea, and the Kathisma church—Mary's resting place on the way to Bethlehem—and

The Dome of the Rock in Jerusalem, built by the caliph 'Abd al-Malik b. Marwan in 691–692 CE.

possibly even the famous Hagia Sophia in Constantinople. The Dome of the Rock was thus designed as a monumental concentric structure, not designed for public worship, and resembled pagan temples, shrines, or churches that were focused on a holy place or memory. What was the 'memory' in the case of the Dome? It appears that the Muslims at this early stage associated the spot in fact with the Temple of Solomon and with Jewish traditions relating to the End of Days. Furthermore, they actually held various rituals which emulated those of the Jewish Temple. According to various Muslim sources, Jews as well as Christians assisted the Muslims in the upkeep and performance of these rituals. Jerusalem itself was called by the Muslims 'Bayt al-Maqdis', an Arabic version of the Hebrew 'Beit Ha-Miqdas', or the Temple.

The Dome of the Rock, view of inner arcade that encircles the stone at the building's centre.

Why did 'Abd al-Malik choose to invest in such an extravagant structure on the Temple Mount? It is not easy to be certain, but our historical sources offer a number of indications, which together hint at 'Abd al-Malik's shrewdness as a politician in turbulent times. First, he had a strong internal political motive as he was faced with the rebellion of 'Abdallah ibn al-Zubayr; 'Abd al-Malik therefore sought to provide an alternative political and religious centre to Mecca. Secondly, the abundant churches and their ostentatious crosses all over Jerusalem no doubt motivated him to build a dazzling monument that would rival the Christian sanctuaries of Jerusalem and the Holy Sepulchre in particular. Moreover, 'Abd al-Malik could present himself as the redeemer of the Temple, God's Throne, from the squalor that the Christians had left it in, thus rebuking the haughty Byzantines.

Although the Dome is the most prominent building on the Temple Mount, it did not stand alone; 'Abd al-Malik, or his successor al-Walid (705–715), also built the mosque of Al-Aqsa, a rectangular house of prayer. This mosque in fact was identified as the location of the furthest mosque where Muhammad was taken at night by God and shown 'our signs' (Sura 17:1), a passage upon which an elaborate tradition was later developed that told of a wondrous winged creature which brought him there and of how Muhammad met with various biblical prophets as well as with God himself. Other features relating to the Temple Mount included a few smaller domed buildings, the outer walls and the gates. In addition to all these, four monumental structures, most probably intended to serve the rulers and their administration, were erected outside the Mount, along its south-west corner. One of these was a two-storied palace with a bridge that provided direct access to the mosque of al-Aqsa. It thus seems that the intention was to build a political and religious hub on the Temple Mount and in its vicinity.

Though the Temple Mount's sanctity in Islam was by then well established, the caliph Sulayman ibn 'Abd al-Malik (715–717) chose to move the political and administrative capital of Palestine elsewhere, to a new city which he named Ramla after the sands that lay about it. Like the garrison towns which the Muslims founded in Iraq, Ramla was situated near an important ancient city, Lydda, and also followed their layout: an orthogonal street plan, a governor's palace, and a congregational mosque. It was surrounded by a wall with eight gates, each leading in a different direction as the city was located at the crossing of routes going from Egypt to Syria and Jordan to the Mediterranean. It also had sundry markets and is described by the geographer al-Muqaddasi, writing in 985, as a beautiful and prosperous city. The White Mosque of Ramla, still standing today, was most probably founded in the Umayyad period, though no clear evidence for this has survived, the original mosque having been destroyed along with the rest of the city in an earthquake in the 11th century. Excavations in the area have, however, revealed Umayyad houses aligned with the mosque, and the underground water reservoir of the mosque is almost identical to the Pool of the Arches, built in the city by the caliph Harun al-Rashid in 789, supporting an early construction date.

Another city which the Umayyads turned into an important urban centre was Tiberias, which was now declared the capital of Jordan, the province adjacent to Palestine. Unlike Ramla, Tiberias was an ancient town, an important Jewish centre and the residence of the Palestinian Academy (Gaonate, the main legislative body of the Jews in Palestine) before it was transferred to Jerusalem, where Jews and Christians lived together. During

Pool of the Arches in Ramla built by the caliph Harun al-Rashid in 789 CE.

the Umayyad period the city became an important administrative hub. In its centre a congregational mosque was built; to the north of this the governor's house and administrative headquarters were founded upon a former basilical building dating between the 4th and 6th century, and to the south of it a Hamam or bathhouse was built.

Two other visible signs of the presence of the new rulers were roads and residences. Several milestones engraved in Arabic script on slabs of stone have been found along the road from Jerusalem to the coast, from Tiberias to Damascus, and from Jerusalem to Jericho. The milestone at Khan Hathrura, on the way to Jericho, mentions that it lies 109 miles from Damascus, which makes clear that the Muslims renovated the Roman road from Jerusalem to Damascus, since this had gone through the Jordan valley via Tiberias, and they also opened a new ascent from Tiberias towards Damascus, as is indicated by the milestone from Fiq. Yet though he followed the routes of the Roman road system, 'Abd al-Malik broke away from the Roman tradition of using pillars as milestones and chose to use flat stone slabs bearing in Arabic a pious message as well as road information, presumably as part of his new policy to define and enhance Islamic identity. Contributing to this policy, though in a very different way, were the elite residences, the ruins of which are still found strewn about the Levant. Most are found in Jordan, and only three—Khirbat al-Mafjar by Jericho, and Khirbat al-Minya and al-Sinnabra near Tiberias—are situated in the Holy Land. Most blend Byzantine and Persian architectural and artistic styles in a way that can be seen as distinctively Islamic. Unlike the Temple Mount, which, despite the Byzantine artistic influence, is purposefully aniconic—undoubtedly due to theological considerations—these private palaces and villas were completely free of these restrictions and openly exhibited bold figurative images.

As well as the grand building projects of the Umayyad rulers and their allies, there were small private initiatives as well. A good example of this is the mosque in the Negev town of Shivta, Byzantine Sobata, where an established Christian community lived in the centuries prior to the conquest. Sometime during the 8th century a small mosque was attached to the external wall of one of the city churches. Arabic inscriptions found on

Milestone in Arabic script at Khan al-Hatrura (Jericho) on the Damascus road erected by the caliph ʻAbd al-Malik.

Floor mosaic in the palace of Caliph Hisham (724–743), Khirbat al-Mafjar, near Jericho, depicting a lion and gazelles under a pomegranate tree.

the walls include Qur'anic verses as well as a dedicatory inscription indicating that the mosque was instigated by local Muslim inhabitants. This reveals that though there was no massive immigration and settlement of newly arrived Arabs in Palestine, Islam was nevertheless penetrating slowly into rural and desert areas. An intriguing case is the commemorative church of the Kathisma, which marks the spot where Mary sat down to rest on her way to give birth in Bethlehem. During the 8th century one of the rooms in the church was turned into a mosque with a prayer-niche (*mihrab*) and a new mosaic with a palm tree was installed. However, unlike the case of Shivta, where it seems that the local Muslim population needed a place for prayer, here the trigger for the addition of a mosque within the church was apparently the common veneration of Mary. The Muslims, it seems, accepted the site of the Kathisma as the place where Mary gave birth to Jesus under a palm tree, which provided her after her birth with fresh dates, as related in the Qur'an (19:23–5). These and other enterprises, both public and private, made manifest the presence of the new rulers of the Holy Land and gave a significant thrust to the process of the spatial Islamization of the Holy Land that would continue, though in a somewhat different manner, throughout the early Islamic period.

What impact did these developments have on the local population, Christian, Jewish, and Samaritan? The answer is that it varied from group to group. The leading Christian community in the Holy Land, which belonged to the Chalcedonian or imperial Byzantine church, went through a great crisis, as it had lost its status as

A mosque adjoining the outer wall of the church of Shivta in the Negev.

representative of the ruling empire and now found itself on a par with all the other sects. Jews and Samaritans, as well as non-Chalcedonian Christians, went through the transition much more smoothly, for they had suffered during the 5th and 6th centuries from a gradual yet persistent loss of their civil rights due to the Christianization of empire and its adherence to the Chalcedonian dogma. To this must be added the hardships that the Samaritans endured following the suppression of their uprising in Samaria that lasted from 529 to 531. As a result, some of these communities actually viewed the coming of Islam favourably. Archaeological as well as written sources indicate that after the initial dramatic upheaval of the conquest, the local population continued to conduct their lives much as before. There are numerous examples of churches and synagogues that were renovated during this period. A striking example is found in the town of Umm al-Rasas, where a new church, with an elaborate mosaic floor, was built next to an older one that was still functioning. In the centre of this new mosaic, framing the nave, appear depictions of eight cities west of the Jordan and eight to its east, all of which were part of the Patriarchate of Jerusalem.

It is important to remember that Christians continued to form a majority of the population of the Holy Land for some centuries to come, and they were employed in substantial numbers in the Umayyad civil service in influential positions. Such was the case of one Athanasius bar Gumoye, a scribe from Edessa in Mesopotamia, who was the senior administrator in the 690s for the governor of Egypt, who was the brother of the caliph ʻAbd al-Malik, and who amassed while there 'gold and silver like pebbles and had 4000 slaves'. Similarly, the famous theologian of the Byzantine church, John of Damascus (d. *c.*750), a member of the Christian Arab Mansur family, held, like his father before him, a high position in the Umayyad treasury before withdrawing to the monastery of Mar Saba in the Judean desert. Often, such people had been employed previously in the local Byzantine administration and simply continued in their jobs, bringing with them valuable knowledge and experience. It may be surmised that this smooth integration between the conquering and the conquered population was at least partially a result of former contact between the Arab conquerors and parts of the local communities. Despite what is often supposed, both sides were not unfamiliar with the language and culture of the other, a fact that must have made the adjustment much easier.

The Jewish and Samaritan communities actually benefited from the change of rulers. Jews had managed quite soon to circumvent the Byzantine prohibition of them living in Jerusalem, which the Muslims initially renewed; it seems that this was due to their participation in restoration work on the Temple Mount and in rituals in connection with the Dome of the Rock. This is evidenced by a text from the Cairo Geniza, a large depository of old books and documents of the local Jewish community which fell out of use. The 11th-century document describes an agreement that was made with the Muslims through the arbitration of ʻUmar I ibn al-Khattab, according to which seventy Jewish families were allowed to live south of the Temple Mount. The Samaritans, too, achieved some gains; they were no longer afflicted with the

Central mosaic in St Stephan's church at Umm al-Rasas (Kastron Mefa), dated 785 CE.

penalties and curbs that the Byzantine authorities had imposed on them and some were granted tax exemptions in return for acting as spies on behalf of the Muslims. Reflecting this, the Samaritan chronicle notes that the Umayyads, like their prophet, 'did not harm anyone'.

Of course there were many who were adversely affected by the conquests and change in rulers, especially those who had served in or felt close to the Byzantine imperial government. Many of these naturally chose to leave for Byzantium with the arrival of the Muslims. Arrangements for their departure are specified in some of the agreements. Houses and businesses that were forfeited by their owners seem in many cases to have been taken over by the Muslims. Along the coastline the change was especially striking. The coastal cities had been the economic and social heart of Byzantine Palestine. Unlike the towns and settlements inland, the Muslims, anxious to secure the coast against recurring Byzantine raids, had built fortified strongholds (*ribats*) and lured Muslims and non-Byzantines to settle there by various material as well as spiritual inducements. In some cities the local population was exiled or encouraged to leave. Many residents of Caesarea, which had been taken by the Muslims after a long siege, were taken captive and made servants of the Muslim elite near Medina. Excavations show dramatic changes in the plan of the city following the conquest. Most striking are the governor's house and the houses of the affluent who had emigrated, which had now become the gardens of others who took their place. The destination of those who fled the coastline was most often Byzantium, although there seems to have been some internal emigration from the coastline inland. Such internal emigration may also explain the exceptional flourishing of the Christian towns and villages east of the Jordan during the 7th and 8th centuries. A contemporary Samaritan chronicle describes how the wealthier members of the community living along the coast left their belongings with their brothers in the area of Neapolis and left for Byzantium, believing that the trouble would soon be over and they would then return.

The conquerors also went through a transition. During the first fifty years the Arab rulers had been content with running the empire based on the capitulation agreements, employing the same local administrators who had previously served the Byzantines, their affairs usually conducted in Greek as before. They saw themselves as inheritors of their Byzantine predecessors and therefore minted coins that looked just like those of the Byzantine emperors with the caliphs' names written in Greek. With the caliph 'Abd al-Malik we witness a significant change. Fighting to assert his rule against multiple challengers, 'Abd al-Malik realized that he needed to strengthen the identity of the regime in the face of both Muslim rebels and the conquered population. He therefore initiated a reform in which Arabic was declared the official language, coins were minted in Arabic without images, and official scribes were now required to write in Arabic. It was also at this time that the Muslim religion became the overt source of legitimacy of Arab rule. This reform does not mean that Arabic was not used before 'Abd al-Malik, as indeed it was; only that from this time onwards Arabic was declared as the official language. A large corpus of administrative papyri found in Nessana in the Negev contains various documents from the 6th and 7th centuries, and there is a change from Greek only documents, to Greek and Arabic ones to Arabic only documents. It took decades, however, before this policy was fully implemented. In tandem with it went 'Abd al-Malik's building work on the Temple Mount, both projects being intended to augment and emphasize Muslim identity.

Another important process that followed in this reform's wake was to have long-lasting consequences for the non-Muslim inhabitants of the Caliphate, the local inhabitants of Palestine included. Around the turn of the 8th century, possibly in the wake of the failed Muslim siege of Constantinople in 717, the Muslim government became less liberal regarding the behaviour of non-Muslims in public. The freedom that was promised to them in the conquest agreements was now being debated amongst Muslims, and slowly but surely various limitations were starting to be imposed, including restrictions on their personal appearance and behaviour (hair style, dress, riding on horses, and more). These regulations heralded a growing change in attitude towards the non-Muslim population that would find its expression in the coming centuries in Palestine as well.

Later dynasties: Abbasid, Tulunid, Ikhshidid, and Fatimid rule (750–1099)

Towards the middle of the 8th century Umayyad rule faltered. The discontent of many of the Arabs and non-Arabs throughout the caliphate resulted in the rise to power of a new dynasty, the Abbasids, and a great massacre of the members of the Umayyad dynasty. Many of them found refuge in Palestine and Arabia where they were sought out by 'Abdallah ibn 'Ali, the governor of Syria. 'Abdallah treacherously ordered the murder of the last seventy members who capitulated at Antipatris, or Abu Futrus, east of modern Tel-Aviv, purging all but one, who managed to flee to Cordoba and establish an Umayyad caliphate there. Unlike the Umayyads, whose military and political power base was in Syria, the Abbasids established their power base in the eastern parts of the caliphate and founded a new capital, Baghdad, just north of the old Persian capital of Seleucia-Ctesiphon. This administrative decision meant that the provinces of Palestine and Jordan were no longer at the centre of the caliphate, and that from then on they would receive much less attention from the caliphs. The great surge of investments was over. There would still be reconstruction, especially at Jerusalem, whose position as the third most holy site in Islam was secure. Thus after the al-Aqsa Mosque was damaged in an earthquake in 749, just prior to the rise of the Abbasids, the caliph al-Mansur had it restored, albeit financing the work by removing the gold and silver plates which covered its doors and melting them down into gold and silver coins. But no further grand building projects were undertaken, only small scale works, such as the addition of great water cisterns to the mosque of Ramla by Harun al-Rashid (786–809) and the construction of a new harbour at Acre during the reign of Ahmad ibn Tulun (878–884).

Changes in settlement patterns

At the beginning of Abbasid rule, in 750 CE, the coastline of Palestine was no longer the main backbone of the Christian community and trade with Byzantium was virtually non-existent. The Christian communities were to be found mainly in the areas of the Judean mountains, the Judean lowlands (Eleutheropolis), and the Hebron hills, western Galilee, Tiberias, and in Transjordan, as well as in an enclave at the southern coast of Palestine around Ascalon and Gaza. The Jewish population lived mainly in eastern lower Galilee, their main centre after the decline of Sepphoris during the 7th century being the city of Tiberias, in villages in the area of the Golan and in the area of the southern Hebron mountains; Jews were also to be found living in mixed cities like Jerusalem and Ascalon. Samaritans were now living mainly in the area of Samaria, though they could be found living in mixed population centres as well. This situation would change significantly by the 9–10th centuries. Archaeological finds indicate that while Muslim centres like Ramla and Tiberias, and mixed cities like Gaza and Ascalon, continued to flourish, many other places, rural areas in particular, went from the 9th and 10th centuries onwards into continuous decline, some even being abandoned. By the 11th century many settlements were, to use the words of the archaeologist Gideon Avni, 'in dire straits'.

Jerusalem seems to have been an exceptional case, and continued to thrive, predominantly as a Christian city, expanding outside the walls for at least three centuries after the conquest. Yet, although it was still mainly a Christian city, the Muslim presence which began in the vicinity of the Temple Mount gradually spread into areas around the Holy Sepulchre. This being said, the population of Jerusalem too had declined substantially, from 50,000–70,000 in the 6th century to only around 20,000 in the 11th century. In addition, at some point, maybe sometime in the 10th century, new city walls were constructed, encircling now a much smaller area. All of these changes are well reflected in the dwindling and altered map of the bishoprics of the Patriarchate of Jerusalem.

We encounter further change when we examine the composition of the population, as newly arrived Muslims either settled beside the local community, as was the case in various cities or in many villages in Samaria, or took places over, as for example in the case of Susiya and Eshtamoa, two Jewish villages in the southern Hebron mountains, where the synagogues had been turned into mosques around the 9th century. Thus, while in the early periods we find examples of coexistence in prayer houses, as in the aforementioned case of Shivta or the Kathisma, later we find the Muslim population taking the place of the former inhabitants and appropriating their prayer-houses, especially in small villages and towns. In some cases it is also likely that the inhabitants remain the same but they are converting to Islam, and indeed the two processes might go hand in hand, the movement of a few Muslims into a place acting as a catalyst for the conversion of the indigenous population.

The presence of Muslims in Palestine towards the end of the period under discussion is found first and foremost in Ramla, Lydda, Hebron, Jerusalem, and Tiberias, cities with a mixed population, in the coastal cities, including Acre, Caesarea, Arsuf, Jaffa, Yubna, Ashdod (Azdud), Ascalon, and Gaza, and also in Samaria. According to the Muslim traveller Ibn al-'Arabi, who spent six months there, Ascalon was an especially important centre of Muslim learning, 'a sea of belles-lettres (*adab*)', as also was Acre. Indeed the whole coastline was, so he says, full of scholars of various schools of learning. Al-Muqaddasi and Ibn al-'Arabi mention the big mosque of Tiberias, as well as that of Nablus, the capital of the region of Samaria. It had been populated by Samaritans for many centuries, but due to a series of revolts against the Byzantine authorities at the end of the 5th and in the 6th century, the Samaritan population had dwindled considerably. This vacuum attracted Muslims, whose presence there is noted in the accounts of the Samaritan Chronicle from the 9th century onwards.

Spatial Islamization

The changes were in fact much more dramatic than just the reshuffling of population. The newly arrived Muslims encountered a Christian land, dotted with crosses, churches, monasteries, and Christian holy places. Christianity was present everywhere. In the coming centuries, religious and political motives came together to transform the character of the Holy Land and give it a new Islamic garb. This process, called spatial Islamization, was a long-term one that started in the 7th century and was to continue for many centuries to come. Sites were sanctified, new traditions of sanctity replaced former ones or were invented, and rituals were established, expressing the beliefs and ambitions of the new rulers and inhabitants of the land.

The most important symbol of a Muslim presence was of course the mosque. Circa 980 al-Muqaddasi mentions altogether twenty-two mosques in Palestine and Transjordan. Another important Muslim marker were graves and shrines of holy figures. These were found not only in central locations but were also spread throughout the countryside. Sites previously sacred to the Christians and Jews received a new Islamic look; hills, vales, trees, and stones were also granted new Islamic significance. Apart from the holy places there were also many new structures that were distinctively Islamic, such as madrasas (Islamic schools), milestones, palaces, and public buildings flaunting calligraphic inscriptions in Arabic.

First and foremost of these new features in the landscape was the Temple Mount in Jerusalem with the impressive structures of the Dome of the Rock and the mosque of al-Aqsa. Alongside these were many other smaller buildings that represented various traditions, some of them of Jewish and Christian origin, such as the cradle of Mary, the Dome of the Chain, where according to Jewish and Islamic tradition David used to judge the children of Israel using a chain of light, the Dome of the Ascension of the Prophet (Qubbat al-Mi'raj), and many more. In the city of Jerusalem itself various other traditions had been Islamized such as *Mihrab Dawud* (today's David's tower), where according to Byzantine tradition David wrote the Psalms, Mary's tomb in Gethsemane, the Church of the Ascension on the Mount of Olives, the valleys of Hinnom and Kidron, which already from biblical times were connected to the events of the End of

The Ascension in a 9th- or 10th-century icon from St Catherine's monastery.

Times, and many more. Also new in the landscape of Jerusalem were tombs of the Sahaba, Muhammad's companions.

The ancient city of Hebron (*Masjid Ibrahim* or *Hibra*) with the Cave of the Fathers in its centre (*al-Haram al-Ibrahimi*) was sanctified already in the 8th century. In the 10th century, when it became an important centre, Joseph's bones were 'found' and his tomb was added, many hostels were built and more praise literature about the city was written. Ramla, though a new city, also adopted traditions of sanctity in order to enhance its position, linking itself to Qur'anic passages and to Muslim eschatology. Thus the hill and the fountain to which God led Jesus in Qur'an 23:50 were identified as belonging to Ramla. Ascalon, described as one of the brides who will be led to paradise at the End of Days, was conceived as the 'summit of al-Sham (greater Syria)', and boasted the place where the Shi'ite martyr 'Ali ibn Husayn's skull was kept (*mashhad Husayn*). Sanctity was attached also to other coastal cities including Acre, Caesarea, and more.

The city of Nablus became an important centre for the Muslim population living in Samaria, and the region acquired its own cluster of traditions of sanctity. According to an early tradition Jabal Nablus was the most beloved mountain in the country. It was also believed by the Muslims to be the place where Abraham was thrown into the fire by king Namrud for denying the idols and was miraculously saved, a tradition that was based on Jewish legend. The many Samaritan holy places that dotted the countryside of Samaria were also given an Islamic makeover, as was the site of biblical Shilo (*Saylun*), the place where the ark had stayed, which was now identified as The Temple of the Shekhina (*sakina*), God's divine presence. Similarly, the tomb in which John the Baptist's head was buried in Sebastiya was now deemed sacred to Muslims.

The effects of the political events

Most of these significant changes in the landscape took place after the accession of the Abbasids, which was a period of significant change in the conditions in Palestine. Constant revolts and rampant local rebellions were the cause of unceasing anarchy; these culminated in an internal Muslim conflict, oddly named 'The War of the Watermelon', which took place during the last decade of the 8th century. This saga was followed by prolonged and uncontrolled anarchy throughout the caliphate following the death of Harun al-Rashid in 809. While these events were ostensibly internal Muslim affairs they had immense effects on their surroundings; according to local Christian and Samaritan sources, they caused considerable loss of lives and property and generated a feeling of constant instability, insecurity, and anxiety on the part of the local inhabitants. For the Christians the most traumatic of these incidents was the death of twenty monks in Mar Saba in the course of Bedouin raids on the area of the famous monastery in 797.

These troubles were exacerbated by natural disasters such as locusts, droughts, plagues, and earthquakes which abounded during this period. Natural disasters had always been part and parcel of the lives of the inhabitants of the area. However in previous times they were managed, mitigated, and repaired by the authorities, while at this time they went unheeded.

As a result of these frequent catastrophes many places were left desolate; unprotected villages, monasteries in rural and desert areas, and small towns were the most vulnerable, and seem to have been the first to be incapacitated and abandoned. The roads became unsafe and communication and traffic were diminished. Although the reports about the destruction of the cities of Gaza and Ascalon, and that of the monasteries of Mar Saba and Euthymius in the Judean desert following the disaster of 797, did not mean their final demise, these places undoubtedly suffered heavy damage. The new situation compelled the inhabitants of the desert monasteries to retreat into the protected areas and to reinforce their fortifications. Jerusalem managed to hold back the attack of the marauders in 796 with much effort only due to its strong walls and gates, while its environs were looted and burned, as were also Eleutheropolis, Sariphea, and even Gaza and Ascalon. The new circumstances thus created a major change in the settlement pattern: while until then numerous villages and towns were spread out in open territories, in the wake of these events the population now clustered in and around a small number of fortified cities.

In addition, the continual calamities were the cause of massive emigration of Christian inhabitants abroad, to Cyprus and Byzantium, an event described by the Byzantine chronicler Theophanes in his entry for the year 812. News of these tragedies reached the West, and in particular the story of the Twenty Martyrs of Mar Saba was told there. Charlemagne, who had been conducting diplomatic relations with Caliph Harun al-Rashid, came to the aid of the Christians of the Holy Land. A survey of the churches and monasteries in Jerusalem and in the Holy Land is preserved in a unique document called The Memorandum of God's Houses (*Commemoratorium de Casis Dei*) that was prepared for Charlemagne. Following this survey we learn that the Roman Emperor built monasteries, a hostel, a library, and a market in Jerusalem. All of these were supported by the income from estates that he had bought in the vicinity of Jerusalem.

Such events were not, however, of limited duration. Rather, they seem to have formed a pattern. From the 9th century until the Crusades, Palestine was beset with internal strife, was torn between rulers of Egypt and the Abbasids in Iraq, and became the captive of various diplomatic struggles between Byzantium and sundry Muslim powers in the East. The first half of the 9th century was characterized by anarchy and strife caused by the war over the control of the caliphate between al-Amin and al-Ma'mun. The next decades were followed by numerous revolts against the authorities, which caused havoc in Palestine; the rise to power of Ahmad ibn Tulun as an independent ruler in Egypt and Syria brought apparent stability but was not good news for the non-Muslim population, as will be seen below; and during the rule of his successor the country was the battle ground between the Tulunids and the Abbasids. Thirty years of complete anarchy followed, after which in 935 the Ikhshidids and then in 969 the Fatimids came to rule in Egypt and in Syria. Though Egypt flourished under the Fatimids, based at their new capital, Cairo, Palestine remained troubled by the

Monastery of Mar Saba in the Judean desert.

activities of dissidents and Bedouin. In fact the period between 969–1029 is known as the 'sixty-year war', a time when various Arab groups and other elements including the Isma'ili Karmatians, Turks, and others wreaked havoc throughout the land. Byzantine emperors took advantage of this opportune moment and managed to conquer major parts of Syria and Palestine, making an alliance with local Arab tribes who fought against the rulers. Though the conquest was short-lived Byzantine influence continued throughout the 11th century. Finally, from 1070–1098 Palestine was ruled by the Turkomans, only to be taken back by the Fatimids a year before the arrival of the Crusaders. Throughout all of this the local population was left mostly to struggle on its own, and even worse, to supply the demands and follow the regulations imposed on it by the changing rulers. Thus, for example, Ahmad b. Tulun, ruler of Egypt, who ruled Palestine from 878–884 CE, confiscated from the Samaritans working animals and actually kidnapped people most probably in order to serve as a labour force for building the harbor in Acre.

The arrival of Byzantium on the scene also had a bearing on the circumstances of the non-Muslim population in the Holy Land. When the Arab allies supported by Byzantium had the upper hand the position of the local Christians was strengthened and the Jews were exposed, while at other times it was the Christians who suffered.

In 966 the church of the Holy Sepulchre was attacked and robbed and the Ikhshidid ruler of Jerusalem burned the church with the Patriarch of Jerusalem, Yuhanna ibn Jami', alive inside it. On the other hand, after truces or peace agreements were signed between the Fatimids and the Byzantines the conditions of the Christians improved considerably; the Holy Sepulchre was rebuilt, and lavish Easter processions were led openly in Jerusalem in the presence of the local governor. However when relations between the two deteriorated again, the Fatimid ruler al-Hakim ordered the destruction of all churches in his domain; among these was the Holy Sepulchre, which was destroyed in 1009, an order that was revoked just a few years later. The church was rebuilt again in 1042, with the help of the Byzantine Emperor Constantine Monomachos. Several years later, in 1056, the Fatimid caliph al-Mustansir Bi-Allah (1036–1094), having heard that a prayer for the well-being of the Abbasids had been said in Constantinople, ordered the church to be robbed of its treasures. The Byzantine support of the Christians worsened the plight of the Jews in Palestine, and in Jerusalem in particular, and their situation declined significantly during the 11th century, as is made clear by documents from the aforementioned Cairo Geniza.

The deteriorating conditions also served as a strong catalyst for the process of conversion to Islam in Palestine which will be discussed in the section dealing with that topic below. The changes which occurred in the land throughout this period are clearly reflected in the new map of the Patriarchate of Jerusalem; most of the former bishoprics and even archbishoprics which previously played a pastoral role, serving the local communities, had now become titular bishoprics and their bishops were actually sitting in the court of the Patriarch in Jerusalem; only sixteen of the former thirty-one active bishoprics continued to exist. New emphasis was now put on the holy places, the strategic assets of the Patriarchate of Jerusalem, where several new bishoprics were founded. These included Nazareth, Thabor, Sebastiya, Neapolis, the Jordan Monasteries, Sinai, and Pharan.

The legal status of the non-Muslims

During the 8th and 9th centuries the legal and social status of the population was also going through a major transformation. The status of the non-Muslim population in the conquered lands was based on Sura 9:29 in the Qur'an: 'Fight those who do not believe in God or in the Last Day and who do not consider unlawful what God and His Messenger have made unlawful and who do not adopt the religion of truth from those who were given the Scripture—[fight them] until they pay the *jizya* according to their ability, while they are humbled.' The *Jizya* was a special tax imposed upon non-Muslims of the 'People of the Scripture' (in Palestine referring to Christians, Jews, and Samaritans), who thereby acknowledged the authority of the Muslims in return for becoming *dhimmis* or Protected People. In fact, throughout the 7th century, the payment of the *Jizya* was the main, and at many times, the only requirement from the non-Muslim population who submitted to the Muslims, mostly by signing surrender agreements that were made usually with specific cities or regions. As noted above (in 'The conquest of Palestine'), these agreements included specific clauses guaranteeing the personal and communal property of the conquered, their prayer-houses, their religious freedom, and in general their right to continue their lives as before. This meant that unless a city was conquered by force, when often property was confiscated and people were taken captive, life was not disrupted and a sense of continuity prevailed despite the tumultuous events. Moreover, the Muslim presence seems initially not to have been felt in everyday life.

All of this was changing, slowly but surely, in the two following centuries, as the Muslims secured their position as lords of the land, and their presence was felt more and more throughout the caliphate in general. The changing social equilibrium brought with it a gradual change in the social status of the non-Muslims who from the reign of 'Umar II (717–720) were required to change their appearance in the public sphere in order to differentiate themselves from the Muslim population (e.g. ride on a pack-saddle rather than a regular saddle, wear their hair differently, wear a special girdle, and not wear certain prestigious articles of clothing). In the second half of the century the caliph al-Mansur issued various orders regarding non-Muslims, one of which was the tattooing of their hands. This trend became regularized after the year 800 when a rigid set of guidelines regarding the appearance and social behaviour of the non-Muslims called 'The Pact of 'Umar' (*Shurut 'Umar*) became the accepted rule, and replaced the former liberal surrender agreements. This new 'treaty', allegedly signed by 'Umar al-Khattab during the conquest, included a prohibition on building new prayer-houses, a list of restrictive measures regarding religious customs such as refraining from calling to prayer by beating a wooden clapper (*naqus*), praying loudly, forming public processions on holidays and funerals, displaying crosses and lights on the roads, and selling pigs and wine. Other clauses refer to the appropriate behaviour towards Muslims, including the obligation to give them priority in seating and on the road, to respect them, not to peek into their houses, be buried next to them, or own Muslim slaves. A series of stipulations regarding signs of differentiation (*ghiyar*) include the obligation to wear a distinctive girdle (*zunnar*) and clothing of a certain colour, and prohibitions on imitating the appearance of Muslims, bearing arms, using saddles, adopting Arabic seals, and teaching their children Arabic.

Although laws and regulations can easily become dead letters, in this case there are not only unequivocal reports that these laws were imposed by the caliph al-Mutawakkil (847–861) as well as several other caliphs throughout the caliphate, but that they were in fact strictly enforced in Palestine in certain periods. The Samaritan Chronicle, which is a contemporary witness, describes in great detail the enforcement of al-Mutawakkil's restrictions and the efforts made by the Samaritans to evade some of them, specifically the demand to affix 'a wooden idol' to their doorpost, an order which after significant intervention was replaced by the image of a candelabrum. These same restrictions, almost word for word, are again imposed on the non-Muslims of Palestine in the reign of Ahmad ibn Tulun (in Palestine 878–884). One should take into account that the region of Samaria was mainly a rural one, whose population was composed by the second half of the 8th century not only of Samaritans but of newly arrived Muslims as well. This report indicates the attention to the enforcement of these restrictions by these rulers. Although one cannot vouch that the regulations listed in the Pact of 'Umar were consistently imposed, they seem to have nevertheless set some sort of standard regarding the inferior social position of non-Muslims living among the Muslims.

Arabization

While the Muslims were establishing their own status and defining their identity in the face of the local inhabitants, the identity of the local population was going through a highly significant change as well. Although Arabs were not a new arrival in Levantine society, they had been a marginal element. Following the conquest, the tables were turned: Arab language, manners, and culture were now those of the ruling strata. The effects of this change were dramatic as the three non-Muslim communities in Palestine went through a rapid process of Arabization. Already towards the end of the 7th century bilingual Greek-Arabic administrative documents are found among the papyri discovered at the Byzantine frontier town of Nessana in the Negev desert. During the 8th century Arabic would become the common spoken as well as the common written language among the various non-Muslim communities in the Holy Land: Christians, Jews, and Samaritans. The adoption of the Arabic language was accompanied by various other elements such as the Arabic name form (patronymic, i.e. son of x, and surname giving origin or profession or the like, e.g. al-Antaki/of Antioch, al-Haddad/the blacksmith), Arab dress codes (which as noted above created at times social tension with the ruling elites), Arab literature and literary conventions, and so on. At the same time that the Arabs were assimilating a whole body of knowledge from the late antique world that was passed down to them by non-Muslim scholars, the non-Muslims in their turn were embracing Arab culture.

Among the Christians of Palestine we find that already in in 772 a hagiographical composition on the Martyrs of Sinai is translated from Greek into Arabic. Psaltaria in Arabic exist already in the 8th century, some of which are bilingual or multi-lingual (Greek-Syriac-Arabic), and by 885 Easter hymns for Good Friday are sung in the Arabic language. This rapid transition may be explained by the fact that during the Byzantine period the bulk of the local Christian community spoke a local dialect of Aramaic called Christian Palestinian Aramaic (CPA) while only the leadership was versed in Greek. The literary corpus of this community was based completely on translations from Greek; thus, on the one hand, there was no cultural heritage to lose by translating the texts yet once more, while on the other the transition to Arabic from a similar Semitic language was both simple and advantageous. The manifestation of this rapid transition is to be found in the vast translation endeavour which took place in the monasteries of the Judean desert during the first centuries of Islam, when hagiographical literature, sermons, writings of church fathers, and Scriptures were translated from Greek, often via Aramaic, into Arabic, which had clearly become the language of the local Christian community. Unlike in the case of CPA, a few original Christian theological compositions are also known in Arabic, a fact which testifies to the depth of penetration of the language. The members of this community also adopted Arab name forms, as well as the Hijri dating system (counting from Muhammad's migration from Mecca to Medina in 622), which is used in almost all of the known Palestinian Christian manuscripts written in Arabic starting from 772 CE.

Among Jews, too, the Arabic language replaced Aramaic from an early stage, and much material in or about The Land of Israel (*Eretz Yisra el*) in Arabic is to be found in the Cairo Geniza. Jewish manuscripts in Arabic are to be found already in the 8th century. However, unlike the Christians, who wrote Arabic in Arabic letters, the Rabbinic Jews transliterated the Arabic into Hebrew letters (Qaraite Jews, who accepted only the Jewish Bible without later Rabbinic material, preferred to write Arabic in Arabic letters; Samaritans used both Arabic letters and the traditional Samaritan script). At first this transliteration was random and depended on the writer, but around the turn of the 10th century a conventional system of transliteration was established. The great scholar R. Sa'adya Gaon played a central role in systematizing the transliteration, as well as the translation of the Bible and the Jewish prayerbook (*siddur*) into Arabic. The dialect, called Judeo-Arabic, was interspersed with Hebrew and Aramaic words.

Despite this rapid and wide transition to Arabic, Jews continued to fully use both Hebrew and Aramaic in their writing, mostly in sentences which were dispersed within the Arabic texts. Jews used Arabic not only for everyday business, including letters and documents, but also for Bible commentaries, rabbinic responsa, and legal literature. Moreover, Jews also translated from Arabic into Judeo-Arabic classical Arabic literature, including the Qur'an, and literary classics such as *A Thousand and One Nights*. While in the field of prose Judeo-Arabic pushed aside the other languages this was not the case with poetry, which had developed in the Land of Israel in late antiquity and had become very popular. It continued to be composed in Hebrew even after Arabic had become the spoken language of the Jews, adopting along the way some characteristics of Arabic poetry. Thus, unlike the Christians, the Jews seem to have taken

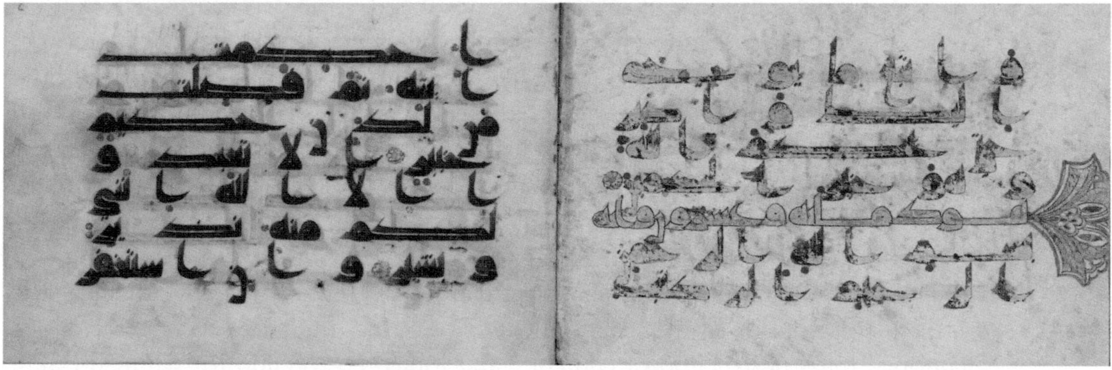

The beginning of Surat Hud from a 9th-century Qur'an written in Kufic script.

An Arabic manuscript dated 885 CE from the Palestinian monastery of Mar Sabas, containing fragments of spiritual and ethical treatises attributed to St Ephrem.

some more care to differentiate themselves linguistically from their Muslim surroundings and to preserve their identity. Judeo-Arabic was in fact a distinct dialect that drew a line between the two communities. The Jewish community also continued to preserve the special status of Hebrew as the ancient Holy Language.

Conversion to Islam

The wide-ranging process of Arabization testifies to the familiarity between the Muslim society and the non-Muslim communities in various areas of life. This close interaction was no doubt one of the factors that paved the way for the other process that was slowly starting to occur, the process of Islamization of both individuals and groups from the non-Muslim communities. It should be noted that Islam, as a rule, was against forced conversion. This view was based on a Qurʾanic passage: 'There is no coercion in religion' (2:256). An exception occurred during the days of the Fatimid caliph al-Hakim bi-Amr Allah who ruled in Egypt and was in control of Palestine between 996–1021. During his reign a series of harsh restrictions was imposed on non-Muslims, including unusual measures such as the above-mentioned mass destruction of churches, and forced conversion to Islam. Al-Hakim retracted these restrictions after a few years, and, making an exceptional decision, allowed non-Muslims who had been forced to convert to return to their religion. However, this was an unusual occurrence, and the process of Islamization was mostly a voluntary one (though of course economic and social pressures played a part in individual decisions to convert).

Very little explicit information exists regarding the Islamization of the non-Muslim communities. What we do know is that by the beginning of the 16th century, when the Ottomans carried out a census in Palestine, Muslims were in a majority. We can therefore deduce that the process of Islamization occurred in the 900 years between 634 and 1516. Nevertheless, diverse pieces of information allow us to piece together an outline of the process. The sources indicate that on the eve of the Crusader conquest of Palestine there was still a non-Muslim majority, first and foremost Christians, as well as Jews and Samaritans. The geographer al-Muqaddasi, who writes *c.*980, notes when describing Jerusalem that 'few are the learned here, many are the Christians, and these make themselves repugnant in the public places...The Christians and the Jews are predominant here and the mosque devoid of congregations and assemblies.' He also emphasizes that in Palestine the majority of the scribes and physicians are Christian, while bankers, moneychangers, and tanners are Jews. The information regarding the scribes is corroborated by other sources as well. Despite his discontent with the Christians, he nevertheless lists the Christian feasts and months, and cites Christian proverbs like: 'When St Barbara's feast arrives (rain season) the builder takes up his flute', or 'When the Kalends (1 January) come, keep warm and stay at home.'

This indicates clearly that Christian traditions and customs still prevailed in al-Muqaddasi's time. A contemporary of his, al-Tamimi, who was a Jerusalemite Muslim physician, tells about the building of churches, the wide dissemination of wine-drinking and pig breeding, both of which were prohibited to Muslims, and describes the extent of viniculture in the area of Jerusalem. He too notes that most physicians in the land are Christian, having himself studied with a Christian physician. One hundred years later Ibn al-'Arabi, a Muslim traveller from Seville to the Holy Land, recounts how 'we argued with its Christians, the land was theirs, they are tilling the land, cling to its monasteries, and attend its churches'. During the Crusader period the court that ruled for non-Muslims in the land was called the 'Court of the Syrians', indicating that most of the population were still Christians who had in the past spoken Aramaic (*suryaye* was the local word for Christians who spoke Aramaic, particularly the dialect known as Syriac). In 1280 the famous traveller Burchard of Mount Zion notes that 'Syrians live in the land and the country is full of them'. All this indicates that there was no massive process of conversion to Islam in the early Muslim period.

For instances of conversion we are mostly reliant on chance mentions in our sources. We have, for example, an anecdote about a monk who embezzled money and in order to evade punishment chose to convert, as well as several hagiographies that tell about Christians who converted to Islam but chose later to revert to Christianity.

The penalty for such defiance of Islam under Muslim law was death, and after having been forewarned three times these converts elected to die as martyrs. These hagiographic stories only imparted this information in order to serve as edifying tales for the Christian community, warning of the dangers of conversion and the merit of staying true to their faith. From Jewish sources we have the example of Ya'qub ibn Killis, a Jew who had served as the supervisor of the merchants in Ramla and who, on account of financial trouble, had converted to Islam and become a powerful figure under the Fatimid administration of Egypt. And in the Cairo Geniza there is information regarding Jews in Egypt and in Palestine who were forbidden to divorce their wives after having converted to Islam.

The Samaritan chronicle provides us with more substantial information. On several occasions it reports openly about occasions of mass conversion to Islam. Only one of these has to do with forced conversion by a local Muslim thug, while three others all talk about extreme situations of financial and physical difficulty, at a time of rising prices and taxes, and especially the *jizya* tax, which was an extra load, unique to non-Muslims, all of which drove many families to convert to Islam out of desperation. It should be kept in mind, however, that the area of Samaria, which was sparsely settled at the beginning of the period, drew many Muslims to it, and the Samaritans were by the 8th century a comparatively small and vulnerable community. Such mass conversion to Islam during this period cannot therefore serve as an indication of similar mass conversion among the Christian and Jewish communities, who were still much more resilient and unlike the Samaritans also had backing from their communities outside of Palestine. Nevertheless the open reports in the Samaritan chronicle are an important indication of the mechanism that could lead to the mass conversion of families of the various communities to Islam. There is therefore good reason to believe that by the end of the 11th century there was still a majority of non-Muslims living in Palestine, and most scholars believe that an accelerated process of Islamization took place only after the Crusades, during Ayyubid and Mamluk rule.

Culture and innovation

The Patriarchate of Jerusalem, led by the monastic community of the Judean desert, had grown to be an important cultural centre within the Byzantine church in the 4th to 6th centuries. Despite the trauma caused by the Muslim conquest it continued to hold this position until the beginning of the 9th century. This continuity was due probably to the nature of Umayyad rule, which was characterized by political and economic stability. Members of the Greek elite of the Patriarchate continued to cultivate Greek learning. In fact, during the 8th century, a period of dearth in cultural activity in Constantinople that was at the time struggling for its survival, Greek culture in Palestine flourished. During the 7th and 8th centuries sundry figures that were part of the leadership of the local church continued to write hymns, saints' lives, sermons, and philosophical and theological treatises in Greek. Most famous among these is John of Damascus (d. *c.*750), the last of the Greek church fathers and the greatest theologian of his time, a renowned fighter against the Iconoclastic movement, who wrote the famous 'Fountain of Knowledge' as well as various polemical treatises and hymns. Other leading cultural figures are Patriarch Sophronius (d. 638), a hymnographer, philosopher, and theologian, and his good friend Maximus the Confessor (d. 662), the famous theologian; Andrew of Crete (d. *c.*740), known for his sermons, theological treatises, and hymns, and Michael the Syncellus (d. 846) who wrote among other things a Greek grammar around the year 800. It is important to note that all of the figures mentioned here were locals who were naturally versed in the local languages (CPA and later Arabic), yet wrote in Greek as this was their literary language.

While the leadership of the Patriarchate would continue to write Greek well into the 11th century, there is ample evidence that beginning in the second half of the 8th century the greater part of the community, including the monks of the Judean desert, were already translating into Arabic and even drafting original compositions in Arabic. Most famous among the writers in Arabic at this period was the theologian Theodore Abu Qurra. Born in Harran, he is reported by contemporary sources to have spent long periods in Mar Saba monastery and considered himself a disciple of John of Damascus. Beside this exceptional figure, there were some indigenous writers who are known to have written in Arabic, such as Stephen of Ramla, who in 877 penned a treatise on the Trinity and the Incarnation and an anonymous essay called 'The Book of Proof', which among other things emphasizes and enumerates thirty sacred sites in the Holy Land. However, the deteriorating conditions, the lack of security, droughts and plagues, and excessive taxation described above were not conducive to the well-being of monasteries and their inhabitants. The great monastery of Mar Saba continued to preserve the heritage of the Patriarchate, but it was now gradually losing its standing as a liturgical centre to Byzantium.

A similar pattern can be observed for Jewish spiritual life in the Holy Land, namely a vibrant burst of creative energy in late antiquity and Umayyad times, but then a slow decline under Abbasid rule. Cultural activity was now more centred in the Jewish communities of Babylonia and Cairo where conditions were much more favourable. The Jewish community of Palestine did nevertheless make one contribution of immense importance in the 10th century. The family of Ben Asher, living at the time in Tiberias, was responsible for the standardization of pronunciation, paragraph and verse divisions, and cantillation of the Jewish Bible (*Tanakh*), thus generating the Masoretic text of the Hebrew Bible that has been in use ever since. The Palestinian Gaonate, both an academy and a legislative authority, continued to be active in Jerusalem during most of the 11th century, although its output was meagre in comparison to that of the Babylonian Gaonate, which was considered superior.

As for the Muslims of Palestine, although they were the lords of the land, they too suffered from the unstable situation. We are familiar with a number of writers, such as those of the Praises of Jerusalem Literature or al-Muqaddasi, who were based in

The Aleppo codex, a tenth-century Masoretic text of the Hebrew Bible written in Tiberias.

Palestine, and we can find in biographical dictionaries lists of religious scholars (*'ulama*) who composed legal and theological texts during this period, but in comparison to the centres in Iraq, Egypt, and Spain it is true that Palestine saw much less literary activity and produced much fewer leading lights of scholarship and science. Evidently the deterioration of the political, economic, and security situation in Palestine from the middle of the 8th century had left its mark on all the communities living in the Holy Land.

CHAPTER 8
The Holy Land in the Crusader and Ayyubid Periods
(1099–1250)

CAROLE HILLENBRAND

'If I forget thee, O Jerusalem, let my right hand forget her cunning.'
(Psalm 137, verse 5)

Moses said to his people... 'My people... go into the holy land (*al-ard al-muqaddasa*) which God has ordained for you.'
(Qur'an, chapter 5, verses 20–1)

A brief historical overview of the Holy Land, 1099–1291

WHEN Pope Urban II made his famous call to Crusade in 1095, the vast Muslim world, stretching from Spain to Central Asia, was divided in both politics and religion. The two great empires of the time, the Shi'ite Fatimids of Egypt and the Sunni Seljuqs of Iran, were in serious decline; Syria and the Holy Land were governed by mutually hostile Turkish chieftains. In the later 1090s Jerusalem was in the hands of two Artuqid Turcoman brothers, Sukman and Il-Ghazi, vassals of the Seljuq Turkish sultans further east. In 1098 al-Afdal, the vizier of the Fatimid caliph, seized Jerusalem just before the arrival of the Franks in 1099.

So the forces of the First Crusade reached a Muslim world which was disunited and unprepared. Never had it faced an attack from such an unexpected quarter. Moreover, the religious concept of *jihad*, which had rallied the faithful in earlier centuries to defend and extend the frontiers of Islam, had long lain buried and forgotten. It was a perfect moment for Western Christian Europe to strike.

The fall of Jerusalem in 1099 and the subsequent formation of four Crusader states—Edessa, Antioch, Jerusalem, and Tripoli—was accomplished with little Muslim resistance. A military response from the Muslims was slow to come. There was an isolated Muslim victory in 1119 under the Artuqid ruler of Mardin, Najm al-Din

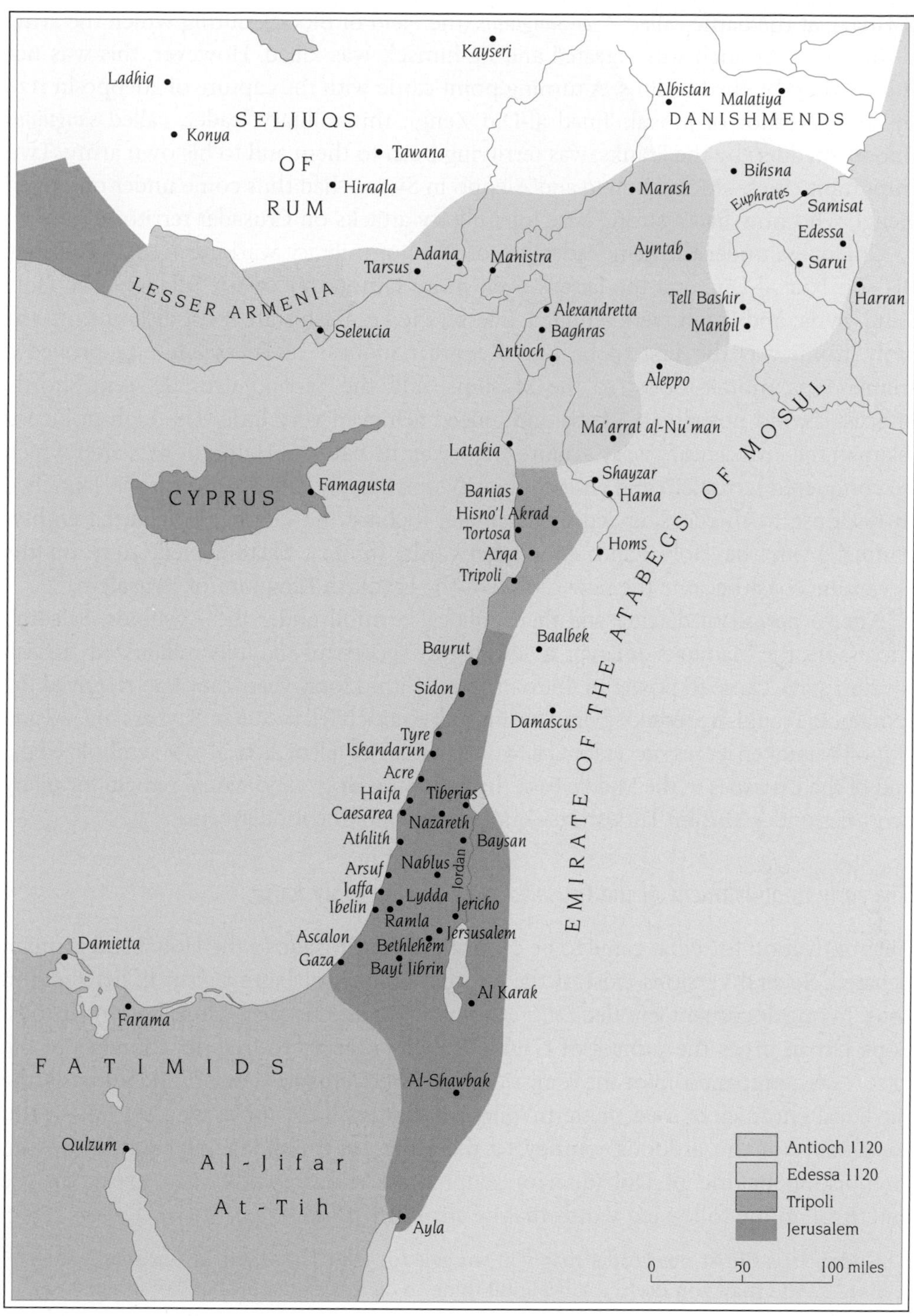

6. Map of the Crusader states in Palestine, Syria, and Anatolia

Il-Ghazi, at the battle called *Ager Sanguinis* (the Field of Blood), during which the army of Roger of Antioch was defeated and he himself was killed. However, this was not followed up by the Muslims. A turning point came with the capture of Aleppo in 1128 by the governor of Mosul, 'Imad al-Din Zengi; this military leader, called *sanguinus* (blood-shedder) by the Franks, was terrifying both to them and to his own army. Two important cities—Mosul in Iraq and Aleppo in Syria—had thus come under one ruler, Zengi, who now had a strong base for military attacks on Crusader territory.

Gradually, under the firm leadership of Muslim military warlords—such as Zengi, his son Nur al-Din, and the latter's even more famous successor Saladin—the Holy Land, Syria, and Egypt were reunited. Edessa, the Frankish state most distant from the Holy Land, was the first to be lost. Zengi's conquest of Edessa in 1144 proved a tremendous morale boost to the Muslims, and the Second Crusade, sent shortly afterwards, did not regain Edessa and indeed achieved very little. The high point for Islam in the 12th century was Saladin's victory at the battle of Hattin in 1187, after which he conquered Jerusalem and entered the city in triumph. The Third Crusade, launched in response to this loss, ended in stalemate, Richard the Lionheart departed empty-handed from the Holy Land; soon afterwards, in 1193, Saladin died. Acre on the Levantine coast became the new capital of the Frankish Kingdom of Jerusalem.

After a period of détente and then political turmoil under the Ayyubids, Saladin's successors, the Mamluks of Egypt, a new, highly successful and fully militarized Turkish Muslim state, came to power in Cairo in 1250. Within forty years they had removed the remaining Frankish presence from Muslim soil; Antioch fell to Sultan Baybars in 1268 and Tripoli was taken by his successor Qalawun in 1289. The fall of Acre in 1291 symbolized the end of the Crusades in the Middle East; thereafter the Holy Land would remain for many centuries under Muslim Turkish rule until the dawn of the modern era.

The early establishment of the Crusader states in the Holy Land

The motivation for what came to be called the First Crusade to the Holy Land is much debated. Several versions exist of the famous sermon of Pope Urban II, delivered in 1095. In one document, entitled *Letter of Instruction to the Crusaders*, dated December 1095, Pope Urban urges the princes of Gaul and their subjects 'to free the churches of the East.... as a preparation for the remission of all their sins'. In view of this emphasis, the medieval chroniclers used the term 'pilgrims' (*peregrini*) for those who set out east in 1096–1097 on the arduous journey to the Holy Land seeking salvation. However, Archbishop Baldric of Dol (d. 1130), emphasizes a more militaristic aspect of the enterprise in the following words that he attributes to the Pope:

> Under Jesus Christ our Leader may you struggle for your Jerusalem, in Christian battle-line.... And may you deem it a beautiful thing to die for Christ in that city in which he died for us.*

* See Further Reading for sources of all extracts in this chapter.

Modern statue of Saladin in Kerak, Jordan.

On 10 March 1098, Baldwin of Boulogne took over the Armenian Christian principality of Edessa and founded the first Frankish state in the Middle East—the County of Edessa. On 3 June of the same year the main body of Crusaders captured Antioch and in January 1099 the Principality of Antioch was established under the rule of Bohemond of Sicily. The Holy City of Jerusalem fell to the Franks on 15 July 1099. On Christmas Day 1100 Baldwin of Boulogne was crowned king of Jerusalem in Bethlehem. A fourth Crusader or Frankish state, the County of Tripoli, formerly a small principality ruled by an Arab family, the Banu ʻAmmar, was founded there in 1109.

The Frankish Kingdom of Jerusalem was the largest and most important of the four Crusader states. At its greatest extent, the Kingdom occupied most of historic Palestine, bordering in the north on the County of Tripoli and in the south reaching as far as Aila on the Gulf of ʻAqaba. The area of three of these states was a long thin maritime strip; only one of them, Edessa, was situated inland. And it was the first to be lost to the Muslims. So geography dictated that the Franks had only a precarious grip on their territories and were always vulnerable.

The County of Edessa and the Principality of Antioch protected the northern and northeastern borders of Syria. The Kingdom of Jerusalem, comprising the Holy City itself, the port of Jaffa, and a few coastal and highland towns, was inevitably the most prestigious Frankish state. The provenance of the Frankish rulers was reflected in three of the states that they governed; Antioch was settled predominantly by Normans, Tripoli by Provençals, and Jerusalem by the French. Edessa, a Christian Armenian city, continued to be populated largely by Armenians.

It seems clear that in 1099 there was a general massacre of the local population, Jews as well as Muslims, by the Crusaders. On conquering the coastal towns, the Franks either killed the Muslim and Jewish inhabitants or drove them out. Most Franks settled in the towns and allowed the Eastern Christians to stay there. Some Franks, however, did live in the countryside, in or near castles or in fortified villages. Other elements of the rural population in the Frankish states included Arabic-speaking peasants, either Muslim or Eastern Christian, as well as some small Jewish communities in Galilee, the Druze in the mountains above Sidon, and the Samaritans near Nablus. This, then, was a multi-confessional land.

Only Franks and Eastern Christians were allowed to live in Jerusalem itself, in addition to a frequently changing pilgrim population. Between 1100 and 1120 the Jerusalem population was so small that only the earlier Christian quarter near the Church of the Holy Sepulchre was inhabited. King Baldwin I moved Syrian Christians from Transjordan and settled them in the former Jewish quarter of the city. By the 1180s the population of Jerusalem numbered between 20,000 and 30,000. According to John of Würzburg, who visited Jerusalem in the early 1160s, the residents of the city were mostly French, with some Italians, Spaniards, and Germans, as well as Eastern Christians of many sects.

Within Jerusalem the victorious Franks did not destroy the Dome of the Rock and the al-Aqsa Mosque. But centuries of generally harmonious coexistence between the

Jerusalem: the Dome of the Rock and the al-Aqsa Mosque.

three Abrahamic faiths were shattered by the European newcomers. They broke taboos and literally occupied these two sacred Islamic sites in Jerusalem. Moreover, a large golden cross was placed on the top of the Dome of the Rock, dominating the whole city.

Until 1187 the city of Jerusalem would remain the administrative centre of the Frankish Kingdom. Seven of the nine rulers of the Kingdom were crowned there, and the last coronation ceremony, that of Guy de Lusignan and Queen Sibylla, took place there on 20 July 1186. Legal matters were dealt with in the Tower of David and to the east of it a new royal palace was built.

Once the 'sacred geography' of Frankish Jerusalem had been established, special events in its history were celebrated. The conquest of the city in 1099 was commemorated by a solemn event on 15 July every year. A procession led by the patriarch moved from the Church of the Holy Sepulchre to the al-Aqsa Mosque, renamed the *Templum Domini* (the Temple of the Lord). Pilgrims on their sacred itineraries also visited the Temple of the Lord and the Dome of the Rock, renamed the *Templum Solomonis* (the Temple of Solomon). When a coronation ceremony took place in Jerusalem, the royal processions moved from the Church of the Holy Sepulchre to the Temple of the Lord, where the king laid down his crown on the altar.

The European newcomers to the Holy Land had no experience of the conditions and way of life there. They were in an alien place. They rarely knew Arabic. They were not Muslims. They were dressed in a different way from the indigenous populations in the Holy Land. Inevitably, after the initial exultation of victory had begun to recede there were problems to be solved; above all, how to survive as a foreign minority in the land they had conquered.

During the next few decades the Franks extended their rule over the whole of the Holy Land, using a variety of strategies, including alliances, treaties, and military conquest. There were frequent examples of pragmatic, opportunistic, short-lived economic and military alliances across the ideological divide during their early presence in the Holy Land. Shared local interests were more important, especially when hostile Muslim aggressors came from outside the region; 'We do not want anybody from the east' was the slogan of local rulers, both Frankish and Muslim, in the Holy Land. In 1108–1109 King Baldwin I of Jerusalem and the Turkish ruler Tughtegin of Damascus agreed to share the revenues from the harvests of lands west of Lake Tiberias and the upper Jordan. In 1115, when the Seljuq sultan Muhammad sent an army into Syria, the Muslim armies of Aleppo and Damascus actually allied with Roger of Antioch, defeating the sultan's forces at the battle of Danith. In this way, the Franks could slot easily into an already existing context of small, fleeting alliances between the Muslim rulers in the region, and they were able to exploit this situation to their own advantage.

On the other hand, the Franks were keen to consolidate their position and also to expand their hold on the Holy Land by military means. From a very early stage their leaders depended a great deal on the assistance of the Italian maritime republics who provided a de facto navy. In return for helping the Franks to conquer the Levantine ports, the Italians received commercial privileges and special quarters in some of the ports. Baldwin I was helped by the Genoese to take Arsuf and Caesarea in 1101 and by the Pisans to capture Acre in 1104. The Venetians assisted in conquering Sidon in 1110 and, after their participation in the conquest of Tyre in 1124, they were rewarded with one-third of the city and were almost completely exempt from the payment of customs duties. The result of this cooperation between Frankish leaders and the Italian maritime republics led to the formation of separate enclaves within the ports, which were not under the jurisdiction of the Frankish ruler, and which were administered by officials sent from Italy. In the mid-13th century, the situation deteriorated, leading to internal conflicts amongst the Italians, which came to be known as the 'War of St Sabas'.

The Frankish need to have access to the Levantine ports was crucial. By gaining possession of these, reinforcements in men and supplies could be sent safely from Europe. The necessary human resources would not only be military men; experts in building techniques, quarrymen, stonemasons, merchants, shopkeepers, millers, armourers, grooms, doctors, priests, scribes, and many other categories of worker were needed.

The greatest concentration of Frankish settlement was along the Levantine coast, in Antioch, Tripoli, Tyre, and Acre; by the 1120s Acre had replaced Tyre as the major market of that area. In these ports with their flourishing markets, alongside the Italians, the Frankish settlers acted as middlemen, using their contacts in a countryside inhabited predominantly by Muslims and with local urban manufacturing workshops. The resident merchants bought products for their own use, such as textiles, glassware, and ceramics, either from local manufacturers or imported from further east. Silks from Antioch and Tripoli and cotton fabrics woven in Tyre were in demand in Europe. The markets traded in sugar, spices, and slaves. The Frankish states also had agriculturally rich areas which produced sugar, fruits, wheat, olives, and wine. Muslim geographical writings and Jewish merchants' letters, found amongst the famous Geniza documents in Cairo, both emphasize that a major export from the Holy Land was olive oil and its by-products, including soap.

In matters of trade, commercial considerations prevailed over ideology and Franks and Muslims engaged in trade with each other throughout the time of Frankish rule in the Holy Land and thereafter. The German scholar Michael Köhler has argued that, especially during the first half of the 12th century, many commercial treaties were signed between Franks and Muslims. In order to protect their mercantile interests, Muslim traders needed access to the Levantine ports, most of which were in Frankish hands for long periods of time. The Damascene chronicler, Ibn al-Qalanisi, mentions in his account of the year 1111 that the Muslim governor of Ascalon, Shams al-Khilafa, made a truce with Baldwin because he was 'more desirous of trading than of fighting'. The Spanish Muslim traveller, Ibn Jubayr, who visited Acre in 1184, describes it as 'the focus of ships and caravans, and the meeting-place of Muslim and Christian merchants from all regions'. Some Muslim, and even more Eastern Christian scribes were employed by the Franks. According to Ibn Jubayr, there were Arabic-speaking Christians working in the customs house at Acre.

The military Orders in the Holy Land

A crucial element in the continuing survival of the Franks in the Holy Land were the Knightly Orders. Amongst those orders that were present there, two major ones stand out—the Knights Hospitaller and the Knights Templar. There were also Teutonic Knights.

In the middle of the 11th century merchants from Amalfi in Italy had established the Hospital of St John in Jerusalem in the vicinity of the Church of the Holy Sepulchre; those who worked there were practising Benedictine monks, who cared for the sick and for pilgrims. In 1113 they were recognized by Pope Paschal II as a separate religious order, the Hospitallers of St John; their Grand Master, Gerard Thom, was given the title of Rector of the Hospital. Soon, from 1136 at the latest, a key military role emerged for the Hospitallers, and under the leadership of Gerard's successor, Raymond du Puy, they took up military duties alongside their medical ones. They were recognizable by their uniform of a red surcoat decorated with a white cross and by the Maltese cross in their capes. Their standing army of skilled cavalry proved to be invaluable to the Frankish

Model of a Teutonic knight; note the powerful simplicity of his dress, with its dramatic contrast of black and white and its emphasis on the cross.

kings and their castle-building skills were famous, as will be discussed shortly. They were often charged with the duty of protecting pilgrims from Europe for whom they hired troops to accompany them on the coastal route to and from Jerusalem. The Hospitallers benefited from generous charitable funding from Europe. By the 1170s the Hospital could house up to 2000 patients, and Saladin, after his triumphal entry into Jerusalem in 1187, was so impressed with the Hospital that he allowed it to stay open for a year so that it could leave its affairs in good order.

Another military order, the Knights Templar, was established by Hugh de Payns and Godfrey de Saint-Omer in 1119. They made a very favourable impression on King Baldwin II and he gave them the al-Aqsa Mosque for their headquarters, near his own residence at the southern extremity of the Temple Mount (the *Haram*). This proximity to the Temple Mount led to their acquiring the name 'Templars'. They repaired the underground area of the al-Aqsa Mosque, called Solomon's Stables, and used it to accommodate many horses and grooms. They protected pilgrims by organizing military convoys on the route from Jaffa to Jerusalem. They wore white surcoats and mantles with red crosses on their front.

Both these orders of warrior monks soon played a key role in the defence of the Holy Land under Frankish domination. Theirs was the responsibility of looking after the castles and citadels built or rebuilt by Frankish rulers. The military skills of the military orders were also of enormous benefit to the Crusader states in their expansionist aims. The wealth of these orders was used to assemble large armies, permanently mobilized. Their Muslim opponents, who greatly feared them, singled them out for unusual severity when they took them prisoner. The Hospitallers and the Templars put down permanent roots in the Holy Land, but the relationship of the Frankish rulers with these increasingly powerful and independent-minded military orders proved problematic as time went on. After the fall of Edessa in 1144 their role became even more important in the states of Tripoli and Antioch as they became more vulnerable to Muslim attacks.

The role of the Hospitallers and Templars was underpinned by two major concepts—the monastic life and knightly chivalry. The Archbishop of Jerusalem, William of Tyre, writing between 1170 and 1174, had mixed views about the military order; he writes positively about their early activities:

> Certain noble men of knightly rank, religious men, devoted to God and fearing him, bound themselves to Christ's service in the hands of the Lord Patriarch. They promised to live in perpetuity as regular canons, without possessions, under vows of chastity and obedience.

He stresses that their primary duty was that 'of protecting the roads and routes against the attacks of robbers and brigands'. However, his early rosy picture of the Templars recedes over time. Indeed, he specifically criticizes their immense wealth, accusing them of taking away tithes from God's churches, and saying that they 'have made themselves exceedingly troublesome'.

Muslim leaders feared and loathed the Knights Templar and Hospitaller. It is not surprising that they regarded these fighting monks as their most implacable enemies.

The Arab chronicler Abu Shama (d. 1268) quotes Saladin as saying: 'I will purify the earth of these two filthy races.... They are the most wicked of all the infidels.' And Saladin did indeed treat the Templars and Hospitallers with extreme severity after the battle of Hattin in 1187.

Frankish religious monuments and castles: a new visual landscape

What was the impact of the Franks on the Holy Land? In a word, they transformed the landscape. They did so in the most literal sense by the buildings that they erected—most obviously, their ecclesiastical monuments. The capture of Jerusalem in 1099 triggered a frenzied building boom of staggering proportions. It was in the Holy City itself that this became most evident, and the result was to make it the most intensively sacralized city on earth, putting Rome itself in the shade. This did not happen by accident. It would be at once futile and disingenuous to propose that all this construction activity was entirely religious in its aims, even though there was a very heavy concentration on buildings with a religious function. A mid-12th-century map of Jerusalem (Cambrai, Centre culturel, ms. 437, f.11) reflects this reality. Triumphalism certainly had its part to play. In a sense, every new Frankish monument was a proclamation of political and military victory. But there was more to it than this. Buildings are facts on the ground. They occupy land and in so doing they make a permanent claim to it. When that land is contested, and contested not only politically but in the extra dimension of religious faith, the stakes rise. The buildings themselves also rise accordingly, and in a very literal sense. The more impressive they are—the more lofty, the more extensive, the more richly decorated—the more of a statement they make. And here the Frankish monuments had a built-in advantage over both local Muslim structures and those of the local Eastern Christians. Over much of Western Europe, by the year 1100 Romanesque architecture, from Santiago da Compostela to Cluny to Durham to Worms, had produced abundant masterpieces from cathedrals to abbeys to parish churches, featuring massive towers, lofty barrel-vaulted naves and triple-arched west fronts packed with figural sculpture of high quality. This was the style which was imported into the Holy Land, and the impact that it must have had is hard to exaggerate. Neither the Muslims nor the local Christians could compete, especially in their post-Umayyad monuments. The religious buildings of the Eastern Christians in the Levant for the most part faithfully reflected the minority standing that these Christians had had for almost half a millennium. They were modest and did not call attention to themselves by their external form. And Jerusalem itself had little of significance to offer in the way of Muslim buildings apart from those on the Temple Mount (Al-Haram al-Sharif) itself. Very quickly, then, Jerusalem, thanks to the torrent of new buildings put up by the Franks, took on the outward semblance of a Western European city—with this crucial difference, that the proportion of religious to secular buildings was much higher. So its look was aggressively Latin Christian. And in that time and place that look had powerful implications. It claimed the holy place in the city for Frankish and not Eastern Christianity. And it expressed the confidence that the Crusaders were there to stay. Even the Dome of the Rock and the al-Aqsa Mosque, the Islamic jewels in Jerusalem's crown, were requisitioned by the Crusaders. In the al-Aqsa Mosque the Templars added large sections, mainly in the front of the building, and they refurbished the facade. The Dome of the Rock was converted into a church and consecrated on 9 April 1141. So the Jerusalem of 1185 would have been unrecognizable to anyone who had lived there a century earlier; it was propelled to a much higher visibility than it had experienced for many centuries.

The Crusader building boom, which generated over 400 ecclesiastical structures, was by no means confined to Jerusalem itself. Commemorative and other churches, as well as abbeys and monasteries, were built by the score, especially on sites with biblical associations. Thus an abbey was reworked from an ancient building in Bethany under the auspices of Queen Melisende (her sister Iveta became abbess there) and a church was built over Lazarus' tomb. Some sites became multi-confessional: at Hebron, Jews, Christians, and Muslims alike visited the remains of the Old Testament patriarchs—Abraham, Isaac, and Jacob. Given the huge scale and quantity of all this building activity, which was moreover, mostly fitted into a mere ninety-odd years, and has been faithfully recorded in a multi-volume work on Crusader churches by Professor Denys Pringle, it is noticeable that so little of it remains in good condition, though physical traces of over 200 churches remain. The virtual disappearance of such a huge body of architecture is no accident. Rather, it was an almost inevitable consequence of the Muslim reconquest, not least because the mass departure of the Franks left most of these buildings unused. Saladin died quite soon after recapturing Jerusalem, and before his death he had the Third Crusade on his hands, so he had no time to get very far with the serious task of de-Christianizing Jerusalem, let alone with giving the city a Muslim facelift. But it is significant that he did begin the long process of repurposing some Frankish Christian buildings to Muslim functions. And as in Jerusalem, so in the rest of the Holy Land. Once the Franks had gone, their religious buildings would face either transformation or ruin.

So much, then, for the ecclesiastical foundations erected in the Holy Land, which unquestionably lent town and country alike a certain Western European character. What of the secular buildings erected by the Franks? If one excludes domestic and industrial architecture, the inevitable by-products of Crusader social and commercial life—and the excavations of Israeli archaeologists have shed a flood of light on such structures, modest though they mostly are—it becomes very clear that the principal legacy of the Franks is their castles. While some of these were deliberately destroyed in the campaigns of Baybars from 1260 onwards to mop up the remaining Crusader resistance, the obvious military utility of many such castles meant that they were simply taken over by the triumphant Muslim Mamluks—after all, apart from the occasional chapel, they did not serve religious functions. Considered as a group, they neatly complement the ecclesiastical heritage of the Frankish states, with its mixed messages of religious, political, and military triumph. But here the proportions are

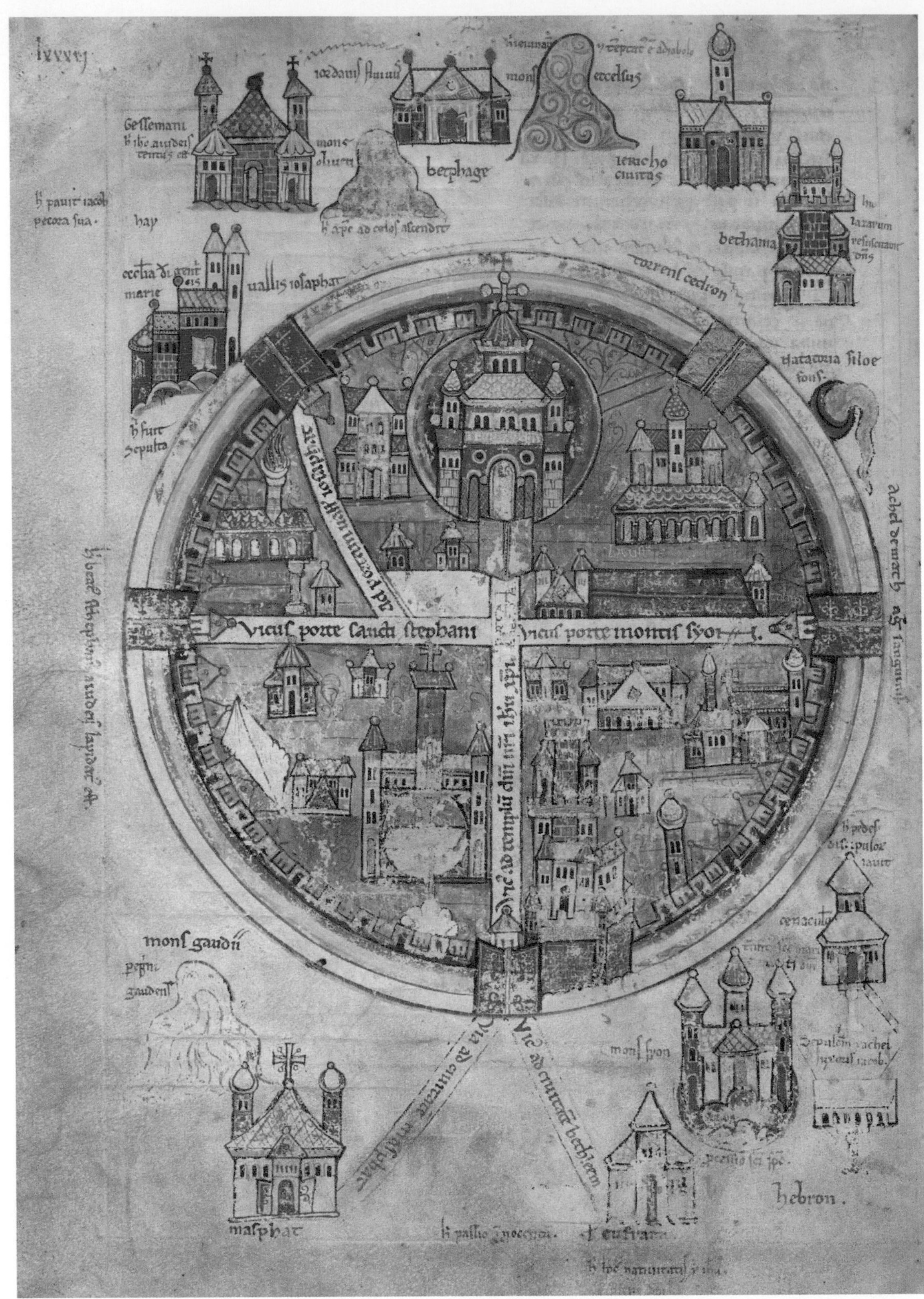

Jerusalem as medieval Christians saw it.

Crac des Chevaliers, perhaps the most perfect of medieval castles, held by the Hospitallers from 1144 to 1271.

reversed: the castles proclaim military, political and, by implication, religious supremacy. They too claim the land, and in a much more brutally obvious way than ecclesiastical architecture can. For they plainly defend that land by force of arms. The ramparts and multiple towers of Acre show the same mindset at work in an urban context.

Fortified cities were no novelty in the Muslim Near East around 1100, as the walls of Cairo, Antioch, and Diyarbakr show, but it is instructive to note that the great fortified urban complexes of Syria and the Jazira—Aleppo, Damascus, and Harran among others—postdate the great Crusader castles of the 12th century and clearly owe much to them in a technical sense. However, the matter goes deeper than this. It was the Crusaders who so decisively militarized the Syro-Palestinian landscape, lands which before their arrival had no need of castles. The isolated Muslim castles of Palestine and Syria—ʻAjlun, Shayzar or the many Ismaʻili Shiʼite examples—are therefore also a response, though of poorer quality and on a much less ambitious scale, to the Crusader challenge. A parallel may be drawn with the many Armenian castles scattered all over Cilicia—'Little Armenia'—which also reflect the inherent political instability of that short-lived kingdom, struggling to survive in a hostile environment.

Much can be deduced from both the sheer quantity of Frankish castles and their careful siting. Seen together rather than separately, they are clearly part of a strategic plan to appropriate and secure all the land that the Franks had conquered and were afraid to lose—hence their distribution across the length and breadth of the Frankish principalities. This aim explains their sometimes out-of-the-way location, such as that of Wuayra, near Wadi Musa beside Petra in the inhospitable extreme south, which had oversight of the route to the Red Sea. Many castles dominated important roads and could therefore threaten the enemy's communication and trade networks while simultaneously protecting Christian pilgrims. Even a small garrison could with impunity sally forth from such castles in lightning attacks on caravans of merchants or Muslim pilgrims. The mere threat of such attacks was enough to inhibit travel. The disadvantages of a remote location could be offset by ensuring intervisibility and communication between castles, whether by means of fire, smoke, or reflected light. Not surprisingly, therefore, steep hilltop sites (which also discouraged the use of enemy siege engines, used by Saladin to devastating effect at Belvoir) were at a premium, as were coastal sites. Pigeon post was used for longer communications. Since the Franks were a beleaguered minority that suffered from a chronic and acute manpower shortage, castles were an ideal method of making a few men do the work of many, and they did not have to be huge to be effective. The early ones were hall keeps on two floors, or tall thin towers; as many as eighty small towers have been identified in the Kingdom of Jerusalem alone. A relatively small garrison could easily store enough water and provisions to make a small castle impervious to siege. A visitor to Margat in 1212 said that the castle contained enough provisions for five years. It was a good example of those castles that were built on a much more ambitious scale to serve as bases from which to invade enemy territory or to halt enemy attacks on Frankish territory, or indeed had an important offensive role—the dispatch of raiding parties to extort tribute from surrounding Muslim areas. Small wonder, then, that some of the castles were described by Muslim chroniclers as being a bone in the throat of the Muslims. Their sheer number and their wide distribution made them a constant and irritating reminder of the Frankish presence all over the Holy Land. So although the web of control represented by the castles was at best thin, it held, and thereby exerted psychological pressure on the Muslims.

In the 12th century castle building was concentrated in three areas: northern Galilee, the south-west frontier facing Ascalon, which was in Fatimid hands, and Transjordan, from Kerak in the north to Aila in the Gulf of Aqaba in the south. By the end of the 12th century, enclosure castles were being built in remote areas to provide refuge for the whole Frankish population living there. In the 13th century, as the Franks were pushed westwards, more castles, which were fine examples of military architecture, were built towards the coast to defend what remained of Frankish territory.

The Franks brought with them the most up-to-date technology in the building and design of castles, information which had been acquired the hard way in faction-torn Western Europe with its robber barons in their impregnable keeps. And they brought the necessary experts too. These included not only architects of the highest calibre, but also stone-quarriers, masons, stone-carvers, and carpenters. The Franks did not take any short cuts in their building materials. They used massive square masonry, despite the costs involved. And they introduced numerous defensive devices that had been perfected in Europe, such as moats, dogleg entrances, projecting towers, spiral staircases that disadvantaged attackers, long expanses of smooth glacis, multiple lines of defence, including secondary ramparts which exposed the enemy to unexpected fire, and the choice of a rocky site that defeated sappers. The quality of stonework was far in advance of local Muslim work. But there was very little decoration. These castles were practical instruments of control. And the Frankish military architects could not only build on the most forbidding sites but could also tackle jaw-dropping challenges. Examples include Saone/Sahyun, which Lawrence of Arabia described as the 'most sensational thing in castle-building I have ever seen'. Here a landlocked peninsula was turned into an effective island by removing the entire mass of rock, many thousands of tons of it that joined the site to the mountains behind, leaving only a slender column of rock, easily defended, to carry a drawbridge. Monte Reale in Jordan belongs in the same heroic category, with its gigantic rock-cut well-shaft leading down 375 steps to the water source. These castles were designed to be self-supporting—hence their long gloomy galleries for stables and provisions and their vast cisterns. In case of trouble they could also serve as a safe haven for the local villagers who in happier times would provide their supplies; for it was common practice for the garrison to live in peaceful symbiosis with the nearby villagers.

A crucial advantage for the Franks was the involvement of the military orders, principally the Templars and Hospitallers (but also the Teutonic knights, who built Starkenberg/Montfort), in the entire castle-building enterprise. Their wealth allowed them to restore and maintain a network of castles and they themselves lived in them. The Hospitallers seized an existing castle in Northern Syria in 1142; their rebuilding and refurbishment of it made it the most famous of all Frankish castles—Crac des Chevaliers. It well deserves its accolade as the most perfect castle ever built. Its strategic position defended the northeastern frontier of the County of Tripoli and obstructed Muslim routes to the Levantine coast.

The involvement of the Templars and Hospitallers in the phenomenon of the castles meant that the manning and maintenance of these crucial buildings was the responsibility not of some local warlord, here today and gone tomorrow, but was in the safe hands of a corporate body of highly motivated fighting monks who had taken vows of poverty and chastity and who owed unswerving obedience to their superiors in a chain of command all the way up to their Grand Master. These orders had been set up by papal charter and their constitutions deliberately kept them apart from the petty

Sahyun or Saone castle, 12th century: the needle of rock to carry the drawbridge required the removal of thousands of tons of surrounding stone by the Franks.

political squabbles of the day. They were envisaged to last for centuries and noble families across Europe provided them with recruits.

Aspects of Frankish government and society

The Kingdom of Jerusalem imported a European model of social hierarchy, but it did not correspond exactly to that of feudal Europe. Apart from the clergy, there were only two classes below the monarch: the nobility who provided the main military forces of the Kingdom, and the merchant class, known as the burgesses. Apart from the four ruling families of the Frankish states, almost all the nobles who came there were parvenus. But such newcomers could succeed, especially by shrewd marriage alliances. The notorious Reynald of Chatillon, whose escapades down the Red Sea shocked the Muslim world and whom Saladin had personally vowed to kill, made two advantageous marriages, and Guy de Lusignan became King of Jerusalem by marrying Queen Sibylla. The burgesses comprised all those who were not nobles. In the Frankish Kingdom of Jerusalem they made up the majority of the population, but in the other three Frankish states they were outnumbered by Eastern Christians. The burgesses were in charge of local small-scale trade, but not of the international commerce which was handled by the Italians.

Muslims and Jews were not debarred from entering the Holy City for the whole time of Frankish rule there. In due course they were allowed in to conduct business and to pray, as the evidence of the famous 12th-century Arab writer of memoirs, Usama b. Munqidh, shows. No doubt, they were also needed by the conquerors to undertake crucial jobs which the Crusaders could not or would not do, serving as vendors, bath-attendants, dyers, and in other practical capacities.

There is evidence that the Franks carried on certain Muslim administrative practices that they found in place on their arrival. For example, they adopted the concept of the *muhtasib (mehtesseb)*, an official whose duty it was to visit the markets daily and to ensure that proper weights and measures were used in the markets. Moreover, it would seem that, certainly in some Frankish areas at least, Muslims were required to pay a poll tax, to the Christian Frankish government, just like the poll tax *(jizya)* Muslim governments had imposed on their Christian and Jewish subjects in the pre-Crusading period. When writing about Nablus, Ibn Jubayr mentions that its Muslim subjects 'lived as subjects of the Franks who annually collected a tax from them and did not change any law or cult of theirs'.

The population of the rural areas remained the indigenous inhabitants, Muslims, Eastern Christians, and Jews. They were responsible for the agriculture on which the Frankish cities depended. However, unlike in Europe, there were no close links between the lords who lived in the towns and the peasants who worked their lands. Ironically, too, the Western European Christians, who had come out east to rescue their Eastern co-religionists, did not provide the latter with a better life. But it is difficult to discover how Muslims lived under Frankish rule. Neither Frankish nor Muslim chroniclers show any interest in the legal or other internal administration of the subject peoples. Isolated references cannot be taken to indicate widespread practices.

Recorded external relations between the Franks and neighbouring Eastern Christian polities mostly involved marriage alliances. Links with Byzantium had not begun well. The contact between the Frankish armies en route to the Holy Land and the Christian Byzantine emperor, Alexius Comnenus, in Constantinople in 1097–1098 was not a good start. The Franks broke their promises to Alexius to hand over any territory they might gain on their way across Byzantine Anatolia. Anna Comnena, Alexius' daughter, writes in her memoirs about her father's attitude to the Crusaders:

> He feared the incursions of these people, for he had already experienced the savage fury of their attack, their fickleness of mind, and their readiness to approach anything with violence.

Nevertheless, in the absence of suitable women from Europe, the Frankish upper classes were obliged to arrange marriages with Eastern Christians. Amalric I married the Byzantine princess Maria Comnena, whilst the wife of King Baldwin II was the Armenian princess Morphia of Melitene.

In the Crusader states there is some evidence of conversion from Islam to Christianity. Some converted Muslims were employed by Frankish rulers, such as Godfrey of Bouillon or King Baldwin I of Jerusalem, or they fought in Frankish armies. Some Franks married Muslim women after they had been baptised. The Egyptian chronicler al-Maqrizi (d. 1442) mentions that the Franks often forced Muslims to convert to Christianity. James of Vitry (d. 1240), Bishop of Acre, baptised a number of Muslims, and Franciscans and Dominicans conducted successful missionary activities in the 13th century. Conversely, a number of Franks are reported to have converted to Islam, both in the heat of war and in times of peace.

The Muslim response and recovery, 1099–1187

When the First Crusade burst into the Holy Land with its dreadful carnage and bloodshed, en route to and especially in Jerusalem, the local Muslims were shocked and terrified. They had little idea of who their attackers were or why they had come. Local Muslim poets used images of rape and pollution to describe the coming of the Franks. The Frankish occupation of the al-Aqsa Mosque and the Dome of the Rock was seen as an act of grave desecration in Muslim eyes. Muslim political disunity and an absence of *jihad* feelings undoubtedly gave the zealous armies of the First Crusade the ideological edge. Even allowing for the rhetoric and exaggeration aroused by feelings of grief and humiliation, the Muslim accounts of the fall of the Holy City bear witness to terrible destruction and bloodshed. The Arab chronicler, Ibn Muyassar (d. 1278), records laconically that the Franks destroyed shrines, killed nearly all the inhabitants of the city, burned copies of the Qur'an and stole gold and silver candelabras from the Dome of the Rock. Indeed, all Muslim accounts express shock and horror at the

Minbar (pulpit) of Nur al-Din, made in anticipation of the Muslim recapture of Jerusalem, 1168–c.1174 and duly placed by Saladin in the al-Aqsa Mosque (destroyed by arson, 1969).

massacre of Muslims and Jews at the hands of the victorious Franks. And the extent of the bloodshed is confirmed by the Frankish sources themselves. The *Gesta Francorum* (The *Deeds of the Franks*) relates: 'The slaughter was so great that our men waded in blood up to their ankles.' Similar brutality was shown in other towns conquered by the

Franks, such as Ma'arrat al-Nu'man in 1098 and Haifa in 1100. A large number of Muslims were enslaved by the invaders. The fate of some cities was less brutal; Nablus, for example, surrendered without bloodshed, and in 1110, as Fulcher of Chartres (d. 1127) reports, Muslim peasants in Sidon chose to stay so that they could cultivate the land for King Baldwin I.

From 1100–1125 the military response from the Muslim side against the Franks was very limited. Isolated military victories, such as the battle of Danith or the Field of Blood, were not followed up. The joining of the Holy Land, Syria, and Egypt under one strong military ruler, combined with a revitalization *of jihad* spirit, were necessary before the Franks could be ousted from the Muslim Levant. At first the stirrings of *jihad* feeling were only minimal. Early on, during the Frankish occupation, one solitary voice, that of a Damascus preacher, al-Sulami, spoke out, warning of the dangers of allowing the Franks to take the coastal towns, and urging Muslims to wage *jihad* against them before it was too late. In his *Book of Holy War* (*c.*1106), al-Sulami blamed Frankish success on the spiritual decline and political fragmentation of the Muslim world, and he called for religious rearmament; the local Muslims must wage a personal spiritual struggle before conducting war against the Franks. These prescient words went unheeded.

Zengi is praised after his conquest of Edessa in 1144 in the Muslim sources as a martyr (*shahid*) but their portrayal of his conduct leading up to this event falls far short of the panegyrics they give to his son Nur al-Din and to Saladin the Kurd after him. These two are the *jihad* warriors par excellence; the terrifying, brutal military commander Zengi does not fit that model at all. A true yearning to repossess Jerusalem was made concrete by Nur al-Din and Saladin. Both placed the reconquest of Jerusalem at the heart of their ambitions. The Holy City simply had to be taken and it was the hitherto dormant spirit of *jihad* which triggered the unification and encirclement of Frankish lands, the necessary basis for its eventual conquest. An increasingly intense campaign of *jihad*, promoted through an alliance between the warlords and the Sunni religious classes, was focused, not on the borders of Islam, but right within the Islamic world itself, on the city of Jerusalem. According to Islamic sources it is with Nur al-Din that the *jihad* phenomenon which underpinned the eventual Muslim recapture of Jerusalem began in earnest. Both Nur al-Din and Saladin are presented in the Muslim sources as being model *mujahidun* (fighters of *jihad*), who are pursuing both the greater *jihad* (*al-jihad al-akbar*) which is a spiritual striving in the path of God to improve one's inner self, as well as the lesser *jihad* (*al-jihad al-asghar*) which is fought militarily to defend and extend the borders of Islam.

A genre of religious writing, known as the *Fada'il al-Quds* books (the *Merits of Jerusalem*) and already current in the 11th century, now regained popularity with Syrian Muslims in the time of Nur al-Din and thereafter. They became a powerful tool in the

---

Right: Muslim soldiers on parade, *Maqamat* of al-Hariri, 1237: the banners bear the text of the *shahada*, the Muslim creed.

وتحمل القفص والجبالة والقفص والذبالة انها لضغث على ابالة فانضاعت تنفض مدرجها

وتنشد مدرجها فلما دانتني قرنت بالرقعة درهما وقطعة وقلت لها ان رغبت في المشوف المعلم

واشيري الى الدرهم فوحي بالسر المدهم وان ابيت ان تشرحي فخذي القطعة واسرحي

فمالت الى استخلاص البدر التم والابلج الهم وقالت دع جدالك وسل عما بدا لك فاستطلعتها

طلع الشيخ وبلدته والشعر وناسج بردته فقالت ان الشيخ من اهل سروج وهو الذي وشى

spiritual and political *jihad* programme aimed increasingly at the Muslim reconquest of Jerusalem. Almost all the compilers of such works came from the Holy Land and Syria. It is easy to suggest clear and convincing reasons for the phenomenon of the virtual 'explosion' of works on the *Merits of Jerusalem* at this time. Such books emphasized the factors which contributed to the importance of the Holy City for Muslims, such as the associations of the Prophet with the city, his Night Journey into heaven, the special value for Muslims of dying in Jerusalem, and its role as the site of the Day of Judgement. These books were read out publicly to large audiences from 1160 onwards and helped to build up the expectation that the Holy City would be recaptured. New works of this kind were composed. In addition, an earlier *Fada'il* work by al-Raba'i (d. 1043) was read out in public in April 1187 just when Saladin's forces were preparing for the Jerusalem campaign. The Muslim concept of *jihad* was now given a more tangible focus than it had had for centuries. This programme of *jihad* was keenly supported by religious scholars in the new Sunni *madrasas* built in Damascus and Aleppo through the patronage of Nur al-Din and various amirs and bearing grandiose *jihad* inscriptions. Moreover, the *jihad* to regain the Holy City was the subject of sermons, letters, and poetry. A letter from Nur al-Din himself in the 1160s exhorts his military commanders to 'purify Jerusalem from the pollution of the cross' and he commissioned in Aleppo the building of a beautiful wooden pulpit (*minbar*) to commemorate his own role in the reconquest of the Holy City. He was deprived by death in 1174 from fulfilling his aim and installing the pulpit where he wanted it to be placed—in the al-Aqsa Mosque.

Thereafter, during much of his military career—from 1174 until his recapture of Jerusalem in 1187—Saladin presented Jerusalem as the supreme goal of his anti-Frankish propaganda. But first came the summit of his military *jihad*, his celebrated victory on 4 July 1187 over the forces of the king of Jerusalem, Guy de Lusignan, at the battle of Hattin, fought near the western shore of the Sea of Galilee against the *salibiyyin* (the bearers of the cross), as the Muslim sources often called the Franks. This memorable event led to the ultimate triumph. One of Saladin's biographers, his 'spin-doctor, 'Imad al-Din al-Isfahani, declares in a letter in 1186, with the confidence of imminent victory: 'The sabres of *jihad* rattle with joy. The Dome of the Rock rejoices in the good news that the Qur'an of which it was deprived will return to it.' Choosing the best possible day to enter Jerusalem in triumph, Saladin waited to take possession of it until Friday 27 Rajab 583/2 October 1187, the anniversary of the Prophet's Night Journey into Heaven. This event was the climax of Saladin's career, the fulfillment of his *jihad* campaign. This supreme moment of his life is described by his biographers as 'the rebirth of Islam in the Holy Land'. The great gilded cross at the top of the cupola of the Dome of the Rock was pulled down as soon as possible by Saladin's men. As Ibn al-Athir records:

> When they reached the top a great cry went up from the city and from outside the walls, the Muslims crying Allahu akbar in their joy, whilst the Franks groaned in consternation and grief.

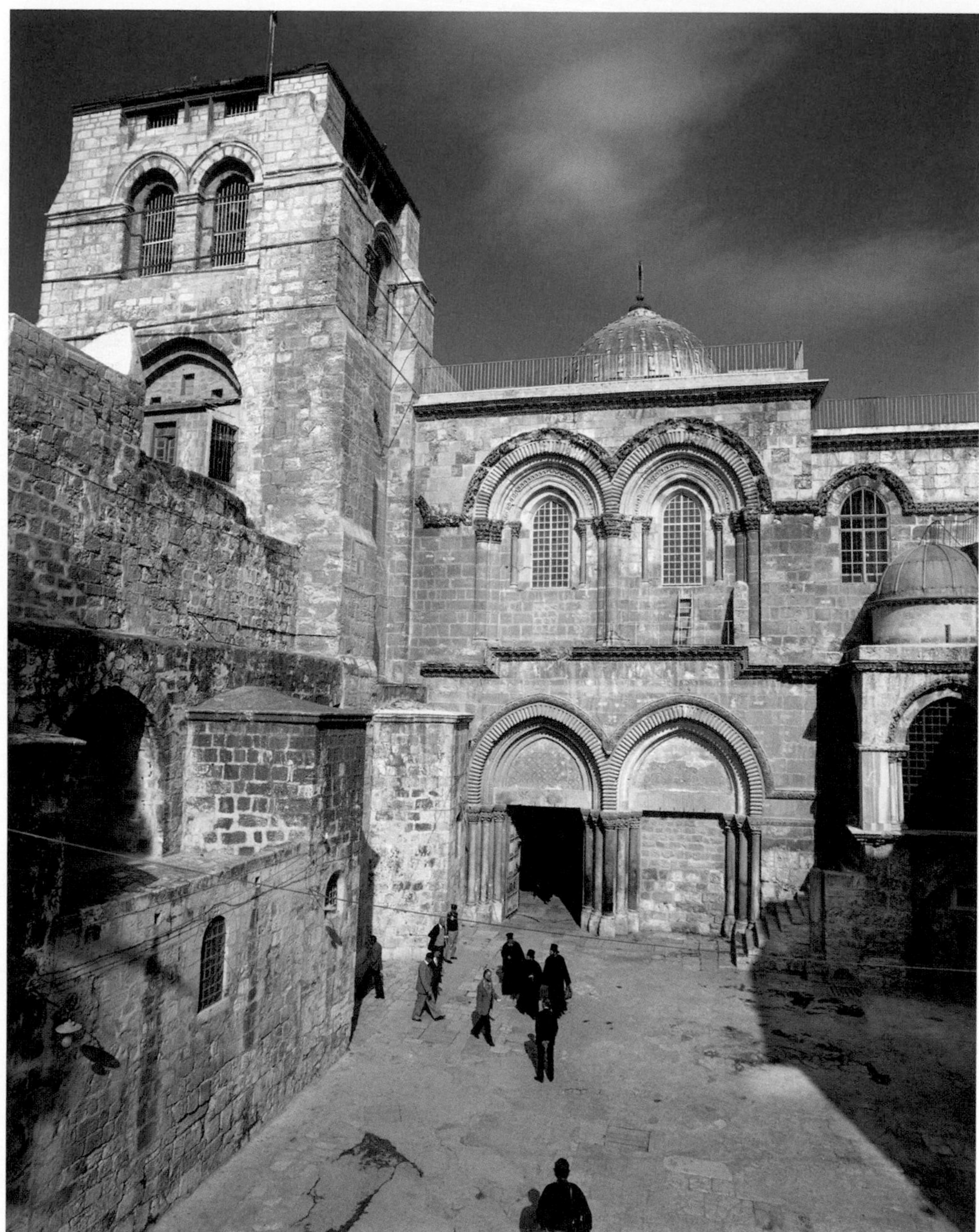

South facade of the Holy Sepulchre, Jerusalem (before 1149).

Saladin resisted the temptation to exact vengeance for the bloodshed of 1099 and was praised by Muslim and Crusader sources alike for his magnanimity towards the enemy in Jerusalem. In his triumphal sermon in 1187, the preacher Ibn Zaki, specially chosen for the occasion, proclaims: 'I praise Him . . . for his cleansing of His Holy House from the filth of polytheism and its pollutions.' On Saladin's behalf, his scribe, al-Qadi al-Fadil, wrote to the caliph in Baghdad about the conquest of Jerusalem, vigorously attacking Christian defilement and the doctrine of the Trinity: 'The earth of Jerusalem has become pure, when once it was like a menstruating woman. God has become the One when he was the Three.' This triumphal letter in Saladin's name to the caliph also records that after the battle of Hattin 'Not one of the Templars survived.'

It would take some time to transform Frankish Jerusalem into a place of Muslim visitation. Saladin made a good start. He set about purifying and re-Islamizing the Holy City. Al-Maqrizi describes this process in some detail:

> The beautiful pulpit was brought from Aleppo and set up in the Aqsa mosque. All traces of Christian worship were removed, and the Rock was cleansed with several loads of rose water. Incense was diffused and carpets spread.

The re-Islamizing of Jerusalem also involved erecting new buildings—*madrasas*, a hospital, and a Sufi hostel—and Saladin and his successors allocated pious bequests to support existing religious monuments as well as to establish new ones. A pragmatic attitude was shown to the Christians. According to al-Maqrizi, 'The Church of the Holy Sepulchre was closed and then opened and a fee determined for those of the Franks who should visit it.' After his reconquest of Jerusalem, Saladin also allowed the Jews to settle there again and they remembered him as a 'second Cyrus'. The Spanish Jewish poet, Yehudah al-Harizi, who came to Jerusalem in 1216, found three Jewish groups there; they were from the coastal town of Ascalon, North Africa, and France.

For the Crusader view of the two crowning moments of Saladin's career, the victory at Hattin and the conquest of Jerusalem in 1187, we are dependent on the inferior accounts of the continuators of William of Tyre. One of them, Ernoul, the squire of Balian of Ibelin, is able to present a favourable picture of Saladin, even in the bitter hour of defeat following the loss of Jerusalem. Ernoul praises Saladin's behaviour in Jerusalem after the conquest, pointing out his pity and kindness towards its defeated Christian inhabitants. Speaking of Saladin's magnanimity to the wives and daughters of knights in Jerusalem, Ernoul writes that he gave them so much that they praised God for it and broadcast to the world the kindness and honour which Saladin had done to them. Later, in 1192, after the truce with Richard, Saladin is shown in this same source as having pity towards Crusader lords.

Frankish-Muslim coexistence from 1099 to 1187

The study of the Holy Land under Frankish rule provides a fascinating example of cultural symbiosis. The Frankish military conquerors from Europe came to the Holy Land with very different religious beliefs, languages, customs, and not least, physical appearance. But over the period of their political dominance in the Holy Land as proto-colonialists they were undoubtedly influenced by living cheek by jowl with Muslims.

Amongst the extant information about the ways in which the Franks adopted aspects of the Muslim way of life two accounts stand out particularly, the *Book of*

Learning by Example, the autobiographical memoirs of the Arab Muslim nobleman, Usama b. Munqidh (d. 1198), and *The History of the Expedition to Jerusalem*, written by Fulcher of Chartres (d. 1127), a Christian priest who took part in the First Crusade and then worked for Baldwin I of Jerusalem. Other valuable sources include the writings of travellers who visited the Holy Land under Frankish domination.

In matters of intellect and in particular medicine, the Muslim sources express feelings of superiority over the Franks. The historian Joshua Prawer commented long ago on the fact that the cream of European scholars did not make their way to the Holy Land when it was in Frankish hands and that no Frankish educational establishment appeared while they were there. This view is supported by Benjamin Kedar who tellingly describes the Frankish clergy as possessing 'lowbrow religiosity'.

Both Muslim and Frankish accounts of the military leaders, such as Richard the Lionheart, Saladin, Guy of Lusignan, and Nur al-Din, show that both sides in the conflict shared similar chivalric values. On their side, the Muslims greatly admired the impressive castle-building skills of the Franks and their courage in war. But on an everyday level, the Franks adopted Muslim customs. They copied Muslim cooking, housing, and clothing. They even abstained from eating pork and began to veil their own women. Muslim craftsmen made works of art for the upper echelons of Frankish society.

Talk of Frankish filth and pollution was not mere rhetoric. Just as the Middle Ages in Europe were described by the 19th-century French historian Jean Michelet as 'a thousand years without a bath', so the perception *and* the reality for Muslims were that the Franks paid little heed to personal hygiene.

The Muslim traveller Ibn Jubayr writes that Frankish Acre 'stinks and is filthy, being full of refuse and excrement'. In the course of time, as Usama b. Munqidh relates with great relish and wit, some Frankish knights eagerly embraced the delights of soap and the bathhouse. However, they did not always conform to Muslim rules either inside and outside the *hammam* and in a series of 'tall stories', told in a condescending and satirical tone, Usama criticizes them for being ill-bred and boorish and lacking in proper pride towards their women folk.

On the other hand, Usama readily admits that he had friends amongst the Templars in Jerusalem who allowed him to pray in a corner of the Temple of the Lord (the al-Aqsa Mosque). Clearly he was not deterred from being in their company, despite the evidence of their filthy bodies, provided by none other than St Bernard of Clairvaux who describes the Templars as follows: 'Never overdressed, they bathe rarely and are dirty and hirsute, tanned by the coat of mail and the sun.' Yet it was these very same unwashed knights who were given permission to use the Aqsa Mosque as their headquarters and who stayed there from 1118 to 1187.

In short, the Franks who *stayed* in the Holy Land became acclimatized, 'orientalized', as Fulcher of Chartres writes:

> Consider, I pray, and reflect how in our time God has transferred the West into the East, for we who were Occidentals now have been made Orientals. He who was a Roman or a

> Frank is now a Galilaean, or an inhabitant of Palestine. One who was a citizen of Rheims or of Chartres now has been made a citizen of Tyre or of Antioch. We have already forgotten the places of our birth... Therefore why should one who has found the East so favorable return to the West?

After Saladin: the Ayyubids and the Holy Land: 1193–1250

The period in which Saladin's descendants, the Ayyubids, ruled the Holy Land can be seen as rather an anti-climax or at best a time of transition before the return of firm government under the Mamluks of Egypt in 1250. The Ayyubids governed a loose-knit and often discordant confederacy. They called themselves in their public discourse '*mujahidun*' but even in their own time they were accused of being lukewarm in their efforts to fight the Franks. The famous Arab chronicler Ibn al-Athir, (d. 1233) writes about the Ayyubids as follows: 'Amongst the rulers of Islam we do not see one who wishes to wage *jihad*.' The Crusader author of the *Rothelin Continuation of William of Tyre* also expresses an extremely negative view of Ayyubid rule; speaking of Saladin and his successors, he writes of Saladin: 'He disinherited many people and conquered more lands than all the unbelieving Muslims who ever lived before him. All his life he succeeded in everything he undertook, but as soon as he died his children lost nearly all of it.'

Whilst it is easy to be critical of Ayyubid rule in the Holy Land after Saladin, it should be emphasized that the years 1200–1250 were a deeply turbulent period for many countries, from Central Asia to Egypt and Anatolia. The Ayyubids tried to hold onto power at a time when there were dangers from both west and east. There was always the fear of further crusades from Europe. But far more terrifying was the threat of the coming of the world-conquering Mongols from the east. Ibn al-Athir in his account of the year 1219–1220 called the Mongol threat the most dangerous that Islam had ever experienced. In the wake of the conquests of Genghis Khan and his successors, seismic demographic shifts westwards began. Soon, on the borders of Ayyubid territory, there lurked groups of Qipchaq Turkish nomads from Central Asia, known as the Khwarazmians, displaced by the incoming Mongols, and themselves terrifying horse nomads. And refugees from Afghanistan and Iran began to flee westwards into Anatolia.

Saladin did not bequeath a centralized state to his heirs; on the contrary, in time-honoured steppe tradition he divided his empire amongst his sons and other close male relatives. It was soon clear that Saladin's brother, al-'Adil, who had been his main adviser and had been especially involved in drawing up the peace treaty with Richard the Lionheart in 1192, would gain the upper hand. He placed his sons in important centres of power—Aleppo, Damascus, and Cairo—and he concluded peace treaties with the Frankish ruler Amalric from 1204–1212. The Mamluk historian al-Maqrizi gives al-'Adil fulsome praise: 'The Franks made peace with him on account of the strength of his resolution, his alert prudence, his capacious intellect, his resource in stratagems.'

When the Fifth Crusade arrived in Egypt (not in the Holy Land) in 1218, al-'Adil despatched his son al-Mu'azzam 'Isa to defend Jerusalem. At that point, al-Mu'azzam

'Isa decided to dismantle the walls of the city in case it should fall into Frankish hands again. The Crusader chronicler Oliver of Paderborn (d. 1227) laments this action, saying: 'In the year of grace 1219, Jerusalem, the queen of cities, which seemed impregnably fortified, was destroyed within and without by Coradin [i.e. al-Mu'azzam].' On the death of his father that same year al-Mu'azzam governed the Holy Land from his centre at Damascus. His brother al-Kamil ruled Egypt.

Dreadful events followed. After the Fifth Crusade the Ayyubid unity that had prevailed in the face of this danger dissipated. In a fateful move in 1226, prompted by fear of his brother, al-Kamil, al-Mu'azzam invited the terrifying new power in the east, the Khwarazmians, to come and provide him with military help. For his part, al-Kamil asked the German emperor, Frederick II of Sicily, to support him. Although al-Mu'azzam was in charge of Jerusalem, al-Kamil offered to hand it over to Frederick. On the death of al-Mu'azzam the following year, al-Kamil seized Jerusalem and Nablus. By 1228 al-Kamil would have been strong enough to take the Holy Land for himself but he had already offered it to Frederick. So in what is probably the most controversial episode of Ayyubid history, the notorious peace treaty of Jaffa, signed on 18 February 1229 and lasting for ten years, Jerusalem and Bethlehem were handed back to the Franks, whilst only the al-Aqsa Mosque and the Dome of the Rock were retained as a Muslim enclave, so that Muslims could continue to pray there. Frederick entered the Holy City in triumph on 17 March that year; he stayed there for only two nights, and on 1 May he left the Holy Land. However, Frederick is shown in the Muslim sources as behaving in a deferential way towards Islam—his long familiarity with Muslims in Sicily would have prepared him for how to behave in Jerusalem.

In the 1240s Jerusalem was the victim of frequent changes of overlord, both Ayyubid and Frank. Internal disunity and rivalries caused individual Ayyubid rulers to make alliances with the Franks against their own family members. Thus the Franks re-acquired Jerusalem still unfortified briefly in the winter of 1243–1244. Once again they had the right to celebrate Christian rituals in the Dome of the Rock and the al-Aqsa Mosque. The Crusader chronicler Matthew Paris (d. 1259) reports that 'the holy city of Jerusalem is now inhabited by Christian people, all the Saracens being driven out'. The Muslim chronicler, Ibn Wasil (d. 1298) describes the situation he himself witnessed at that time in Jerusalem: 'I saw monks and priests in charge of the Rock and I saw bottles of wine for the ceremony of the Mass.' He is deeply disturbed by these Christian practices, which he says have rendered Muslim prayer in the Holy sanctuary invalid. But the Franks were destined to hold the city for only a few months.

As if the previous sordid deals struck over Jerusalem were not enough, Jerusalem was finally returned to Muslim rule in a way which was thoroughly discreditable to Islam and to those Muslims who in Saladin's time had made such sacrifices for the Holy City. After a summons from Najm al-Din Ayyub, the last Ayyubid sultan in Cairo, groups of Khwarazmians crossed the Euphrates and created havoc wherever they went. In the early summer of 1244, they moved south into the Holy Land and arrived outside Jerusalem on 11 July 1244.

Frederick II of Sicily, medieval Renaissance man par excellence.

When the Franks heard about the advance of the Khwarazmians, some 6000 of them left Jerusalem in fear, but only 300 of them escaped the Khwarazmians who then entered the city 'which stood quite empty'. They attacked the garrison in the Tower of David which held out until 23 August 1244 when it surrendered on the promise of safe conduct. The invading forces killed those Christians still in the city, not sparing any of them and taking their women and children into captivity.

The devastation caused in the Holy City was terrible. Both Muslim and Christian chroniclers were ashamed at what had been perpetrated by the Khwarazmians who, after all, were at least nominally Muslims. The Khwarazmians entered the Church of the Holy Sepulchre and destroyed the tomb which Christians believed to be that of the Messiah, removing the marble framework which enclosed the tomb and its carved columns. They also massacred monks and nuns in the Armenian convent of St James, desecrated Christian tombs, including those of the Frankish kings that were in the church, and burned the bones of the dead. For Matthew Paris rhetoric knows no bounds, saying that in the Holy City the Khwarazmians 'cut the throats, as of sheep doomed to the slaughter, of the nuns, and of aged and infirm men'. The Ayyubid sultan Najm al-Din Ayyub condemned the excesses of the Khwarazmians in the Church of the Holy Sepulchre in a letter dated 15 August 1246, addressed to Pope Innocent IV. He said that what had happened there in the way of destruction and desecration had occurred without his knowledge or presence. However, that same year the infamous battle of Harbiyya (La Fourbie), as serious militarily as Hattin, gave the victory to Najm al-Din Ayyub with his Khwarazmian allies over the troops of the Syrian Ayyubids and Franks. This ill-fated collaboration of Syrian Ayyubids and Crusaders was strongly criticized by the Muslim chronicler Sibt b. al-Jawzi (d. 1256) who bemoaned the fact that the Muslims had fought with crosses over their heads, and with Christian priests offering them the sacrament.

After the battle of Harbiyya, a terrible disaster that accelerated the fall of the Ayyubid dynasty, Jerusalem was governed from Egypt. Ayyubid pragmatism toward the Holy City lasted to the very end of their rule; in his testament, Najm al-Din Ayyub, counsels his son, the last Ayyubid sultan of Egypt, as follows: 'If they [the Franks] demand the coast and Jerusalem from you, give them these places without delay on condition that they have no foothold in Egypt.' Clearly the centre of power had shifted to the south.

The end of the dynasty was now fast approaching. Najm al-Din Ayyub died in November 1249 and his slave troops (*mamluks*) staged a *coup d'état* in which they appointed one of their own number as sultan. The Mamluk dynasty had begun to rule.

Looking back over the Ayyubid period, it should be borne in mind that the story of Ayyubid rule in the Holy Land is not just one of disruption and bargaining over the ownership of Jerusualem. It is a saga of desperate survival tactics in a period of great external dangers, when the threat of more crusades from Europe did not recede and when the even more terrible spectre of the Mongol invasions loomed ominously on the horizon. Against this background individual Ayyubid princes could occasionally unite against a common foe. More often, however, what motivated them was sheer pragmatism as they sought grimly to keep hold of their own territories in whatever way they could. Maintaining control of the Holy Land was a secondary consideration in such a situation and its generally unhappy fate in much of the Ayyubid period may rather be seen as a symbol of the widespread fragility of power, both Muslim and Crusader, in these troubled years.

Moreover, Saladin's Ayyubid heirs, men of much lesser vision and prone to endless political squabbles, had little appetite for ambitious construction projects in the Holy Land. Their focus quickly shifted north and south, to Aleppo, Damascus, and Cairo, and that is where their most important buildings are still to be found. But under Mamluk tutelage (1250–1517) Jerusalem was once again transformed beyond recognition, this time by over sixty Muslim monuments, again overwhelmingly of religious function. No Outremer castle held out for longer than six weeks after the Mamluks had begun a siege. Castles also fell to the Mamluks because the inhabitants were offered safe conduct if they surrendered. The Mamluk sultan, al-Ashraf Khalil, laid siege to Acre on 6 April 1291. The city was taken on 18 May. Many of the inhabitants of the city had already left for Cyprus, but the thousands that remained were killed. Very soon the whole Levantine coast finally reverted to Muslim rule exercised by the Mamluks.

A Mamluk *amir* dressed to kill.

Concluding remarks

Three Frankish states managed to implant themselves precariously for almost two centuries in alien territory far from Europe. The length of the Frankish occupation of individual cities within the Holy Land varied considerably; for example, Nablus from 1099 to 1187, Caesarea from 1101 to 1187 and 1191 to 1265, and Tyre from 1124 to 1291. This was possible initially because of the strength of Frankish religious ideology and, by contrast, Muslim disunity and lack of strong leadership under the banner of *jihad*. The network of castles, the military strength of the Knightly Orders, and the assistance of the Italian maritime states in bringing men and supplies to the Holy Land presented a formidable stumbling block to Muslim success in ousting the Franks definitively in the first half of the 12th century. However, under the command of Nur al-Din, Saladin, and Baybars, the Holy Land gradually reverted to Muslim rule, culminating in the fall of Acre, the last bastion of Frankish power on traditionally Muslim soil.

From the death of Saladin onwards, the Holy Land somehow lost its holiness and it reverted under his descendants to the subsidiary political status it had always had since the beginning of Muslim rule in the Middle East. The Ayyubid princes prioritized Egypt and Syria. That, after all, was where the major cities were. The Holy Land contained no city that could serve as a political hub for them. They focused on Aleppo, Damascus, and Cairo as their centres of power. Jerusalem, which had served as a religious and political capital for the Frankish Kingdom, degenerated in Ayyubid times into a political bargaining tool in a power game played between al-Kamil and Frederick II of Sicily. Even worse than that, Jerusalem then became the target for an abominable invasion and desecration perpetrated by rampaging nomadic Khwarazmian Turks who dared to call themselves Muslims. For them even Jerusalem's sacred status meant nothing.

The Crusades were not just about war. The Franks and the Muslims lived cheek by jowl in the Holy Land for almost two centuries and there were frequent periods of peace between them. The Frankish states were skilful in making alliances with neighbouring Muslim states, and, for a while in the Ayyubid period in the 13th century, the remaining Frankish Crusader states—the Kingdom of Jerusalem at Acre, the Principality of Antioch, and the County of Tripoli—almost became an integral part of the political landscape of the Holy Land.

The Mamluks of Egypt, on their seizure of power in 1250, recognized the importance of Jerusalem as the third most holy city in Islam, and they cared for it as a core centre of Muslim piety and pilgrimage. Politically, however, the Holy Land, with its lack of commercial and economic clout and with its absence of large urban centres, was destined thereafter to be ruled until modern times from Cairo and then Istanbul. Fortunately for the Muslims the Holy City still houses Mamluk and Ottoman monuments which testify to the loving care lavished on it by these two long-lived Muslim Turkish dynasties.

CHAPTER 9

The Holy Land from the Mamluk Sultanate to the Ottoman Empire

(1260–1799)

NIMROD LUZ

Defining the period

THIS chapter sets out to tell the story of the Holy Land over a long stretch of time, from 1260 to 1799. During this period two main political powers ruled the Holy Land: the Mamluk Sultanate and the Ottoman Empire. These two very different political entities shared a common heritage and a few characteristics, as they were both of Asian-Turkic origin and relative late-comers to the world of Islam. But before we look at the important role played by the Turks in the Muslim world a few words are in order concerning the periodization of this chapter.

We begin in 1260, the year in which, following the Battle of Ayn Jalut between the Mamluks and the Mongols, the Holy Land became part of the embryonic Mamluk Sultanate. It remained under its rule until the Sultanate's surrender to the might of the Ottomans in 1516–1517. The analysis ends with the failure of the siege of Acre by Napoleon in 1799, which was followed by a hasty and rather chastening retreat. The history of the region, following the waning of the Crusader kingdom in the wake of the Battle of Hattin in 1187, is best understood through the prism of the growing impact of Turko-Islamic political entities and cultures on the Muslim world. Following the battle of Ayn Jalut and the Mamluks' defeat of the Mongols, the Holy Land, as part of Syria, would be under the rule of the Mamluk Sultanate for some 270 years. The changes brought about by this regime and the growing dominance of Turko-Islamic culture(s) are of crucial importance for understanding the history of the region and the major socio-cultural-political and religious developments that occurred.

However, it should be noted that the Ottoman Empire and its Turkish society, though Muslim in its formal expression (much like the Mamluks), was strongly Byzantine in its folk culture. The conquered subjects of the Turks were Christians of the Byzantine and semi-Byzantinized areas such as the Balkans, and the economic

View of Ayn Jalut in the Lower Galilee and its environs.

and cultural life of the Ottomans was greatly determined by these Christian subjects. The economic continuity of Byzantium had important repercussions as well in the Turkish tax structure and administration. Finally, this widespread absorption and survival of Christian populations had a marked effect in the spheres of Turkish family life, popular beliefs, and practices. In sum, these legacies had a significant impact on the Ottomans and meant that their polity differed substantially from that of the Mamluks.

The decision to conclude the chapter with the invasion of Napoleon is based on the subsequent outcomes of this event, which contributed to the region's exposure to the winds of modernization, westernization, and the growing influence of European powers in the Middle East at large and particularly in the Holy Land. Thus, the 19th century, even though still under Ottoman rule and exhibiting a considerable degree of continuity, presents a noticeably different history of the region when compared to the 550 years that preceded it. Indeed, some of the changes were already under way prior to the invasion while others were very slow to follow. Thus the Napoleonic act of bravado was a meaningful and significant marker and gateway to a new period in the history of the region.

The Turks in the Islamic world and their impact on the Holy Land

'Turk' is an umbrella term used by Arab-Muslim sources in order to describe various peoples and tribes of the Eurasian Steppe. Originating in the Turkic Empire that arose in Mongolia in the 6th century, and that for the first time connected the lands from Manchuria to the Caspian Sea, the Turks gave their names first to the tribes that were subject to them and then to all those who adopted the Turkic languages. The rise of the Islamic Empire in the 7th century gave these groups and peoples the opportunity to play a decisive role in shaping Islamic history and the Middle East for over a millennium. The Mamluks and the Ottomans offer two different examples of the Turkish-Islamic phenomenon: the former represents the outcome of the use of Turkish people as military slaves throughout the Muslim world while the latter were the latest and most successful of the free Turkish groups that managed to establish political rule in the Muslim world from the nineteenth century onwards. Let us explore then these two socio-political Turkish manifestations, as they are fundamental to understanding the history of the Holy Land in the post-Crusader periods.

The Mamluk institution and the formation of a Mamluk Sultanate

The Mamluk institution is a unique phenomenon to be found only in Islamic civilization. The term *Mamluk* is generally translated from the Arabic as 'being owned' or 'a slave'. It was a term earmarked mostly for the Turkish slaves of pagan origins, purchased from Central Asia and the Eurasian Steppe by Muslim rulers to serve as soldiers in their armies. A good idea of how these people were perceived and why they became so attractive to Muslim rulers desperately seeking to buttress their authority is given by the following excerpt from al-Jahiz, a ninth-century Arab scholar: 'they care only about raiding, hunting, horsemanship, skirmishing with rival chieftains, taking booty and invading other countries. Their efforts are all directed towards these activities.' These qualities whether grossly exaggerated or even pejoratively analysed suggest what made this reservoir of manpower particularly alluring to Muslim rulers, who spared no efforts in trying to harness and exploit them to supplement their dwindling armies. The harsh climatic conditions of the Eurasian Steppe and consequently the pastoral nomadic lifestyle of its people were apparently the manufacturers of formidable soldiers. Already in childhood these nomads performed brilliant feats of horsemanship and were superb mounted archers, excelling in the operation of the composite bow from the back of their small native horses. They were able to bestow any army with two assets that when joined together proved to be a force to reckoned with: mobility and firepower. These skilled mounted archers proved to be unstoppable and ruthless warriors who, under capable leadership, were able to launch, time and again, massive attacks on Europe, China, and the Middle East.

From the ninth century CE young boys (sometimes as young as eight years old) from the Eurasian Steppe were bought as slaves and were brought to centres of the Islamic world. On arrival they were put through a lengthy and tough military training which prepared them to become the 'praetorian' personal guard of their Muslim master. Isolated and cut off from their former lives, families, cultures, and geography these young soldiers formed a very loyal and cohesive force for their new rulers. This system of using 'Turks' as military slaves became known as the Mamluk institution. It is generally agreed among scholars that the first to heavily exploit Turkish military slaves (henceforth Mamluks) in his army was the Abbasid Caliph al-Mu'tasim (r. 833–842). Following him and in different polities around the disintegrating Muslim world Mamluks began to emerge as the favoured solution for professional armies. Under the Ayyubids (1193–1250), the descendants of Saladin, and particularly during the reign of Sultan al-Malik al-Salih Ayyub (r. 1240–1249), the recruitment of and reliance on Mamluk corps became even more pivotal to the security of the realm. In 1249–1250, while the Sultan was on his death bed, it was the regiment of his loyal Mamluks that stopped Louis IX's crusade from arriving in Cairo and saved the day for the Sultanate. By the end of 1250 and following rather intricate manoeuvres, the Mamluks assassinated the last Ayyubid sultan and consequently became the elite of a new regime and a political entity in their own right: the Mamluk Sultanate.

Nimrod's Castle (Arabic: Qal'at al-Subayba/ Castle of the Cliff'), on the southern slope of Mount Hermon guarding the route to Damascus.

After a decade of internal skirmishes their hour of glory arrived. The young and disorganized Mamluk Sultanate responded to an invasion of Mongol troops that had advanced into the Holy Land and reached as far as Gaza in the summer of 1260. This dire threat to the still disunited Sultanate served as a catalyst to work together against a common enemy. The Mamluk army met the Mongols in south-east Galilee, in the Jezreel Valley (Ar. Marj ibn 'Amr). On 3 September 1260 the Mamluks became the first army to have ever stopped the mighty Mongols in the Battle of Ayn Jalut. This victory not only put an end to Mongol conquests in the Holy Land, but also placed the Mamluks centre stage in world history and served to legitimize their position vis-à-vis the Muslim communities of the region. Since 1260 and until the arrival of the Ottomans in 1516–1517 the Mamluk Sultanate ruled the Holy Land. The slaves of yesterday became the masters of today. Throughout the Mamluk period the Holy Land as part of greater Syria was secondary to the centre in Cairo. However, due to its religious status it attracted attention (mainly Jerusalem) from the sultans and other Mamluk dignitaries. During this long period some major and profound processes took place, such as the intensification of Islamization within the local population, the neglect and intentional destruction of coastal cities, heavy investment in religious institutions, mostly in Jerusalem, and the creation of an elaborate and efficient road system for military use.

The Ottomans

The Ottoman Empire represents another variant of the Turkish-Islamic experience. Apart from the Mamluks, who were brought to the Muslim world as individuals, whole Turkic tribes began to Islamize from the tenth century onwards. This was the outcome of encounters that mostly took place in the Iranian cultural sphere (hence the significance of Iranian Islam for the Turkish tribes), where they were subjected to the twin influences of Sufi mystics and the Hanafi law school. Following the conversion of Turkish tribes a string of Turco-Islamic dynasties emerged on the border of the declining Abbasid Caliphate. The Seljuqs were the most prominent and successful of them all. In 1055, after conquering Baghdad, they succeeded in forcing the powerless Abbasid caliph to bestow on them the title of Sultan, i.e. a supreme executive Muslim ruler who is not a caliph. Under the fast expanding Seljuq Sultanate, Turkish tribes and individuals began to arrive and to destabilize the border areas between the Byzantine Empire and the Caliphate in eastern Anatolia. In 1071 this growing tension and political unrest erupted in the Battle of Manzikert (near Lake Van in today's Turkey) in which the Seljuqs inflicted a stunning defeat on the Byzantine army. Subsequently, the whole of Asia Minor was opened to Turkish peoples and tribes (mostly Oghuz) that gradually diminished the Byzantines' influence and presence in the region. A rebellious branch of the Seljuq family established itself as the Sultanate of Rum (1077–1307) and at its height controlled the better part of the Anatolian Plateau. This new political entity would serve the first Ottomans as a political and cultural model.

While the Seljuq Sultanate suffered internal and external problems and finally collapsed in 1194 the Sultanate of Rum thrived for a few more decades, finally succumbing to the advancing Mongols and, following the battle of Kose Dag (1243), it became effectively a vassal state until its final demise in 1307. During the second half of the thirteenth century a handful of small Turkish emirates (*beyliks*) established themselves on former Seljuq Rum territory. The most impressive and long lasting state was what came to be known as the Ottoman Empire. This political entity ruled at its apogee the entire Middle East, much of North Africa, as well as the Balkans, and penetrated deep into central Europe. The Ottoman state came into existence as a small frontier principality devoted to holy war on the frontiers of the Byzantine Empire. Its initial warrior character influenced its existence for six centuries, in particular its dynamic conquest policy, its military structure, and the predominance of its military class within an empire that managed to hold together and control a mix of disparate religious, cultural, and ethnic elements.

By the time of Sultan Orhan (1324–1362) the Ottomans had already crossed into Europe and captured parts of the Balkans, thus absorbing political and cultural structures from both the Byzantine and the medieval Balkan states. At the end of the fourteenth century they controlled most of Anatolia and almost annihilated the Byzantines. In 1453 the young sultan Mehmet II (1451–1481) conquered Constantinople, the capital of the Byzantine Empire, in one of the most defining moments in world history and made it into the new capital of the Ottoman Empire, Istanbul. Up to this juncture there existed reasonable solidarity between the rising Turkish state and the already established Mamluk Sultanate. In the face of mutual enemies such as a crusading West and ominous Mongol threats these two Islamic entities shared mutual interests. These were soon to expire as the Ottomans began to establish their influence and suzerainty over Turcoman principalities on the buffer zone between them and the Mamluks and their archrival, the Safavids of Iran. Under the active leadership of Sultan Selim I (r. 1512–1520) the Ottomans decided to end the long Mamluk rule over the Arab lands. In 1516 these two Islamic powers engaged in north Syria at the battle of Marj Dabiq, which led to the complete collapse of Mamluk control of greater Syria. A few months later the two parties met again in a battle near the Pyramids in Cairo, which brought about the complete annihilation of the Mamluk army and the demise of the Mamluk Sultanate. From 1517 to 1917 the Ottomans ruled, in varying degrees, the Middle East, and more importantly for us, the Holy Land.

A political history of the Holy Land: Mamluks (1260–1517)

If the Battle of Ayn Jalut and the epic victory over the Mongols mark the beginning of the Mamluk Sultanate's rule of the Holy Land, then the rise to power of Sultan Baybars I (1260–1277) signals the beginning of the consolidation and organization of Mamluk control. During his relatively long reign Baybars was the driving force behind the main processes that would ultimately entrench the Mamluk Sultanate in Syria and

The ruins of Khan Jubb Yusuf, Jacob's Well Hostel, northeast of Tiberias.

eliminate the influence and presence of its two main challengers: the Crusader principalities on the Syrian-Palestinian coast and the Mongol Ilkhanate of Persia to the north. In order to achieve this Baybars engaged in long and continuous military campaigning, particularly against the Crusader Kingdom in the Holy Land. Time and again he launched successful attacks and besieged garrisons, fortresses, and fortified cities.

He ravaged the Palestinian coast, and it remained Mamluk policy throughout its control of the Holy Land to keep former port cities such as Gaza, Jaffa, Arsuf, Cesarea, and eventually Acre in a non-functional condition. This was partly done to deter any new crusaders from landing in the region, but also as part of Baybars' policy to economically pressure the existing Crusader Kingdom. He attacked the very heart of their realm, Acre, in 1263 but failed to reduce it. However, during his reign he managed to thwart all Mongol attempts to advance into Syria. This was facilitated through the establishment of the *Barid*, a system of roads and inns that enabled couriers to move between Northern Syria and Cairo, the capital of the Sultanate, within four days. Thus

Jisr Jindas, or Baybars' Bridge, built in 1273, spanning the river Ayalon near Ramla.

Baybars was able to hold most of his army in Egypt and still respond quickly to intelligence reports forewarning of a coming Mongol attack in the north. The *Barid* has left its mark to this day in a plethora of caravanserais and bridges which attest to the magnitude and efficacy of this institution. This illustrates the point that most of the energies invested in the Holy Land by the Mamluks were aimed to serve their own immediate military purposes.

Yet there is another important aspect to Mamluk rule in the Holy Land which also began with Baybars and which set the tone for the duration of the Mamluk control of the land, namely heavy investment in religious buildings and demonstrations of Islamic piety. In order to understand this aspect of the Mamluk presence in the Holy Land let us examine the inauguration inscription of the Red Mosque which was built by Baybars in Safad shortly after he managed to capture this important Crusader fortress in 1265. Immediately after Safad was taken Baybars initiated the construction of two mosques in the city. The mosque known as al-Masjid al-Ahmar (the Red Mosque) was built in a budding new suburb of Safad. This is the inscription which still decorates the gate of the building:

> In the name of Allah the merciful and the compassionate. This blessed mosque was built by the instructions of our lord the sultan al-Malik al-Zahir, the most great and

> magnificent master, the wise, the just, defender of the faith, warrior along the borders, the victorious, supporter of the faith and the world, sultan of Islam and the Muslims, slayer of the infidels and the heathens, vanquisher of rebels and conspirators, Baybars al-Salahi, partner of the head of the believers, and this in the year four and seventy and six hundred [1276].

This inscription encapsulates the Mamluks' precarious, and at times challenged, position as a military Turko-Islamic elite controlling a mostly Arabo-Islamic population. The Mamluks were fearsome, ruthless, and victorious in the battlefield and yet they, like any other hegemonic power, were in perpetual need of acceptance and legitimation from their population. As newcomers to Islam, who were of a different ethnic affiliation from their subjects, they were often regarded with suspicion by Muslim scholars (*ulama*). In order to overcome this distrust and gain legitimation they had to prove themselves not only as a successful military power and defenders of the population but as pious and observant Muslims. Thus, from Baybars onwards, members of the Mamluk elite established numerous religious endowments (*awqaf*) throughout the Holy Land, though mostly in Jerusalem due to its religious importance. In the above inscription Baybars depicts himself not only as the slayer of the Crusaders but also as a pious believer and the protector of Islam. Be that as it may, after a lifetime of war mongering against the Crusader principalities, Baybars signed a ten-year peace treaty in 1272 with Hugues III, King of Cyprus, probably because he needed to focus his

The public fountain (*sabil*) of Qaitbay on the Temple Mount in Jerusalem.

attention and energy on the growing threat of the Mongols to the north. Thus, when he died in 1277, he still left his successors with the task of eliminating the Crusader presence in the Levant.

In 1291 Acre finally succumbed to the Mamluks and with this ended the 200 years of Frankish settlement in the Holy Land. This strengthened the Mamluks' claim to power and stopped any internal criticism levelled against them. At this juncture the Mamluks had to check a new wave of Mongol attacks, initiated this time by Ghazan Khan, the Muslim ruler of the independent Mongol Ilkhanate of Persia. This proved to be the last time that the Mongols arrived in the Holy Land and threatened the Sultanate's hold over southern Syria. And so, at the beginning of the fourteenth century, the Mamluk state, having rid itself of its two main adversaries and secured control of the Indian-European commercial routes, entered a period of relative peace and prosperity. This coincided with the long and successful reign of al-Malik al-Salih Muhammad Ibn Qalawun (1311–1340). During his reign the Sultan and Mamluk dignitaries alike embarked upon a lavish building spree. Amir Tankiz al-Husami, the governor of Syria (1312–1340) and a close ally of the Sultan, was known to have built a variety of compounds of both civil and religious importance. In Jerusalem, for example, he built religious schools, markets, bathhouses, sufi lodges, and accommodation for pilgrims. Additionally, he was responsible for a massive renovation of the city's main aqueduct and refurbishment of sites on the Haram al-Sharif, the iconic Islamic compound of Jerusalem.

Yet, despite these successes, the Mamluk Sultanate faced many challenges in the fourteenth century. Some were specific, such as the Black Death, which probably arrived from Europe and wiped out anything between 25 and 40 per cent of the population of the Holy Land, and the predations of Timur, a Turko-Mongol warlord who strove to restore Genghis Khan's Empire, though he never entered the Holy Land itself. Other challenges were long term and in the end overwhelmed the Mamluks, in particular the growing pressure of the Ottomans, the mounting insurrections of local Bedouins and the rise of European powers' control of the commercial routes to central Asia and India. The measures taken by sultans to try and meet the challenges usually represented a turn for the worse for the population of the Holy Land. Deteriorating security conditions, forced conscription, new taxes, and other forms of economic constraints—all were becoming more and more apparent as the century progressed.

Early on in the fifteenth century the Ottomans began to challenge the Sultanate within the Holy Land by channelling funding for various religious activities. Yet internal problems seemed to be more crucial at this point. The increasing factionalism among different Mamluk groups based on different ethnic origins became the paramount reason for internal clashes. In 1402 this amounted to an open rebellion of the governor of Gaza against the Sultan in Cairo. The governor and his army were defeated soon after that by a confederation of local Bedouin tribes, operating this time in conjunction with Sultan Faraj (1399–1412). But this was not always the case and this sultan was forced to initiate no less than seven military expeditions across the Holy Land to address escalating insurgencies in Syria.

The increasing political instability of the Sultanate was manifested also in its weakening economic situation. Sultan Barsbay (1422–1438) tried to implement a more rigorous fiscal policy and not only confiscated Christian property in the Holy Land but also banned the use of European currencies by merchants. However, these were desperate and futile measures in a losing battle to preserve the Mamluk machine, which seemed to be ill equipped to adjust at this stage. The burden on the local population (Muslims and non-Muslims alike) increased. In one of the last serious attempts to check Ottoman power and growing interference in the Sultanate, Sultan Qaitbay (1469–1495) ordered the forced conscription of Muslims in Syria and the Holy Land. The local Bedouin population retaliated and pillaged villages and cities, thus exposing publically the weakness of the Sultanate. In one of those many incidents Bedouin tribes from the Jericho area launched an attack on the Mamluk governor of Jerusalem. In their efforts to catch him they chased him into the Haram precinct and rampaged through the city and harassed the local population. In addition, Qaitbay in a desperate attempt to stabilize the much ailing economy, issued decrees that broadened state control over local commodities (oil, soap, etc.) and effectively tried to expand the state's monopoly of the market. But the growing burden of taxes on the local population combined with the corruption of local governors trying to enlarge their own wealth only worsened the situation.

The discovery of the Ocean route through the Cape of Good Hope in 1497 by Vasco de Gama was another blow for the Mamluk economy as it enabled European merchants to bypass the Sultanate on their way back from India. The last Mamluk sultan, Qansuh al-Ghuri (1501–1516) went so far as to send a delegation to the Pope warning him that the Christian sacred sites in the Holy Land would be harmed if the Europeans used this new route, but to no avail. In a sense this was one of those defining moments which would render the Middle East more vulnerable to western powers. In 1512 Salim I became the Ottoman sultan and very soon was engaged in direct confrontations with the Mamluks. Apparently, the Sultanate was no match for the Ottomans and in 1516, following the Battle of Marj Dabiq, the Holy Land, as part of Syria, surrendered to the Ottomans. By early 1517, the Ottomans crossed the Sinai Desert and met the Mamluks in the outskirts of Cairo. Using firearms and cannons, it took less than an hour for the Ottomans to deal the final blow to the Mamluks and the Mamluk Sultanate was no more. A new power was in place that would control the Holy Land for the next four hundred years.

A political history of the Holy Land: Ottomans (1517–1799)

After the conquest of the Holy Land Selim I made very few changes in the new provinces that succumbed to his rule. Initially he relied on the former Mamluk officers to manage the provinces of Egypt and Syria on his behalf. However, this was soon to change as the local Mamluks revolted and tried to overthrow the Ottomans. The period of unrest ended in 1525 in the course of which Selim's son and successor, Suleiman I (known also as the Magnificent to the Europeans, or the Law Giver to his own people), crushed all local resistance. As a result of this Mamluk insurgency the

Ottomans resorted to a new policy. New governors, new laws, new borders, and censuses were all implemented for a better control of the land. Suleiman's reign is usually considered as a time of prosperity for the Holy Land. The Ottomans invested money to improve safety along the highways, developed efficient local administration, and oversaw the formation of a more centralized tax system. Suleiman was also heavily investing in construction projects, particularly in Jerusalem. In addition to limiting new regulations so as to encourage commerce and boost the local economy, he was responsible for a comprehensive and impressive building spree in the city. The walls, formerly dismantled by the Ayyubids (1219), were newly constructed and survive today as one of the more impressive landmarks of the city. The water supply to the city was greatly improved, new water dispensaries (*sabil*) and bath houses were built, and caravanserais were renovated. New oil presses were needed to attend to the growing supply of olives, and soap factories were also built in the city. In the northern town of Safad a new industry of silk- and wool-working was introduced by the Jewish immigrants from the Iberian Peninsula that completely changed the city's history, if only for a brief time. Due to the relative safety and prosperity of the Empire the products were exported to lucrative markets in Europe through the port of Acre.

Depiction of the walls of Jerusalem.

Citadel of Jerusalem, or Tower of David, substantially expanded by Suleiman I.

Most major cities of the Holy Land experienced strong demographic growth at this time, as Ottoman censuses inform us. But this glory period came to an end shortly after Salim II (the Sot) succeeded his father on the throne in 1566. In the last quarter of the sixteenth century a monetary crisis affected the Ottoman Empire. This resulted from global changes, such as the arrival of precious metals and lucrative goods from the 'New World' and changes in the fabric industry that enabled the Europeans to flood the market with cheap high-quality materials at the expense of local industry in the Holy Land. Thus cities like Safad that had experienced prosperity, population growth, and a rich social and cultural life began to deteriorate towards the end of the sixteenth century. That said, by the end of the century the Ottomans were able to consolidate their hold on the Holy Land, giving it a distinctively 'Ottoman' colouring. They replaced the Mamluk fiscal and legal system with their own version (referred to as the *Qanun*) as well as their own understanding of economic and governmental institutions. And yet, even as the region slowly acceded to the Ottoman sphere of influence, it also experienced a variety of challenges from local warlords and noble families. A typical case in point is the family of a certain Turabay ibn Karaja, the sheikh of a Bedouin tribe from the northern part of Samaria who was appointed by Selim I as Amir al-Darbayn, literally the person in charge of the two roads leading from Damascus to Cairo and to Jerusalem. As a reward for his loyalty to the sultan he and his family were granted the lease for the taxes levied on the region of Nablus and its environs. The Turabay family kept its prominent role in the region until its power dwindled by the beginning of the eighteenth century.

The provinces of Syria were for much of the Ottoman period secondary and marginal to the dynasty's main interests that lay mostly with Western Anatolia and the Balkans (Anadolu and Rumeli respectively). Accordingly the Ottomans generally entrusted their Syrian possessions to people of local influence. This strategy allowed them to invest as few resources as possible to retain their hold. Thus, from the late sixteenth century to the end of Ahmad al-Jazzar's rule of the northern parts of the Holy Land (1804), the Ottomans maintained their rule through provincial governors who acted at times as their proxies and at times ran their own self-serving polity. As would often happen when their protégés became too autonomous, the Ottomans would take measures to diminish their power. This was usually done by manipulating other local authorities against their former chosen leaders.

A good example is provided by Amir Fakhr al-din II, a Druze dignitary whose family (al-Ma'an) controlled the better part of the Lebanon prior to the Ottomans' rule. From 1590 to 1634 he controlled most of Syria and the Holy Land. As part of his efforts to extend his authority to Jerusalem he tried to obtain support from Christian European leaders by promising them to 'redeem' the city from the Muslims and to win it back for the Christians. Indeed during his time the Christians gained permission to renovate churches and monasteries after a long period of being denied such activities. His period in office was a time of prosperity in the Holy Land and in the areas under his direct control. Fakhr al-Din initiated the introduction of the mulberry tree as a way to boost the local silk industry. He was also involved in advancing other industries such as the manufacture of oil and soap (both extracted from local olives) and cotton, and cattle rearing. This was all part of his effort to augment his revenues, for all these goods were exported to Europe. To do that he also invested in renovation of the local road system, bridge construction, and development of the long-ruined port of Acre. His mounting power finally incurred the wrath of the Empire. The Ottomans encouraged local leaders to unite against him and check his power. In 1634 Fakhr al-Din surrendered to an Ottoman military delegation and was sent, following a Sultanic decree, to Istanbul where he was executed in 1635. Muhammad ibn Farukh was one of the leaders who was very active in the efforts to rid the region of Fakhr al-Din's influence. Unlike other local leaders Ibn Farukh was not of Bedouin-Arab lineage but a son of an Ottoman officer of Circassian origin. His father served among other things as the governor of Jerusalem and was instrumental time and again in subjugating local rebellions of Bedouin tribes. When he died in 1621 his son Muhammad succeeded him as governor on behalf of the Sultan and extended his iron-fist policy towards the local population. Their period is notorious for the persecutions of non-Muslim (Dhimmi) communities and the abandonment of villages in the hinterland of Jerusalem.

As the central government continued to distance itself from the region's management, local governors became more and more crucial to the ongoing political affairs of the Holy Land. This was the backdrop to the attempts of a succession of local leaders to gain control of territories within the Holy Land, ostensibly in the name of Istanbul. 'Umar al-Zaydani was a Bedouin tribe leader appointed by a certain Amir Bashir, himself an Ottoman-appointed governor of Mount Lebanon, as tax collector (*multazem*) of the northern region of Safad circa 1700. The Zaydani family remained influential long after Bashir died in 1707. The sons of 'Umar and his brother inherited their family status and became local rulers in Galilee. Around 1720 'Umar's son Daher al-'Umar was officially recognized by the Ottomans as the governor of Tiberias. Over the next few years Daher skilfully used this position to expand his authority over more territories due west and north of Tiberias. Beginning in 1746, once the Sultan realized he was a force to be reckoned with, he was officially appointed by the Ottoman governor (*wali*) of Sidon as the governor of Galilee. From his new heavily fortified palace at Dayr Khanna in the central Lower Galilee Daher continued to establish his authority and strengthen his ruling position on the northern and central parts of the Holy Land, gaining control over the port city of Acre and later the emerging port city of Haifa. By the 1770s Daher had extended his zone of influence as far as Jaffa and Gaza. However, when he made a move on Jerusalem he apparently crossed a line with the Ottomans. Following a Sultanic decree Ottoman land forces arriving from Damascus were joined by an Ottoman fleet and jointly besieged Daher in Acre. While the city was enduring heavy shelling Daher fled the scene, but at long last his luck gave out and he was killed on route northwards by a random shot. In all he had played a central role in local politics for well over fifty years. Although he did not always obey orders coming from Istanbul, he was never more than a highly successful tax collector and he always

View of Tiberias *c.*1890.

accepted the legitimacy of Ottoman control over 'his' lands. Daher was successful as long as the Empire was unable to exert its power (for all sorts of reasons) on remote provinces such as the Holy Land. But once the Sultan was able and resolute enough to do away with this independent-minded and unpredictable underling Daher's fate was decided.

The person entrusted by the Sultan with this task was an officer notorious for his fearless and ruthless nature, Ahmad Jazzar Pasha. Formerly a Christian, probably from Herzegovina, he converted to Islam when he became part of the court of Ali Bey, the ruler of Egypt. He earned his highly pejorative nickname al-Jazzar (literally 'the butcher') for his role as his patron's chief executioner. He reaffirmed his fearsome reputation while serving as governor and dispensing stiff punishments on his recalcitrant subjects and was known to order the mutilation of his staff when they failed in their duty. Following the annihilation of Daher and the end of his long reign, al-Jazzar was appointed governor of Sidon, although he resided in Acre. He kept this status and title until his death in 1804. For twenty-nine years (probably the longest serving Ottoman governor in the region) he ruled large parts of the Holy Land with an iron fist and shrewd political understanding which helped him sustain his precarious position as governor vis-à-vis the Sultan on the one hand and his population and local rivalries on the other hand. His first years in power were dedicated to establishing his authority and securing his realm. After diminishing the influence of the Zaydanis he sought to check the growing power of the Shi'ite population of the upper Galilee and southern Lebanon of today, locally known as Mutawallis. Once he had annexed their region he could address the most unstable and menacing factor that could have seriously challenged his authority: the Bedouin tribes that roamed the areas west and east of the Jordan Valley. Although he was not able fully to subjugate them he succeeded in keeping them in check and in reducing their raids on his sedentary (and tax-paying) population. This relative security naturally facilitated an upturn in commerce and local industry. Al-Jazzar abolished in his lands the long existing system of *Iltizam*, a form of tax-farming in which the state leased taxation rights to local people of influence. It was a highly ineffective system and on the whole encouraged excessive and disproportionate taxes. Al-Jazzar made sure that all taxes were levied directly to his treasury and by cutting out the middlemen he was able not only to meet his obligations to his Ottoman masters but also to enjoy a surplus that could be used to sustain his army, improve local infrastructure, monumental building projects, and so forth. Furthermore, he monopolized the key industries (cotton, wheat, silk) and was generally well disposed to European merchant activity along the shores of the Levant. During his long time in office Acre thrived: its port became the central exit point of goods exported to Europe and it hosted a range of monumental projects such as the renovation of its main aqueduct, the enlargement of its walls, new markets, and an ambitious mosque known as the al-Jazzar mosque fashioned in contemporary Istanbul style.

His uncanny ability to remain in office was tested once again in 1790 when his deputy, a certain amir Salim, organized a coup, probably with the quiet consent of the Sultan. Al-Jazzar found himself betrayed by his own troops and officers and yet was able to organize the local population and thwart this challenge. When he learned that the French merchants were supportive of the move to remove him from power he revoked their trading rights in Acre. In doing so he directly opposed his masters in Istanbul who ordered him to restore European trade rights in the Levant. True to form al-Jazzar stood his ground but was willing to overlook French unofficial commercial activities in his province. This dispute was shortly to be forgotten, however, as the Holy Land like other provinces of the Empire was engulfed in the political storm that overwhelmed Egypt in 1798 in the shape of the Napoleonic invasion. Napoleon's ambitious campaign to the Orient exposed once again the relative weakness of the Empire and its diminishing abilities to counter the might of European powers. Within a very short time the French army was standing in front of the Walls of Acre, al-Jazzar's capital and the most important city of the region. It is to al-Jazzar's credit that

Mosque of al-Jazzar, Acre.

Napoleon failed in his highly ambitious plan to proceed from the port of Acre to Istanbul and from there to return to Europe as the unchallenged new emperor. Aided by a British fleet and a French military expert, a former colleague of Napoleon, the city under al-Jazzar's command withstood the siege. The Napoleonic invasion and its ultimate failure will serve us here as the terminus of this political survey. Its ramifications are manifold and surely represent a turning point in the history of the land regardless of its immediate outcome. Al-Jazzar himself remained in power until his death in 1804 and with him ended also the period of semi-independent local rulers.

Administration patterns and the status of the Holy Land

The history of the Holy Land was for the most part dictated by external forces, and the Mamluk and Ottoman periods were no exception. This was a natural outcome of the geostrategic position of the land as a central junction of historical roads and a passageway connecting the Levant with Egypt and the Arabian Peninsula. Following the Mamluk takeover of the region the Holy Land became once more a peripheral

View of the land walls of Acre.

region within a bigger administrative unit. The centre of the Mamluk Sultanate was firmly established in Cairo. Indeed, the Syrian region occupied the Mamluks mostly only as a military buffer zone sheltering the core of the Sultanate: Egypt and especially Cairo. In the event of an approaching enemy it allowed the Sultan in Cairo time to recruit from his power base in Egypt and to address the military challenge accordingly. This policy was put to the test during a series of Mongol invasions in the last quarter of the thirteenth century.

The centrality of Cairo meant that posts in the Holy Land were viewed by the Mamluk elite either as a temporary setback in their upwardly mobile career or as a punishment for those who fell out of grace with the Sultan. Either way, the time in office would be spent mostly in exploiting the land financially while waiting for a better post. As long as the Sultanate was in a stable condition its northern provinces, including the Holy Land, fared reasonably. However, these were also the provinces where any instability in the realm and internal factionalism were immediately apparent. Thus, during the turbulent years of the latter parts of the fifteenth century, when the Mamluk Sultanate was facing mounting challenges due to the rising power of the Ottomans and the economic supremacy of its European adversaries, the local administration of the Holy Land was highly dysfunctional and rather oppressive.

Administratively, the Holy Land was considered part of *al-Sham* (Syria) which consisted of seven provinces (*mamlaka* or *niaba*). The governors were nominated by and answered directly to the sultan in Cairo. The Holy Land consisted chiefly of the province of Gaza in the south and the province of Safad in the north. Jerusalem and its hinterland, as well as the eastern area of the Jordan Valley, were administered through Damascus until 1376. Thereafter the city became an independent province and its governors answered directly to the sultan. This is a clear indication of the city's special standing within the Sultanate which was mostly due to its revered religious status in Islam. The city was politically inferior to the other two provincial capitals, Gaza and Safad, but enjoyed distinction nonetheless. This is clearly attested in the plethora of religious endowments built by Mamluk officials that still adorn the streets of the Old City of Jerusalem. The daily governance of the Holy Land was entrusted to the governor of Damascus, who was in charge of the nomination of officers and clerks responsible for all aspects of life throughout Syria: taxation, maintenance of the main urban systems, water supply, religious endowments, protected communities, pilgrimage, and so on.

The transition from Mamluk to Ottoman rule was relatively easy for the local population. After all, this was nothing but a change in the external Muslim power controlling the land. After a long period of general misconduct, inept administration, and frequent illegal and forced taxation it would seem that the locals were not devastated by the political change. On the contrary, the new regime was better equipped to address the recurrent problem that preoccupied local administration and impinged on the safety and well-being of the population: frequent invasions of Bedouin nomadic groups. As under the Mamluks, this region was marginal in the Ottomans' geostrategic understanding of their territories. Indeed, this would only change during the latter part of the nineteenth century following the opening of the Suez Canal and the growing interest of European powers in the region (*nahiya*). When the Holy Land became part of the area controlled by the governor (pasha) of Damascus the province (wilayet or eyalet) was subdivided into counties (*sanjak*, or *liwa*) and each of the counties was further divided into districts (*kaza*) consisting of a number of villages and sometimes small towns (*nahiya*).

The area of the Holy Land comprised five sanjaks, centred on Safad, Lajun, Nablus, al-Quds (Jerusalem), and Gaza. The original administrative system and division lasted until the beginning of the seventeenth century. In 1614, following an imperial decree, the governor of Damascus was ordered to construct a new administrative unit from the sanjaks of Beirut, Sidon, and Safad. Consequently the regions of Galilee, southern Lebanon, and the shoreline up to Beirut were amalgamated into the new province of Sidon. This was a response to the growing challenges that faced the governor of Damascus and his apparent inability to check local warlords' private initiatives to exert their sway over this region. Thus, from the beginning of the seventeenth century onward the Holy Land was divided between two main administrative units: its northern parts were under the control of the governor of Sidon and its central and southern parts answered to the governor of Damascus.

Population: demographic trends and interfaith relations

The earliest surviving registers which comprise reasonably reliable quantitative data of the Holy Land's population are the Ottoman *tahrir* of the sixteenth century. This means that until the first wide-ranging population survey conducted by the Ottomans in 1525–1526 most understandings of demographic statistics of the region are highly speculative. Thus, for example, estimations of the ratio of Muslims to Christians in the Crusader Kingdom of Jerusalem are no more than assumptions, learned though they might be. Therefore, essential issues such as the rate of religious conversion and Islamization of the region and the cultural and political relations between different communities are rather difficult to assess. In what follows let us focus on one important demographic issue, namely the proportion of Muslims in the general population and its ramifications for interfaith relations.

On the eve of the Muslim conquest of the region the majority of the population of the Holy Land was Christian. The conquest set in motion forces that eventually transformed the area into a predominantly Muslim one. Nevertheless, even as late as the end of the tenth century the noted chronicler and former Jerusalem citizen al-Muqaddasi (d. 985) could still lament that the city was dominated by Christians. Throughout the Crusader period one may still find significant Christian communities in Palestine. Yet according to the first Ottoman survey of 1525–1526 the majority of the population was Muslim. This means that only sometime during the Mamluk period did Islam become the dominant religion in the Holy Land. One may thus conclude that conversion to Islam and more importantly the transformation of Muslim communities into the demographic majority was a very slow process, taking some seven to nine centuries.

The Ottoman survey of 1525–1526, which registered only tax payers, informs us that there were just six major cities in Palestine at the time and none of them extended beyond 6000 inhabitants. Most of the population lived in villages, although it is almost impossible to arrive at a total number. What is rather consistent in all places surveyed since 1525 is the existence of a Muslim majority in the region. However, even with the invaluable data supplied by the Ottoman registers it is difficult to establish accurate figures for the entire population of the region, though estimates tend to set the number at between 250,000 and 300,000 people by the end of the sixteenth century. In the absence of accurate statistical data for the seventeenth and eighteenth centuries we are left with European travellers' estimates, which suggest that the entire population of the land did not exceed 300,000 on the eve of the Napoleonic invasion.

In addition to Arab Muslim communities there existed a plethora of ethnic and religious minorities. Turkoman and Kurdish tribes were settled in cities and villages alike. Druze communities occupied rural areas, mostly hilly places in Galilee. The northern parts of Galilee harboured also a few Shi'ite villages. Among the more

Napoleon in the Pesthouse at Jaffa.

influential populations were nomadic Bedouin tribes, which time and again conducted raids and during the latter part of the Ottoman period became heavily involved in local politics. These were all Muslim communities, but the population of the Holy Land consisted also of resilient communities of Jews and Christians. These had enjoyed a special status since the early days of Islam and were recognized as *Ahl al-Dhimma*, which means protected people.

What, then, were the ramifications of these demographic trends, in particular regarding the relations among communities of the Holy Land? It would seem that both the Mamluk and the Ottoman sultans were keen on keeping peaceful interfaith relations. As long as they were able to restrain local Muslim communities and keep hostilities at bay, authorities were rewarded with minimal expenses on policing local communities and enjoyed uninterrupted revenues from Christian and Jewish pilgrimage. So it would seem that both regimes had little incentive to change the status quo regarding minorities' rights. Consequently, cases of organized and deliberate harassing of minorities by authorities were uncommon. Of course, there were specific episodes during which orders arrived from above dictating that Christians or Jews vacate a certain site which they owned or pay additional (usually illegal) taxes. An example is the expulsion of the Franciscans from their monastery on Mount Zion in Jerusalem. In the latter years of the Mamluk Sultanate the movement of non-Muslims was restricted in this area as the Muslims sought better access to the Tomb of David. Efforts in this direction were renewed by Sultan Suleiman I when he launched his grand project of renovating the walls of the city in the 1530s. This time it was not about gaining better access for Muslims to the holy site inside, but about applying mounting pressure to oust non-Muslims from the area. Not only were the Franciscan monks of Mt Zion forced to pay large sums to fund the project, but soon after its completion the Sultan made sure that the legal mechanism would be found to allow him to ban them from the area. This ultimately took place by 1545 and from then until the nineteenth century Christians were forbidden to enter their holy sites on Mount Zion.

But while the authorities mostly maintained a practical and generally tolerant approach to minorities, things were strikingly different at the grassroots level. Hostility and the infringement of non-Muslim rights were increasingly common as the Muslims came to constitute a majority of the population. During the latter years of the Mamluk Sultanate local Muslims in Jerusalem were engaged in various activities against their rival communities, culminating in 1473 in the destruction of the Jewish Synagogue on Mt Zion, despite an express Sultanic decree forbidding it. The Christians were also vulnerable to more and more cases of religious extremism and violation of their long established protection. The most conspicuous activity of this nature was the construction of two minarets flanking the Holy Sepulchre towards the end of the fifteenth century. However, during the seventeenth century and even more so during the eighteenth century, Christian communities found themselves shielded under the patronage of European powers that were engaged in an escalating contest to enlarge their sphere of influence in the region. Yet the struggle over sacred places entailed also internal conflicts among Christian communities. This was attested time and again in the Holy Sepulchre in Jerusalem, but also in different locations within the Holy Land, such as the struggle over control of the sites on Mt Carmel between the Greek Orthodox community and the Catholic order of the Carmelites during the second half of the eighteenth century.

Locals, travellers, and pilgrims: narrating the Holy Land

In contrast to the peripheral political position described hitherto, the Holy Land remained a mesmerizing and an alluring destination for pilgrims and travellers of a variety of religions and backgrounds during the Mamluk and Ottoman periods. The numerous accounts are an invaluable source and contain information that more rigid and 'official' chroniclers may consider to be of lesser importance or would simply be oblivious to and thus might fail to mention. Precious details, such as diets, currency rates, religious landmarks, peasants' way of life, daily life among different communities, even the very existence of previously unknown communities, are all pertinent examples that spring to mind. This list is far from exhaustive and represents nothing more than a rudimentary selection from a bounty of narratives. Informed and accurate as some of these may have been, their personal preferences, background, and agenda demand at times a more critical approach to and awareness of their inherent biases.

Mujir al-Din al-Hanbali al-Ulaymi was a Jerusalemite judge who wrote the most informed and detailed local description of the Holy Land of the late Mamluk period (1495). His narration is concerned with what he as a devout Muslim and a proud denizen of Jerusalem holds to be important, dedicated mostly to the Muslim parts and people of the city. As a member of the educated elite he elaborates for example on religious luminaries who resided in Jerusalem and enriches us with nuanced descriptions of public landmarks as well as various historical events which took place in the city. His book is not dedicated solely to Jerusalem and so we enjoy also his knowledge regarding other cities and places. His pride in his city is well attested in the following general description of Mamluk Jerusalem:

> And as for the way Jerusalem is viewed from afar, it is a marvel renowned for its radiance and its fine appearance . . . If Gods allows an aspiring visitor to reach the noble al-Aqsa Mosque and the noble Tomb of Abraham, from the moment he sees these glorified places, he will receive so much delight and joy as can scarcely be described, and he will be relieved of hardship and fatigue.

Throughout his lengthy description Mujir al-Din stresses time and again the pivotal role of the religious centre of the city that is at the heart of the sanctuary, the Haram al-Sharif. He also talks much about the streets surrounding the holy precincts that were laced according to him with bustling markets, bath houses, pilgrimage lodges, schools, and Sufi centres. He is far less generous when it comes to Christian or Jewish locales within the city and his descriptions are full of disdain for these communities and their places. Thus the Holy Sepulchre is called in his description *Kanisat al-Qummama* (church of garbage) as opposed to *Kanisat al-Qiyama* (church of resurrection). Such expressions of contempt were not rare during the Mamluk (and Ottoman) era.

As the sultanate's power eroded over the course of the fifteenth century, the animosity between sectarian groups took a sharp turn for the worse. An indication of this growing intolerance is given in the lengthy, perceptive, and rather critical narration of Felix Fabri, a Dominican monk who travelled a few times to the region (1480, 1483) for a relatively long duration. In his 'Book of Wanderings' he alludes to the construction of the minarets adjacent to the most sacred Christian site in Jerusalem: 'From this tower they shout all day and night as is the custom of the "cursed religion" and they engage in such activities with the utmost disrespect to the Crucified and as an insult to Christendom.' Fabri had a sharp eye and regularly broached topics that far exceeded the ordinary purview of other Christian travellers. His vitriol comes in

View of the Church of the Holy Sepulchre in Jerusalem with flanking minarets.

response to his astute appreciation of Christianity's inferior position in Jerusalem during the late fifteenth century and of the growing intolerance of the local Muslim community.

In 1521 Rabbi Moshe Basola from the Italian town of Pesaro embarked on his own trek to the Levant. His in-depth account of the region is the outcome of a year and half of travels. He landed in Tripoli and from there travelled by foot to Beirut, Sidon, Tyre, and northern Galilee. He arrived in Safad in late October 1521 and spent some three weeks visiting a string of Jewish pilgrimage sites in its environs. His arrival in the Holy Land only four years after the Ottoman conquests makes his account among the best informed about this transition period. As might be expected he focuses on Jewish life and communities but does not fail to comment on more general issues, such as the commercial layout in Jerusalem. The city boasts, according to him, four covered markets consisting of small dedicated markets, such as the cotton market, the vegetable market, and so forth. While describing Safad he reveals that the town's Jewish community consisted of three hundred families—both established residents and new immigrants—and a few synagogues. Although the Mamluks had already been ousted from the region in 1517, it is safe to say that the modest town of Safad did not undergo drastic changes in the four years that had elapsed between the Ottoman conquest and Basola's journey.

In 1569, while confined to a prison cell in Sanaa, Yemen, a Jewish poet named Zechariah wrote down his travels in the Levant in a book he titled 'The Book of Morals'. The book was written in rhymed prose and contains a vivid description of Jewish lives in regions under Islamic rule. In 1567 he travelled through the Holy Land on his way from Syria to Egypt. While visiting Tiberias he visits a relatively big Yeshiva funded by 'an eminent woman from the great city of Constantinople that was closely connected to the powers that be'. Zechariah relates here too one of the most enigmatic episodes in Jewish history under the Ottomans. The wealthy and eminent woman in Zechariah's narrative is Gracia Mendes-Nasi. Dona Gracia, as she is often referred to, was born in Lisbon in 1510, to the noble *converso* family of Benveniste. She married Francisco Mendes-Nasi, a member of one of the largest international trading and banking firms in the world. Following the death of her husband she settled in Antwerp, which was then a free city and enabled her, as a Christian convert suspected of Jewish ancestry, to enjoy relative safety. After a lengthy ordeal involving some of the main political figures of the Europe of her time, this formidable lady and her untold wealth landed in Ottoman Istanbul in 1552. There she joined her nephew Joseph Miques (or by his Jewish name, Don Joseph Nasi), who was already a prominent figure in the politics of the Ottoman Empire. In 1558 she was appointed as the *muqtaaji* (tax collector) of the region of Tiberias by Sultan Suleiman. Apparently, while serving in this capacity, she invested in the region's economy and infrastructure in order to prepare it to absorb Jewish and *converso* refugees. It is suggested that she intended to transform Tiberias into a major centre of Jewish settlement, trade, and learning. The yeshiva seen by Zechariah in 1567 should be considered as part of these endeavours. However, these highly imaginative plans (for which very little documentation exists) came to a sudden halt upon Dona Gracia's death in 1569.

Mehmet Zilli was an Ottoman Turk born in 1611 in Istanbul who over the course of forty years had made a series of long journeys throughout the Ottoman Empire. He is better known by the name Evliya Celebi under which he published his collected notes in a ten-volume work called *Seyahatname* (Travelogue). He spent two years travelling in the Syrian region from 1648 to 1650 and left us with copious and detailed descriptions of the land. The following is his account of his visit to Nablus, a small town in Samaria:

> This is a Samaritan *sanjaq* in the province of Damascus. The annual fixed sum for the post of governor therein has been set aside by the Sultan to be 29,645 aqshe a year. The *sanjaq* has seven sub-counties (*za'amet*) and forty-four taxable fiefdoms (*timar*). The revenue of this *sanjaq* is granted to the commander of the caravans of Pilgrims to Mecca in Damascus. The fief-holders are ordered to accompany him with the inhabitants of their districts to the honored town of Mecca... The governor receives a yearly income of seventeen thousand piasters; the noble office of the qadi is endowed with one hundred and fifty *aqce* a year. There are two hundred villages in this district and yearly revenue of six thousand piasters accrues to the judge.

Evliya's narrative is highly informative on administrative issues and explains clearly how the Ottoman system operates at the local level as well as the possible repercussions of the dependency of various office holders on revenues cropped within their district.

In July 1653 the senior Russian monk Arsenij Sukhanov submitted his pilgrimage report (*Proskinitarij*) to the newly elected head of the Russian Church, Patriarch Nikon. This work was the outcome of a two-year voyage which took him from Moscow to Alexandria and the Holy Land and then back to Russia through Georgia and the Caucasus. The report consists of three parts of which two address internal polemical issues that troubled the Russian Orthodox Church at the time both internally and vis-à-vis its Greek-Orthodox counterpart. The second part of the work is dedicated to a description of Christian pilgrimage and sacred sites in the Holy Land. In the following passage he recounts the Christian pilgrimage to the Baptismal sites near Jericho on the Jordan River:

> All the peoples that have come to Jerusalem from all the lands, from around the world to venerate the sacred sites, old and young, monks and laymen, women and men, Greeks, Franks, Armenians and the rest of those infidels who are called Christians, all are exiting Jerusalem on the second day of the week of agony... some are leaving the city through Gethsemane Gate, some through Zion Gate. Passing through the Valley of Tears they all meet, on foot and mounted on horses, on the road to the Jordan. At the same time the Governor of Jerusalem leaves the city with his army to defend the pilgrims from the Arabs of the Jordan Valley desert... Everybody walks to the spring of Elisha... and they spend the night near Jericho; it used to be the city of Jericho but now the place is deserted and one cannot see the town... it is a village inhabited by Arabs.

Sukhanov draws a very gloomy picture not only of the land but also of the internal relations among Christian groups. Nevertheless, his narrative tells us much about the relations between pilgrims and local authorities and the taxes demanded at each and every sacred site.

As we draw to the close of this survey of the Holy Land under the Mamluks and Ottomans let us conclude with one of the most astute, informative, and reliable observers of the region, Constantine François de Chasseboeuf, Comte de Volney, who spent three years there (1782–1785). He published the account of his travels in a two-volume book in 1787 under the title *Voyage in Syria and Egypt*. It is a rigorous and exhaustive scientific report which reads as a geographic survey supplemented with vast ethnographic descriptions and penetrating political analysis. His narrative is furnished with ample data on administration, economy, agriculture, population numbers, and many other issues. He holds the political system and indeed the Ottoman sultan responsible for the wretched situation of the Levant as he found it during his long sojourn. Unlike other Europeans who arrived on the Eastern shores of the Mediterranean he is well aware of his own bias as an outsider from another place and culture: 'we must place ourselves in their situation in order to feel what they are influenced by and the consequences which result'. Yet, he says, 'the observer should be circumspect, but not timid'. Timid he is certainly not, but he tries to remain as objective as possible in his rather bleak reports on the state in which both Egypt and Syria are found. As a typical product of eighteenth-century European ideas of enlightenment and progress he muses time and again on the power of science and personal freedom and their absence in Syria. He concludes his description of his lengthy voyage in the region with an almost prophetic statement on the imminent collapse of the Ottoman control of the Holy Land:

> The account I have given shows how the abuse of authority, by causing the misery of the individuals, becomes eventually destructive to the power of the state and what we may safely venture to predict will soon go to prove that the ruin of the nation sooner or later rebounds upon those who have been the cause of it.

De Volney takes a rather dim view of the state of a Holy Land that he saw and experienced rather intimately during his lengthy travels. He is adamant in his assertion that the despotic political system of the Ottomans should be held accountable for the misery and poverty he witnessed. Be that as it may, De Volney touches on one of the more demanding topics that haunts scholars of the region studying the latter periods. This is usually treated under the heading; the decline of the Ottoman Empire. With respect to the Ottoman Empire one might simplify the issue by asking: was the Empire in decline from the late sixteenth century as previously suggested by doyens of the field? Is it really a decline and if so how can one measure such a condition? What are our frames of reference, indeed what do we compare it with? Certainly we need to adopt a very cautious approach; to quote De Volney once again: 'we have not only to combat the prejudices we meet in our way, but to overcome our own!' And indeed, we would do well to remember that the Ottomans, as indeed also the Mamluks, were among the longest surviving dynasties, and surely their empire could not have been in decline throughout its existence. If anything, this survey suggests that during the long periods of sovereignty of these Muslim-Turkish regimes there were times of prosperity, cultural vibrancy, building sprees, and positive encounters among different communities, which should be set against the periods of decline, social unrest, economic uncertainty, and tyrannical behaviour on the part of the ruling powers.

CHAPTER 10

From Napoleon to Allenby

The Holy Land and the Wider Middle East

ROBERT FISK

'WE must go to the Orient; all great glory has always been acquired there', Napoleon told his secretary Bourienne. The French Directory believed his expedition to Egypt would occupy a mere six months. Once he arrived in 1798—and before he fought his way down to Cairo with increasingly mutinous French troops—Napoleon issued a proclamation in 'inelegant' Arabic script in which he told Egyptians that he had not come to fight them, and that his purpose was to free them from the oppression of the Mamluks who were (up to a point) creatures of the Ottoman Empire. This propaganda sheet, whose contents would acquire a weary familiarity in the future colonial history of the region, was run off on a printing press aboard the French flagship *L'Orient.* Napoleon ordered his own soldiers to respect Muslims and even assured Egyptians that the French were themselves true Muslims who had deposed the hateful Pope. The French arrival, he said, was the will of Allah.

A hundred and twenty years later, the British would not go quite so far when they invaded the Arab world, but their professed respect for Muslims in Palestine and Mesopotamia was remarkably similar: 'our armies do not come into your cities and lands as conquerors or enemies, but as liberators', proclaimed General Frederick Maude in Baghdad in 1917 (the words were written by the woeful Mark Sykes). '[Y]our citizens have been subject to the tyranny of strangers…[your] safety from oppression and invasion must ever be a matter of the closest concern to the British Government.'

Napoleon was not pious. He decorated the local Arab sheikhs with tricolour badges and informed his men that they must show special courtesy towards Muslim women. But he took a quixotic view of the land he wished to develop—perhaps to colonize—and mixed his sensitivities towards Islam with a profoundly childish attitude towards its people. He flaunted himself in Oriental regalia and ordered the revolutionary French tricolour to be flown from Cairo's minarets, an idea which predictably went down very badly indeed. He wished to encourage the Arabs to rise up against their Turkish masters, another idea which would be borrowed 120 years later. T. E. Lawrence would admit his debt to Napoleon's military tactics in Egypt; that the quality of his soldiers must be better than the quantity of his enemy's forces. 'Napoleon, in his pregnant valuation of the Mamluks in terms of French soldiers, first gave me the idea', he wrote after the 1914–18 war. Lawrence, whose cruelty towards his enemies was clear even in the pages of *Seven Pillars of Wisdom*, noted elsewhere how 'Napoleon had spoken in angry reaction against the excessive finesse of the eighteenth century, when men almost forgot that war gave licence to murder.'

Napoleon showed little military finesse in his expedition to the Middle East. Setting an example of butchery for many other European adventurers, he ordered, during his 1799 Syrian campaign, the execution of 4500 Turkish prisoners outside Jaffa—they were driven into the Mediterranean, and shot or bayoneted to death—on the grounds that he had neither rations nor escorts for them. When Egyptians rose up against the French occupation, Napoleon rounded on them with Saddam-like ferocity and bombarded the great Al-Azhar mosque and the Citadel. His cannon-balls are still embedded in the walls. 'Here in Cairo', Napoleon wrote to one of his generals, 'I have heads cut off at the rate of five or six a day.'

There was always something frenzied about Napoleon, his sudden, brilliant military concepts balanced by his almost Roman fixation with constitutional law, his intuitive—and often poorly conceived—desire to act justly, often combined with his all too obvious wish to show off his genius for improvisation. The Muslims of Egypt must have noticed this. Did they really think his removal of the Pope made him a friend of Islam? How, then, is one to address the story—and scholars have responded to this with varying degrees of credibility—that Napoleon sought to restore the Jews to the land of their forefathers? After storming north into Syria, Napoleon's plan was to capture Acre from the Ottomans and then triumphantly enter Jerusalem, even pressing on to Damascus. It was during his ultimately hopeless sixty-three day battle for Acre—finally defeated by plague, massive casualties, the British Navy's capture of French guns, the pugnacity of the Ottoman defenders, and the knowledge that Ottoman reinforcements were approaching—that Napoleon apparently issued a proclamation to the Jews 'of Asia and Africa' to 're-establish the ancient Jerusalem', adding that he had already given weapons to Jewish 'battalions' outside Aleppo. The sadistic ruler of Acre, Ahmad Pasha al-Jazzar (*jazzar* means 'butcher' in Arabic), whom we encountered in Chapter 9, was principally assisted in military as well as banking advice by Haim Farhi, whose prominent Jewish family came from Damascus. Was Napoleon's generous proclamation intended to persuade Farhi to change sides and support the French army? Farhi did not do so although since he was later blinded by his ruler, it might have been a good idea.

The source of the 'proclamation' was the French revolutionary newspaper *Le Moniteur Universel* and it was published in Paris, quite by chance, scarcely twenty-four hours after Napoleon had abandoned his siege of Acre. Did he really believe that such a promise would bring Farhi to his side—as the British, rather more realistically, thought they could encourage Jews to join the Allied cause in 1917 with a more credible declaration of support? Or was this mere propaganda, demonstrating to Europeans that he was genuine when he demanded the emancipation of the Jews of Europe, merely seeking their help, such as it may be, in his Syrian campaign? They had been given full citizenship after the French Revolution and there is evidence enough of Napoleon's admiration for the Jewish people he found in Malta on his way to Egypt. But Napoleon appears to have issued his promise, which also referred to Jews as 'the rightful heirs of Palestine', in the third week of April 1799, when his siege of Acre had lasted more than a month and when failure must already have seemed a likely outcome. At such a moment, suborning the Pasha's Jewish adviser might have seemed worth the effort. It certainly seems to have prompted the rabbi of Jerusalem to urge his people to join Napoleon's forces. But if he had formulated a grand plan for a Jewish 'return' to Palestine, why not publish this proposal earlier in his campaign—or even before leaving Egypt?

Napoleon knew the history of the Jews, and Theodore Herzl, a founder of political Zionism, briefly referred to Napoleon in a letter to the Kaiser, but to regard the Emperor-to-be as some kind of original Zionist thinker seems to be cloning late nineteenth-century history onto a leader who would come to see the Jews of France as a benefit to his own country rather than to a plague-infested land that had brought about his first military defeat. Napoleon, like other generals, was a man who breathed in antiquity as the oxygen of warfare; he was following the path of history. He did see that Jews could be a political force, and he realized that the Ottoman Empire was probably in a terminal state. But he was before his time. The British struck in 1917 at a perfect political moment—for the Allies and for the Zionists.

Like Rommel almost a century and a half later, Napoleon wanted to destroy Britain's Indian trade routes. But being a dangerous romantic, he also wished to copy Alexander the Great by continuing his Egyptian adventure all the way to India. Yet Napoleon also believed in an early form of the French *mission civilisatrice,* the perfidious system of colonizing natives by giving them the benefits of western society without the privilege of becoming members, a system which the Algerians would have to endure later. Yet only nine years after the French Revolution, there was real sympathy for the poor of Egypt, the *fellahin* of the Delta, and the Nile Valley, thousands of whom Napoleon's army had killed in its initial Battle of the Pyramids but whose ancestors, along with an appropriate number of slaves, had supposedly built the ancient tombs from which the battle took its name.

Although Napoleon ordered his men to respect Christians as well as Jews and Muslims in Egypt, the Revolution which sent him there would never regard itself as a Christian movement. This was left to the English. Lloyd George would ask Allenby to give him Jerusalem as a Christmas present, but for decades the British—and later the Americans—had regarded the Middle East as an essentially biblical land which had been lost to them a thousand years before. Missionaries were the NGOs of their time, and their desire to re-establish a strong Christian presence in the Middle East would cause great offence, even to those ancient Christian sects whose ancestors had never left the Holy Land. The search for Christian roots would come to obsess Europeans and, later, Americans, as they sought to discover their own lost faith in a region of the

The Last Crusade. Lloyd George wanted Jerusalem as a Christmas present—and *Punch* magazine believed Richard the Lionheart thought the same. Despite official efforts to avoid the Crusades as a symbol of Allenby's entry into the city in 1917, writers and cartoonists in London felt compelled to emphasize the British Army's biblical achievement in the Holy Land.

world that did not belong to them. Neither future admiral nor future emperor may have understood the language or the irony, but Nelson isolated Napoleon after destroying the French fleet and its flagship *L'Orient* in the waters off an Egyptian Arab town named after the father (*Abu*) of a Cypriot Christian martyr called Cyrus (*Qir*): Aboukir Bay. The English preferred to call it the Battle of the Nile.

But the French Revolution brought a unique gift to Egypt which would transform the people of the Middle East; for Napoleon, a literary and mathematical man, brought with him a battalion of civilians—scientists, archaeologists, doctors, technicians, map-makers, and chemists, whose contributions to the French expedition were more important than any military endeavour. New hospitals, mills, agricultural projects, land taxes—collected by Christian Copts, it should be noted—impressed the sheikhs; one of Napoleon's more astringent biographers was moved to record how he issued orders 'for the erection of street lanterns every thirty yards through the main thoroughfares of Cairo'. The general's *Institut d'Egypte* created the science of Egyptology and, in the year after Napoleon's invasion, discovered the Rosetta Stone, which allowed the French to decypher Pharaonic hieroglyphs. The Institute's modern premises were to be burned out in Egypt's 2011 post-revolutionary violence—an 'awakening' originally regarded in France and other European countries as a progressive event—along with 200,000 volumes and an eighteenth-century map of Lower and Upper Egypt.

Murad and Ibrahim, the Mamluk Beys who effectively ruled Egypt and treated their Ottoman masters with contempt, believed in 1798 that their horses would easily overwhelm Napoleon's army—an arrogance to be repeated by other Arab rulers in the twentieth and twenty-first centuries—and the early nineteenth-century Egyptian scholar Abdulrahman al-Jabarti regarded their misrule as responsible for the easy French invasion, and thus for the effective collapse of Ottoman rule in Egypt. Indigenous Egyptians regarded the Mamluks as descendants of enfranchised slaves. Indeed, Napoleon's invasion marks a symbolic moment in the miserable decline of the imperial government in Constantinople, a tragedy—for so many of the Empire's people—which would reach its climax when Generals Maude and Allenby marched into Baghdad and Jerusalem respectively. The 119 years between Napoleon's landing and the Allied capture of Damascus in 1918 is the story of the end of an empire which ruled most of the Middle East—and, for a time, a large portion of Europe—since the start of the fourteenth century. It was to expire in the betrayal of the Arabs, the temporary military defeat of Turkey, and the greatest act of bloodletting in the Middle East in modern times.

Empires have a habit of subsuming the nations which they rule. They rub up against local history and leave us with the invading rulers' narrative of events and discoveries, and a subsidiary literature of poorly archived and often sloppily indexed accounts by those whose fate was to live in submission. Thus we see Napoleon's occupation largely through French eyes, or those of the Ottomans who did not believe that Napoleon's soldiers were 'sincere friends of the Ottoman Sultan and enemies of his enemies' and who subsequently declared war on France with the opportunistic support of the British Navy. In fact, Napoleon's rule was doomed by the heavy taxes imposed on both the

All our pomp of yesterday. Only months after General Maude's 1917 'liberation' of Baghdad from the Ottomans, British war artist Donald Maxwell travelled up the Tigris and painted this Turneresque view of a British steamship approaching an Iraqi sailing boat. On the bleak horizon, oil fires are burning. The West would try vainly—through occupation, dictatorship and invasion—to control Iraq for the next century.

middle classes and the poor, by French looting—accompanied by the usual atrocities, including the hanging of the governor of Alexandria—and, as al-Jabarti says, the expropriation of property. Despite its revolutionary clothes, the French *were* Christians—those Muslim Egyptian women who married Napoleon's soldiers invariably converted—and the Muslim people turned to their preachers in al-Azhar to lead them in their opposition to the highly intelligent and scientifically-minded infidels.

This produced a form of psychological as well as military chaos not dissimilar, perhaps, to that which followed the Anglo-American invasion of Iraq in 2003. In al-Jabarti's words, the French invasion of 1798 was 'the beginning of a period of great battles, terrible events, disastrous occurences, ghastly calamities, ever increasing misfortunes...persecutions, disorders...continual terrors, revolutions, administrative disorders, catastrophes and general devastation'. Could there be a better description of the Middle East in the second decade of the twenty-first century?

Napoleon was to abandon his Egyptian adventure, his army, and his married French mistress in just over a year. The remaining French forces swiftly surrendered to the Ottomans whose armies included Mohamed Ali, a ruthless young Albanian mercenary in the Turkish expeditionary force. He would subsequently rule Egypt and much of the region after variously fighting the Mamluks, defeating the British, and absorbing many of the French. The heads of all three groups were displayed on spikes in the streets of Cairo over the coming eleven years, the Mamluks themselves finally vanquished when their leaders were invited to enjoy a banquet in the Citadel and, on attempting to leave down a narrow rock passageway, were massacred by Mohamed Ali's killers. In all, perhaps 4000 Mamluk grandees and kinsmen were slaughtered in Cairo alone, their houses plundered, their friends hunted down and beheaded. Napoleon's head-chopping was modest by comparison.

Mohamed Ali subsequently set out for Arabia to administer Ottoman justice to rebellious tribesmen of the Sunni Wahhabi faith—a temporary victory because a century later, the Wahhabi Al Sauds would conquer almost all of the peninsula including Mecca, ultimately controlling much of the Arab world's oil. Out of this world would later spring a wealthy young guerrilla fighter called Osama bin Laden. Abdul Aziz Al Saud had inherited his faith from his father Mohamed's alliance with Abdul Wahhab, the eighteenth-century preacher who—like so many clergymen, before and since—believed that a catastrophe visited upon his co-religionists was the punishment of God; in his case (and he took his cue from an even earlier Syrian theologian), the Mongol subjugation of Islam meant that God had abandoned Muslims and that Muslims must therefore return to a life precisely the same as that of the Prophet and his companions.

All objectors to this harsh creed must be eliminated, all reverence for anything other than God must be destroyed, those caught in adultery stoned to death. Mohamed Ibn Saud was later assassinated, and his son Abdul Aziz subsequently declared himself the successor to Wahhab after the latter's death in 1792. In 1802, Abdul Aziz conquered the Mesopotamian city of Kerbala, slaughtered 2000 of its Shia citizens—a sect of corrupt deviants, in the eyes of the original Abdul Wahhab—and captured Medina, where his men smashed the tombs of the Prophet's companions. They did the same to the Prophet's supposed birthplace in Mecca. Those who now have to tolerate the twenty-first century might be forgiven if they saw the mirror image of these grim events—the mass killing of Shia Muslims, the destruction of tombs and historical sites, the vicious punishment of those who have transgressed the strictest Islamic laws—in their own age. They would be right. The 'Islamic Caliphate' which would proclaim itself in 2014, was the direct descendant of this fateful eighteenth-century alliance.

Its mistake—until the House of Saud re-emerged as a more powerful tribe decades later—was to challenge Ottoman power. No better man than Mohamed Ali, then, to act on the sultan's behalf. He destroyed Abdul Aziz's forces and packed the latter's son and heir to Constantinople for decapitation. Slicing off the heads of his enemies was clearly not confined to the Mamluks. But, educated in Salonika, Mohamed Ali understood western (and specifically French) history and military culture—the future Mustafa Kemal Ataturk, final liquidator of the Ottoman Empire, would be born in the same city a few years later—and used French advisers to remodel the Egyptian army and redesign the country's economy. This was the same army which would overwhelm the Greeks at the beginning of the war of independence, and conquer Sudan.

Mohamed Ali created a unique and symbiotic relationship between nationalism and French learning, drafting Egyptians into his army, planting cotton fields in the Delta, building canals, and introducing secular schools, while sending students to France to breathe in the language of Reason. Only in Lebanon, where the Maronite church communed with the Church of Rome, did 'local' culture become neo-European in the manner in which it developed in Egypt. But the presence of Al-Azhar as a centre of Islamic learning and thus a storehouse of Arabic literature, as the Arabic scholar John Haywood would observe, gave Cairo (at least to start with) a distinct advantage over Beirut.

The Arabic language had to be adapted to modern science. Of the forty-four officers, including his grandson, whom Mohamed Ali first sent to France, the most impressive was Rifa'a al-Tahtawi. He was to become the counterpart of all those Frenchmen who arrived in Egypt thirsting for Pharaonic knowledge and Arab history. Al-Tahtawi

Egypt's first feminist in her early years. Huda Shaarawi drank the fruits of French literature and culture as an antidote to British occupation, studied the Koran, and became an accomplished pianist.

learned fluent French, translated European science books into Arabic, and read Racine, Voltaire, and Rousseau; he even edited a newspaper and thus, along with Mohamed Ali who founded *al-Waqai al-Misriyya* ('Egyptian Events'), became the father of Arab journalism. Before he died in 1873, he was the most modern of Egyptians, lighting a fire for the country's feminists forty years later—though he never called for the abolition of the veil—by demanding girls' education and opening the first Egyptian girls' school. His belief that Islamic law should be reinterpreted might have cost him his life a century and a half later.

Mohamed Ali courted the friendship of the Maronite 'Emir of Lebanon', Bashir Shihab II, officially only an Ottoman tax-collector but, like Mohamed Ali, another intellectual—ruthless as well as erudite—who encouraged Lebanon's literary renaissance and believed in education and foreign cultural contact. His crushing of his own Shihabi rivals—their leaders were blinded, imprisoned, banished, hanged, or assassinated—was achieved with a thoroughness that must have impressed the 'Viceroy of Egypt'. Bashir's Druze opponents were humiliated, only the poor chief of the Jumblatt clan holding out until Bashir prevailed upon the Pasha of Acre to hang him. Butcher and despot, he also had more than a little in common with Napoleon, whose ambitious siege of Acre he declined to support but whose artistic pretensions he emulated in building the glorious palace at Beit Eddin—which exists to this day under the tutelage of the descendants of his old enemy Jumblatt.

Bashir's educated elite included Nasif al-Yaziji, a Christian Greek Catholic scholar who could, reportedly, not only recite the entire works of the early Iraqi poet Mutanabbi but the entire Koran as well. Teacher and versifier—it is difficult to find anyone today who actually *enjoys* Yaziji's writing—he lived with his emir at Beit Eddin and later taught at the missionary Syrian Protestant College, which would become the American University of Beirut. Grammarian and rhetorician—rhetoric being an essential although increasingly decadent element of Arabic poety at the time—he also mythologized the benevolence of Christian rule in Lebanon, suggesting that the land was a nation in itself rather than a tribal area of Syria. But Bashir was no more an all-popular feudal leader of Christians, Sunni, Shia, and Druze than Saddam would be a beloved patriarch of all Iraqis 150 years later. Lebanon's writers, mostly Christian—Nikola al-Turk, Boutros Karama, Amin al-Jundi among them—were courtiers and worked for the Emir.

Thus Lebanon's 'Europeanization' came about not through invasion—although there were plenty to come, just as there are Maronites today who would suggest this phenomenon began with the Crusades—but through the Maronite conception of Lebanon as a country. It was to be psychologically separated from its Syrian-Ottoman landscape in which Arab nationalism—on an inter-Arab scale, stretching down to Arabia and Egypt—would usually be represented by the Sunnis (and in Lebanon to some extent by the Greek Orthodox minority) rather than the Christians. In Austria, for example, Metternich regarded Lebanon as a country in its own right; thus it was inevitable that a mere provincial entity of Ottoman Syria would attract foreign intervention.

No hint of war: scarcely twelve months before Edward Lear painted this romantic view of Beirut in 1861, around 10,000 Christians and Druze had been massacred in the mountains on the right of the painting.

Maronite–Druze conflict was partially responsible for Bashir's downfall and the subsequent Druze–Christian civil war of 1860. This horror brought French troops to Beirut to defend the Christians—they pitched camp in the pine forest where the French embassy stands to this day—and elicited a promise of support for the Druze from the British, who offered their leaders' sons the dubious reward of education at an English public school. History has largely forgotten the far more terrible massacre of 12,000 Christians in a single day in Damascus, perhaps because the Ottomans responded with appropriate brutality, hanging a hundred of those held responsible, including the Pasha of Damascus. A Beirut conference of the six major European powers—Britain, France, Russia, Germany (Prussia at the time), Austria, and Italy (or 'Sardinia')—then recognized the privileged Ottoman Sanjak of 'Mount Lebanon'. No one disputed that this was part of Syria, whose own existence as a pseudo-state was only recognized three years later when the *Vilayat* (Governorate) of Damascus was renamed the *Vilayat* of Syria. But Lebanon and especially the great old Roman city of Beirut were doomed to become a 'jewel'—fake perhaps, as false as the propagandists who would later claim it to be the Paris of the Middle East—in the crowns of both Ottomans and Europeans.

For if Lebanon could be a nation, then it could also rid itself of Ottoman suzerainty. A Christian nationalist could be an Arab Lebanese nationalist, even an Arab Syrian nationalist; Arab Muslims, however, could feel themselves Ottoman as well as Arab since the Ottoman state was for them also the State of Islam. To be secular and Arab usually meant to be Christian. American and British missionaries perhaps unwittingly fed into this new and precarious 'history', translating the Bible into modern Arabic with the help of local teachers, both accentuating and softening the differences between faiths. The American-taught scholar Boutros al-Boustani was among these Bible translators and would become one of the great intellectuals of late nineteenth-century Lebanon, a Maronite convert to Protestantism who spoke of a secular Arab, albeit Ottoman, nationality. He founded the most famous and challenging of Lebanese-Syrian educational institutions, the National School, for children of every religion—Maronite, Christian, Sunni, Shia—and built houses for Christian and Muslim teachers to educate pupils in a non-religious environment. Speaking Hebrew, Greek, and Latin, al-Boustani also edited an Arabic dictionary and encyclopedia. It is a grim reflection on the Arab world's concern for its own intellectual history that today the school lies in ruins, its entrance vestibule collapsed, its classrooms decayed into run-down Pepsi parlours, its great goitered arches crumbling behind a concrete wall. The school-teachers' houses now sprout trees.

The Lebanese historian Kamal Salibi, a Protestant scholar who wrote speeches for the civil war Maronite leader and president-elect Bashir Gemayel who was murdered in 1982, convinced himself that the Christian Arabs of Syria–Lebanon were the first advocates of Arab nationalism, partly because the Christian Copts of Egypt spoke Arabic but were not ethnically Arab in origin. While Mesopotamia (Iraq) remained an essentially eastern and poor Arab Ottoman land—historically invaded by Persians, its writers inevitably influenced by Persian poetry—and the sandpit of Trans-Jordan was a mere part of the Damascus *vilayat*, Palestine, like Lebanon, found itself, for obvious reasons, a target for Christian missionaries. Catholic, Protestant, and Greek Orthodox schools, printing presses and hospitals flourished amid a population of 600,000, 10 per cent of them Christians and the rest mostly Sunni Muslims. In 1880, almost two decades before Theodore Herzl, the founder of Zionism, travelled to Jerusalem, Jews numbered only around 25,000 in the lands which would become the British mandate of Palestine after the 1914–18 war, and which, later still, would include the State of Israel. By 1890, they would be a majority of the population in Jerusalem.

Arab–Muslim relations with the tiny Jewish minority were peaceful, with Arab Christians, they were friendly. Indeed, Palestine was to be the only Arab land—then or in the future—in which virtually no tensions existed between Muslim and Christian. The great Muslim families held all the senior municipal posts in Palestine, but Christian schools provided better education than Muslim Turkish schools and the growing commercial class was largely Christian. At the same time, European and American Christian sects poured in from abroad, one of them fully believing that they would meet the Messiah on the road to Jericho.

Just why resistance to Ottoman rule was so late in reaching the Arab world is not difficult to understand. The Ottoman Empire was notable for its anti-colonial instincts.

'When I remember thee in days to come…' wrote Theodore Herzl, the founder of Zionism. Jerusalem in 1898 was still countryfied, and stagecoaches were waiting for tourists outside the Jaffa Gate—through which General Allenby would walk on foot nineteen years later.

Although in its final century it ruled most of the Arab peoples—sometimes brutally, often feebly, and always capriciously—it never attempted to colonize the land, as the French did in Algeria and as the Zionists would do in post-mandate Palestine. While Europe taunted the Turkish Ottomans for their political and military weakness and successfuly sought to destroy the Empire in the 1914–18 war, Britain and France had found reason to support the Turks in the mid-nineteenth century when Russia was about to seize Ottoman territory. Whether or not Tsar Nicholas I invented the phrase 'the sick man of Europe' for Turkey, the 1853–1856 Crimean war was caused—these origins are largely ignored today—by a dispute between the rights of Christian minorities in the Holy Land (the French supporting the Catholics, the Russians the Greek Orthodox). British and Turkish Muslim troops were thus fighting and dying on the same side sixty years before the Ottomans suicidally chose to join the German and Austro-Hungarian Empires against the Entente in 1914.

Until that world tragedy there was still hope that Arabs might prevent or at least delay the Ottoman collapse. Under Turkey's 1876 constitution, they were elected to the Parliament in Constantinople. Members from Jerusalem, Jaffa, Nablus, Acre, and Gaza took their seats in 1908 and 1912. The prominent Lebanese Sunni businessman and politician Selim Salaam represented Beirut in Constantinople, although he later opposed the Empire as well as the French mandate which followed. His son Saeb became prime minister during the Lebanese civil war and in Beirut would proudly show off Selim's official Ottoman pass to the parliament buildings in Constantinople, which hung on the wall of the family's home in the suburb of Musaytbe. Salim always wore the traditional *tarbush* hat, Saeb favoured his own trademark red carnation. Contrary to the image of a decaying empire, the Ottomans blessed Beirut with a new port, paved roads, public gardens, and a fine steam train route over the mountains to Damascus. The locomotives were state-of-the-art Swiss rack-and-pinion engines and carried the Damascus-bound Kaiser Wilhelm of Germany to Sofar on the heights above Beirut during his state visit to Syria–Lebanon in 1898. Christian residents sought the Kaiser's help in protesting what they claimed was their minority status in the Empire. 'Then become Muslims!' the Kaiser is alleged to have replied. But the West remained a visionary second home for many Christians in the Middle East.

Thus, around the shores of the Arab Mediterranean, a Christian minority—in Egypt, in Palestine, and in Syria–Lebanon—would, for religious, cultural, and commercial reasons, look towards Europe, enthusiastically supported by a growing Muslim middle class. But the notion that this would somehow create a bridgehead between the two great societies, between the East and Europe—or between the 'Muslim world' and 'the West' as politicians and journalists would revealingly call these potential antagonists many decades later—was a precarious one. Arabs would be welcome to imbibe the wisdom of 'civilization' in Paris, London, or Rome. But in return, Europe sent to Egypt, to Palestine, and to Syria–Lebanon an army of Orientalists, whose writing, sketches, and paintings would warp our western understanding of the Middle East for at least a century and a half, producing a vindictive cocktail of romance, beauty, lechery, wonder, fantasy, awe, and disgust for those who became addicted to it.

Executioner and military failure: Jemal Pasha, one of the three Turks who led the Ottoman Empire throughout the First World War, stands with his staff in Jerusalem. Despite hanging Arab nationalists—journalists, soldiers, intellectuals, and clerics—he failed to destroy the Arab revolt.

At its most seductive, this cultural invasion, as persuasive and dominating as satellite television would prove to be in the Middle East, produced fine works of art. At its worst, in the sexual grotesqueries of Flaubert, for example, and the cruel sectarian analyses of Lamartine—who carved his name on one of the ancient cedars of Lebanon like a twentieth-century graffiti kid—it depicted the Muslim world as sexually depraved, socially decadent, and untrustworthy. The late and audacious Palestinian scholar Edward Said, who will always be associated with the word 'Orientalism' because he endowed his groundbreaking work with the same title, spoke of this phenomenon as an 'enterprise', almost as if it was a colonial project, carefully planned and organized as a victorious military campaign. That may have been the effect. It pretended to be a medium through which the Arab Muslim world could be understood while at the same time turning its people into aliens. It corrupted the most basic terminology of our language; the very expression 'Middle East' employed in this chapter is itself a potent and enduring example of this sense of superiority. 'Middle', for us, means halfway to the 'Far' East. But East of what?

This mysterious environment—of desert warriors, harems, oases, whirling dervishes, half-dressed women, slaves, naked children, Muslims at prayer—was portrayed in a mixture of styles; Impressionist, pre-Raphaelite, even Rubenesque. Arab faces are often painted with great sensitivity (Etienne Dinet's *Le lendemain de Ramadan, aprés la prière*, for example) and depict a people who are both sincere and intelligent as well as violent. The opulence of their carpets and silk gowns—in mosques, souks, private homes—is matched by the sensuousness of women whose traditional modesty is replaced on canvas by *odalisques* (Frederick Bridgeman's *L'aprés-midi, Alger*) and whose scarcely concealed nudity suggests an Arab world more interested in sexual pleasure than submission to God. This art was given integrity not only by its photographic precision but by the renown of the painters who travelled to the Arab world, Eugene Delacroix among them.

Yet one theme almost exclusively dominated their work: antiquity rather than modernity, ancient mosques with cracked walls, unpaved streets, men dressed in long robes and turbans, tableaux that might have been painted in the fifteenth and not the nineteenth century. The Middle East which the Orientalists painted was in reality also a world of modern industry, of railway trains, the telegraph, the Suez Canal, even the early telephone. In the cities of the late nineteenth and early twentieth century, Arab men wore the modern *tarbush* rather than turbans, suits rather than robes, and the Arabs were fascinated by photography and western music as well as European literature. True, many of these objects were imported from Britain and France—de Lesseps' canal was itself a colonial undertaking which helped to bankrupt Egypt—but they demonstrated quite clearly that Arabs wished to be part of the age of steel and industrial technology as well as of Islam.

Most of the Orientalist painters visited Cairo in the 1860s and 1870s when the rule of Ismail and Tewfiq Pasha coincided not just with technological progress—railways, canals, and ports—but political agitation, including military protests against Egypt's

No hint of modernity: when Leon Belly painted his timeless portrayal of pilgrims on foot and camel trekking towards Mecca in 1861, steam locomotives were already pulling passenger trains from Cairo to Suez, and de Lesseps was only eight years from completing the Suez Canal.

bankruptcy and Ismail's feckless policy of indebting his country to European powers. Yet the Orientalists chose to ignore these exciting—and, one would have thought, artistically graphic—events. The Viennese painter Ludwig Deutsch was in Cairo in the years immediately following Britain's 1882 invasion, the bombardment of Alexandria, and the catastrophic battle (for Ahmad Orabi and for the 2000 Egyptians who died there) of Tel el-Kabir. Yet Deutsch occupied himself by painting tombs, Nubian dancers, and a magnificent canvas of Muslim students reading the Qur'an and praying in the courtyard of Al-Azhar. Several photographs were taken of the aftermath of the British military victory; one image shows the corpse of an Egyptian soldier lying beside a dead camel, a poignant historical and political statement of Egypt's courage, loss, humiliation, and future occupation. Here, indeed, was ideal subject matter for any painter.

But not for the Orientalists. If they were not transmitting images of a glorious Arab past that still (in theory) existed, they were also implicitly stating that these people *lived* in the past, that they were therefore socially backward and thus decadent—and, by extension, *sauvage*. David Roberts' paintings of Pharaonic and Roman remains—the temples of Edfu and Baalbek, for instance—depict a world of antiquity whose titanic and ruined buildings appear architecturally more modern than the broken streets and laneways of nineteenth-century Cairo. Nothing which suggested that Arabs appreciated the comforts, privileges, and culture of the time was permitted on their canvas. The Arab world was a key to a previous age rather than to the future, to the broken theatres, temples, and architecture of a non-Arab Pharaonic or pan-European Classical Roman history. For Delacroix on his visit to Morocco, 'Rome is no longer in Rome itself. Antiquity has nothing more beautiful.'

But injected into this same *oeuvre* was a more proselytizing art form, the depiction of places and shrines sacred to Christians, for whom the 'Middle East' was really the 'Holy Land' and whose history was immortalized by William Bartlett's steel engravings of the churches of Jerusalem and Bethlehem and the caves of Old Testament prophets. In his pictures, Muslims are relegated to the role of miniature bystanders, their religion symbolized by distant minarets. The British traveller and writer John Carne, whose father was a Wesleyan, felt able, in his text accompanying a three-volume set of Bartlett's illustrations in 1836, to write of an Arab people who were 'a prey to indolence and apathy', describing Islam as 'the selfish system of manners, and false faith, of the Qur'an'. The text is also anti-Catholic. But there is no doubt of the social perspective of Carne's publishers. The desire of future tourists to see the ancient biblical sites, they wrote in a preface, will be 'strengthened by...the various incentives to enterprise held out by science, by commerce, and by the gradual progress of European ideas and civilisation'.

If Muslims were regressive, so also were the Jews portrayed—of whom Carne writes in the spirit of a nineteenth-century anti-Semite—presenting 'a picture of poverty and dejection, as well as recklessness of heart, veiled to every proof that their law and traditions are passed away for ever'. Carne notes that many Jewish women are 'remarkably handsome'—thus comforming to the Orientalist obsession with female beauty—but cruelly describes a Jewish street hawker as 'a true Hebrew, anything to turn a penny'. More than fifty years later, when Christian tourists were now flocking to the Middle East, *Murray's Hand-Book for Travellers in Syria and Palestine* was to speak of Sunni Muslims as 'proud, fanatical and illiterate...regardless of truth, dishonest in their dealings, and secretly immoral in their conduct'. While the upper classes were 'mentally feeble' (because of polygamy and 'degrading vices'), the peasantry were 'robust and vigorous, and much might be hoped for from them if they were brought under the influence of liberal institutions'. For 'liberal', of course, read European. While acknowledging that the Jews of Palestine 'were driven from the home of their fathers' eighteen centuries earlier, 'the Jews of Palestine are foreigners. They have come from every country on earth...[but] under the fostering care of Baron Edmond Rothschild and others, Jewish colonies are springing up in many parts of the Holy Land, and some of them are really in a flourishing condition.'

But God, in His various manifestations, seems always to have had a baleful influence on the birthplaces of the world's great monotheistic religions. Much though God would be worshipped, revered, sought after, loved, and fought for, his presence—Quranic, Biblical, Judaic—would come together in spiritual, political, and colonial agony in the land called, with varying geographical boundaries and end dates, Palestine.

By the end of the nineteenth century, Muslims claimed their right to the territory because they lived in it, owned most of it (insofar as Ottoman land documents were title deeds) and because the Prophet Mohamed had travelled to heaven from the very centre of Jerusalem. Christian claims were based on the Bible, the birthplace of Jesus which lay just twelve miles from the city, and a largely unexpressed belief that the Crusades should have been successful. Jewish adherence to Palestine had almost always been religious; the heritage of the Jewish empire, the expulsion from Jerusalem, the Bible, the prayers of every Jew for centuries, and the population of Jews who still lived in that most holy and most dangerous of cities.

For a 'land without people', there were a lot of Arabs in Palestine. Two 19th-century Bethlehem girls in local embroidery and with coins sown into their headdress.

But the late nineteenth-century origin of the Jewish demand for a state in Palestine was primarily political, intended to resolve the generations of anti-Semitism that had afflicted the Jews of Europe. Theodore Herzl's *Der Judenstaat* (The Jewish State), a pamphlet written, ironically, in the language of the future killers of his people, was a prescient and extremely eloquent proposal to end the generations of persecution; indeed, so powerful are its accounts of Jewish suffering, that it might have been written in the 1930s. But in 1896, Herzl was imagining 'the restoration of the Jewish state' and in one paragraph wrote, in essence, the founding declaration of a future Israel: 'Let the sovereignty be granted us over a portion of the globe large enough to satisfy the rightful requirements of a nation; the rest we shall manage for ourselves.' The problem, as Herzl saw for himself, is that another people, the largely Muslim Arabs of Ottoman Palestine, already lived in this 'portion of the globe'. 'An infiltration [of Jews] is bound to end badly', he wrote. 'It continues till the inevitable moment when the native population feels itself threatened, and forces the government to stop a further influx of Jews. Immigration is consequently futile unless we have the sovereign right to continue such immigration.' Herzl thought that a portion of Argentina as much as Palestine might become the Jewish homeland. Yet within a year, the First Zionist Congress, chaired by Herzl himself, declared that 'the aim of Zionism is to create for the Jewish people a home in Palestine secured by public law'.

But who would 'grant' the 'sovereignty' of which Herzl wrote? And who would donate the 'sovereign right' to immigration? It certainly wouldn't be the Palestinian Arab population—who at this stage had no sovereign national identity and, in Herzl's words, would 'feel itself threatened'. Napoleon had been dreaming. The Kaiser showed no interest. The Sultan would permit only limited Jewish immigration to other parts of his empire. Ruhi Khalidi, the nephew of Jerusalem's mayor and a newly elected member of the Ottoman parliament, sought vainly in Constantinople to halt Jewish immigration, telling members that Zionists—he sought to differentiate Jews from Zionist colonizers—were forming a militia in Palestine. But 'Herzl viewed the [Arab] natives as primitive and backward', an Israeli historian would later write, 'and his attitude toward them was rather patronizing. He...did not consider them a society with collective political rights over the land in which they formed the overwhelming majority.' Herzl 'hoped that economic benefits would reconcile the Arab population to the Zionist enterprise in Palestine'. Like Napoleon, Herzl thought his people could bring the benefits of western 'civilization' to the Arabs.

The casual, almost promiscuous way in which this civilization would shove aside the fears and aspirations of the Arabs in the First World War would prove only that the superpowers of the time—as now—cared exclusively for their national interests. In retrospect, the infamous correspondence of Sir Henry McMahon, the British High Commissioner in Cairo, to Husain Ibn Ali, the Sherif of Mecca, can be seen as the deceiptful and disingenuous promise that it represented. Far from offering Husain a caliphate across the Middle East in return for an Arab uprising against the Turks, it 'cabin'd cribb'd, confin'd' Husain's state, setting aside lands which 'cannot be said to be

'...in the name of God, let Palestine be left alone', Yusuf Diya-uddin Pasha al-Khalidi, mayor of Jerusalem in 1899, wrote to the chief rabbi of France who showed it to Theodore Herzl, the founder of Zionism. Herzl replied to al-Khalidi to tell him that if the Zionists were not wanted in Palestine, 'we will find elsewhere what we need'.

purely Arab' (goodbye to much of Syria, all of Lebanon and, by extension, Palestine) or which required 'special administrative arrangements' (goodbye to most of modern day Iraq). The equally mendacious Sykes–Picot agreement which carved up the Middle East into British and French zones—later to be honoured with the name of 'mandates' by the post-war League of Nations—merely formalized European ambitions, albeit kept secret until the Bolsheviks revealed their contents after the 1917 Revolution.

The public Balfour Declaration of the same year—a single sentence in a short letter to Lord Rothschild, a leader of the British Jewish community—bore no relation to the post-war justice for the Middle East which the victors proclaimed as their ambition. One of the purposes of the Great War, as it was called at the time, was to destroy the Ottoman empire; its territories could therefore be promised to anyone whose assistance might prove necessary to defeat the German-Austrian-Ottoman alliance. After the bloodletting at Verdun and the Somme and the French army mutinies on the Western Front, such undertakings were easily given by the Allies, especially when they might earn the allegiance of Jewish communities in America, Britain, post-revolutionary Russia, and Germany itself.

The British government's support for a 'national homeland for the Jewish people' in Palestine was itself deeply ambiguous. 'National' implied statehood. 'Homeland' suggested something less, a 'protected' area, perhaps, rather like the Maronites enjoyed on Mount Lebanon. It implied—but did not offer—all of Palestine to the Jews. But it was perfectly clear that the final part of the crucial sentence was worthless. The 'homeland' would be established, Balfour wrote, 'it being clearly [*sic*] understood that nothing shall be done which may prejudice the civil and religious rights of existing non-Jewish communities in Palestine'. 'Understood' by whom? And what were the 'civil rights' of the 'non-Jewish communities' if they were not a right to the very lands upon which the Jewish 'homeland' would be established? Churchill was more cursory, writing in 1919 of the collapse of the Ottomans and of 'the Jews, whom we are pledged to introduce into Palestine, and who take it for granted that the local population [*sic*] will be cleared out to suit their convenience'.

While the boundaries of the 'Holy Land' have always been uncertain, it would be perverse to exclude the land of Saint Paul and the possible burial place of the virgin Mary—not least because inside modern Turkey and its hinterland, the Christians of the Middle East suffered their greatest martyrdom amid the upheavals of the early twentieth century. In the Armenian Quarter of Jerusalem today, you can trawl through the catalogues of Armenian cities, towns, and villages from which this ancient Christian people were dispossesed by the Ottoman authorities. A million and a half of them were put to death, beheaded, knifed, and starved, the women raped and the children murdered on death marches into the deserts of northern Syria. Churchill himself was to call this greatest war crime of the 1914–18 conflict a 'holocaust'.

At the end of this awesome catastrophe, General Allenby, still mourning the death of his only son on the Western Front less than five months earlier, walked on foot into Jerusalem in an act of Allied humility before the world's three great religions. His total

A 'holocaust' to be repeated: Armenian victims of the October 1895 Erzerum massacre are buried in a mass grave—precursor of the world's first 'holocaust' in 1915 when up to a million and a half Armenians were slaughtered by the Ottoman Turks.

victory at Megiddo in September 1918, comparable to the final Allied offensive in France a year later, broke the Turkish army—although not its ability to fight on after the armistice. General Maude arrived in Baghdad to declare his soldiers 'liberators', but to die of cholera a few days later because he declined to boil his milk. T. E. Lawrence, the train wrecker of the Hejaz, finally and after much butchery helped the Arabs to liberate Damascus—only to hear Allenby explain to Husain's son, Prince Faisal, in the Victoria Hotel, that Syria would be controlled by the French.

Already, however, the torture wheels of the future Middle East had been set in place: the Arab-Zionist battle for Palestine and the subsequent Arab-Israeli wars, the Arab nationalist struggle against the colonial powers—and later against the Americans—and the puritan Islamist creed that would brook no argument or infidel upon its lands. The bloodletting of 1915 casts its shadow over the Middle East today. Fresh bones now

An Armenian Christian woman strokes a dead child on the desert floor outside Aleppo. Exactly 100 years later, Christians will be killed in this same desert by ISIS.

lie atop the ancient skeletons of the Armenians. Borders which were shaped at the start of the nineteenth century and set down on colonial maps at the start of the twentieth century were erased with bulldozers. Most Middle East citizens, however, would find one fact of life unchanged. To use Maude's expression—ghost-written by Mark Sykes—they still live 'under the tyranny of strangers'.

CHAPTER 11

Pilgrimage

PETER WALKER WITH ROBERT G. HOYLAND

IF all human life can be seen as a journey—through time and places, from the known into the unknown, from the past into the future—then it is no surprise that, in many religious systems, the life of faith is also understood in terms of a journey; nor that significance has often then been given to particular physical journeys—whether to major sites (such as the River Ganges, Mecca, or Jerusalem) or to more local sites (such as shrines, tombs, or churches)—which somehow evoke this 'journey of faith'.

Thus, not coincidentally, each of the three major world religions which are particularly invested in the Holy Land, look back to the figure of a wandering nomad, Abraham. His journeying into what the Bible later calls the 'land of promise' can be seen as setting an enduring pattern for the 'journey of faith'—a responding to a sense of call and travelling into the unknown. In Judaism, Christianity, and Islam, Abraham can be seen as an exemplar, an archetype of the journeying which all human beings are invited to embark upon—the life of 'pilgrimage'.

Nor is it any coincidence that the Holy Land has become an area filled with 'pilgrims'—people setting out on journeys which have a religious intention: Abraham arriving at Bethel, the Israelites entering the Promised Land, the annual pilgrims going up to Jerusalem to celebrate Jewish festivals, Jesus going up to Jerusalem, Byzantine Christians seeking out the 'holy places', Muslims seeking to pray on the Temple Mount. All these, even if very different, have this same capacity to resonate with the 'journey of faith'. Moreover, they have each indelibly left their mark on the Holy Land. Any history of the Holy Land would thus be incomplete without noting the effect on the land's history of so many individuals choosing to set out on pilgrimage.

The biblical background

Journeying within the Holy Land (the Old Testament period)

The opening books of the Hebrew Bible are all about journeys. In Genesis Adam and Eve are expelled from the Garden of Eden and Abraham departs his country in accordance with God's instructions; Jacob is led down to Egypt to live with his sons and with Joseph. In Exodus the journey works in reverse as the Israelites under Moses set out to return to the land enjoyed by their patriarchs. Eventually they cross the River Jordan into the Promised Land. Only then does the narrative, as it were, 'settle down'.

Yet, even in the midst of the journeying, there is a call to the Israelites to 'journey' in worship towards their God, Yahweh: his tabernacle (with the Ark of his Presence) is in the midst of the camp, and they are reverently to approach his holiness through his appointed priesthood and sacrifices. Once settled in the Promised Land, this ongoing 'journey' of worship becomes associated first with Shiloh and eventually with the temple in Jerusalem. This then becomes the place at the centre of the Israelites' corporate life, the place to which they are to 'go up' on pilgrimage. As recounted in one of the 'Psalms of Ascents' (Ps. 120–134, sung by pilgrims 'ascending' to Jerusalem on pilgrimage):

> I rejoiced with those who said, 'Let us go up to the House of the Lord'. Our feet are standing in your gates, O Jerusalem.... That is where the tribes go up to praise the name of the Lord according to the statute given to Israel. (Ps. 122:1–2, 4)

Jerusalem becomes the central focus of Israelite pilgrimage. Hence over 20 per cent of the Psalms make reference to Jerusalem or its temple (e.g. Ps. 46, 48, 84, and 132). According to rules set down in Deuteronomy (16:16) all Jewish males over the age of twelve were supposed to 'appear before the Lord ... at the Feast of Unleavened Bread, at the Feast of Weeks, and at the Feast of Booths' (that is, the three feasts of Passover, Pentecost, and Tabernacles). Even if this was not strictly observed, this vision ensured that annual pilgrimages to Jerusalem would become an integral part of religious life throughout the Old Testament period. Yes, these festivals could also be celebrated locally and within the family, but many individuals would go up to Jerusalem to celebrate in a corporate context. This would, of course, then do much to foster a sense of national identity—gathered together as one people serving the one Lord, Yahweh.

These pilgrimages to Jerusalem were seen, in part, as a celebration by the Israelites of the way their God had given them the entire land. Psalm 68 portrays God himself, as it were, in a triumphal journey from Sinai to Zion, moving from where he first appeared in the wilderness to Jerusalem as the place now of his settled dwelling. The Israelites had been wandering in the desert, but now they had been given a land to settle in: pilgrimage to the temple then gave them a public means of celebrating this gift. Thus in Psalm 81 worshippers are called to 'raise a song' because this is a statute given to them by their God, the 'Lord who brought you up out of the land of Egypt' (vv. 1, 4, 10). The act of pilgrimage—a physical action in real space—was a response to God's gracious generosity which had given them a physical space (the land). Pilgrims, traversing through the land of Israel, went up to Zion to thank God for the gift of the land through which they had just walked.

Another aspect of pilgrimage was the motif of approaching God's 'holy presence'. The temple's structure manifested a clear division between the profane and the holy, with its innermost sanctuary being termed the 'holy of holies'. Psalm 24 then evokes this sense of journeying towards God's holiness when it asks: 'who may ascend the hill of the Lord and who shall stand in his holy place?' And the answer comes back: 'He who has clean hands and a pure heart...' It ends with a sense of worshipful approach into the sanctuary: 'lift up your heads, O gates! And be lifted up, O ancient doors, so that the King of Glory may come in!' (v. 9). Here pilgrimage has a keen sense of destination, an anticipation to encounter the King of Glory in worship—something that perhaps was not possible elsewhere.

Yet both these aspects of pilgrimage (the gift of the Land and the place of God's holiness) are challenged within the Old Testament's own history and theology. In due course (in 587 BCE) the people would be exiled from the land and the temple destroyed. So, now that the gift had been taken from them, they were forced to ask a different question: 'how shall we sing the Lord's song in a foreign land?' (Ps. 137:4). And Ezekiel has a vision of God's holy presence (the *Shekinah* glory) departing from the Temple and going over the Mount of Olives to the east (Ezek. 11:23).

Eventually some of the exiles would return and the temple would be rebuilt—albeit in a much more modest form. Yet the practice of pilgrimage would inevitably thereafter have a note of ambiguity. For the next 500 years Jewish pilgrims would continue to flock to Jerusalem from the diaspora (especially for the mid-summer feast of Pentecost) but there were perhaps some haunting questions: 'in what senses do we still possess the land that we were once promised as a gift?' and, more acutely, 'where *is* our God?' These ambiguities were matched by biblical texts which seemingly looked beyond this narrow focus on Jerusalem to a more universal vision of God's presence being manifested to people of 'all nations' and to the 'ends of the earth' (e.g. Ps. 65, 67, 87; Isa. 2:2–4; 25:6–10; 42:6; 49:6). Pilgrimage to a particular place was being subsumed under a larger vision which was more universal. How would this tension be resolved?

Going out from the Holy Land (the New Testament period)

This reality of Jewish pilgrimage forms a vital backdrop for events described in the New Testament. By the time of Jesus' adult ministry (*c.* 30 CE) pilgrimage had indeed become 'big business'. Nearly fifty years earlier Herod the Great had commissioned a colossal rebuilding of the temple, vastly expanding the area of its outer courts (the 'court of the Gentiles'). This had triggered a further increase in pilgrim numbers, such that Jerusalem's population rose from *c.*20,000 to perhaps 200,000 during festival seasons. For the pilgrims flooding into Jerusalem—whether from Galilee or from the diaspora—these festivals became powerful expressions of their Jewish national life—social, religious, and, yes, political. Precisely because these festivals looked back to God's redemptive acts in the past they inevitably fuelled ardent prayers that God might act powerfully once again—not least to oppose the pagan might of Rome. Political tensions at Passover ran high.

John's Gospel makes plain that Jesus went up to Jerusalem not just for Passover (John 2:13; 13:1) but also for the Feast of Tabernacles (John 7:2) and for Hanukkah (a fourth major festival celebrating the rededication of the temple in 167 BCE after its desecration by Antiochus Epiphanes: see John 10:22). So his final journey up from Galilee to Jerusalem can indeed be seen as a 'pilgrimage' (he was surrounded by other Galilean pilgrims). Yet it had certain unique, even subversive aspects within it, such that pilgrimage might never be quite the same thereafter. For a start Jesus had a radical message for the temple: 'Not one stone will be left on another' (Mark 13:2). Then he overturned the money-changers' tables, proclaiming 'My house shall be a house of prayer for all nations!' (Mark 11:17, quoting Isa. 56:7)—a 'prophetic sign' which scholars have seen as a 'portent of destruction'. In word and deed he was signalling the temple's imminent demise.

In due course his followers would conclude that Jesus had been accomplishing something radically new during his pilgrimage to Jerusalem: he had offered his life as a 'sacrifice for sins' (which effectively eclipsed the temple's sacrificial system) and in his words at his Last Supper he had established a different 'table' around which his followers could derive the full benefit of that sacrifice. If so, what continuing need for the temple remained? Moreover, if (as they believed) this pilgrim had indeed been the true Messiah and the embodiment in person of Israel's God; if (in other words) his pilgrimage to Jerusalem had more truly been a unique visitation by Yahweh to his people, then Jerusalem's rejection of this pilgrim, which culminated in his crucifixion, was no slight matter. They would now sense the full force of Jesus' words as he wept over Jerusalem: '[Your enemies] ... will not leave one stone upon another, because you did not recognize the time of God's coming to you' (Luke 19:44). Like a bride on her wedding day rejecting her bridegroom, so Jerusalem, the city of God, had rejected the one whom God had uniquely sent.

In due course these new perspectives, which questioned the continuing role of both the city and its temple, were articulated by various New Testament writers: for example, Paul (a former Law student in Jerusalem) would say: 'the present city of Jerusalem is in slavery with her children, but the Jerusalem that is above is free' (Gal. 4:25–6; see also Heb. 12:22; Rev. 11:9; Eph. 2:14–22).

However, in the weeks after Jesus' pilgrimage had come to an abrupt end with his untimely death, Jesus' followers were presented with two further factors to consider: the Resurrection of Jesus and the gift of his Spirit. Those who became convinced of these as realities then found they now had a motivation for going on a pilgrimage in entirely the reverse direction—not towards Zion, but away from it. As Jesus had said: 'when the Holy Spirit comes on you, you will be my witnesses in Jerusalem ... and to the ends of the earth' (Acts 1:8). In this way, Isaiah's vision might find a fresh fulfilment: 'The law will go out from Zion, the word of the Lord from Jerusalem' (Isa. 2:3).

So pilgrimage undergoes a fundamental change of direction within the New Testament. Instead of a centripetal movement towards Jerusalem, there has now been launched a strong centrifugal dynamic. Luke, the writer of both the Gospel of Luke and the Acts of the Apostles, has reflected this transition in the very structure of his two-volume work. Thus, on the one hand, his Gospel is Jerusalem-centred

A mosaic depiction of the 'heavenly Jerusalem' (Heb. 12:22; Rev. 21–2) to inspire worshippers in the mid 6th-century church of San Vitale in Ravenna.

(starting and ending in the temple, and with Jesus' journey up to Jerusalem being given an extended focus). In the book of Acts, by contrast, Luke tells how the Christian message spread out from Jerusalem to Rome: the apostles went out with this message, but so too, presumably, did the Jewish pilgrims who had gathered for Pentecost (as described in Acts 2)—the news about Jesus thus going out from Jerusalem 'to the ends of the earth'. Luke-Acts has a chiastic structure (up to Jerusalem/away from Jerusalem), with the central events in Jerusalem acting as the pivotal fulcrum around which the narrative turns.

In the New Testament pilgrimage thus suffers a strange reversal. In the forty-year interval between Jesus' prediction of the temple's demise and its eventual destruction in 70 CE, there was a 'twilight season' in which Christian believers could still honour the Temple and continue the pilgrimage-dynamic towards Jerusalem (as does Paul in Acts 21, though with other motivations). However, the perennial attraction of Jerusalem as the goal of pilgrimage had been severely tarnished. For, in the experience of Christian believers, the powerful Spirit of Christ had brought to them (wherever they were located) a fuller measure of God's presence than Jerusalem could ever offer; and in their eyes, they had been offered something far better as the ultimate goal of their spiritual journey. We can sense this best in the Epistle to the Hebrews, written by an unknown Jewish author to fellow Jewish Christians (almost certainly in the early CE 60s). The epistle is really an extended sermon based on the theme of pilgrimage. He reminds his audience of the Israelites' journeying through the wilderness (Heb. 3–4), of Abraham's wanderings (11:8) and of Jesus' own journey to the cross (12:2; 13:12–13)—all this, in order to encourage them in their own journey of faith. And where will their own journey reach its goal? Precisely *not* in the physical Jerusalem, but rather in the 'heavenly Jerusalem' (12:22). 'For here', he reminds his Jewish audience with their natural affection for the physical Jerusalem, 'we do not have an enduring city', 'but we are looking for the city that is to come' (13:14; cf. 11:16). Jesus' pilgrimage to Jerusalem means pilgrimage can never quite be the same again.

Returning to the Holy Land (the era of the early Church)

Yet that is not the end of the story. Pilgrimage does not suddenly end with the coming of Jesus. Instead, once Christian believers in subsequent generations had come to see a much deeper significance in that coming, it had the power to give to the practice of pilgrimage a whole new rationale: for where else in the world, Christians now began to ask, could one visit places which had been touched by the feet of God's own Son? So, even if we have sensed a 'change of direction' in pilgrimage during the New Testament era, the seeds of a yet further reversal have been sown. It will not therefore be too long before the tide starts flowing in the opposite direction.

The process takes approximately 300 years. In some ways the dedication of the church of the Holy Sepulchre (over the site of Jesus' crucifixion and resurrection) in September CE 335 marks that moment when the process has 'come full circle'. The Jesus who in his day had been rejected, crucified, and buried in a stranger's grave is now proclaimed by the Roman Emperor's court official as the ultimate King of Kings. A dramatic reversal indeed! And the result, for the practice of pilgrimage, was the opening of the floodgates: a veritable deluge of pilgrims now flocked to Jerusalem. News spread that the Holy Land was open for business.

Christian pilgrimage

The quiet years (from 70–325 CE)

Back in September 70 CE, however, such a scene would have been hard to imagine. Jerusalem's temple buildings lay in ruins, the surrounding city dwellings smouldering from the fires lit by the soldiers of the Roman emperor's son, Titus. Two generations later in 135 CE, there would be another dark day in Jerusalem's history: Emperor Hadrian razing the city to the ground and superimposing over its ruins the grid of a standard Roman army camp; he also put an 'exclusion zone' several miles around Jerusalem to prevent any Jew from setting eyes on it again, and even scrubbed the name 'Jerusalem' from the records: henceforth it would be called by the pagan name Aelia Capitolina. This affected both Jews and Christians: the previous Jewish practice of making pilgrimage to the burial sites of Hebrew prophets was made far more difficult, but so too was any visit to Jerusalem by Christians. Indeed, strictly speaking, from 135 to 325 CE, 'Jerusalem' did not even exist.

What do we know of Christian pilgrimage up to, say, 230 CE? We know the names of just three Christians who visited in those first 200 years after Jesus: Melito (the bishop of Sardis), Pionius (a man later martyred), and Alexander (a Cappadocian who later became Jerusalem's bishop). The latter, according to Eusebius of Caesarea (*Church History* 6:11.2), came 'in order to enquire about the places and to pray'—a combined phrase which marks the first known instance of what we would recognize as Christian 'pilgrimage'. However, absence of visitors does not equal absence of local memory. For throughout this period there were Christian believers resident in the land. In the Galilee region, for example, there were Jewish Christians living in Capernaum and Nazareth—including some of the wider family of Jesus (Eusebius mentions the grandsons of Jesus' brother, Jude, who were poor farmers in the area: see *Church History* 3:20). These Christians will have preserved a faithful memory of key sites, such as the homes of the Virgin Mary (in Nazareth) and of Simon Peter (in Capernaum). Meanwhile, in Jerusalem, the Christian community in the early third century was still worshipping in a building on Mount Zion associated with the day of Pentecost; they also had a small library which contained a list of the bishops since James (it had Jewish names up until Hadrian's expulsion of the Jews in 135 CE, Gentile names thereafter).

That major break in population in 135 CE must indeed be borne in mind when we consider the possible continuity of local traditions. Yet, almost certainly, it will not have prevented the passing on of important memories associated with Jesus' life (there will have been Gentile Christians in the Jerusalem area throughout this period). Thus we should take seriously the traditional location both for Jesus' birth in a cave in

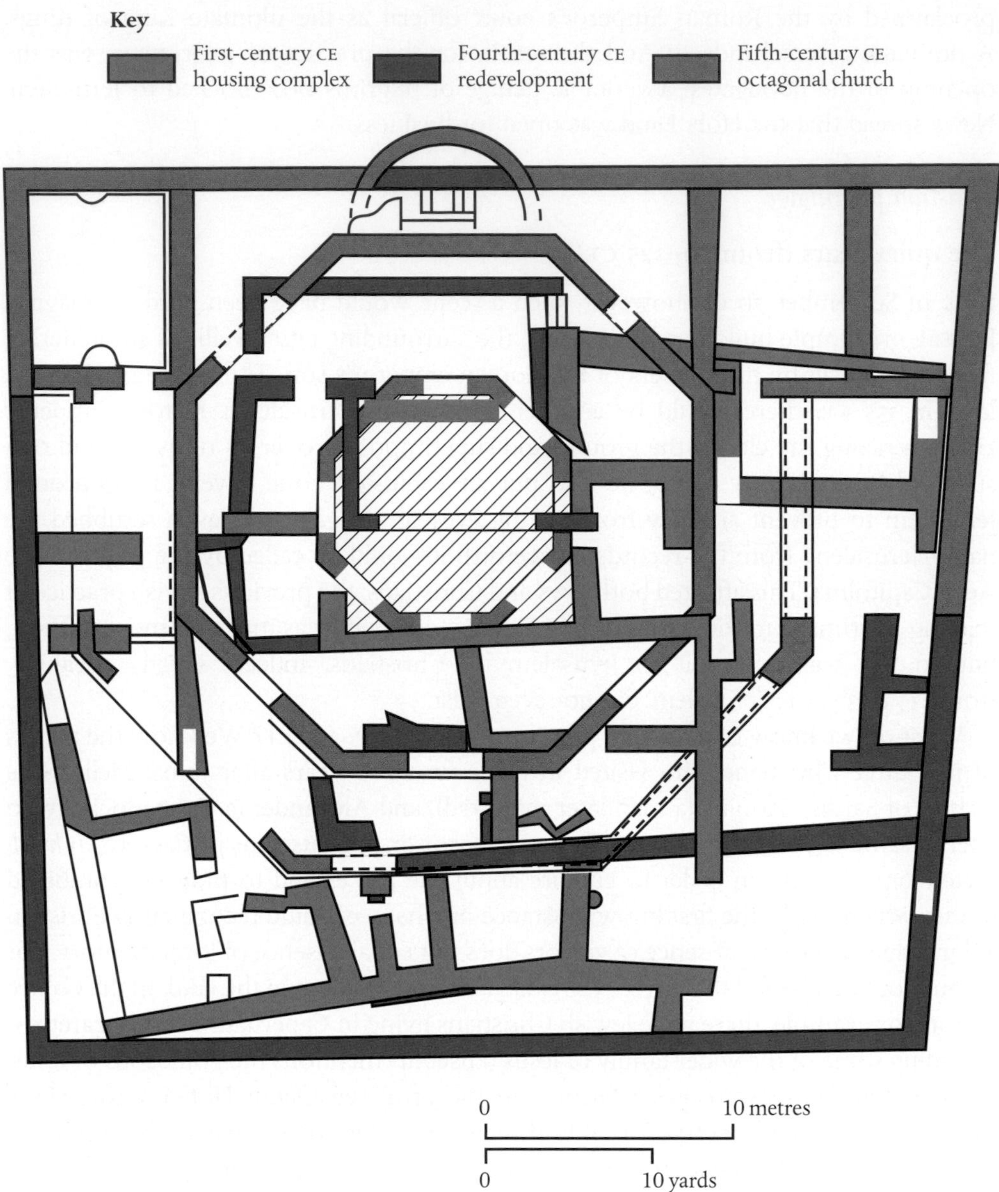

Floor plan of the various church structures built around the traditional site for the home of Simon Peter in Capernaum.

nearby Bethlehem (reference is made to this from as early as *c.*135 CE in an apocryphal Christian text called the *Proto-Evangelium of James*) and for Golgotha. Yes, Hadrian had regrettably covered this site of Jesus' crucifixion with a new forum (close to the centre of his repositioned Aelia Capitolina), but this did not obliterate the local memory; if anything, it only preserved that memory the more strongly, for Christians now knew full well that the site was sadly inaccessible. In those difficult years, often marked by imperial persecutions, they might ardently pray that those pagan buildings would be removed, but such hopes would remain only a wistful dream.

Later in the third century CE, however, the tide of pilgrimage seems to increase. The great biblical scholar, Origen, establishes his impressive library in Palestine's capital Caesarea Maritima. In his *Commentary on John* he indicates that he himself has visited 'Bethany beyond the Jordan' (referred to in John 1:29); and in *Contra Celsum* 1.51, he refers to the Bethlehem cave which is 'shown' to visitors and 'much talked about, even by enemies of the faith'. And, two generations later, his scholarly successor, Eusebius, claims that visitors have been coming from 'all over the world' to visit Bethlehem and to overlook the ruins of Jerusalem from the Mount of Olives (*Demonstration of the Gospel* 6:18). Strictly speaking, this terminology does not give us any real idea of how *many* such visitors there were—only that they came from a wide variety of places. Yet we sense that Christian interest in the Holy Land—a somewhat unexplored jewel—is only increasing.

Around 290 CE Eusebius himself compiles a gazetteer of biblical places (the *Onomastikon*), listing biblical sites in alphabetical order, in which (whenever possible) he identifies the site's location. This clearly evinces a growing interest in biblical history and geography. As a church historian, Eusebius knew that history matters. Yet even he could probably not see the great turning-point within history that was coming over the horizon. In the *Onomastikon*, his brief entry on Golgotha simply states: 'It is pointed out to the north of Mount Zion.' Some thirty years later, however, he would find himself standing on that precise site, but now surrounded by a vast church, built to cater for pilgrims longing to see the place where Jesus had died: Eusebius was that 'court official' mentioned above—the bishop appointed to preach the sermon at the dedication of the church of the Holy Sepulchre for the absentee Christian emperor, Constantine.

The flowering of pilgrimage (325–638 CE)

Eusebius gave that speech in 335 CE. He was now in his seventies and, as he looked back over his life, he must have been amazed at how much had happened in such a short time. After his early career, based in Origen's library in Caesarea, writing works of history and apologetics, he had then lived through a violent and long spate of persecution (which he described in his *Martyrs of Palestine*), after which he was consecrated the bishop of Caesarea, with 'metropolitan' responsibilities for the whole province of Palestine. So, when the Emperor Constantine had come to power in the eastern half of the empire after the battle of Adrianople in 324, Eusebius had found himself one of those invited to the council of Nicea in 325. There he had met Constantine for the first time (he would later be his biographer, writing the *Life of Constantine*) and had also become involved in some private conversations between the emperor and Macarius, bishop of Jerusalem, about an exciting project back in Jerusalem: would the Emperor be willing to commission an archaeological excavation over the likely site of Golgotha? Constantine had graciously agreed. And a few months later, back in Jerusalem, the most amazing discovery had been made—none other than the tomb of Jesus! Constantine had then written further letters of instruction, casting his vision for a magnificent church over this 'august location' (*Life of Constantine* 3:29–32). And now, just ten years later, Eusebius was standing to speak at the church's dedication. In a few days' time, moreover, he would travel to the new imperial capital, Constantinople, and there deliver this speech again—this time in a private audience with the emperor himself.

Thus begins the golden era of Christian pilgrimage, as detailed by Konstantin Klein in Chapter 6 above. Although it begins suddenly and dramatically, with the gift of hindsight we might sense there was something inevitable about it: after 300 years of comparative neglect (enforced by imperial opposition to the Christian faith), the time had surely come when Christians might express their historical and devotional interest in the scenes of the Incarnation. And if, as some have argued, Constantine had a conscious and intentional 'Holy Land Plan', that too makes eminent sense: what better way could there be for giving his new 'Christian' empire a distinctive and fresh focus? Even so, the suddenness of it all caught Eusebius 'on the wrong foot'. We might presume that, as Palestine's metropolitan bishop, he would have been delighted in these developments. Yet, in fact, his long-established theology had been quite dismissive of focusing on physical places; Christian hope, he had argued, was to be focused on 'things above', on the 'heavenly Jerusalem', and not on particular 'holy places'. Now he found himself at the front of an upsurge of Christian interest in what Constantine and others were already calling 'holy places'. Such language sat quite uneasily with his own viewpoint, so his choice of words in his final pieces of writing (including his speech in the Holy Sepulchre) becomes quite contorted—as he tries to steer this new devotion to pilgrimage and 'holy places' in a more spiritual direction.

By the time Constantine died (in 337 CE) Palestine had already been significantly transformed. He himself had never been able to visit it (though, intriguingly, Eusebius records how he had hoped to be baptized in the River Jordan); yet, despite his absence, his finger prints, as it were, would leave an indelible mark on the Holy Land and provide the strongest possible impetus for further Christian pilgrimage. Thus by the year 400 CE we can see how much had been built on that firm foundation. By that date, for example, further churches had been built, new Christian communities and monasteries had been established, and suitable liturgies had been developed, such that Holy Week, for example, becomes a colourful and exhausting pageant of prayer. In addition, there had been a significant development in what might be called the 'pilgrim trade', with pilgrims returning home with mementos of their visit—perhaps small containers (or *eulogiae*) with some soil or dust, or even substantial relics.

So much has happened in a short length of time that one wonders whether there is any one individual who, after Constantine, can be credited with this development. To this the answer is yes: Bishop Cyril of Jerusalem (*c.*320–384). Cyril will have grown up as a child of the new era, surrounded by the freshly emerging Christian Jerusalem. Whilst still in his twenties he is consecrated as the city's bishop and he continues in that

The 'Stone of Anointing' (located in the church of the Holy Sepulchre between the traditional sites of Jesus' death and burial)—an evocative place for modern pilgrims to identify with the story of Jesus' Passion.

role for another thirty-five years. During that time he puts Jerusalem on the Christian map and makes the pilgrims' experience something they would never forget. The evidence for this can be found in two main written sources: first, Cyril's own *Catechetical Lectures* (delivered to baptismal candidates in the Holy Sepulchre *c.*348 CE) and, secondly, the travel narrative of a Spanish nun, called Egeria (who made an extended visit to the Levant in the years 381 to 384 CE).

In his *Lectures* Cyril advances a strong case for the importance of Jerusalem. Unlike Eusebius, who had never described it as a 'holy city' and occasionally used its pagan name 'Aelia', Cyril was in no doubt that Jerusalem was indeed a 'holy city'. Thus Matthew's reference to the 'holy city' (Matt. 27:52–3) was not a reference to the *heavenly* Jerusalem (as both Origen and Eusebius had argued), but rather a plain reference to 'this city in which we are now' (*Cat.* 14:16). He was well aware of Jesus' predictions of destruction but saw those words as applying exclusively to the temple, not to the city. He noted how on Palm Sunday Jesus had been rejected by Jerusalem but drew a vital distinction: '*that* Jerusalem crucified Christ, but that which *now* is worships him' (*Cat.* 13:7).

Instead Cyril highlighted the events which had uniquely taken place in Jerusalem: it was the scene of the eucharist's institution, of the Cross, the Resurrection, and the Ascension; more broadly, it was the city of the Incarnation and would also be the place of Christ's return (*Cat.* 16:34; 14:23; 18:33; 15:15). As such, Cyril concluded, Jerusalem should have for Christians a natural 'pre-eminence in all things' (*Cat.* 16:4).

Cyril is thus laying the theological groundwork for the re-entry of Jerusalem into the Christian imagination. After 300 years of its being on the margins, Cyril is now making a significant bid for it to be placed back on 'centre stage'. Perhaps not coincidentally, the bishopric of Jerusalem would eventually (in 451 CE under Bishop Juvenal) be elevated to being a fifth 'patriarchate' in the worldwide Church.

Cyril pursues the same pattern of logic with regard to the more focused issue of 'holy places'. In contrast to Eusebius' hesitancy on this matter, Cyril had no such qualms but instead developed a deliberate theology of 'holy places'. The gospel sites, he argued, 'all but showed Christ to the eyes of the faithful' (*Cat.* 14:23); they had the power to 'shame', 'reprove', and 'confute' any who were tempted to disbelieve (*Cat.* 4:10; 12:32; 13:4; 13:38). It was as though they were living witnesses to the gospel events.

Loaves and fishes, as depicted in the floor mosaic in the late 5th-century church (now restored by the Benedictines at Tabgha) which was built by Lake Galilee to commemorate Jesus' feeding of the 5000.

This theology, seeing the gospel sites as a testimony to Christ, was then put into practice when Cyril developed appropriate liturgies for pilgrims to use in those sites—as witnessed by Egeria. She constantly remarks on how the selected Scripture readings and acts of worship are so 'suitable' to the precise time and place. And her description of the Holy Week services shows the evocative power of celebrating the story of Christ's Passion in its original location and in the company of fellow-worshippers. Bishop Cyril would have been the leading celebrant in those Easter services. Almost certainly too he was the theologian behind the scenes, crafting the ceremonial in these creative directions. And, when one considers how the shape of the whole Christian year has been influenced by these innovations in fourth-century Jerusalem, one senses the enormous influence of this one personality in the ancient Church. Much of what is seen today in the Holy Land and through the worldwide Christian Church may thus bear the hallmarks of Cyril, that enterprising bishop of Jerusalem.

One of the most famous pilgrims from this era is Jerome, one of the four 'doctors of the Church', who came to Bethlehem in 386 and stayed there until his death in 419, writing his commentaries and translating the entire Hebrew and Greek Bible into Latin. Going down into one of the caves under the Church of the Nativity modern visitors can imagine Jerome working there—translating what he would have seen as the written 'Word of God' just a few feet from the place where he believed had been born he who was the incarnate 'Word'. He also wrote a long letter describing the intensely devotional pilgrimage of his two women friends, Paula and Eustochium, as they travelled up to Galilee and back (*Epistle* 108). Yet Jerome could also be critical of pilgrimage, advising Paulinus of Nola against coming on pilgrimage: after all, he argued, 'access to the courts of heaven is as easy from Britain as it is from Jerusalem'. Nevertheless, Paulinus eventually came to Palestine and would become an enthusiastic pilgrim. His words, written after the event in or around the year 400 CE, neatly summarize for us the motivations of many Byzantine Christians during that momentous opening season of pilgrimage that was the fourth century CE:

> No other sentiment draws people to Jerusalem than the desire to see and touch the places where Christ was physically present, and to be able to say from their very own experience, 'We have worshipped in the places where his feet have stood'. (Paulinus, *Epistle* 49:14)

This period of just over three centuries was a relatively calm one for Christians in the province of Palestine, governed by the emperors in Byzantium, enabling the Christian practice of pilgrimage to develop in an undisturbed fashion. Thus, for example, there had been continual support from the imperial courts: the Empress Eudocia had completed the rebuilding of Jerusalem's walls and the building of a church in honour of St Stephen (the first Christian martyr); and Emperor Justinian had later built a brand new church within the city gates (called the 'Nea' or 'New Church') and completed a significant rebuilding project for the Church of the Nativity, enabling pilgrims to go down into the cave of Jesus' birth (rather than merely looking down towards it from ground level). Futhermore, the phenomenon of desert monasticism had flourished—so much so that, according to some estimates, the number of monks living in cells or monasteries in the Judean wilderness had risen to 30,000. However, all this was greatly disrupted in 614 CE by the Persian invasion. As the soldiers stormed through the desert they put to death all the monks in the monastery of St Theodosius (their skulls are still on display in the monastery's charnel house) and proceeded on their rampage through Jerusalem and Bethlehem—only sparing the Church of the Nativity from complete destruction because of their respect for the Persian headgear of the Magi depicted on the church's facade. Though the Persians were defeated in 628, it was only a few short years before Muslim forces overran the Holy Land and made it their own. The tranquil 'golden era' of Byzantine Christian pilgrimage had come, tragically and painfully, to an abrupt end.

This Christianization of the Holy Land by the Byzantines played a key role in the story of the worldwide Church, providing it with a necessary historical anchor, buttressing its understanding of the Incarnation, and allowing it to develop powerful liturgical practices. Yet, more negatively, Byzantine pilgrimage changed forever the landscape of the biblical terrain (with sites now marked with churches) and, far more

The main nave of the Church of the Nativity in Bethlehem, as rebuilt by the Emperor Justinian (*c.*530 CE) with openings to look down to the original mosaic floors built on the orders of Emperor Constantine and his mother Queen Helena (326 CE).

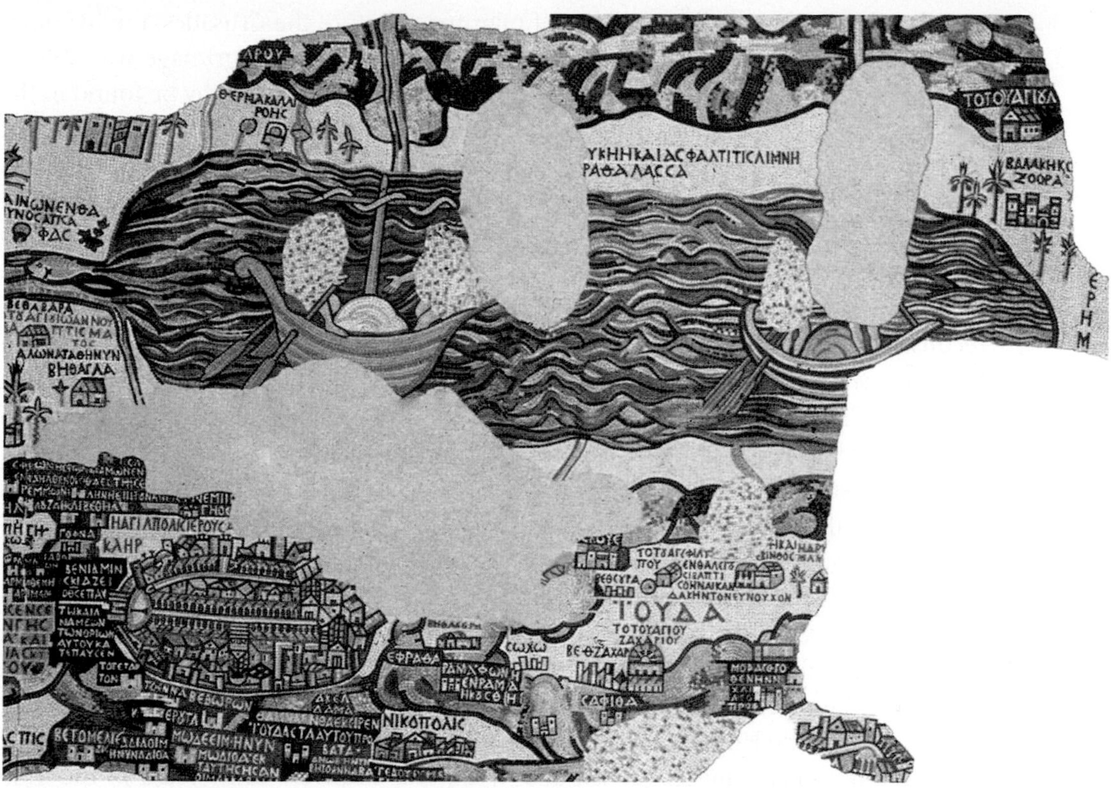

Floor mosaic in the 6th-century church in Madaba (Jordan) depicting the Dead Sea and (below, to the west) the 'holy city of Jerusalem' (with its colonnaded streets and the roofs of its three main churches).

importantly, increased the religious value of the Holy Land in such a way that its later history would almost certainly be one of increased conflict. Would Muslims have so valued Jerusalem, Church historians might venture to ask, if the city had not already been so highly prized by Byzantine Christians? And, more poignantly, if there had been no Byzantine promotion of this 'God-trodden Land' (as Palestine is described in an inscription found far away near the Black Sea), would soldiers have come many centuries later from the far away West to retrieve it from Islamic rule? In the light of this complex history and theology, we can now sense why the entrance of Caliph 'Umar into Jerusalem in 638 CE—however peaceful it was in its own terms—would inevitably have momentous consequences for the Holy Land. The stage was set, irreversibly, for an escalation of tension and contention. Never again would people be able to speak, straightforwardly and without qualification, of Jerusalem as the 'City of Peace'.

Contesting the land: The early Islamic period (638 to 1099)

The new Muslim authorities indeed showed remarkable restraint in the way they took over the land of Palestine, doing little to overturn its economic systems or religious life; and, with their own commitment to the *Hajj*, they respected the Christian desire to go on pilgrimage. Thus, in his overview of pilgrimage before the Crusades, the historian John Wilkinson (1977) suggests that after the arrival of Islam pilgrimage was able to resume 'within, at the most, a single generation'. Evidence for this may be found in the thriving picture of pilgrimage we can glean from the Frankish bishop Arculf's account later in the seventh century (see Table 11.1), but also from archaeology: thus, although the Muslim presence caused the abandonment, over time, of perhaps half of the local churches, only one-fifth of the pilgrimage sites fell into disuse. Wilkinson then analyses the practicalities of such travel in this period (entirely on foot or donkey) and highlights its attendant dangers (whether being robbed or attacked by lions). He also reconstructs the routes pilgrims would have used: the main one would have been from Caesarea, *via* Antipatris to Jerusalem, but with optional visits to Hebron, the Jordan River, or Galilee. And he notes that Jerusalem itself would have been for pilgrim visitors 'unexpectedly monumental and open'.

All this suggests that, even if on a more modest scale than in the heyday of Byzantine rule, the volume of pilgrims continued throughout the next 400 years—primarily from the Eastern Church but also from the Latin West. For example, in 808 CE an official document (the *Commemoratorium*), drawn up because of the good relations between Charlemagne and the Muslim authorities, makes clear that Christian institutions in the Holy Land were flourishing. Charlemagne never himself visited the Holy Land (despite many later stories to the contrary), but his ambassadors did receive a set of keys to the Holy Sepulchre from the Orthodox patriarch. These were peaceful years in the united Church of East and West, and relatively calm years in the long history of the Holy Land, punctuated only by occasional disasters, such as the devastating earthquake of 746 CE and the rule of the mad Fatimid Caliph al-Hakim (996–1021), who wielded his power cruelly against both Jews and Christians. First he seized the property of churches, next he banned the Palm Sunday procession over the Mount of Olives, and then he ordered the destruction of the church of the Holy Sepulchre. This resplendent church, which for nearly 700 years had so spectacularly affirmed to pilgrims the centrality of their faith in the Resurrection, now lay in ruins around their feet. In the last decade of his reign, however al-Hakim relented and allowed non-Muslims to worship freely once again. His son allowed the Holy Sepulchre to be rebuilt and pilgrimage to the Holy Land resumed—as evidenced, for example, in the accounts of Adhemar of Chabannes and Ralph Glaber (both writing in France in the second quarter of the eleventh century).

The era of the Latin Kingdom (1099 to 1187)

Although the desperate need of the Byzantines for military support and the desire of the popes to strengthen their hand against the Holy Roman Emperor were the key factors in the launch of the Crusades, the increasing difficulties being experienced by western pilgrims must be recognized as at least one of the factors motivating the Crusaders. There was a genuine desire to ensure that pilgrimage could have a lasting future and that pilgrims have a safe passage. The perceived need of western Christians to have some tangible links with the Holy Land had been expressing itself continuously

TABLE 11.1 Named pilgrims and written accounts (638–1291)

Arculf (*c.*680)	in Adomnan's *The Holy Places*
Epiphanius the Monk (*c.*690?)	in a guidebook (*c.*750–800)
Willibald (724–730)	in Hugeburc's *Life of Saint Willibald*
Jacinthus the Presbyter (*c.*750?)	From Spain
Bernard the Monk (870)	*A Journey to the Holy Places and Babylon*
Eutychius (*c.*940)	*The Book of the Demonstration*
Adhemar of Chabannes (1034)	from France, died in Jerusalem
Rodulphus (or Ralph) Glaber	*History of his own Time* (1044)
Saewulf (1101–1103)	from England
Rorgo Fretellus (*c.*1130)	from France
Daniel the Abbot (1106–1108)	more personal; from region near Kiev (later Ukraine)
King Siguror of Iceland (1220–1236)	bathed in Jordan
Peter the Deacon (1137)	
Abbot Nikulas Bergsson (*c.*1140)	from Munkathverá, Iceland
Hugh of St Victor (before 1141)	
Belard of Ascoli (1155)	
Benjamin of Tudela (1166–1171)	
John of Wurzburg (*c.*1170)	from Germany
Theoderic (1169–1174)	from France
John Phocas (1185)	From Byzantium (?)
Wilbrand of Oldenburg (1211–1212)	
Theitmar (1217–1218)	
Ernoul (*c.*1231)	
Louis IX of France (1251)	
Marco Polo (1271)	
Friar Maurice (1271–1273)	
Burchard of Mount Zion (1274–1285)	
Philip of Savona (1285–1289)	
Riccoldo of Monte Croce (1288–1289)	

Drawn from Wilkinson (1977), Wilkinson et al. (1988), and Pringle (2012).

throughout the previous centuries: hence the cult of relics (especially of the True Cross) and the building of sepulchres in the West that more realistically matched the original in Jerusalem, a phenomenon which had been developing strongly since at least the 950s. Actual pilgrimage to the Holy Land was also increasingly in vogue—brought about, no doubt, by the opening up of a new land route through Hungary under its

Christian King Stephen in 1001 and also perhaps by the significance of the 'millennial' years which were observed in 1000 and 1033. This was a season when large groups were making the 'great pilgrimage'. As Glaber commented (writing in 1044):

> an innumerable multitude from the whole world, greater than any man could have hoped to see, began to travel to the Sepulchre of our Saviour in Jerusalem;...finally (and this was something that had never happened before), numerous women, noble and poor, undertook the journey.

So, when the Latin Kingdom was established in the Holy Land, we can be sure that pilgrimage itself once again picked up momentum. By 1128 the Crusaders had liberated all the gospel sites from Muslim control (apart from Caesarea Philippi); numerous churches were built; a new site for Emmaus was discovered and promoted (at Abu Ghosh, not Nicopolis); there was much searching for relics and bones (for example, the 'nails of the cross' and the body of St George found in Lydda). Within Jerusalem itself, the Dome of the Rock was taken over by the Franks as a church. Above all, pilgrims in the city could now freely commemorate all the events of Jesus' Passion. If there was a sense in which the Crusading movement as a whole was, as Wilkinson has suggested, 'an international way of the cross', then the individual pilgrim could now enjoy their own, more intimate, 'way of the cross' along Jerusalem's Via Dolorosa. Moreover, from now on the Latin term *peregrinus*, which previously had simply meant a 'traveller' of any kind, now referred expressly to a 'pilgrim'. Thus the rededication of the Church of the Holy Sepulchre in 1149, marking the fiftieth anniversary since the arrival of the First Crusade, was a great celebration of this distinctive aspect of Christian devotion—pilgrimage. Believers were once again able to see with their own eyes 'all the places where Christ our God had walked for our salvation' (Daniel the Abbot) and the whole land, now freed from enemy control, was an 'allegory of Paradise' (Fretellus).

With hindsight, that moment on 15 July 1149 was a zenith, a high point in the ebb and flow of pilgrimage. For in the next decades Crusader power began to crumble. From that time onwards pilgrims could only view the sites around Lake Galilee (only sixty miles from Damascus) from the safety of Mount Tabor; and twenty years later, on the hills above Tiberias, the Crusaders would be engulfed in the throes of Saladin's army.

The end of the Crusading era (1187 to 1291)

With Saladin's victory in 1187, the number of Latin pilgrims to Jerusalem inevitably dropped dramatically. The Muslim authorities regained control over the Dome of the Rock (thus causing the previous route of the Via Dolorosa to change to its present form) and immediately removed Latin clergy from the Holy Sepulchre (now given entirely to the care of the Orthodox); but some pilgrims continued to be allowed into the city—so long as they paid an appropriate tax. An overview of pilgrimage texts dating from this period (Pringle, 2012) yields the names of seven or eight pilgrims (see Table 11.1) and includes several other anonymous accounts, general descriptions, and maps. Some boats in the 1240s, Pringle notes, would carry on board around 1500 passengers, so pilgrimage was still very much in business.

In that troubled century, however, when the land was subject to numerous raids by conflicting armies, pilgrims increasingly commented on how more and more sites were coming under Mamluk control. Many pilgrims indeed never reached Jerusalem, instead travelling to Damascus or Mount Sinai, or, if nothing else, to Nazareth (though the church there was destroyed by Sultan Baybars in 1263). Eventually, as the Crusaders' presence was pushed back to the port of Acre, many pilgrims had to be content with staying within Acre itself. However, because during that century the offering of indulgences (to be remitted against years spent in purgatory) had gradually been connected with pilgrimage, such pilgrims might not return to Europe 'empty-handed'; for, according to 'The Pilgrimages and Pardons of Acre' (1258–1264), there were now over forty places and activities within the city which could yield many years' worth of indulgences. Paradoxically, then, a pilgrimage to the Holy Land could in that sense be successful even though the pilgrim had not visited any of the biblical sites.

This reveals some of the motivations which fuelled Holy Land pilgrimage from the West in the medieval period. Increasingly it was seen as a work of penitence. In his sermons on pilgrimage, James of Vitry (bishop of Acre from 1216 to 1228) emphasized

Interior of the Greek Catholic church of St Andrew in Acre, built in 1765 within the ruins of the Crusader cathedral church of St Anna (destroyed in 1291).

its hardships, poverty, and simplicity. Sometimes this penitential act was undertaken voluntarily, sometimes vicariously (on behalf of someone who had given money in their will for someone to go on a pilgrimage on their behalf), and very often as a requirement or punishment. Thus, for example, in 1203 the community of Osney Priory (just outside Oxford) considered sending an adulterer 'to Jerusalem' but he was 'too poor' to do so. The net effect in Jerusalem, however, of sending so many people there for some kind of religious offence or criminal activity was not entirely positive. Thus Burchard of Mount Zion (writing *c*.1274–1285) comments:

> We Latins are worse than all the other inhabitants.... When anyone has been an evil-doer he crosses the sea as a penance;... but in truth they change their sky but not their inclination.... Because of [their] sins, the land itself with the place of sanctification comes into contempt. (para. 13)

In terms of both quality and quantity, the year 1291 thus marks the ultimate nadir in the story of pilgrimage. Having sunk so low, could it ever be restored?

Rediscovering the Holy Land: the centuries of calm (1291 to 1800)

Thus the era after the Crusades was inevitably a quiet one in the history of pilgrimage. After their humiliating defeat, the nations of Europe would not be getting politically involved in the Levant for many centuries to come; and the prospect of making a pilgrimage to a Palestine now under such firm Muslim control would seem a rather hazardous and foolhardy enterprise for all but the bravest of western pilgrims. The only vestige of western (or 'Latin') Christian influence in the Holy Land was the small Franciscan community to whom the Pope gave the role of guarding the Christian sites. The *Custodia Terrae Sanctae* was established in 1342 and would arrange for Latin Catholic monks and clergy from Europe to live close by the gospel sites—a role which has continued to the present day. However, the number of western pilgrims who visited during the fourteenth and fifteenth centuries would have been but a trickle. Then came the Reformation in western Europe. Once both Luther and Calvin had spoken out so sharply against the practice of medieval pilgrimage (not least because of its associations with 'works' of penitence, but also its focus on physical relics rather than the person of Christ), it would be a long time before western Christians within the newly emerging Protestant churches would consider a pilgrimage to the Holy Land in positive terms.

As a result, for five long centuries (from 1300–1800), pilgrimage was mostly practised by Eastern Christians—primarily the Greek Orthodox and Armenians. According to Titus Tobler (who provided some estimates for pilgrim numbers from 1666 to 1845) the number of Western pilgrims (estimated at 2000 to 3000 each year) rose somewhat during the eighteenth century so that by the early 1800s the number of pilgrims at Easter was approximately one-third Greek Orthodox, one-third Armenian, and one-third Roman Catholic and others (such as Greek Catholics, Copts, etc.). So, at the dawn of the nineteenth century, pilgrimage was still taking place on an annual basis. Moreover, the Christian communities in Jerusalem itself had continued to be an active presence: thus in the year 1800 it is estimated by the Israeli historian Yehoshua Ben Arieh (1984) that Jerusalem's Christian population totaled 2775 (50 per cent Greek Orthodox, 20 per cent Armenian, 20 per cent Roman Catholic).

Yet all this was about to change: during the nineteenth century there would be a meteoric and almost frenzied explosion of interest in the Holy Land. Before 1800 the Holy Land had been a 'closed book', a *terra incognita*, a sad backwater, and a derelict province of a declining Ottoman empire; however, after Napoleon's visit in 1799, the Orient was ripe for rediscovery.

The nineteenth century: a new development

Motivated by a combination of vital interests (historical, theological, and political) the western world rediscovered the Levant, a unique area which lay at the very root of its own civilization and which was already strangely familiar—because they were the lands of the Bible. Now too there were new opportunities for commerce and for exerting political influence. All these important historical and technological developments would inevitably have an effect on the number of individuals going on 'pilgrimage' of some kind. Yet, arguably, the converse may also have been true—namely that those larger historical movements were themselves fuelled by this instinct for 'pilgrimage'.

In sum, there emerged between 1800 and 1850 a distinctly 'Protestant' variant of the 'pilgrimage' mentality. Protestant visitors, even if prayerful and deeply Christian, revealed a quite new 'touristic' mentality which was markedly different from more 'Catholic' styles of (what we shall now call) 'traditional pilgrimage'. Yet, before looking at these two parallel versions of pilgrimage, we should note that Protestants also revealed their love of the Bible in many other ways: for example, enquiry into the overall geography and terrain of the Bible Lands; scholarly research into biblical sites and their archaeological excavation; Christian missionary work amongst the Jewish and Muslim populations; educational ministries and medical service; and even eschatological vision and 'millenarian' hope, inspired by biblical prophecies, for the future reign of Christ. These are strictly separate from their acts of 'pilgrimage' and thus will not be covered in this chapter but they can rightly be seen as very closely related. They were all aspects of Protestants' deep respect for the Bible.

'Traditional pilgrims'

From 1800 to 1850 there was a modest increase in the number of Greek Orthodox, Armenians, and Roman Catholics visiting the Holy Land. Although there was a devastating fire in 1808 which destroyed much of the church of the Holy Sepulchre, that event does not seem to have lessened the number of pilgrims. In 1834 a monk called Neophitus estimated that the pilgrim numbers had risen from 3000 (in 1800) to around

One of the famous lithographs by David Roberts (1839), depicting his fellow pilgrims encountering the land's Arab inhabitants by the Dead Sea near Jericho.

10,000. In that year some 14,000 people (including local residents) were in the church of the Holy Sepulchre for the 'Holy Fire' ceremony; tragically, another fire broke out, causing a stampede which left over 100 people crushed to death by the main doorway. Another writer in that decade (Isidore Taylor) thought these pilgrim numbers were returning to levels previously seen in the eighteenth century—helped by the fact that the Egyptian authorities had recently abolished any tax on pilgrims; he noted that the majority of the pilgrims indeed came for Easter, but actually arrived by sea the previous November. During this long stay some might venture up to Galilee: for example, the painter David Roberts was allowed to join a party of 4000 Eastern pilgrims going up to Galilee just after Easter in 1839. However, the vast majority would insist at the least on going down to the River Jordan (often on the day before Palm Sunday), in order to be 'cleansed' and to experience a catharsis prior to the celebration of Holy Week.

Right: Russian Orthodox clergy and pilgrims preparing to renew their baptismal vows by the River Jordan (*c.*1900).

The climax of their pilgrimage was indeed the 'Holy Fire' ceremony. According to Eduard Schulz (1851), the Turkish authorities, in order to police the crowds safely, had now insisted this take place not on Easter Day but twenty-four hours earlier—at 2 p.m. on Holy Saturday. In this ceremony (which continues to this day) the 'holy fire' was received by the Greek Orthodox patriarch in the tomb of Christ and then passed out to the thronging crowds; each pilgrim, holding their bundle of thirty-three candlesticks (one for each year of Jesus' life), would then pass on the flame to their neighbour, whilst proclaiming 'Christ is Risen!' In these and other liturgical events the pilgrims were encouraged to immerse themselves in the mystery of the incarnation, identifying with Christ in both the place and season of his death and resurrection. This event was very much the highlight of the Orthodox year. One of the significant developments, then, by the end of the century would be the marked increase in the number of Russian Orthodox pilgrims. Back in 1829 the Russian government had taken on an overall responsibility for Orthodox pilgrims and residents within the Ottoman Empire. In due course the 'Russian Compound' was built just to the north-west of the Old City, catering for up to hundreds of pilgrims (each of whom received some money from the Tsar towards their pilgrimage). Meanwhile, there was an increased number of Catholic pilgrims (from Italy, Spain, Austria, and France)—helped along by various factors, for example: the Pope's installation of a Latin Patriarch in 1847; the opening of Jaffa as a port for Austrian and French ships; and the visit of the Austrian emperor Franz Josef II in 1869. In addition to St Saviour's, a hostel located in the Old City, these pilgrims were accommodated in newly built facilities, such as the Austrian Hospice and the Notre Dame Centre just outside the 'New' Gate.

So at the dawn of the twentieth century traditional pilgrimage was developing strongly. Jerusalem in the Easter season could become intensely crowded—not helped, it should be noted, by Muslim authorities often setting up rival pilgrimages for Muslims to the Dome of the Rock at precisely the same time. Christian 'traditional pilgrimage' was thus continuing in its own world of incarnational piety—a world which could trace its roots all the way back through the Crusades to Bishop Cyril and the flowering of Byzantine pilgrimage. In some ways it was locked in a 'time-warp' of its own. Yet all around it the wider world was changing at a great pace. And the very expansion and development of pilgrimage was paradoxically dependent on that wider world—not only for the technological developments which made travel to the Holy Land so much easier, but also for the heightened awareness of the importance of the Holy Land for Christian believers. Surprisingly this incentive—to value the Holy Land more highly for its 'pilgrimage potential'—had come, so several scholars argue, from a paradoxical alternative source—namely Protestant Christians who, officially, did not really believe in 'pilgrimage'.

Protestant 'pilgrims'

The years from 1800 to 1880 have been termed by Ben Arieh in his comprehensive study of those who visited the Holy Land in the nineteenth century the 'Era of Rediscovery' (1979). He estimates that from this period we know the names of 2000 travellers who wrote, between them, over 5000 books or articles about their visit. Remarkably, 1700 of these travellers visited between 1840 and 1880—a forty-year period which must therefore be seen as marking the effective launch of the 'tourist' trade within the Holy Land. And the overwhelming majority of these visitors were Protestants (see Table 11.2). Ben-Arieh observes that most of the visitors were 'Protestant missionaries and clergymen, coming on the wave of economic prosperity in Europe and America and of the religious revival of the period' (p. 153). Though keen Christians they did not practise 'pilgrimage' in its traditional form but rather pursued interests such as geographical fieldwork, missionary enquiry, or geological research. As for their overall impressions of what they saw, Ben Arieh concludes: 'they marveled at the country but were appalled by its desolation' (p. 16).

The culmination of this initial period of exploration is widely recognized to have been the visit in 1838 of Edward Robinson, Professor of Biblical Literature at Union Theology Seminary (New York). In his landmark publication *Biblical Researches in Palestine* (1841) Robinson focused expressly on the particular sites and 'holy places' mentioned in the Bible. He was very sceptical of 'local monkish traditions' and thought the church of the Holy Sepulchre was a 'pious fraud'; but he can be credited for identifying successfully gospel sites such as the Siloam Tunnel and Capernaum's synagogue—as well as the now famous 'Robinson's arch' on the south-west corner of the Temple Mount. From then on things began to develop rapidly. In the 1840s and 1850s the Ottomans introduced reforms in their treatment of non-Muslim minorities, which encouraged, for example, the creation of the Anglican/Prussian shared bishopric in Jerusalem (from 1841) and of consulates in Jerusalem for all major European powers. These consuls could then defend the interests of Christian pilgrims. Travelling was becoming easier. Thus, during the decade from 1840 to 1850 no less than 300 books were written by Protestant visitors.

During the 1860s there were visits from two famous individuals: Albert, the Prince of Wales (later King Edward VII) and Samuel Clemens (known to us by his pen name Mark Twain). Mark Twain was a journalist on board the USS *Quaker City*, which set sail for Palestine in 1867, and who later wrote up his account in *The Innocents Abroad* (1869). His witty and acerbic comments did much to dispel the 'Romantic' and poetic visions of the Holy Land promulgated by its first explorers. Posing as a 'new American vandal', he saw the Holy Land with jaded eyes as a 'country of disappointments', as 'hopeless, dreary and heartbroken'. 'What Palestine wants is paint! Each detachment of pilgrims

TABLE 11.2 Some significant Protestant visitors (1800–1870)

1806	Jasper Seetzen (German)	
1812	Johann Burckhardt (Swiss)	
1814	Lady Hester Stanhope	excavated at Ashqelon (dressed as a man to avoid having to wear a veil)
1823	Josiah Conder	*The Modern Traveler* (1825)
1834	Robert Curzon (British MP)	descriptions Holy Sepulchre aroused Christian concern
1838	Joseph Russegger (Austrian)	pioneer of geology (calculating depth of Dead Sea)
1824	Frederick Catherwood	maps of Jerusalem; 6 weeks' access to the Muslim-controlled Temple Mount
1836	John Stephens (American)	*Incidents of Travel* (1838?); first self-styled 'tourist'
1839	David Roberts (Scottish)	lithograph drawings
1833–79	The Revd W. M. Thomson (American)	most travelled individual explorer: authors *The Land and the Book* (London, 1870)
1838	Andrew Bonar & Robert McCheyne	Church of Scotland missionaries
1847	William Lynch (American)	detailed surveys of Jordan Valley (calculating depth of Lake Galilee)
1835	Titus Tobler (Swiss)	topography of Jerusalem
1845	Ernst-Gustav Schulz (German consul)	later publishes memoirs
1846–1901	Conrad Schick (German Pietist)	55-year long residency in Jerusalem, charitable work, and studies in archaeology.
1843	Ridley Herschell	converted Jew writes: *A Visit to my Father Land*
1851–63	James Finn (British consul)	memoirs
1858	H. B. Tristram	pioneering work on Palestine's fauna and flora
1867	Samuel Clemens (Mark Twain)	*The Innocents Abroad* (1869)
1868–72	William Holman-Hunt	artist's extended second visit
1869	Albert, Prince of Wales (later Edward VII)	travels with A. P. Stanley (Dean of St Paul's Cathedral)

The large wall of the platform constructed by the workmen of Herod the Great during his extensive rebuilding of Jerusalem's Temple (from *c.*15 BC), and showing the spring of an arch (now named after the American professor, Edward Robinson, who uncovered it in 1838).

should give it a coat!' He was explicitly angry with previous authors for their overblown praise of the country and heaped sarcasm on the way visitors would start to cry on seeing Jerusalem—a city which he and others thought instead was 'fetid, squalid and mean in the extreme'.

In a sense the 'bubble had burst' and the honeymoon was over. In the 1860s there was an observable shift in perceptions of the Holy Land from romanticism to reality, or perhaps from more 'mystical' approaches to more 'materialistic' ones. There was also a shift from visitors travelling on their own as lone pioneers to visitors being part of organized groups. Many of these groups were scientific expeditions of various kinds—for example, those sent out by the Palestine Exploration Fund, established in 1865, to create Ordnance Survey maps or to investigate archaeological features. Other groups, however, were precursors of the modern tourist party: the days of mass tourism had started. Thus with hindsight Mark Twain's visit can be construed as the first ever 'package tour' from the USA. Two years later, in 1869, Thomas Cook & Sons would lead the first of their many tours from the UK (normally involving a full month under canvas, starting out from Alexandria); this became very attractive to British Christians and by 1891 Cook's would have taken over 12,000 visitors to the Holy Land. As a sign of the shifting times, the Prince of Wales (whose visit in 1869 had coincided, to his annoyance, with Thomas Cook's first group of dreaded 'tourists') now thirteen years later arranged for his two sons, Prince Albert Victor and Prince George, to travel under the auspice of Thomas Cook & Sons. Travel to the Holy Land was no longer the preserve of lone rangers and scholars, but very much for all.

Thomas Cook, himself a staunch Evangelical General Baptist, particularly attracted low-church Protestants, who then articulated some very negative reactions to the non-Protestant aspects of 'traditional pilgrimage' which they encountered. One visitor, the British Baptist minister Samuel Manning, speaking of the church of the Nativity in Bethlehem, wrote: 'the degrading superstition and the disgraceful discord which prevail here are a scandal to the birth-place of Christianity'; another, writing of the Holy Sepulchre, wrote: 'Nothing can possibly be more opposed to the simplicity of Christ than [its] gorgeous decorations, costly shrines and superstitious ceremonies' (Burns). Here we see the stark contrast between Protestant and Catholic approaches to pilgrimage. In Jerusalem this contrast would lead to a Protestant counter-proposal for the site of Jesus' death and resurrection. Ever since Robinson's critique of the Holy Sepulchre, the search had been on for an alternative site that Protestants would find both more historically plausible and more appealing to their spiritual tastes. So, when in 1867 an ancient tomb was discovered north of the Damascus Gate and close to a cliff-face with a rock formation resembling the features of a skull, there were many who were convinced that modern archaeology had discovered what ancient tradition had obscured: the true site of Golgotha and Jesus' tomb. Influenced by the ideas of General Gordon (who stayed in Jerusalem in 1882–1883, not long before his famous death at Khartoum), the Garden Tomb Association was created in 1895 to purchase the nearby land and to preserve the tomb which many thought to be that of Joseph of Arimathea.

Protestants thus loved coming to the land of the Bible but what motivated them was different from what inspired 'traditional pilgrims'. They loved things which confirmed the veracity of the Bible—such as seeing the towns which Jesus had cursed now lying in ruins. They loved anything which connected with the pictures of Bible events drawn by their childhood imaginations. Above all, they were moved not by sites but by scenery: the River Jordan, the Dead Sea, the fields near Bethlehem, a storm on Lake Galilee, or their first views of Mount Sinai or Jerusalem from a distance: 'There is nothing imposing or impressive in the sight and yet every traveller halts; even the most frivolous are awed into silence. Not a few gaze with tears upon the scene' (Manning: evidently taking a softer line than Mark Twain!). And they had their own 'Protestant' ways of expressing their emotions: being baptized in the Jordan, or lying down prostrate in the Garden Tomb. Yet, arguably, such expressions of devotion brought

Watercolour depicting Kaiser Wilhelm and his wife, Augusta Victoria, entering through the newly opened Jaffa Gate on Saturday 29 October, 1898.

them closer to Catholic and Orthodox patterns of religious devotion than they might have liked to admit. And, in their writings, they continued to use the language of 'pilgrimage'. They might view themselves as being involved in something quite different from 'traditional pilgrimage', but the majority of them were visiting as Bible-believing and earnest Christians who hoped to derive real spiritual benefit from their visit. So they were more than mere 'tourists'; but what, then, was the right label? 'Religious tourists'? Or, perhaps even, 'non-religious pilgrims'?

Some of these ambiguities within Protestant 'pilgrimage' come to the fore in the most famous visit to Jerusalem at the end of the century—the imperial pilgrimage made by Kaiser Wilhelm II in 1898. Travelling with his wife, Augusta Victoria, from Germany, the royal couple entered Jerusalem on Reformation Day, 31 October, for the dedication of the Redeemer Church (built about 100 yards from the church of the Holy Sepulchre). Elaborate preparations had been made: stray dogs on the streets of Jerusalem had been poisoned, and the historic Jaffa Gate was destroyed because it was too narrow for the imperial carriage. Outwardly the visit was a great a success. Yet, behind the scenes there were rumblings of unease. The German Catholics were disappointed not to get their (Protestant) emperor's backing for their attempted purchase of the Coenaculum (the traditional site of the Last Supper), being offered instead a site where they would later build the Dormition Abbey. Theodore Herzl, who came with four other Zionists to meet the Kaiser, was also bitterly disappointed with the emperor's negative response to their vision for a homeland—a negative response which the Kaiser underlined privately the very next morning to the Anglican Archbishop at St George's Cathedral: 'there can't be any future for them!' And, as for his own impressions of the Holy Land as a pilgrim, this Protestant emperor was also very negative, expressing explicitly his disappointment with the Holy Sepulchre, with Jerusalem and indeed with the Holy Land as a whole: 'What a dismal arid heap of stones Palestine is! ... Jerusalem is very much spoiled by the large modern suburbs .... The Church of the Holy Sepulchre ... looks like something between a bazaar and a Chinese temple, but certainly not like a church!'

Conclusion

In these three small cameos relating to the visit of Kaiser Wilhelm we can observe in a nutshell some of the religious tensions and political complexities of pilgrimage—complexities which would then be played out throughout the century following the First World War until the present day: tensions between Catholics and Protestants; tensions between Christians and others who have their different desires for the Holy Land (be they secular Zionists, religious Jews, or practising Muslims); and the tension between believers' previously imagined pictures of what that land should look like and the harsh, very different, realities on the ground. For the story of Christian pilgrimage to the Holy Land, as we have seen, is indeed a complex one—not least because it has to be practised alongside people of other faith-traditions who have their own interest in this same plot of land as a *terra sancta*.

We have seen its ebb and flow, its highs and lows; there have been times when the primary direction of the travel has been, as it were, *away* from the Holy Land, but much of the time, the direction has been firmly fixed towards it. Yet this ebb and flow reflects ongoing tensions that are intrinsic within the very core of the Christian tradition itself—the tensions between a focus on Christ's incarnation or his exaltation, the tensions between the faith's historical or spiritual aspects. For some Christians, the biblical message 'He is *not here*, he is risen!' says it all; but others want to reply, 'But that means that, once upon a time, he *was here*!' This dialectic first came to clear articulation in the era of Constantine, being seen in the two contrasting strands of thought developed by Eusebius and Cyril. It can be seen again, in a slightly different guise, in the two very different approaches to pilgrimage—'Catholic/Orthodox' or 'Protestant'.

The last 1700 years can therefore be seen as, in essence, the story of the subtle and complex interweaving of those two equally vital strands, which occasionally appear as though they inhabit two different worlds or speak two incomprehensible languages. Yet, there is, much deeper down, a fundamental unity. In the words of the historians Ruth and Thomas Hummel: 'they are communicating in two dialects of the same language, sharing one underlying faith in the person whose earthly home they find so enchanting'.

Muslim and Jewish pilgrimage

In contrast to Christian pilgrimage, much less attention has been paid to Muslim and Jewish pilgrimage to and within the Holy Land. This is perhaps because the focus for both faiths has been on their canonical pilgrimage, that is, pilgrimage that is prescribed by Scripture: Deuteronomy and the Qur'an respectively. This canonical pilgrimage became restricted to the past in the case of Judaism and to Mecca in the case of Islam. Yet the adherents of both faiths, partly influenced by late antique Christianity's zeal for reverencing holy persons and places, developed an enthusiasm for visiting places and persons of recognized religious significance. The word for this practice in Arabic is *ziyara*, which simply means 'visit', and Jews often used it too for lack of a simple Hebrew expression for voluntary non-canonical pilgrimage. There was sometimes an element of competition in this phenomenon—claiming sites of divinity for one's own faith over against a rival, but there was also the genuine desire to seek blessing and favour, to commemorate celebrated events and persons of the past, to make atonement, and even to satisfy a desire for travel to exotic lands.

Jerusalem was the most important focus of this sort of pilgrimage for both Muslims and Jews. For the latter the Jerusalemite Temple had served as the crux of Jewish pilgrimage (*aliyya laregel*) until its destruction by the Romans in 70 CE (see above under 'Journeying within the Holy Land (the Old Testament period)'). Many Jewish scholars at first decreed that this event nullified the former veneration of this sacred building, but its draw proved too strong and it soon became a symbol of what had once been and what would one day be again. The sole part of the Temple that had remained relatively unscathed, the Western wall, assumed mythic stature and soon attracted crowds of pilgrims, as it still does today. Initially it was a rather mournful practice; a fourth-century Christian pilgrim from Bordeaux describes how Jews would enter Jerusalem on Tisha B'Av (9 July or August), the anniversary of the destruction of the Temple, and would 'bewail themselves with groans and rend their garments'. But as time went on, and especially in the Islamic period, when Jews could once again move freely and settle in Jerusalem, it acquired a more positive ethos. Thus a text from the medieval Jewish archive of Cairo suggests that it was still necessary 'to rend your garments for the Temple', but also recommends the prayer: 'We give you thanks, O Lord our God, that you have given us life, brought us to this place and made us worthy to enter your House.' And during this time the Jerusalem Academy (*yeshiva*) would lead a procession through the city on the seventh day of the Feast of Tabernacles (*sukkot*) around the Temple Mount and up the Mount of Olives for singing and prayer. Frankish rule (1099–1187) limited Jewish travel to the Holy City, but did not halt it, and once it ended there was a marked upturn in the number of Jews seeking to visit the Holy Land, in particular from Europe, and from this time on pilgrimage accounts by Jews and lists of pilgrimage sites for Jews begin to proliferate.

In the hearts of Muslims, too, Jerusalem enjoyed a special status. Allegedly, the second caliph 'Umar (634–644) commissioned the construction of a mosque on the

Temple Mount, and there was certainly a 'Saracen house of prayer' at that location by 670, when it was inspected by the Gallic Christian pilgrim Arculf. At an early date this mosque became linked with 'the furthest mosque' (*al-masjid al-aqsa*) mentioned in Qur'an 17:1 as the endpoint of a journey made by God's 'servant', assumed to be a reference to the prophet Muhammad. Only a few yards distant lay the rocky tip of Mount Moriah, on which Abraham had initiated the sacrifice of his son, an event recounted in the Qur'an as well as the Bible, and where, some said, Muhammad's feet had alighted at the end of his heavenly journey. This only increased the sanctity of the Temple Mount for Muslims, and the caliph 'Abd al-Malik (685–705) capitalized on this fact by building the dramatically beautiful octagonal shrine that became known as the Dome of the Rock. Some said that he did this to divert the pilgrimage from Mecca and Medina to Jerusalem, and if this probably overstates the case it is nonetheless true that it was widely accepted that travelling to pray on the Temple Mount, even if voluntary, ranked not far behind worship at the two Arabian cities.

Some of the most popular pilgrimage sites were connected with holy persons, in particular prophets and patriarchs. Many of these were revered by all three Abrahamic faiths, even if in different measure, and so were shared or contested. King David was particularly important to Christians as the founder of the dynasty from which Jesus descended, and they paid respects at his tomb on Mount Zion (though Bethlehem had been postulated as its location before the seventh century). But David also makes an appearance in the Qur'an, and so his burial place came to attract Islamic attention too, as is noted by Muslim writers of the tenth century. Around the beginning of the twelfth century the old Byzantine Church of Zion, which had been plundered in 966, was rebuilt on a grand scale by the Crusaders, and in one corner a chapel was established to commemorate the tombs of the House of David, including that of David himself. Jewish travellers challenged the identification of the site, beginning with Benjamin of Tudela, who visited in around 1170 and stated that, contrary to what the Christians say, 'the exact site (of David's tomb) cannot be determined'. Christians and Jews struggled for control of it in the fifteenth century, but the Muslim authorities stepped in and in 1452 the tomb of David was converted into a mosque, though this of course did not stop the site being a draw for Jews and Christians.

Abraham had many places associated with him across the Middle East, but the most well known was the cave of Machpelah at Hebron. There he was said to be buried along with Isaac and Jacob, and the wives of all three of them, as is already attested by Arculf in the seventh century. The Crusaders built a monastery there and claimed, in 1119, to have discovered the actual tombs of the patriarchs, which seems to have created some tension. The Jews of Acre warned Petahiah of Regensburg, who ventured to Palestine in the 1170s, that the Christians 'have placed three corpses at the entrance to the cave and they say "these are the patriarchs", but they are not'. However, reports Benjamin of Tudela, for a fee, but only for Jews, 'the custodian of the cave will open a gate of iron which was constructed by our forefathers, and then one can descend below... where there are six sepulchers, those of Abraham, Isaac and Jacob, respectively facing those of

The Herodian fort-like construction surrounding the ancient 'cave of Machpelah' at Hebron which is revered in both Judaism and Islam as the burial place of Abraham, Isaac, Jacob, and their wives.

Sarah, Rebecca and Leah'. Another Jewish visitor of the twelfth century, Jacob ben Nathaniel, takes this idea even further and claims that Christians are prevented from seeing the real tombs, and when once some priests tried to get to them 'a wind arose and slew them'. This theme of the secret burial place, the indulgent custodian and the miraculous wind occurs in the account of the Muslim pilgrim 'Ali al-Harawi, who went to Hebron around 1192 and relates how a colleague of his bribed the guard to take him to the lower cave after hours: 'They descended approximately seventy steps and came to a large spacious grotto where the wind blew; it contained a slab upon which lay Abraham covered in a green garment and the wind was playing with his hair.'

There is an interesting pattern here of identification of/claim to sites of biblical figures by the Crusaders, which was then challenged by Jewish authorities, who felt they knew better, and then there was often a struggle for control of the location, usually involving the Muslims too. The case of the prophet Samuel illustrates this well. According to the Bible he was buried in Ramah, which in Byzantine times was linked with the village of al-Ram, north-east of Jerusalem. However, the Crusaders selected a site to the north-west, probably for strategic reasons, since it controlled access to the Holy City, and they built there a church and monastery dedicated to Samuel (at present-day Nabi Samwil). Benjamin of Tudela angrily accuses the Christians of violating the original tomb of the prophet and removing his bodily remains to their church. The Crusader structure was razed by Saladin and incorporated into a new mosque. The anonymous *Elleh ha-Massa'ot*, a thirteenth-century list of Jewish pilgrimage itineraries, records this mosque of Samuel, along with the tomb of his mother Hannah and a well that was her ritual bath (*mikveh*), as stops on a Jewish pilgrimage circuit. Other sources tell us that on the day of Samuel's death (28 May) people would come to prostrate and kindle torches by his tomb and that during the Feast of Weeks (*Shavu'ot*) they would bring Torah scrolls from Jerusalem to be read out there. This site was, therefore, shared between Jews and Muslims, often in peace, sometimes in conflict, as in the fifteenth century when, according to the Italian pilgrim Isaac ben Meir, the Muslims tried to stop Jews praying at the tomb. Thereupon Samuel rose up, saint-like, to grab the offending Muslim by the throat and demand he return the key to the Jews, for 'they are my children, not you'.

In general, though, Muslims and Jews seemed to enjoy a special understanding over the issue of shrines, or at least that is how many Jewish writers liked to portray it. The Florentine merchant and pilgrim Meshullam of Volterra (1481) tells us that the Muslims showed respect for the Jewish veneration of 'tombs of the ancestors' (*qivre avot*) and 'tombs of the righteous' (*qivre saddiqim*): 'They honor all these places and they have an oral tradition like ours.' It is pointed out time and time again that Muslims would visit these graves of Jewish holy persons seeking healing and intercession, and this includes post-biblical figures, whom Christians would seem never to have acknowledged. A comparison between the list of Muslim pilgrim destinations in al-Harawi (1192) and Jewish ones in the *Elleh ha-Massa'ot* reveals a fair degree of overlap. For example, there is the burial site of Jethro, identified by Muslim tradition as the Arabian prophet Shu'ayb, at the village of Hittin above the Sea of Galilee. The author of *Elleh ha-Massa'ot* is keen to point out that there is no conflict here, for 'it is the custom of the Ishmaelites to build their prayer houses next to the tombs of the righteous'. Then there is the tomb of Jonah ben Amittai—Nabi Yunus in Arabic—in Cana, north of Nazareth, where there was, according to the same source, 'a beautiful building, a house of prayer (*bet tefillah*) for the Ishmaelites'.

In some cases the two texts reveal that, though there was agreement between Muslims and Jews over the sanctity of a site, each community nevertheless revered there a different holy person. At Yavneh, for instance, the Jews paid homage to Rabban Gamaliel, considered a founding father of rabbinic Judaism, whereas the Muslims visited it to pay their respects to Abu Hurayra, one of the most beloved of Muhammad's companions. The most dramatic example of this is found on the upper slope of the Mount of the Olives, near the Church of the Ascension. From at least the sixth century Christians had identified a cave there to be the last resting place of Pelagia, a wealthy *bonne vivante* of Antioch who had converted to Christianity, given away her riches to the poor, and then lived out the rest of her life as a hermit in this cave on the Mount of Olives. Much later the same cave was claimed by the Muslims as the burial place of the famous female mystic Rabi'a al-'Adwiyya (d. 801), even though all her life had been spent in fasting and prayer in the Iraqi city of Basra. Later again the site became attached to the Jewish prophetess Huldah, who foretold how King Josiah would be spared God's punishment because of his repentance. Consequently, notes Yehosef Schwartz (1804–1865) disapprovingly, 'sometimes there are three kinds of people there: Jews, Christians and Ishmaelites, all come to pray in that place'.

Of course the landscape of sanctity is a complex and multiple arena. In his guidebook for pilgrims 'Ali al-Harawi very frequently notes that several persons are venerated at a single site, or that one person is celebrated at several locations. He is acquainted, for example, with four tombs each for Abu 'Ubayda ibn al-Jarrah and Abu Hurayra, Companions of Muhammad, and with two each for the biblical figures Jonah, Elisha, and Jethro (Mecca as well as Hittin). He usually indicates this with the subtle comment that we have also visited the tomb for this person at another place 'but God knows best (about which is the right one)'. It is also often the case that one spot will be associated with different sacred traditions that are not necessarily contradictory, though they may provoke communal rivalry. For instance, at Acre there is the Ox Spring, whence, says al-Harawi, an ox emerged to plough the fields of Adam, and it is also the site of a shrine to 'Ali ibn Abi Talib, son-in-law of Muhammad. The Franks had wanted to make it into a church, but 'Ali gave a warning in a dream to the overseer, who told his Frankish masters, and, after the death of a foreman, they allowed it to remain as a mosque.

The very fact that there was no sanction for this type of pilgrimage—visits to tombs and shrines for blessings, intercession, and memorializing—in Scripture or in the Law meant that some Jews and Muslims were suspicious of it, or even downright hostile to it. The tenth-century theologian and Jerusalemite Sahl ben Masliah leaves us in no doubt about his views: 'How can I be silent while certain idolatrous practices are rampant among Israelites? They pass the night among tombstones. They make requests of the dead, entreating "O Yossi of Galilee, cure me, grant me a child". They light candles upon the graves of the righteous ones, burn incense before them and tie knots on the date palm of the saint in order to cure a host of illnesses. They go as pilgrims (*hogegim*) to the tombs of these dead saints and make votive offerings to them.' This lament reveals a set of practices and expressions that were shared by Christians, Jews, and Muslims in their visits to holy persons, and it is precisely this inter-confessional mingling and ambiguity that increased the antipathy of some religious authorities.

Many Muslim theologians were wary of *ziyara*, because it looked like imitation of Christian practice and because it had the potential to serve as a substitute for the canonical pilgrimage to Mecca. As with the quote of Sahl above, their condemnations convey an idea of what sort of rituals were involved. For instance, the Baghdadi theologian Ibn 'Aqil (d. 1119) castigated people for 'innovations such as venerating tombs and honoring them with what the Law forbids: kindling lights, kissing and

One city, three faiths; the two Muslim domes of the 'noble sanctuary' (*Haram esh-Sharif*) stand above the Jewish Western Wall, with the Christian Church of the Ascension seen beyond them on the Mount of Olives.

perfuming them, exhorting the dead, writing petitions on scraps of paper, taking earth away as a blessing, pouring fragrances over graves, journeying to them, and throwing rags on trees'. This anti-*ziyara* trend has remained a part of Islam until today, but it was by no means the dominant view and even those who supported it often made subtle distinctions. Thus the Syrian theologian Ibn Taymiyya (d. 1328), who was perhaps the most vocal critic of any hint of a Muslim 'cult of the saints', distinguished between legal *ziyara*, which meant visiting tombs to pray on behalf of the dead, and illegal *ziyara*, visiting tombs to seek intercession for oneself from the dead. And most tended to agree that there were certain benefits to *ziyara*, such as, in the words of one of the greatest Muslim theologians of all time, al-Ghazali (d. 1111), 'remembrance and contemplation . . . and seeking blessings (from God)'.

Epilogue

There were, then, many disagreements among different religious groups about the merits and de-merits of pilgrimage to the Holy Land, as well as heated debates about where certain sacred events had occurred, about which events and holy persons should be commemorated, and about where and how such commemoration should be carried out. These disputes were not just between Jews, Christians, and Muslims, but between different factions within these three faiths. And yet much more united the different parties than divided them. All felt an investment in and attachment to the Holy Land, and Jerusalem in particular, albeit for different reasons. All played up their historical associations with the land: it was where King David had ruled, where Jesus had walked, where Muhammad had alighted on his journey from Mecca. Some of these historical events were even shared, such as Abraham's sacrifice of his son on Mount Moriah. Finally, as was pointed out at the beginning of this chapter, journeying was crucial to all three faiths: it had been a key aspect of the lives of their founding figures and so it is not surprising that it became integral to the lives of their followers.

CHAPTER 12

Sacred Spaces and Holy Places

RICHARD S. HESS AND DENYS PRINGLE

THE Holy Land is full of places where the physical world and the numinous appear to intersect. They range from the place where Moses encountered the divine in the burning bush on Mount Sinai, to those where Jesus passed his life on earth and appeared again after his crucifixion, to that from which the Prophet Muhammad ascended briefly into heaven.

Just as religion itself may be regarded as an aspect of human culture, holy places—whether artificial constructions or natural features—are culturally defined, regardless of whatever divine revelation may be held to account for them. Some, like Elisha's Spring in Jericho or the summit of Mount Sinai where Moses was handed the law, may attain the status of a site visited and venerated by pilgrims while still apparently retaining their original natural form, while others like the burning bush may be represented by simulacra erected on the same supposed site. Others are claimed by their adherents to present more concrete evidence of a connection with past people or events through the physical remains of built structures (including caves), the tombs of prophets, saints, and martyrs, or movable relics. In others, however, no such connection may be claimed and a sacred space such as the holy of holies of a temple or the sanctuary of a church may be an artificial space in which a divine presence is invoked through the imprecations of the worshippers and the liturgies enacted around them. A feature of all sacred spaces, however, is the way in which they are delimited from normal space, with access to them often being restricted to a select group of people.

The multitude of holy places that cover the Holy Land today and continue to draw in pilgrims from around the world testify not only to the antiquity of religious practice in the land, especially by the followers of the three principal monotheistic faiths of the Abrahamic tradition, but also of the ability of holy places both to unite and to divide people. At different times and in different places examples can be found of sites being shared or contested by adherents of different religions or of different traditions within the same religion. At times, such friction has led some to seek the holy in solitary places, but even these may come to be contested by later followers, underlining again that holy places are as much a product of human culture as of divine inspiration.

Here we make use of both archaeological and historical evidence to trace the history of holy places in this region from the earliest beginnings until the end of the Ottoman period.

Pre-Bronze Age (c.10,000–3300 BCE)

The earliest evidence for sacred religious spaces in the Holy Land is represented by a series of circles of standing stones in the Negev Desert and southern Jordan. These circles can date as early as 10,000 BCE, in the Mesolithic period, and are comparable in date to Göbekli Tepe in Turkey, until recently regarded as the oldest example of a religious sacred space. The unworked stones themselves range from less than a metre to many metres in height and most likely represented deities or ancestors, who continued to receive veneration. The standing stones often occur in groups of seven or nine and face eastward. Offering benches and ash pits have been found in front of or at the centre of these groups, while others mark burials. Over a hundred such sites are known, including some that appear much later and some that were in use for many millennia.

Also found in the Negev are dozens of open rectangular sanctuaries, marked off by single or double rows of stones. They have no walls or roof and no floor other than the desert sand. The corners face the cardinal points of the compass; one of the corners sometimes contains a group of standing stones, facing east. Open sanctuaries occur in Pre-Pottery Neolithic times from *c.*6000 BCE onwards. Artificial piles of stones on hilltops near to ancient tracks announced to passers-by the location of special burials, standing stones, or open sanctuaries. Other sites that were evidently regarded as sacred during this period are those containing human burials, both adult and infant. In the adults' case, the skulls were often removed. In Jericho, such burials have been found below house floors, while the discovery of skulls with the features of the head restored in plaster suggests a continuing cult of ancestors within the houses themselves.

The Chalcolithic period (*c.*4500–3300 BCE) witnessed the development of formal cemeteries and new types of public sanctuaries. For the first time in the Holy Land cemeteries were regularly separated from settlement sites. In the northern Negev and lower Jordan Valley, differences in tomb construction, including circular graves with offerings, cist graves, and small tumuli in cemeteries, may reflect social ranking. Such cemeteries occur at northern sites such as Tulaylat al-Ghassul, at Shiqmim, and Kissufim in the Negev, and at Eilat on the Gulf of ʻAqaba. Near the coast burials are found in caves. A natural cave used for burials in the Wadi Qana in western Samaria included eight gold and electrum ring-shaped ingots, the largest concentration of such objects found in the Levant in this period. Characteristic of these cemeteries are box-like ossuaries, often carved with a nose or whole face forming the front. The original purpose of the stone circle of Rujm al-Hiri (Rogem Hiri) in the Jawlan (Golan) is

Massebot from the Uvda Valley in the Israeli Negev.

uncertain, whether funerary, astronomical, or for exposure of the dead, but in the Early Bronze Age it would become a burial centre.

At Tulaylat al-Ghassul, on the east side of the lower Jordan Valley, colourful frescoes depict ceremonial processions and human and animal figures of mythical origin. At En-Gedi, west of the Dead Sea, a sanctuary consisting of several structures and a larger cultic building was surrounded by a stone wall. The main building measured 20 by 5.5 m and formed a rectangular broadhouse. The entrance was on the south, opposite a niche containing ash and a clay statuette representing a bull. A piece of white limestone at the back of the niche may have provided a base for a venerated image. The remarkable collection of 416 copper maces, crowns, and other artifacts from the nearby cave in Nahal Mishmar (Wadi al-Sufaysif) may also have been used in rituals at this regional centre, while excavations at Gilat in the northern Negev have revealed seven strata of rectilinear buildings with more than 200 'incense burners', standing stones, violin-shaped figurines, and small zoomorphic and anthropomorphic vessels and statuettes.

Some of the archaeological features of this early period, including groups of standing stones, specialist art and metalwork, and the separation of burials from living areas, suggest a growing association of religious activities with defined sacred spaces, something that would be more fully developed in the next period.

It had three steps at its entrance and two incense altars as well as two standing stones (*massebot*). The larger altar corresponded to the larger stone, leading some scholars to hypothesize that this represented Judah's God, Yahweh, while the smaller altar and stone represented his consort, Asherah. The Iron Age II texts from the site, representing written correspondence dating mostly from near the end of the period of Judean independence in the early sixth century BC, mention only the deity Yahweh. At nearby Beersheba a single four-horned altar of cut stone was also found dismantled and reused in a wall.

At Kuntillat 'Ajrud, an Iron Age fort or road station in the northern Sinai desert, excavations have revealed a room just inside the entrance lined with benches evidently intended for offerings and containing pottery and stone vessels incised with drawings and inscriptions, with similar decoration painted on its plastered walls. Blessings invoking Yahweh and Asherah appear with other texts that mention Yahweh, Asherah, and Ba'al. A similar blessing to Yahweh and Asherah is inscribed at a burial site at Khirbat al-Kum in southern Judah. At the cult site of Deir 'Alla in the east Jordan Valley, dated *c.*800 BCE, an ink inscription on plaster mentions a vision of the priest-diviner Balaam, son of Beor (Num. 21–4; 31:8), regarding a divine assembly of 'gods' and other groups of West Semitic deities, whose names or titles find echoes in the names applied by the Bible to Israel's God.

Elsewhere on the borders of the traditional areas occupied by Israel we find Iron Age cult sites. The Philistine temple at Tel Qasile (on the northern outskirts of modern Tel Aviv) includes a central space whose roof was supported by two columns. Tel Miqne (Khirbat al-Muqanna'), identified with Philistine Ekron, contains its own temples, one with an Aegean-style hearth at the entrance, reflecting the Mediterranean origins of the Philistine people and culture. More impressive are the horned altars, a form that was widely used in Israel and Judah. At Ekron they are found throughout the site, including the areas of major olive-oil presses, indicating how sacred spaces could appear in both domestic and industrial contexts. The already mentioned Geshurite stele from al-Tall (Bethsaida) bore a carved image reflecting the moon cult. Its location at the main entrance to the city, defining a sacred area where visitors could pour out a libation, also points to cultic activity related to Aramean cultures to the north.

A variety of tombs are found in the Holy Land. By the latter part of the Iron Age II period, however, the body was first laid out on a bench cut into the side of a cave. After decomposition, when only the bones remained, they were added to other bones of the family ancestors in an ossuary pit in the same tomb (hence the description of the departed being 'gathered to his/her people' in Gen. 25:8 and elsewhere). The tombs reveal evidence of eating and drinking vessels. It is unclear whether these items were intended to service the perceived needs of the deceased or to provide a memorial meal of some sort for the living.

A number of tombs dating from *c.*600 BCE have been discovered in the area of Old Testament Jerusalem. Among the finds from tombs on the western shoulder of the Hinnom Valley are two small silver scrolls, which were found, when unrolled, to contain portions of the Blessing of Aaron (Num. 6:24–6) and possibly other references to Yahweh from the Pentateuch. In the wider region surrounding the city, some twenty artificial mounds or tumuli have also been found. These have been related to the biblical references to twenty-one kings from David to Zedekiah (for the exception, see 2 Chron. 21:19), who were remembered after death by the construction of a sacred mound and the performance of rituals connected with fire.

The Bible witnesses to the continued religious use of Solomon's temple in Jerusalem until its destruction by the Babylonians in 586 BCE (1–2 Kgs; 2 Chron.; Jer.). For both Israel and Judah the sacred spaces and the altars and texts that accompany them attest to two parallel traditions. The first tradition links surrounding cultures in the worship of more than one deity at a shrine. This practice is reflected in texts such as those discovered at Kuntillat 'Ajrud. The second tradition, whether indicated by a single altar or by texts like those from the Hinnom valley tombs, involves the worship of a single deity at a shrine. Evidence for the second tradition becomes stronger later in the period.

The Babylonian, Persian, Hellenistic, and early Roman periods (586 BCE–70 CE)

The Persian period (586–330 BCE) saw the foundation and building of a new temple in Jerusalem on the same site and with the same orientation as the earlier temple built by Solomon (Ezra 3:8–10). In this way Judaism sought to preserve its religious identity. The post-exilic prophet Haggai observed how diminished the rebuilt temple appeared when compared with the magnificence of the earlier structure (Haggai 2:3). It was finished around 515 BCE and was enclosed within the square precinct of the Temple Mount, which defined the sacred space.

The Jewish historian Josephus Flavius, writing in the first century CE, records the building of a Samaritan temple on Mount Gerizim in the fourth century BCE, though excavations now put its foundation somewhat earlier, in the mid fifth. As in Jerusalem, the sacred space around the temple was defined by a rectangular enclosure some 96 m square. Gates gave access to it from the north, south, and east but not from the west, suggesting that as in Jerusalem the inner sanctuary and holy of holies—later obliterated by other buildings—would have been on that side.

The Hellenistic period (*c*.330–363 BCE) witnessed the destruction of some earlier temples, largely through the zealotry of the Jerusalem-based dynasty of the Hasmoneans. The Samaritan temple on Mount Gerizim, for instance, was destroyed by John Hyrcanus I (*c*.110 BCE); and in the second century BCE, Jonathan Maccabee was remembered for having destroyed a Philistine temple at Ashdod (1 Macc. 10:83–4; 11:4).

Sometime around the end of the third century BC, the high priest Simon II repaired the Jerusalem temple, strengthening its foundations in order to create a higher and stronger structure (Eccles. 50:1–2). After taking power in 175 BCE, the Seleucid king Antiochus IV Epiphanes passed through Jerusalem and stripped the temple of its adornments. He constructed the Akra, a fortress south of the Temple Mount of that time, where in 167 BCE he offered pigs and unclean animals as sacrifices to Zeus

(1 Macc. 1:54). The Maccabean Revolt led three years later to the recapture of the temple and the dedication of the new altar, an event remembered in the Feast of Hanukkah. In 141 BCE, Simon Maccabee also destroyed the Akra. The dynasty begun by the Maccabean family, known as the Hasmoneans, extended the Temple Mount to the south, constructed a fortress in the north-west corner and embellished the temple itself and its surrounding sacred space.

The Roman assault on Jerusalem led by Pompey in 63 BCE ended in the destruction of the Maccabean fortress, the capture of the temple and Pompey's entrance into the holy of holies; however, Josephus records no desecration. Indeed, the final decades of the first century BCE saw Rome's client king, the great builder Herod the Great (37–4 BCE), focusing his efforts on increasing the temple's size and splendour. So impressive and sacred was this structure that centuries after its eventual destruction both the Mishnah and the Talmud devoted large sections to describing its construction and use. The Dead Sea Scroll community also composed a vision for a rebuilt temple that was apparently based on it, while Josephus gives us a detailed description of what he saw of it before its destruction.

Herod's works included extending the temple precinct further south and bolstering the retaining wall that supported its porticoes with massively drafted stones, which can still be seen today. Inside the older square enclosure of the Temple Mount stood the balustrade and screen, known as the *soreg*, marked with signs prohibiting non-Jews from approaching any closer on pain of death. Twelve monumental steps gave access to the main court east of the temple, known as the court of women, where men and women seem to have been separated. This court, with four chambers and surrounding porticoes, could accommodate 6000 worshippers. From it another flight of steps led west to the terraced court of the Israelites, from which another series of monumental steps rose up to the court of the priests. This lay before the altar of the burnt sacrifice, which was perhaps 14.5 m square with a ramp leading up to it.

To the west of the court of the priests, twelve steps led up to the porch enclosing the entrance to the sanctuary or holy place of the temple. According to Josephus (*War* 5.207–26) this building appeared to be 150 feet (*c*.45 m) high and 150 feet broad, but behind the facade it narrowed to 90 feet (*c*.27 m) in width and would have been some 200 feet (*c*.60 m) in length. Large parts were covered in gold, while the rest was white. Golden spikes prevented birds from settling on the roof. Internally the sanctuary was divided into an outer and inner chamber, the outer being 30 feet (*c*.9 m) wide, 75 (*c*.22 m) long and 135 (*c*.40 m) high. A pair of golden doors, hidden from public view by a great red, blue, and purple linen tapestry, opened into the inner chamber. This was 30 feet (*c*.9 m) wide and 90 (*c*.27 m) long but only 90 feet high and was itself divided into two parts by a great veil. The western part, 30 feet square, represented the holy of holies. In the Roman period this was bare, but the place where the Ark of the Covenant had stood may have been marked in some way. Here the high priest sprinkled blood on the Day of Atonement for the forgiveness of the sins of Israel (Leviticus 16). The temple would continue to function until the Romans destroyed it at the time of the Great Revolt in 70 CE.

In addition to his work on the Temple, Herod the Great recognized two places sacred to the Jews, both of them in the region of Hebron south of Jerusalem. A few kilometres north of Hebron he constructed a temenos wall of large drafted masonry similar to that of the Jerusalem temple around a venerable oak, identified as the oak of Mamre or of Abraham, in the place where the patriarch was thought to have pitched his tent and entertained three angels (Gen. 13:18; 14:13; 18:1). In Hebron itself, another massive precinct wall with external pilasters, built in a similarly monumental style using huge smoothly drafted blocks of stone, was erected around the traditional site of the cave of Machpelah, where Abraham, Isaac, and Jacob and their respective wives, Sarah, Rebekah, and Leah, were buried (Gen. 23:1–20; 25:9; 49:31; 50:13).

Elsewhere, new forms of sacred space were emerging in this period, involving both the living and the dead. In the first century CE, in the period leading up to the First Jewish War with Rome, both the New Testament and archaeology attest the existence of synagogues in the Holy Land. In the gospels Jesus teaches in the synagogues in Galilee, while building remains of pre-Revolt synagogues have been excavated at Masada, Herodium, and Gamla. An inscription known as the Theodotos inscription, found in the excavation of the city of David, south of the Temple Mount, also mentions the building of a synagogue together with a guest room and other chambers in the late first century BCE. In the diaspora, however, synagogues are attested by inscriptions from as early as the third century BCE. Jewish tradition as reflected in the Mishnah also projects the existence of a body concerned with the interpretation of biblical law and known as the Men of the Great Synagogue back to the sixth century BCE, suggesting that the setting aside of specific places in which Jews could gather together to study, pray, and discuss the Torah may have begun at the time of the sixth-century exile.

Synagogues at Gamla in the Golan and at Herodium to the south of Jerusalem appear as rectangular structures with roofs supported by stone columns and stone benches around the inside face of the walls. A similar synagogue at Masada, as rearranged by the insurgents during the Revolt, contained four tiers of stone seats along the walls and a smaller chamber partitioned off in one corner, in which were found fragments of biblical manuscripts. A fourth structure associated with a ritual bath and a courtyard has been excavated west of Jericho and identified as a synagogue of the first century BCE.

The Dead Sea Scroll community at Qumran set aside sacred spaces throughout the complex in the form of ritual baths (*miqvaot*) for purification. The baths bear architectural witness to a greater emphasis on ritual purity than is observable elsewhere. Indeed, the entire community gave itself to the observance of the strictest priestly rules of purity and discipline. *Miqvaot* have also been found at approaches to the Jerusalem temple and in cities such as Sepphoris in Galilee, which included some Jewish citizens. Tombs outside Sepphoris and Nazareth resemble those dotting the hills around early Roman Jerusalem. Many of them were for individual burials, a departure from the earlier practice of family burial.

Synagogue at Masada.

The late Roman and Byzantine period (70–636/7 CE)

Even before the Jewish revolt of 66–74 CE and the subsequent progressive integration of the Holy Land more fully into the Roman empire, Roman pagan cults, including worship of the emperor, were making their presence felt in a land that from the time of the Hasmoneans had been essentially monotheistic. Herod the Great had himself established temples of Augustus in Caesarea and Samaria. After the Bar Kokhba revolt and Hadrian's refounding of Jerusalem as Aelia Capitolina in 134 CE, a capitoline temple of Jupiter (Zeus) was built, probably on the Temple Mount, and a smaller temple of Venus in the new forum covered the place where early Christians believed that the tomb of Jesus lay. Among other pagan Roman temples built in the second century CE were those dedicated to Hadrian in Tiberias and to Zeus Akraios in Beth Shean (Scythopolis). A temple of Zeus Hyposistos (the Supreme) also replaced the destroyed Samaritan temple above Flavia Neapolis (Nablus) in 160 CE, in an example of syncretism similar to that in Baalbek (Heleopolis) in modern Lebanon, where a massive temple of Zeus Heliopolitanus was built in the first century CE at a sanctuary earlier associated with Ba'al.

Samaria (Sebaste): the surviving podium and steps of the temple of Augustus, built by Herod the Great around 25 CE.

The destruction of the Jewish temple and the exclusion of Jews from Jerusalem by Hadrian encouraged the development of synagogues as a focus for religious teaching, prayer, and worship in places where Jews were settled, notably in parts of Judea away from Jerusalem and above all in Galilee and the Golan. Some indication of the cultural make-up of these congregations is indicated by their synagogue inscriptions, which tend to be in Greek in the coastal areas, the major cities, and Lower Galilee, but in Hebrew or Aramaic in the remoter parts of Judea, Upper Galilee, and the Golan. Synagogues also acquired additional meaning in this period as holy places reflecting the sanctity of the destroyed Temple. They were more usually oriented towards Jerusalem; and the Torah scroll, instead of being brought into the hall for readings and removed afterwards, was accorded a permanent place of honour in a shrine, often in a niche (bema) or apse. Somewhat curiously, however, in Palestine there is a hiatus of almost two centuries between the Temple's destruction and the building of the next datable synagogues in the mid third century. The high point for synagogue construction was in the fifth and sixth centuries.

At one time it was thought that differences in the form of surviving synagogues reflected a chronological development, but more secure dating now suggests that such

The torah shrine and mosaic floor of the fourth- to fifth-century synagogue at Khirbat Susiyya, near Hebron.

variations are more likely to have been due to the social, cultural, and architectural preferences of those who commissioned and built them. Some layouts follow earlier practice, with a columned interior and stone benches set around three sides facing a bema or apse, while others have a broadhouse plan, with the bema set in one of the longer walls and the entrance in one of the shorter ones. There are also basilican types, similar in plan to early churches (see later in this section), with three or sometimes five aisles divided by colonnades and the Torah shrine located in an apse or niche opposite the entrance. While in some synagogues the decoration is austere, with no figural representation of humans or animals, others are richly decorated with mosaics and in some cases sculptured figural decoration.

At Beth Alpha (Khirbat Bayt Ilfa) in the Jezreel Valley, a synagogue of the early sixth century is laid out as an aisled basilica facing south, preceded by a narthex and atrium. The central aisle of the basilica is paved with a mosaic containing three panels. A panel immediately in front of the bema shows the Torah ark, flanked by two seven-branched candlesticks, two lions, and various other religious objects, including a palm frond, citron, ram's horn, and incense shovel. The central panel represents a square containing two concentric circles. In the inner circle the sun god Helios (or Sol Invictus) drives his four-horse chariot though a dark sky containing a crescent moon and stars. The outer ring is divided into twelve segments, each containing a sign of the zodiac, while the four corners of the square contain personifications of the seasons. Finally, the third panel, just inside the door, shows the story of Abraham's sacrifice of Isaac (Gen. 22). Similar pavements, in which God the ruler of heaven and earth is represented in the guise of the Graeco-Roman sun god, are found in the synagogues at Hammat Tiberias, Sepphoris, Na'aran ('Ayn Duq, near Jericho), and Susiyya (near Hebron), while at En-Gedi the signs of the zodiac with their corresponding months are simply listed in Hebrew, along with a list of the righteous ancestors from Adam to Azariah.

The site of the Samaritan temple and associated Hellenistic city on Mount Gerizim had lain unoccupied since their destruction by John Hyrcanus in 114–111 BCE, but in the fourth century CE the Samaritans defied Roman decrees excluding them and constructed a synagogue. Dedicatory inscriptions in Greek recording monetary offerings as well as coin finds indicate revitalized religious use of the sanctuary, though whether this included animal sacrifice is uncertain. A number of Samaritan synagogues were also built elsewhere in Samaria during this period. One excavated at Khirbat Samara, between Nablus and Tulkarm, consisted in the fourth century of a barrel-vaulted rectangular hall measuring internally some 8.4 by 12.4 m with walls over 2 m thick. It was aligned east–west, with the door facing west and two tiers of stone bench seats around the walls. Originally the Torah ark seems to have been placed in the centre of the south wall, but in a secondary phase it was relocated to an apse built in the west wall towards Mount Gerizim. The floor was paved with mosaics and the building was approached through an atrium and narthex. A comparable synagogue, also oriented towards Mount Gerizim, has been excavated in the same area at al-Khirba, near Bayt Lid.

The early Christians, being converts from Judaism, may also be expected to have continued to worship in synagogues, though archaeological evidence for Judeo-Christians has proved difficult to identify. As specifically Christian liturgical practices developed and as more gentiles joined the new religion, however, new architectural forms developed. Because of persecution both by the Jewish religious authorities and by the Roman state, the early Christians tended to meet secretly in private houses.

One of the earliest examples of a house-church has been excavated in the city of Dura-Europos, on the Euphrates in present-day Syria. This was adapted from a private house around 232 CE but was buried under earth and rubble in 256–257 CE, when the city was fortified against an impending Sassanian attack. It was built around a central courtyard with an entrance on the north. The south range consisted of a meeting room, formed by combining two earlier rooms, with a raised dais for the president at the east and a vestry behind. A room on the west is interpreted as a 'school room' for instructing catechumens (those not yet baptized), while the north range contained a baptistery.

In 324 CE, following Constantine's defeat of the rival emperor, Licinius, at Chrysopolis (Scutari) on the Bosphorus, Christianity became the official religion in the Eastern

The monastery of St Mary in Choziba, in the Wadi al-Qilt between Jerusalem and Jericho, established from an earlier hermitage by John of Thebes between *c.*480 and *c.*530. It was rebuilt by the Greeks in the 12th century, at the time of the Latin kingdom, and is still an Orthodox monastery today.

Roman Empire as it had been in the West since 312 CE. At the Council of Nicea (325 CE) Constantine would have met Palestinian bishops, including Macarius, bishop of Jerusalem, and it was probably as a result of these encounters that the temple of Venus in Jerusalem was demolished on the emperor's orders and excavations took place to uncover the tomb of Christ beneath it. The details of the buildings that Constantine subsequently built over and around the exposed tomb are now hard to appreciate. From a combination of Eusebius's account in his *Life of Constantine*, the description given by a Spanish pilgrim named Egeria in 384 CE and the results of recent archaeology, however, we know that by the end of the fourth century the rock around the tomb had been cut away, so that it appeared as a free-standing chapel or aedicule enclosed by a timber-roofed rotunda with a colonnaded ambulatory supporting a gallery. The form of the aedicule is represented by a small-scale model surviving in Narbonne and by pictures on glass flasks (*ampullae*) for holding holy water or oil preserved in Monza and Bobbio in Italy. In 333 CE, a pilgrim from Bordeaux also mentions that the rock of Golgotha stood in the corner of a courtyard separating the rotunda from a basilican-style church to the east. This church, which was certainly the one built by Constantine, had five aisles with an apse towards the west containing twelve columns representing the Apostles. On the east it was preceded by an atrium and a porch or propylaea facing on to the main north–south street of the city. The church was dedicated in September 335 CE, the thirtieth year of Constantine's reign.

Work on the Holy Sepulchre would have been well advanced when the empress Helena, Constantine's mother, travelled to Jerusalem to pray at the Holy Places, probably in 327. Her journey was of great importance, not only for the legends that subsequently developed around it, such as her discovery of the relic of the True Cross and the building of countless churches, but also for the official boost that it gave to the practice of pilgrimage. Eusebius ascribes to Helena the building of the churches at Bethlehem and on the Mount of Olives, though we may assume that the emperor actually provided the means.

In Bethlehem, the raised sanctuary of the basilica covering the cave of Christ's Nativity was enclosed by an octagon. To the west the basilica was preceded by a spacious atrium, around which monasteries for men and women and hostels for pilgrims were later erected. Following a disastrous fire in the early sixth century, the church was rebuilt under Justinian with a cross-shaped east end and a longer nave, which is how it survives today. On the Mount of Olives another church enclosed the cave where Jesus taught his disciples. Meanwhile, alerted to the pagan use being made of the Herodian enclosure around Abraham's oak at Mamre (Tall al-Rumayda), near Hebron, Constantine instructed Macarius to build another church, remains of which may be identified in the central cell of a series of five constructed across the east side of the precinct.

Many other basilicas, both large and small, were built between the later fourth and early seventh centuries. Basilicas of the Constantinian type, though later in date, may be seen at Kursi (Gergesa) on the north-eastern shore of the Sea of Galilee and at Oboda ('Abda) and Shivta (Sobata) in the Negev (Naqab). Typically such buildings have roofs supported by colonnades with a central nave lit by clearstory windows and flanked to each side by one or two aisles. The nave terminates to the east with a semi-circular apse, while the aisles end either with smaller apses or with rectangular sacristies, in which the eucharistic vessels and the offerings of the people were kept. The doors into the nave and aisles would usually be preceded by a narthex and atrium—a court surrounded by porticoes with a vaulted cistern below it. Some churches also have a baptistery. In the north church at Sobata this took the form of a small room on the south side of the church with an eastern apse containing a cross-shaped stone font. Catechumens would have entered this from the western bay of the church and after receiving baptism would have proceeded to another apsed room to be anointed with oil by the bishop before continuing back into the body of the church.

Other forms of church building also existed besides the basilica. The rotunda built by Constantine to enclose the tomb of Christ, for example, mirrored a building form

Sobata (Subayta): the interior of the south church, showing the triple-apsed east end, raised sanctuary, and colonnaded nave. The church was probably built in the late fourth century, but was altered in the sixth and partly repaved in 640 CE.

commonly used for imperial mausolea, such as his own in Rome, which in 328 CE was used instead for the burial of St Helena. As with mausolea, centrally planned churches provided a focus for the memorialization of objects, such as relics or the tomb of a saint or a biblical personage, or a place associated with biblical events. This explains the octagonal form of the timber-roofed church built in the mid fifth century enclosing the exposed rock on which the Virgin Mary is supposed to have rested between Jerusalem and Bethlehem and possibly the similar design of that dedicated to St Mary by the emperor Zeno in 484 CE on the site of the destroyed Samaritan temple on Mount Gerizim, though here the intention seems to have been to supplant the Samaritan holy place rather than draw attention to any particular spot. Other octagonal churches were built over the supposed site of the house of St Peter in Capernaum, in Gadara (Umm Qays), in Bosra (Busra, 512–513 CE) and possibly over the tomb of the Virgin Mary in Gethsemane (*c.*600 CE), while circular churches are found in Beth Shean (Scythopolis), Jarash (Gerasa, 531 CE), and on the Mount of Olives, where one, albeit largely unroofed, enclosed the rocky outcrop from which Christ was believed to have ascended to heaven.

From the later fourth century onwards, St Helena's example of travelling to pray in the Holy Places was followed enthusiastically by others from the West, resulting in the

The aedicule and rotunda enclosing the tomb of Christ in the church of the Holy Sepulchre (or Resurrection) in Jerusalem, as depicted by Cornelius De Bruyn in 1698 (from Corneille le Brun, *Voyage au Levant, c'est à dire dans les principaux endroits de l'Asie Mineure dans les Isles de Chio, de Rhodes, de Chypre &c., de même que dans les plus considérables villes d'Egypte, de Syrie, et de la Terre Sainte,* Delft: H. de Kroonevelt 1700, pl. 144).

provision of appropriate facilities for pilgrims. Another factor leading to the explosion of church-building in the fifth and sixth centuries was the development of monasticism. St Hilarion had established a monastery at Tavatha, near Gaza, around 308 CE and St Chariton established one in the Judean wilderness at Pharan around 330 CE. In the later fourth century a number of monasteries for monks and nuns were established on the Mount of Olives and in Bethlehem. Cyril of Scythopolis (*c.*525–660 CE) records the lives of seven Palestinian monastic saints. Among them was Euthymius (376–473 CE), an Armenian who in 411 CE founded a monastery with Theoctistus in the caves of Wadi Muqallik between Jerusalem and Jericho. In 428 CE, he established the monastery that was later named after him and whose ruins may still be seen at Khan al-Ahmar. Sabas (439–532 CE) was a Cappadocian who came to Palestine in 456 CE and joined

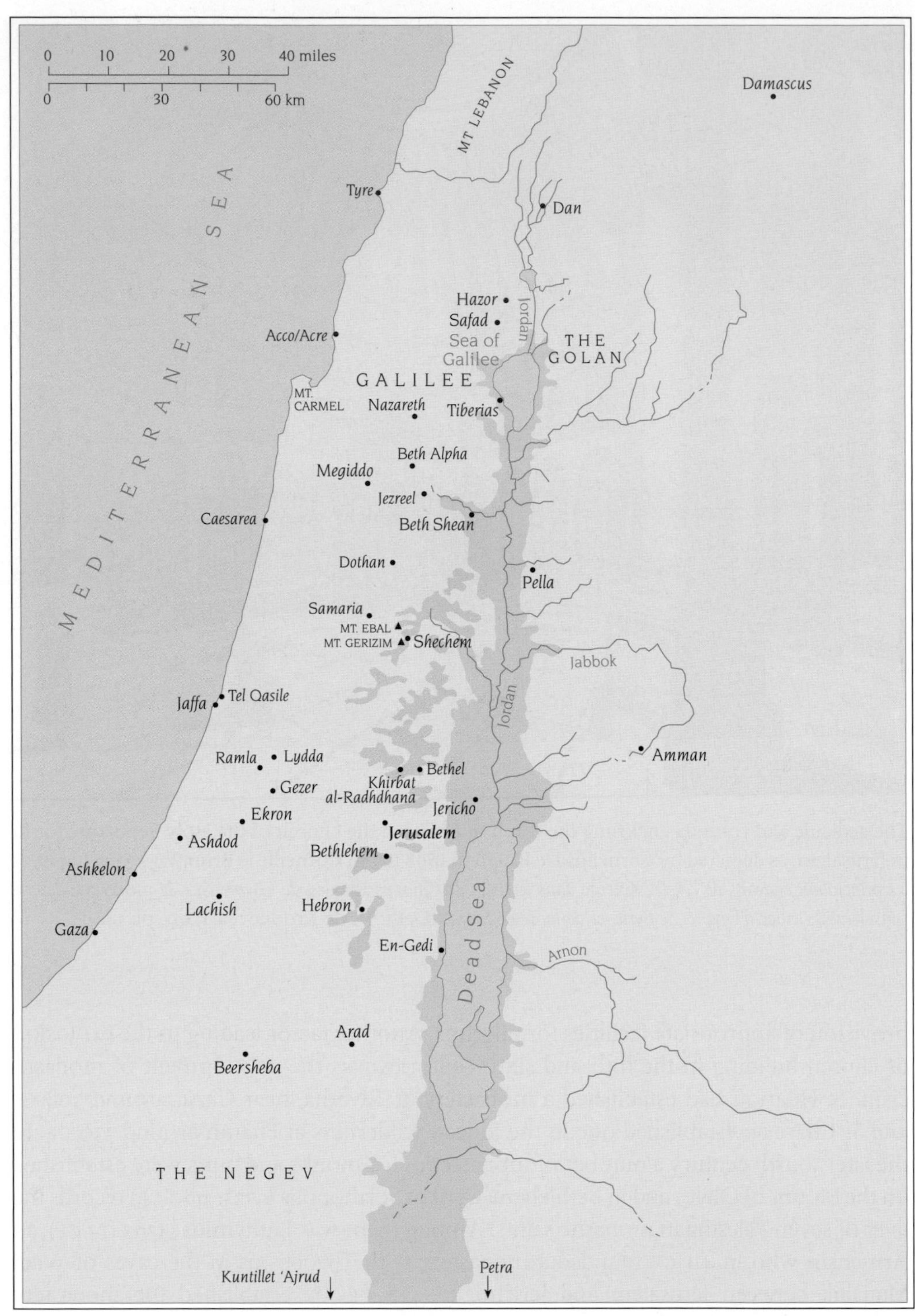

7. Location of sacred spaces and holy places

Euthymius. In 483 CE, he also established his own monastery in the Kidron Valley east of Bethlehem, now known as Dayr Mar Saba. Typical features of such monasteries were a church, a refectory or dining room, individual cells (often caves) for the monks, a cemetery, and outside the monastery a hospice for pilgrims and travellers. In 530, after a Samaritan revolt, Sabas appealed directly to the emperor for money for the repair of churches, the defence of the desert monasteries, and the construction of a grand new church and hospice in Jerusalem. The results of his appeal may still be seen in the large stone towers that protect Dayr Mar Saba and the excavated foundations of Justinian's massive 'New Church' (*Nea Ekklesia*) of the Mother of God in today's Jewish quarter.

The early Islamic period (636/7–1099 CE)

In 634, a Muslim Arab army led by 'Amr Ibn al-'As advanced from the Hijaz to 'Aqaba at the northern end of the Red Sea. The Christian Arab tribes who were supposed to defend the Roman frontier abandoned their positions and although the governor of Palestine, Sergius, hurried south with provincial troops, he was defeated and killed at Dathin (Anthedon), near Gaza. Palestine and Syria fell quickly. In 635 Damascus was occupied and the following year the Muslims defeated the emperor Heraclius himself at the battle of the Yarmuq. Jerusalem fell in 638 and Caesarea, the provincial capital, in 640.

After the death of Muhammad in 632, political leadership of the Islamic movement fell to his tribe; but in 656, the governor of Damascus, Mu'awiya, staged a revolt and had himself installed as the first of a dynasty of caliphs, known as the Umayyads. The Umayyads used monumental architecture as a means for both emphasizing their own status and proclaiming the victory of Islam over other religions—in particular Christianity. In Jerusalem, which remained predominantly Christian, the principal surviving religious buildings from the Umayyad period are those grouped within the 'Noble Sanctary' (Haram al-Sharif), the former Jewish temple precinct.

Principal among the buildings in the Haram al-Sharif was the Dome of the Rock (Qubbat al-Sakhra), an octagonal structure surmounted by a leaded timber dome on a masonry drum, supported internally by an annular colonnade. Originally it was decorated inside and out with brightly coloured glass mosaics. The structure is dated by a mosaic inscription to 691/2 CE, indicating that its builder would have been the caliph 'Abd al-Malik (685–705 CE), though his name was later replaced by that of 'Abdallah al-Ma'mun (813–833 CE) without altering the date. The local geographer al-Muqaddasi wrote around 984 CE that 'Abd al-Malik had it built to record the victory of Islam over Christianity and to rival the dome of the Holy Sepulchre; but an alternative story recorded by al-Yaq'ubi (874 CE) alleges that the caliph intended it as a place for Muslim pilgrimage to rival Mecca and Medina, which at the time were in the hands of an alternative caliph, Ibn al-Zubayr. Indeed, the form of the building is similar to that of a Byzantine martyrium, like that of St Simeon at Dayr Sim'an (Syria), with a broad ambulatory surrounding a central sacred space, in this case the exposed natural rock that probably represents the place of sacrifice of the destroyed Jewish Temple. Here in 333 CE a Christian pilgrim from Bordeaux had witnessed Jews mourning and rending their garments. The surviving decoration of the Dome of the Rock gives few clues about the original meaning of the building, though the internal mosaics, depicting plants relating to paradise, may perhaps allude to the Last Judgement, which was expected to take place between the Temple and the Mount of Olives.

The principal congregational mosque in Jerusalem, known as al-Masjid al-Aqsa (the Farthest Mosque) on account of its association with Muhammad's legendary Night Journey and brief ascension to heaven alluded to in Qur'an 17:1, occupies the southern part of the Haram al-Sharif, making this for Muslims the third holiest place of pilgrimage. Arculf, a bishop from Gaul, describes around 684 CE what appears to have been a building site while a Greek papyrus document records work still in progress in 715–716 CE; but little is known of this early building as the mosque was rebuilt by the Abbasid caliphs al-Mansur and al-Mahdi in the later eighth century. Another building that is also most likely the work of 'Abd al-Malik, despite its Byzantine style, is the double gate, known to Muslims as the Gate of Mercy (Bab al-Rahma) and Gate of Repentence (Bab al-Tawba) respectively and to Christians as the Golden Gate, which gave access to the Haram from the Kidron Valley to the east, while to the south of the Haram stood the caliphal palace complex (Dar al-Imara).

The replacement of the former religious focus—often a church or cathedral—by a congregational mosque was the most obvious change brought about by the advent of Islam to the religious landscape of Middle Eastern cities, towns, and villages. In this building the entire male Muslim population was expected to congregate each Friday—though there might also be other smaller mosques and shrines. One of the problems in identifying a Muslim presence in the earliest period of Muslim settlement is that early mosques have no obvious distinguishing features. Congregational prayers could be held in the open air, for example in an enclosure (as in the Ka'ba in Mecca) or in the courtyard of a house. It was only in 707/9 CE that al-Walid I is recorded constructing a *mihrab*, or small rounded niche, in the *qibla* wall of the mosque in Medina, itself formerly a house, to indicate the direction of prayer. Once *mihrab*s became common features of mosques, it is easier to identify them. One early mosque with a *mihrab* is built into the entrance portico of one of the churches in Shivta (Sobata), while elsewhere in the Negev in the countryside near Oboda the conversion of settled Arabic-speaking farmers (*fallahin*) to the new religion is illustrated by inscriptions and the building of open-air mosques.

In some towns churches were converted into mosques by suppressing the eastern apse and inserting a *mihrab* into the south wall, which in Syria and Palestine is the direction of Mecca. This happened in Homs, Hama, and Aleppo, where churches were divided between Muslims and Christians. In Damascus the cathedral, built by the emperor Theodosius I (379–395 CE), was located within the precinct (*temenos*) that had formerly surrounded a first- to fourth-century temple of Jupiter. After 635 CE, a mosque was established in the eastern part of the *temenos*; but when al-Walid I became caliph in 705 CE, he pulled down the church and extended the mosque across the full width of the longer south side of the *temenos*. The mosque's prayer hall has three aisles, bisected by a central transept aligned north–south and focused on the *mihrab* in the centre of the south (*qibla*) wall. To the right of the *mihrab* would have stood the *minbar*, or pulpit, from which the sermon was delivered and the statement of loyalty to the caliph was pronounced. The area around the *mihrab* was enclosed by a screen (*maqsura*), less out of piety (as with a Christian chancel screen) than to protect the caliph, two of the first four of whom were murdered in mosques. Since Muslims are required to wash before prayer, most mosques are also provided with a washing place and toilets. Most Friday mosques also have a tower, or minaret (*manara, midhana*), from which the call to prayer is made; in the case of Damascus, there are four, built at the four corners of the Roman temple precinct. An early square-plan minaret, possibly of Abbasid date, also survives attached to the Mosque of the Forty in Baysan (Beth Shean), in the Jordan valley just south of Tiberias.

The conversion of churches into mosques, however, was a relatively rare occurrence while there were still large Christian populations making use of them. Indeed, a story tells how when in 638 the patriarch of Jerusalem, Sophronius, invited the caliph 'Umar I ibn al-Khattab (634–644 CE) to pray in the church of the Holy Sepulchre, 'Umar declined and instead established a small mosque in the atrium of the church, forbidding Muslims to enter the church itself. In Ayla ('Aqaba) the early Islamic settlement, including the mosque, lay outside the existing Byzantine city walls and was enclosed within a rectangular fortified enclosure resembling a Roman fort. Ramla, the capital of *Filastin* established in the coastal plain near Ludd (Lydda) by Sulayman just before he became caliph in 715 CE, also occupied a virgin site. Its mosque, known as the White Mosque, stood in the marketplace, though the city also contained churches and synagogues. In Jarash and Tiberias, however, recent archaeological work has revealed that large congregational mosques were established in the Umayyad period at the very centres of existing Byzantine cities. In Tiberias, the layout of the mosque, which was misidentified by earlier archaeologists as a Byzantine 'market building', represents a half-scale copy of the great mosque of Damascus.

The Muslim conquest of Palestine and Syria involved no mass migration. Its success was due to the takeover of military and political authority by a new Muslim elite, followed by the gradual conversion of the local population. Christians and Jews, as 'peoples of the book', were allowed to continue to practise their religion but were subject to special taxes and circumscribed in other ways. For example, although they were able to keep and maintain their religious buildings, they were not allowed to build new ones and the ringing of bells was forbidden. Despite this, it is clear that in some places, such as Madaba, east of the Jordan, new churches were being built and decorated well into the eighth century; and although some scholars have interpreted the destruction of images of animals and people on some mosaics as evidence for the enforcement of the Muslim prohibition of the representation of living creatures, it now seems more likely that it was the result of a more general wave of iconoclasm that affected both Islam and the Byzantine empire from the mid eighth century.

Despite a general degree of religious tolerance in the early Muslim centuries, religious minorities were not entirely free from persecution—sometimes by other minorities. In 939, for instance, the church of St Mary the Green in Ascalon was destroyed by a mob of Muslims and Jews and the bishop was forced to flee to Ramla. In 1009, the deranged Fatimid caliph al-Hakim (996–1021) ordered the destruction of all Christian churches in his domains, a purge so thorough that in the Holy Land only the churches in Bethlehem and Mount Sinai escaped undamaged. In Jerusalem the church of the Holy Sepulchre (or Resurrection) and the tomb of Christ were demolished, though the resulting pile of debris helped preserve the lower parts of both structures. Soon afterwards, however, al-Hakim relented and allowed the Christians to begin rebuilding their churches. The church of the Holy Sepulchre was already being used for the Easter services in 1027 and would have been essentially restored by the time that it was seen and described by the Persian scholar Nasir-i Khusraw in 1047. The rebuilding, however, did not include Constantine's basilica but only affected the courtyard and rotunda, which now served both as martyrium and church by having a choir and apse added to its eastern side, extending into the courtyard. The rotunda was flanked on the south by a series of three chapels, the central one domed and containing a baptistery, and on the north by another one. The style of the reconstruction includes both local and metropolitan Byzantine elements, perhaps reflecting the assistance that successive Byzantine emperors, including Basil II (958–1025), Romanus III (1028–1034), Michael IV (1036–1041), and Constantine IX (1042–1055), gave to the project.

Other churches built or rebuilt in this period tend to be small square or rectangular structures, roofed with barrel-vaults or masonry domes rather than timber and with a rounded apse. Some, like the small restored church of St John the Baptist in Sebaste (Sabastiyya) and that of St Mary in 'Abud, were of the Byzantine cross-in-square type with a central dome, while others, like those enclosing the birthplace of St John the Baptist in 'Ayn Karim and the place from which the tree of the Holy Cross was taken, were larger domed basilicas.

The Crusades and kingdom of Jerusalem (1099–1291 CE)

The return of Jerusalem and most of Syria and Palestine to Christian control following the Crusaders' conquest of the city in July 1099, together with the lifting of the restrictions on building work by non-Muslims, paved the way for a huge programme of church building. In the kingdom of Jerusalem alone, nearly 500 churches are known to have been built or rebuilt in the almost two centuries of the kingdom's existence. The building programme reflected two of the principal aims of the Crusade itself: to restore Jerusalem and Palestine to their rightful place in the body of Christendom and to ensure unhindered access for pilgrims to the Holy Places. Although the eastern

Christian communities were also able to take the opportunity to restore their own churches and even built new ones, most of the churches built under Frankish rule were those of the Latin incomers from the West. In any case, as the schism between the Orthodox and Catholic churches was not yet final, the Latin church hierarchy viewed local Greek- and Arabic-speaking (or Melkite) Orthodox Christians as subject to the authority of the Latin patriarch, even if their Orthodox counterparts, including the exiled Greek patriarch, may have thought otherwise. None the less, during the twelfth century the Armenians were able to rebuild their cathedral of St James in Jerusalem and the Greek Orthodox, with assistance from Emperor Manuel I Comnenus, restored the monasteries of St John the Baptist, St Mary in Choziba, St Elias, Dayr Hajla (Kalamon), and St Euthymius in the Judean wilderness, besides participating with the Latins in renewing the wall mosaics in the church in Bethlehem.

In Jerusalem itself the church of the Holy Sepulchre was transformed. The cramped eleventh-century choir and apse were demolished and replaced by a new Romanesque crossing, choir, and apse, with an ambulatory and gallery, taking up all the space previously occupied by the courtyard east of the rotunda. Thus all the holy sites associated with the Passion and Resurrection were conveniently accommodated in a single building, which would also serve as the patriarchal cathedral and principal parish church of the city besides providing a fitting location for state occasions, such as coronations and royal funerals. To the east the church was linked to the conventual buildings of the Augustinian canons who now served it, and to the west and north to the patriarchal palace.

Augustinian canons also served the churches of the Ascension on the Mount of Olives, the Lord's Temple (formerly the Dome of the Rock), where the presentations of both Jesus and his mother Mary were recalled, and St Mary of Mount Zion, where pilgrims could see where Jesus celebrated the Last Supper and appeared to the Apostles after his resurrection and where the Virgin Mary fell asleep. The two Benedictine abbeys of St Mary Latin and St Mary the Great that had been established for monks and nuns respectively near the Holy Sepulchre in the eleventh century were now joined by an abbey for monks at the Virgin Mary's tomb in Gethsemane and abbeys for nuns at the house of St Anne near the Temple and the tomb of St Lazarus in Bethany.

Outside Jerusalem new cathedral churches in the western Romanesque style, albeit with pointed arches and vaulted naves and aisles, were built—and still survive, to a greater or lesser degree—in Beirut, Tyre, Nazareth, Caesarea, Sebaste (Sabastiyya), and Lydda and within the Herodian precinct enclosing the tombs of Abraham and the other patriarchs in Hebron. Some parish churches, such as those in Gaza, Ramla, and Saffuriyya, were no less impressive in scale than the cathedrals, while elsewhere smaller aisled parish churches served rural communities in planned Frankish settlements and small towns or castles such as Yubna, al-Shawbak (Montreal), al-Bira, and al-Qubayba, and still smaller churches with barrel-vaulted naves in some indigenous Christian villages containing Latins such as Fahma, Sinjil, Ziri'in (Jezreel), Jifna, and 'Amwas. Western monastic orders that established houses in the countryside included the

Sebaste (Sabastiyya): the ruined nave of the Crusader cathedral of St John the Baptist, built above the underground Roman tomb in which the saint's relics were rediscovered in 1145. The nave now represents the courtyard to the mosque and site of the tomb is marked by a domed Muslim shrine.

Benedictines on Mount Tabor, where Christ was transfigured, and at Jacob's Well (Balata) near Nablus, where the community serving at the well where Jesus spoke with the woman of Samaria seems to have included both monks and nuns. Although St Bernard of Clairvaux was at first reluctant to send any Cistercians to the Holy Land, Cistercian houses were subsequently founded in 'Ayn Karim and 'Allar al-Sufla (or Khirbat al-Tannur), west of Bethlehem, while Premonstratensian canons occupied the church containing the tomb of Samuel on Mount Joy, from which pilgrims caught their first glimpse of Jerusalem. In the early thirteenth century a group of Latin hermits on Mount Carmel came together to form the Carmelite Order, which quickly established a network of friaries throughout the West. In many of the houses established by religious orders in the Holy Land, careful design of the church and monastic buildings allowed the monks and nuns to maintain their own secluded conventual life while providing access to the holy places and hospitality for visiting pilgrims.

The Crusades also gave rise to a new form of monasticism exemplified by the military orders, whose ministry to the physical needs of pilgrims also extended to fighting to protect them and the kingdom itself. The Templars, established in the former al-Aqsa Mosque, and the Hospitallers, who served in the hospital of St John the Baptist beside the Holy Sepulchre, were recognized as orders of the church in the first two decades of the twelfth century. They are known today primarily for their castles, including the Hospitallers' Belvoir (Kawkab al-Hawa), Bayt Jibrin, Marqab and Crac des Chevaliers, and the Templars' Latrun, Safad, Safitha (Chastel Blanc), Beaufort, Sidon (Sea Castle), and Pilgrims' Castle ('Atlit). These were effectively fortified monastic houses, each containing a conventual dormitory, refectory, chapter house, and chapel. These two orders were joined from the 1190s by the Teutonic Order, whose castles of Montfort and Jiddin still survive in the hill country near Acre, where they had their headquarters.

Jewish travellers who visited the Holy Land in the Crusader period, such as Jacob b. Nathanel (1153–1187) and Benjamin of Tudela (1169–1171), provide us with information about the numbers of Jewish families residing in different places and describe the tombs of holy people (*sadiqim*); but we know relatively little of their places of worship. Similarly, although there was a significant Muslim population in certain areas, especially around Nablus, Tyre, Sidon, and Tibnin, and Muslims still had access to some holy sites now in Christian hands, including the Haram al-Sharif in Jerusalem and sites in Acre, there is scant evidence of any Muslim buildings being newly constructed in the areas under Frankish rule.

The Ayyubid and Mamluk periods (1187–1517 CE)

Following Saladin's destruction of the Frankish army at Hattin on 4 July 1187 most of their kingdom fell quickly to him, including on 2 October the city of Jerusalem itself. In a reversal of the situation that had faced the Crusaders some eighty-eight years earlier, the sultan was now confronted with the work of restoring the city's Islamic character and its position as the third holiest site in the Islamic world. The Haram al-Sharif was therefore cleansed of its Christian intrusions. The gilt cross was pulled down from the top of the Dome of the Rock and dragged through the streets before being smashed to pieces. Inside the building, the paving with which the canons had covered the sacred rock (partly to protect it from the rapacious fingers of souvenir-hunting pilgrims) was lifted and the exposed surface washed with rosewater. Statues were removed and new Arabic inscriptions replaced the Latin ones around the inside of the dome. The Haram was also cleared of the conventual buildings of the Augustinian canons and of the Templars, including their church. In the al-Aqsa Mosque the dividing walls inserted by the Templars were demolished, a new *mihrab* was constructed and the *minbar* that Nur al-Din had commissioned for the mosque in 1168–1169 but had been unable to deliver to it was finally installed.

Although the oriental Christians were permitted to retain their churches, including the Holy Sepulchre, which now became Greek Orthodox once again, the Latins lost all of theirs. Many of them were converted into Muslim religious institutions. The church of St Anne was transformed by Saladin into a quranic school, the Madrasa al-Salahiyya, and the patriarchal palace into a convent or *khanaqah* for Sufis. In 1192, Saladin also established an Islamic hospital in the Benedictine nunnery church of St Mary the Great, and the corresponding male house, St Mary Latin, became a Shafi'i madrasa. Around the same time, the northern part of the adjacent Hospital of St John was made into a mosque by one of Saladin's sons, al-Malik al-Afdal 'Ali; and in 1216–1217, the southern part became a Sufi convent, the Zawiyat al-Darjah. The former cathedral of the Jacobites became the Maymuniyya madrasa in 1197.

Saladin and his Ayyubid successors supported the Sunni tradition of Islam upheld by the Abbasid caliph in Baghdad, as opposed to the Shi'ite form of the deposed Fatimid caliphs in Cairo; and although he himself favoured the Shafi'i school of Sunni Islam, other Ayyubids also made endowments in favour of the alternative Hanafi, Hanbali, and Maliki branches. The Shafi'i school permitted only a single main Friday mosque in each settlement and in Jerusalem this was al-Aqsa. Four smaller mosques, however, including the Masjid al-Afdal and another two within the Haram, were founded in the Ayyubid period as well as six madrasas, six other convents, and a quranic school for children. Other building works included various mausolea, sometimes attached to pious foundations, and a number of smaller domed structures. These included the Qubbat al-Mi'raj, erected beside the Dome of the Rock in 1200/1 to celebrate Muhammad's ascension and built almost entirely of recycled Crusader architecture and sculpture.

In Acre, Saladin established a Friday mosque in the cathedral church of the Holy Cross, occupying the site of the earlier mosque; he also divided the Hospital of St John between a convent (*ribat*) for Sufis and a college of jurists, and made the patriarchal palace into an Islamic hospital. In 1191, however, Acre was recaptured by the Third Crusade and these changes were reversed. Elsewhere, however, former Latin cathedrals and churches in Hebron, Sebaste (Sabastiyya), Tiberias, Ramla, Nablus, Gaza, Fahma, Sinjil, Baytin, al-Bira, Bethany, Yubna, and al-Ram have remained mosques to this day.

Whereas after Saladin the Ayyubids, divided by family squabbles, tended to adopt a diplomatic approach towards the Franks, even allowing Jerusalem to be returned to their control between 1229 and 1244, the Mamluks, who came to power in 1250, pursued a more aggressive and uncompromising policy against the remaining Frankish states, culminating in the fall of Acre in 1291 and the end of the kingdom of Jerusalem. The conquests of Jaffa, Arsuf, Caesarea, and Acre were followed by the destruction of their churches and in some cases the removal of valuable building materials for reuse in Islamic buildings in Cairo. In Jerusalem the northern and western sides of the Haram were lined with magnificent porticos, behind which elegant madrasas, convents, mosques, and mausoleums, endowed by pious donors, jockeyed for the most prestigious positions closest to the sacred enclosure.

Elsewhere in Palestine, three Mamluk mosques including the Red Mosque (Jami' al-Ahmar, 1275) survive in Safad, the regional capital, and others in Majdal near Ascalon (1300) and Bayt Lid (1335–1336) near Nablus. In Ramla Sultan Baybars (1260–1277 CE)

The stalactite (*muqarnas*) portal of the Red Mosque (Jami' al-Ahmar) in Safad, with the inscription attributing its construction to Sultan Baybars in 674 H (1275/6 CE).

completed Saladin's reconstruction of the White Mosque and in 1318 al-Nasir Muhammad added a lofty minaret. In Jaljuliyya, the ruined mosque is named after Shams al-Din Abu 'l-'Awn, a fifteenth-century Sufi, who in the 1480s built a complex of buildings at Haram Sidna 'Ali near Arsuf surrounding the tomb of 'Ali ibn 'Alil, a descendant of caliph 'Umar (CE 634–644), where an annual pilgrimage was held until the 1940s. A similar pilgrimage complex was built around the same time at Nabi Musa, near Jericho, where the burial place of Moses had been identified since the time of Sultan Baybars I. The Mamluk reconquest of Palestine was accompanied by a rebuilding of the road system that had formerly connected it to the Islamic world. Roads were important not only for trade and the movement of troops but also for Muslim pilgrims travelling to Mecca and Medina, as well as Christians travelling to Nazareth, Jerusalem, and Bethlehem, from whom the state benefited economically. The khans or caravanserais in which travellers lodged, such as Khan al-Ahmar near Baysan (Beth Shean, 1308) or Khan Lajjun (1331), usually contained a mosque. In Khan Jubb Yusuf, built from the 1260s onwards on the main road from Damascus to Egypt, north of the Sea of Galilee, there were two: a small one on the south and a larger one near the entrance, apparently intended for Muslim pilgrims who came to see the pit into which Joseph was cast by his brothers. Baybars gave state backing and military support to the annual pilgrimage (*hajj*) from Egypt and later from Syria. It was probably he who built the first khan for pilgrims in 'Aqaba, which was rebuilt and fortified by the last Mamluk sultan, Qansuh al-Ghuri in 1514–1515.

The Ottoman period (1516–1917 CE)

The religious importance of Jerusalem for the Ottomans was underlined from Selim I's entry into the city on 28 December 1516. Under his successor, Suleiman I the Magnificent (1520–1566), the mosaic decoration on the outside of the Dome of the Rock was replaced with locally made glazed tiles depicting floral motifs and patterns in dark blue, turquoise, black, white, and yellow. Around the top of the drum, a text from Qur'an 17:1–20, referring *inter alia* to Muhammad's Night Journey and the destruction of the Jewish temple, not only served to proclaim Sunni orthodoxy but also pointed to Suleiman as the successor to Solomon. Other pious building works in the Haram and throughout the city included the building of numerous fountains, fed from the restored Roman aqueduct from Solomon's Pool, south of Bethlehem. The city walls, destroyed in the thirteenth century, were also rebuilt in 1537–1552, more for symbolic effect than for any serious attempt at defence. Another important Islamic foundation of this period was the Imaret complex of buildings endowed in 1552 by Khassaki Khurrem, a favourite wife of Suleiman I. It included a mosque, a public building comprising a kitchen, bakery, storeroom, latrines, and woodshed for the support of the poor and needy, a convent (*ribat*) containing fifty-five cells, and a khan for travellers. What remains, incorporating the Mamluk palace of Lady Tunshuq (*c.*1388), still functions as an Islamic orphanage and soup kitchen (*takiyya*). Throughout the Ottoman period, both the al-Aqsa Mosque and the Dome of the Rock underwent frequent restorations at government expense.

The Ottoman state also continued to protect travellers, both pilgrims and merchants. At 'Ayyun al-Tujjar (Springs of the Merchants) on the Damascus–Cairo road near Tiberias, two large fortified khans containing mosques, sponsored respectively by the government and the grand vizier, Sinan Pasha, were built in 1581, replacing an earlier Mamluk one, and further south at Ra's al-'Ayn another was built in the 1570s. Local pilgrimage was also promoted to Hebron and to Nabi Musa, where from 1820 an annual festival developed.

From the mid eighteenth century important building works took place in northern Palestine, which fell temporarily under the quasi-independent control of a local Galilean Bedouin leader from the Zaydani clan, Daher al-'Umar (d. 1775), and his successors, Ahmad al-Jazzar (1775–1804) and Sulayman Pasha (1805–1819). Dahir's mosque in Tiberias (*c.*1740) consisted of a cuboid prayer hall covered by a large dome, entered from the north through a triple-domed porch. Similar designs occur in the mosque attached to the palace that Dahir's family built at Dayr Hanna and in the smaller Jami' Malaha (1748) and Sea Mosque (1800s) in Acre. A more grandiose version, however, is the Jazzar Pasha mosque in Acre (1781–1782), which has a five-dome porch on the north and a tall pointed cylindrical minaret; it is set beside al-Jazzar's mausoleum within a quadrangular enclosure surrounded by porticos giving access to some fifty rooms for the mosque attendants and visiting pilgrims. In another of Dahir's castle-palaces at Jiddin, however, the mosque had four bays carried on a central pier, as in the contemporary Sea Mosque in Tiberias.

In 1808 a fire broke out in the church of the Holy Sepulchre, destroying the timber roof of the rotunda and severely damaging the aedicule, choir, and apse. Rebuilding of the apse and aedicule was undertaken in a baroque style by Nikolaos Ch. Komnenos, a Greek architect from Istanbul, and was completed in 1810. During the nineteenth century, however, the persistent rivalry between the different Christian confessions in the Holy Land assumed more serious proportions as France's traditional claim to protect the rights of Roman Catholics was challenged by Russia on behalf of the Orthodox. An immediate result was the Crimean War (1853–1855), from which France allied with Britain, Turkey, and Piedmont-Sardinia emerged victorious. In 1863–1868, however, France, Russia, and Turkey collaborated in rebuilding the dome of the Holy Sepulchre, using the novel technique of a cast-iron frame made in Russia. Nonetheless, in spite of this instance of cooperation, religion continued to be used as a vehicle through which the European powers vied for political influence in the Holy Land.

In 1847, under French influence a Roman Catholic patriarch of Jerusalem was appointed and in the 1860s a patriarchate was built in the Old City, posing a direct challenge to the Greek Orthodox patriarch. In 1856, Sultan 'Abd al-Majid granted Napoleon III the former Crusader church of St Anne, or Madrasa al-Salahiyya, in recognition of French support in the Crimean War, and a seminary for Greek Catholics was subsequently established in it by the White Fathers. By the time of the Great War France was sponsoring over twenty religious institutions in and around Jerusalem, including the hospital of St Louis (1879–1896), the massive pilgrim hospice of Notre Dame de France (1884–1904), convents of the Sisters of St Joseph, St Vincent de Paul, and the Rosary Sisters, and the Dominicans' convent of St Stephen (1880s–1900). Meanwhile the Franciscans continued the work that they had been entrusted with since the fourteenth century of providing facilities for Catholic pilgrims at the Holy Places.

In parallel with this, in 1859 the Russian imperial government purchased land beside the Jaffa Road outside the Old City for use as a camp site for pilgrims. Permanent structures including an infirmary were subsequently provided and in 1864 the cathedral of the Holy Trinity was dedicated. Between 1886 and 1890, an enormous hospice was built, which by 1900 allowed the compound to accommodate up to 9000 pilgrims each year. A large Russian Orthodox monastery was also established on the Mount of Olives in 1870–1878 and the seven-domed church of St Mary Magdalene in Gethsemane in 1888.

The first Protestant church in Jerusalem, Christ Church, was built beside the British consul's house in 1848 as the seat of a joint Anglican and German Lutheran bishopric. The see was engaged in missionary and welfare work, at first among the city's Jewish inhabitants but later more generally among oriental Christians. In 1887, however, the joint venture with Germany was dissolved and Bishop George Blyth began building a new cathedral church of St George with an annexed bishop's house and hostel on the Nablus Road north of the city. Designed by the architect George Jeffery, at the time Curator of Ancient Monuments in Cyprus, this complex, influenced by New College, Oxford, was completed in 1903 and in 1912 a bell-tower recalling that of Magdalen College, Oxford, was added as a memorial for King Edward VII.

Meanwhile in 1869 Crown Prince Frederick William of Prussia had been granted the ruins of the Crusader church of St Mary Latin in the Muristan area of Jerusalem, south of the Holy Sepulchre. The church was subsequently rebuilt and dedicated as the church of the Redeemer on 31 October 1898 in the presence of Kaiser Wilhelm II and his wife Augusta Victoria. In 1906–1910, Wilhelm also sponsored the building of the Augusta Victoria pilgrim hospice on the Mount of Olives, to a design recalling his ancestors' castle of Hohenstaufen and incorporating a church of the Ascension and a lofty bell-tower from which the Mediterranean was visible. Not forgetting his Roman Catholic subjects, in 1906 the Kaiser also built a church commemorating the Dormition of the Virgin Mary on land on Mount Zion granted him by Sultan 'Abd al-Hamid during his visit in 1898. In this case the model was Charlemagne's chapel in Aachen.

The Jewish population of Jerusalem continued to grow during the nineteenth century. The Sephardi community worshipped in four interconnected synagogues named after Rabban Yohanan ben Zakkai. In 1836 Jewish immigrants from Lithuania obtained a *firman* from Mehmet 'Ali to build a synagogue, Menahem Zion, on part of the site of the ruined synagogue of Rabbi Yehudah he-Hasid, which had been destroyed in 1720. After the Crimean War, with diplomatic assistance from Britain and funding from the Jewish diaspora, a major synagogue arose on the site. This was built under the supervision of the sultan's architect, Assad Effendi, in a neo-Byzantine style, and featured a large dome supported on four corner towers. Although officially named after Jacob Mayer de Rothschild, it is more usually known simply as the Hurva, or 'Ruin'. Although Jews had been permitted access to pray at a small area of the western wall of the temple in the Moroccan quarter from perhaps as early as the reign of Suleiman I, attempts to enlarge the area available were unsuccessful before the end of the Ottoman period.

The final decades of Ottoman rule in Palestine also saw the Holy Land become the centre of a new monotheistic religion, when Baha'u'llah (Mirza Husayn 'Ali Nuri), the spiritual leader of the Baha'is, having been banished from Tehran in 1850, was incarcerated by the Ottoman authorities in the prison in Acre in 1868. His burial shrine is next to the mansion of Bahji, near Acre, where he died in 1892, while his son 'Abdu'l-Baha (1844–1921) and the martyred founder of the religion, al-Bab ('Ali Muhammad of Shiraz, 1819–1850), are buried in a mausoleum in the Baha'i gardens in Haifa.

Despite the developing activity of other religions in the area, Palestine remained a predominantly Muslim country under Ottoman rule, as witnessed during its final years by the building of new mosques in Haifa (1897–1998), Bi'r al-Sab' (Beersheba, 1905), and Jaffa (Hasan Bey mosque, 1914–1916). All towns and most villages contained at least one mosque, while in the open countryside small domed shrines marked holy sites and the tombs of Muslim holy men and women, as they had done for centuries and still do today.

CHAPTER 13

Scripture and the Holy Land

ADAM SILVERSTEIN

Introduction

IT has been taken as a given throughout this book that there is such a thing as a 'Holy Land', a land that is endowed with theological significance which sets it apart—and above—all other places on earth. But why should this be so? After all, in the monotheistic religions that concern us here God is believed to have created *all* lands, and He is, moreover, believed to be everywhere, as both the Bible (Deuteronomy 10:14) and the Qur'an (2:115) state. Why, then, should some places on God's earth be preferred to others? Since Hellenistic times adherents of Judaism, Christianity, and Islam have felt compelled to answer such questions, but it should be pointed out that as far as the God of Abraham is concerned no answer is required: a particular region is holy because God said it is, and that, in theory, should be enough for those who believe in Him.

The means by which God communicates His ideas to mankind are, broadly speaking, of two sorts: individual prophets are chosen to convey God's message to an immediate audience; and Scriptures—Holy books—are sent via angels and/or prophets, which contain God's message to the rest of us. In the broadest of strokes, a particular land was singled out as being 'special' in Scripture(s), and it was promised to a particular prophet and his people in exchange for obedience to God; that is, a Holy land was promised to a Holy people in exchange for Holy behaviour. In what follows, this simplified formula will be examined in detail and we shall see that different religious communities understood it in very different ways. They are divided over such questions as: Which book(s) reflect God's communication with us? Assuming we agree on the Scripture, how are we to read and interpret it? Which land is 'Holy' (and what might this mean in practice)? To which *people* has this Holy Land been promised?

In addition to such inter-religious religious questions, we shall also raise some of our own: What constitutes a 'Scripture' in practice? What makes a Holy land 'holy'? And what do the various answers to all of the above questions tell us about each religious tradition? It will likely come as no surprise to readers that there are no unequivocal, simple answers to these questions. The practical ramifications of these disagreements have been surveyed in the preceding chapters, which cover the political-religious rivalries that have dogged the Holy Land over history. This chapter will focus on the theological basis for each religious community's claims to the Holy Land.

Jewish Scripture

The idea that one place on earth is spiritually superior to others is related to the biblical idea that one *people* can be chosen by God, even though He created everyone. In fact, the election of the people and place are described together in the Hebrew Bible's passages on God's promise to Abraham. We are told in Genesis 17:1–9:

> And when Abram was ninety-nine years old the Lord appeared to Abram and said to him: 'I am god Almighty; walk before Me, and be wholehearted. And I will make My covenant between Me and you; and will multiply you exceedingly.' And Abram fell on his face; and God talked with him saying, 'As for Me, behold, My covenant is with you, and you shall be the father of a multitude of nations. Neither shall your name any more be called Abram, but your name shall be Abraham, for I have made you the father of a multitude of nations. And I will make you exceedingly fruitful, and I will make nations of you, and kings will come out of you. And I will establish My covenant between Me and you and your seed after you throughout their generations for an everlasting covenant, to be a God to you and to your seed after you. And I will give to you and to your seed after you the land of your sojournings, all the land of Canaan, for an everlasting possession; and I will be their God.' And God said to Abraham: 'and as for you, you shall keep My covenant, you, and your seed after you, throughout their generations.'

There are four points of relevance to us in this well-known passage. First, there is a deal here or, as God calls it, a 'covenant'. God makes promises to Abraham but also expects things in return. Second, the deal is between God on the one hand, and Abraham and his descendants on the other—the overwhelming majority of beneficiaries have not yet been born and will only come to know about this deal from Scripture(s). Third, the deal promises Abraham two separate things, a multitude of descendants and a particular land for them. Finally, the land is neither empty nor is it otherwise related to Abraham or his clan—it is very specifically the 'land of Canaan'. It belongs to *other* people (Canaan being the grandson of Noah via Ham, whereas Abraham descended from Noah via Shem), for which reason the transfer of ownership to Abraham's people will take place not through peaceful migration but through conquest, as we shall see.

Taken on its own, and devoid of context (as it often is), this passage belies the fact that Abraham already has a 'people' and a 'place'. In Genesis 12:1 we read, 'Now the Lord said to Abram: "Leave your country, and [leave] your kindred, and [leave] your father's house, [and go] to the land that I will show you..."'. In a tribal society such as that of the ancient Near East, people could elevate certain regions over others—one's birth-place, one's adopted place of residence, or one's family's patch of land might be favoured over all other places for obvious reasons. This verse tells us that Abraham (still known here as 'Abram') had a country with all three attributes. What God is doing, therefore, is asking Abraham to forego his native land in favour of another land, which is holy *not* because it is where Abraham is from, lived, or has family ties, but despite the fact that it is none of these things. Put another way, the land is 'Holy' for no other reason than that God said it is. Abraham's willingness to leave his familiar and familial land behind has thus been taken by commentators for centuries as a sign of his faith in God. For our purposes, this deceptively important verse is where the scriptural idea of a Holy Land is born. To be sure, there will be other places—within the borders of the Holy Land and beyond it—where important biblical events take place, thereby imbuing these places with religious significance. Burial plots, sites where treaties were concluded, temples, holy mountains, gardens, bushes, wildernesses, and more will all be encountered in the Hebrew Bible, and they will often be elevated to special status in light of events associated with these places. But the 'land of Canaan' is the only one that is holy simply because God chose it.

The establishment of the 'land of Canaan' as being God's chosen region, and the deal that secures this land for Abraham and his progeny in exchange for upholding God's commandments (limited though they might have been at this pre-Mosaic point in the story), are related to the broader theological issue of 'Landedness' that Genesis introduces. The basic idea is that God rewards us by giving us 'land' and punishes us by withdrawing it from us (or us from it). This theme is already apparent in the Adam and Eve story, where the protagonists' sin is punished by—among other things—expulsion from their 'homeland' (Gen. 3:22–4). The theme can be discerned in the Bible's next major narrative: that of Noah's flood, where 'land' (in this case dry land) is taken away from mankind on account of the corruption they have spread on earth (Gen. 6–10). The next major narrative similarly punishes the culprits—in this case, the architects of the Tower of Babel—by 'dispersing' them all across the earth (Gen. 11:1–9). This is in turn followed by God's command to Abraham that he set off for the land that God has chosen for him. Thus the promise to reward Abraham and his progeny with land is starkly set against a backdrop of divine punishment through landlessness. Rewarding God's people with land, and punishing them by detaching them from it, is one of the major themes of the Hebrew Bible, and we will return to it below (see 'Christian Scripture' section).

Later on in the Pentateuch, the 'five books of Moses', we hear that God has fulfilled the first half of his promise to Abraham, namely that he shall be the father of a multitude of descendants: upon entering Egypt we are told in Exodus 1:7 that 'the children of Israel were fruitful, and increased abundantly, and multiplied, and waxed exceeding mighty; and the land was filled with them'. Thus, although Abraham had been childless at the time of God's promise to him, by the time his descendants left Egypt they numbered some 600,000 men, as well as unnumbered women, children, the elderly, and hangers-on from other nations (Exod. 12:37–8; Num. 1:46 gives the number of men as 603,500). The other half of the promise, however, is only effected in the next section of the Hebrew Bible, 'the Prophets',and the narrative wastes no time in getting to the point. In Joshua 1:1–4 we read:

A traditional Torah scroll written on parchment.

> Now it came to pass after the death of Moses, the servant of the Lord, that the Lord spoke to Joshua the son of Nun, Moses' minister, saying: 'Moses My servant is dead; now therefore arise, go over this Jordan, you and all the people, to the land which I give to them, to the children of Israel. Every place that the sole of your foot shall tread upon, to you I shall give it, as I said to Moses. From the wilderness, and this Lebanon, to the great river Euphrates, all the land of the Hittites and to the Great Sea toward the setting of the sun, shall be your border.'

This passage is important for two reasons, the one explicit the other implicit. The implicit point is that despite doing more than any other person to bring about the fulfilment of the second half of God's promise, Moses himself dies before the Israelites inherit the land. This is yet another example of divine punishment through landlessness: Moses sinned (Num. 20:6–11), for which reason he does not merit entry into the Land (Deut. 34:4). The explicit significance of the passage is in its supposed description of the Land's extent. There are two curious facts about the supposed borders of the Land. First, the borders appear to be determined *not* by God but by the Israelites themselves, and rather haphazardly at that. Can it really be that the detailed terms of God's Covenant with Abraham are determined by wherever the Israelite conquerors happen to tread with their feet? Second, this description of the Land's 'boundaries' is inconsistent with other biblical verses. Joshua 1's Land echoes the description of Deuteronomy 11:24, but does not tally with the much more detailed description of the Land's extent provided in Numbers 34:1–12, which excludes East of the Jordan.

In addition to the geographical clues to the Land's extent, one finds repeated references to the peoples who inhabit the Land prior to its conquest. Thus, already in Genesis 15:18–21 there is a list of the ten peoples who will be displaced by Abraham's descendants upon the latter's inheritance of the Land. Other lists name fewer indigenous peoples (e.g. Exod. 3:8–17; 23:23; 33:2; 34:11), and more often than not the entire list is collapsed into 'all the Canaanites' (Josh. 17:16) or 'Canaan', as in the phrase 'the Land of Canaan' itself. As stated above, the fact that the land that God promises to Abraham belongs to other peoples necessitates that the land will be conquered. As the Conquest is necessary in order for God to deliver on His promise, He makes it clear from the outset that He will enable the Israelite conquest of the land, a promise whose fulfilment is described in the book of Joshua. Joshua 23 describes not only God's role in the Conquest, where 'One man of you has chased a thousand' (v. 10), but also God's threat to make the people 'perish quickly from the good land which He has given you' (v. 16), should the Israelites not uphold their side of the Covenant.

Until now, we have been referring to the 'Hebrew Bible'. This ostensibly descriptive term is imperfect on more than one account. To begin with, it is not entirely accurate in that there are chunks of the text (in the book of Ezra and Daniel) that are not in Hebrew but in the related language of Aramaic. More crucially, the phrase is implicitly 'Christian' in that it implies that there is a 'Bible' that is *not* 'Hebrew', which is what Christians believe (as the New Testament is in Greek) but Jews reject. Another inaccuracy stems from the fact that there is another 'Hebrew' Scripture, one that, moreover, focuses on God's promise of a chosen Land for Abraham and his descendants. This is the Samaritan Pentateuch, which Samaritans call 'Qushta' (lit. 'the Truth'). The only other 'biblical' book of which the Samaritans have a version is the Book of Joshua, though it is more of historical than theological interest to them and is not included in their canon. The centrality of the Holy Land to Samaritan scripture is reflected in the fact that their version of the Ten Commandments includes a commandment (number 10) that focuses specifically on the conquest of Canaan as part of the Israelite inheritance.

For Jews, Scripture is not the 'Hebrew Bible' but the 'TaNaKh', an acronym that stands for 'Torah' (Pentateuch), 'Nebiim' (Prophets), and 'Ketubim' (Writings). Crucial for us is the fact that this three-way division of Scripture is determined by Abraham's descendants' relationship with the Holy Land: the Pentateuch covers the history of the Israelites before they enter the Land, the Prophets concern their history (and future) in the Land, and the Writings detail the fortunes of the Jewish people outside of the Land, having been exiled by God in retribution for their [repeated] disobedience. Aside from the Covenant itself, therefore, it could be argued that the central theme of the 'Hebrew Bible' or 'TaNaKh' is the relationship between God's chosen People and His chosen Land, as the layout of Jewish Scripture itself is guided by land-related matters.

The foregoing overview of the Holy Land in the Hebrew Bible presupposes that the TaNaKh as we have it is the same Scripture that Jews (and Christians) have been reading since antiquity. Discoveries such as those from Qumran (the 'Dead Sea Scrolls') and from Cairo (the 'Cairo Geniza') have to a certain extent supported this presupposition. The differences between the modern and ancient versions of the Pentateuch, Prophets, and Writings are minor indeed and—with the exception of the Samaritan Pentateuch mentioned above—have little impact on the issues covered above. There is, however, one relatively major difference between modern and ancient TaNaKhs, namely the list of books that one might deem to be 'Scripture' at all. It is not so much that modern Bibles include books that were once excluded (the only book of the TaNaKh missing from the Qumran scrolls is 'Esther', for reasons that are unclear and still debated), but that there are books to which ancient Jewish communities clearly attached theological importance, though these books did not (for whatever reason) make it into the Jewish canon. One such book, which is—moreover—of direct relevance to the Holy Land, is the Book of Jubilees. This text is a commentary on Genesis written in Hebrew by a Jewish author in the mid-second century BCE. It presents itself as a Divine revelation and was taken as such by communities of Jews and Christians since antiquity; it is still part of the scriptural canon of Ethiopian Jews and Christians. Interestingly, fifteen copies of this work were found in the library of the Qumran community, suggesting that it was highly popular amongst this group of Jewish sectarians (far fewer copies of some 'canonical' books of the Bible were preserved in the Qumran library).

What is of particular interest about this text is its apparent uneasiness with God's promise and conquest of the 'Land of Canaan' for Abraham's descendants. Writing in a heavily Hellenized milieu, the author of Jubilees seems unwilling to accept that a Just,

Merciful, and Fair God would simply displace the indigenous inhabitants of a land with violence. Or perhaps the Jews in second-century BCE Palestine were being challenged on their right to the Land altogether. After all, it was known even in their own Scripture as 'the Land of Canaan'. He therefore rewrote the story, claiming that Canaan had no right to be occupying the Land. Subsequent to the dispersal of peoples as a result of the Tower of Babel episode, we are told in Jubilees 10:28–34:

> And Ham and his sons went into the land which he was to occupy, which he acquired as his portion in the land of the south. And Canaan saw the land of Lebanon to the river of Egypt, that it was very good, and he went not into the land of his inheritance to the west (that is to) the sea, and he dwelt in the land of Lebanon, eastward and westward from the border of Jordan and from the border of the sea. And Ham, his father, and Cush and Mizraim his brothers said unto him: 'You have settled in a land which is not yours, and which did not fall to us by lot: do not do so; for if you do so, you and your sons will fall in the land and (be) accursed through sedition; for by sedition you have settled, and by sedition will your children fall, and you shall be rooted out for ever. Dwell not in the dwelling of Shem; for to Shem and to his sons did it come by their lot. Cursed are you, and cursed shall you be beyond all the sons of Noah, by the curse by which we bound ourselves by an oath in the presence of the holy judge, and in the presence of Noah our father.' But he did not harken to them, and dwelt in the land of Lebanon from Hamath to the entering of Egypt, he and his sons until this day. And for this reason that land is named Canaan.

As stated, the Book of Jubilees did not make it into [most] Bibles and it would be stretching it nowadays to consider the above passage as 'Scripture'. Nonetheless, the problem to which 'Jubilees' is offering a solution is very much a biblical one and it has exercised the Bible's readership for generations.

The displacement of indigenous 'Canaanites' notwithstanding, God in the TaNaKh is exceedingly consistent and fair in His dispensing of justice regarding the Abrahamic Covenant. The Israelites merit conquest of and subsequent life in the Holy Land by upholding their side of the bargain—Joshua 5 even stresses that upon entering the Land an entire generation of Israelites underwent circumcision, echoing the original Covenant with Abraham. God thus supported the Conquest, which culminated in the creation of Jerusalem (under David) and a Temple (under Solomon). The flipside, however, is that when the Israelites were disobedient God withdrew the Land from them, exiling the northern inhabitants of the Land (the 'Kingdom of Israel') in 722 and the southern ones (the 'Kingdom of Judah') in 587. It is interesting to note that in both cases the Israelites are exiled eastwards, whence Abraham originally came, hinting perhaps at an undoing of the Covenant as much as a suspension thereof.

The TaNaKh relates that, eventually, the Israelites—now 'Jews'—were returned to the Holy Land, as the prophets had promised they would be (Jer. 25:11–12). But this time it was not by Conquest but by royal decree of Cyrus the Great. To be sure, God's role in this Return is made clear and lest anyone misunderstand that Cyrus was the architect of the Return, the Bible emphasizes that he is little more than God's agent

A young man reads from the Torah scroll in a public ceremony.

(Isa. 45:1). Still, unlike the first entry into the Land, this time not all Jews chose to return, and unlike the first entry, God was acting on the People's behalf only indirectly, through agents and gentile ones at that. Some read into this the loosening of God's bond with His People. The prophets, moreover, convey God's message of a New Covenant that will be established (Jer. 31:31), and a messianic figure whose career will be associated with this New Covenant. It is to the New Covenant or 'Testament' that we now turn.

Christian Scripture

Jeremiah himself, in the well-known passage on God's 'New Covenant', makes it clear that this Covenant is not merely a 'renewal of vows' but rather a different *type* of Covenant altogether. It is specifically 'not like the covenant that I made with their fathers on the day when I took them by the hand to bring them out of the land of Egypt, my covenant that they broke, though I was their husband, declares the Lord. For this is the covenant that I will make with the house of Israel after those days, declares the Lord: I will put my law within them, and I will write it on their hearts. And I will be their God, and they shall be my people' (Jer. 31:32–3). But what does this mean? Presumably the message is intended (at least at the outset) for Jews themselves. After

mission beyond the boundaries of the Holy Land generated debate precisely because the association between his mission and the Land was so close. By this logic, the absence of Land-theology in the Gospels indicates not that the land theme was downgraded but that it was unchanged, and it could be argued that the TaNaKh's land-theology was simply transferred to the Christian Scripture and thought.

On the other hand, there are passages that suggest that some of what is new about the New Covenant concerns the status of, and practical relationship with, the Holy Land. For instance, Stephen's speech in Acts 7, reminds its Jewish audience of God's promise of the Land to Abraham, and of Joshua's divinely effected conquest of it. And yet, a somewhat negative tone can be discerned in this speech, as the story of the ancient Israelites includes the implication that God's bond with them was at its strongest when they were in *Egypt*, that is to say, outside of the Land. It is also implied that Solomon's building of the Temple in Jerusalem was 'confining' God within it: 'Who found favour before God, and desired to find a tabernacle for the God of Jacob. But Solomon built him a house. Howbeit the most High dwells not in temples made with hands; as the prophet said, Heaven is my throne, and earth is my footstool: what house will you build me? said the Lord: or what is the place of my rest? Has not my hand made all these things?' (Acts 7:46–50).

In a similar vein, Hebrews 11 recounts God's promise of the Land to Abraham, but also reminds us that he and the other patriarchs were themselves strangers in the Land, and that they were in fact seeking a 'Heavenly country':

> By faith Abraham, when he was called to go out into a place which he should after receive for an inheritance, obeyed; and he went out, not knowing whither he went. By faith he sojourned in the land of promise, as in a strange country, dwelling in tabernacles with Isaac and Jacob, the heirs with him of the same promise: For he looked for a city which hath foundations, whose builder and maker is God. Through faith also Sarah herself received strength to conceive seed, and was delivered of a child when she was past age, because she judged him faithful who had promised. Therefore sprang there even of one, and him as good as dead, so many as the stars of the sky in multitude, and as the sand which is by the sea shore innumerable. These all died in faith, not having received the promises, but having seen them afar off, and were persuaded of them, and embraced them, and confessed that they were strangers and pilgrims on the earth. For they that say such things declare plainly that they seek a country. And truly, if they had been mindful of that country from whence they came out, they might have had opportunity to have returned. But now they desire a better country, that is, a heavenly: wherefore God is not ashamed to be called their God: for he has prepared for them a city. (Hebrews 11:8–16)

Perhaps most surprisingly and tellingly of all is the fact that despite inheriting the Hebrew Bible with its dominant theme of the Land, the New Testament has so little to say of direct relevance to this topic. This is particularly striking in Paul's wide-ranging theological discussions, which do touch upon Abraham, but curiously relegate 'Land' to the margins of theology. Paul merely states (Romans 4:16) that God's promise to Abraham was fulfilled through Jesus (rather than through the Land). This relative indifference to the Land may arguably indicate a downgrading of the Land in early Christian thought. And when we *do* hear of the Temple or the Land in a theological context it is almost exclusively reinterpreted and spiritualized: the Gospel of John (2:18–21) compares Jesus's body to the Temple, which will be destroyed and resurrected.

To an extent, these changes to the TaNaKh's land-theology are understandable. Jesus's career takes place in the Holy Land, yes, but under foreign, Roman occupation. Many Jews at the time were expecting a messiah to redeem them from this occupation and when Jesus arrived, promising the advent of God's Kingdom, they might have expected a physical redemption from a physical oppressor. Instead of defeating the Romans, he disarmingly explained that 'My Kingdom is not of this world' (John 18:36). That the New Covenant was to inaugurate a change was clear from the relevant verse in Jeremiah; and that the original Covenant was land-related is clear throughout the TaNaKh. It is thus not surprising that the New Testament's land-theology would be innovative, and the transfer of God's Kingdom to Heaven encouraged this theological innovation to be spiritualizing.

Related to this is the reality of life in the Holy Land in the aftermath of the Romans' destruction of the Temple in 70 CE. The traumatic event left its mark on both Jewish and Christian scriptural interpretation and attitudes to the Holy Land. Christian theology was based on texts that—for the most part—probably predated 70 CE. But the shaping of these texts into a coherent theology is something that happened only after 70 CE. The spiritualizing readings of land theology would thus trump those approaches that favoured attachment to a physical Holy Land, Jerusalem, and Temple. The Church Fathers could not argue for a worldly Jerusalem and Temple in the aftermath of their destruction. The abrogation and reinterpretation of 'the Law' (argued by Paul) combined with this reality to ensure a new, Christian land-theology based on new Scriptures, as well as new readings of the older Scriptures.

Jewish theology was transformed by the destruction of the Second Temple in another way. Judaism was restructured in this post-Temple world in ways recorded in the Mishnah and its Talmudic elaborations. Hereafter, the Holy Land becomes the focus of yearning, prayers, and planning for a very physical return to a physical Temple. In the two millennia since the destruction of the Temple, Jews have prayed at least thrice daily for the rebuilding of a physical Temple in a physical Jerusalem. Although there were Scriptualists who rejected the authority of the Mishnah and Talmuds, for everyone else these texts are referred to as the Oral Torah. This imbues them with authoritative status in determining Jewish practice and thought, but also suggests that there are *two* Torahs: an oral one as well as the written one. Is the Oral Torah 'Scripture'? Are its attitudes to the Land relevant to a discussion of the Holy Land in Scriptures?

Not only are the boundaries of Scripture open to interpretation here but so are the boundaries of the Holy Land itself. As seen, the TaNaKh provides us with more than one map, and the precise borders are far from certain. Modern scholars such as E. Lohmeyer and R. H. Lightfoot, moreover, have suggested that in the Gospels of

Mark and Matthew one may discern a new Land theology that focuses on the Galilee as a 'new' Holy Land. In the centuries following the Temple's destruction Jews and Christians were debating (amongst themselves and with each other) the precise boundaries of both the scriptural canon and the Holy Land itself. To these questions, and many others, the new religion of Islam offered answers.

Muslim Scripture

When Islam burst onto the scene in seventh-century Arabia, and conquered one-third of the civilized world by the middle of the subsequent century, observers in the conquered lands naturally wondered what was going on. What new message was this new prophet bringing? What was this new religion about? These, from an Islamic point of view, are flawed questions. The Islamic religion—as described already in the Qur'an itself—was nothing new. And the prophet was not starting something, he was finishing it. It is with this in mind that Muhammad is referred to in the Qur'an as the *seal of prophets* (Q. 33:40), the last in a chain that began with Adam and passed through such notable biblical figures as Noah, Abraham, Moses, and Jesus—amongst many, many others. In fact, according to one seventh-century account, by an Armenian cleric,

A father reads the Bible to his daughters.

Muhammad and his new community were doing no less than fulfilling the Abrahamic Covenant by returning 'the Land' to Abraham's Israelite and Ishmaelite descendants:

> He (Muhammad) preached to them (Arabs and Jews) saying: 'God promised that country to Abraham and to his son after him, for eternity. And what had been promised was fulfilled during that time when [God] loved Israel. Now, however, you are the sons of Abraham, and God shall fulfil the promise made to Abraham and his son on you. Only love the God of Abraham, and go and take the country which God gave to your father, Abraham. No one can successfully resist you in war, since God is with you.' Then they all came together (Arabs and Jews)...and they constituted a mighty army. After this they dispatched a message to the Byzantine emperor, saying: 'God gave that country as the inherited property of Abraham and of his sons after him. We are the sons of Abraham. It is too much that you hold our country. Leave in peace, and we shall demand from you what you have seized, plus interest.' The emperor rejected this. He did not provide a fitting response to the message but rather said: 'The country is mine. Your inheritance is the desert. So go in peace to your country.' (pseudo-Sebeos, *History of Armenia*, ch. XXX)

Tantalizing though this may be, it is not how the Islamic tradition itself remembers things, though it too recalls there having been an early association between the Prophet Muhammad and the Holy Land. Before turning to this, a few preliminary points about Islamic Scripture—the Qur'an and its authoritative exegeses—are in order. These points, moreover, are of direct relevance to any discussion of the Holy Land's status in Islam and its Scripture.

First, just as early Christianity's relationship with the Hebrew Bible was 'complex', the Qur'an's perspective on the Judeo-Christian Scripture(s) is beyond simple generalizations. On the one hand, it informs its audience that this book was preceded by 'the Scripture of Moses...and this book has come to confirm it in the Arabic language' (Qur'an 46:12). Just as the Christian community 'inherited' the Hebrew Bible, the Qur'an positions itself in relation to the Abrahamic scriptures preceding it. On the other hand, God did *not* simply send the previous Scriptures to the Arabs in an Arabic translation—the Qur'an shares concepts, characters, and concerns with the TaNaKh and New Testament but it is in no way mistakable as simply being an Arabic rendition of these scriptures. To complicate matters further, Islamic tradition explains this paradox away by asserting that the Qur'an *was* sent through Moses and then Jesus (with other scriptures, such as those of Abraham, alluded to as well) but the receiving communities transformed and falsified them, necessitating a *final* attempt by Allah at communicating with mankind via a prophet bearing a Scripture. Accordingly, inconsistencies between the qur'anic and the biblical versions of events are the result of Jewish/Christian falsifications and corruptions of the Qur'an into what has reached us as the Jewish and Christian Scriptures.

What this means in practice is that the biblical focus on the Land is to *some* extent apparent in the Qur'an, but only clearly in those [re]tellings of the stories of characters such as Moses and Lot, in which the Holy Land is an integral part of the story. To illustrate this, we may take, for example, Qur'an 5:20–6, in which the story of the spies scouting out the Holy Land (Num. 13:1–33) appears:

> And [mention, O Muhammad], when Moses said to his people, 'O my people, remember the favour of Allah upon you when He appointed among you prophets and made you possessors and gave you that which He had not given anyone among the worlds. O my people, enter the Holy Land (*al-ard al-muqaddasa*) which Allah has assigned to you and do not turn back [from fighting in Allah's cause] and [thus] become losers.' They said, 'O Moses, indeed within it is a people of tyrannical strength, and indeed, we will never enter it until they leave it; but if they leave it, then we will enter.' Said two men from those who feared [to disobey] upon whom Allah had bestowed favour, 'Enter upon them through the gate, for when you have entered it, you will be predominant. And upon Allah rely, if you should be believers.' They said, 'O Moses, indeed we will not enter it, ever, as long as they are within it; so go, you and your Lord, and fight. Indeed, we are remaining right here.' [Moses] said, 'My Lord, indeed I do not possess except myself and my brother, so part us from the defiantly disobedient people.' [Allah] said, 'Then indeed, it is forbidden to them for forty years [in which] they will wander throughout the land. So do not grieve over the defiantly disobedient people.'

Second, unlike the TaNaKh and New Testament, the prophet delivering the Islamic Scripture is *not* active in the Holy Land itself. Thus, the *story* of the rise of Islam—unlike the stories of the rise of Israelite/Jewish religion or Christianity—does not take place in the Holy Land at all and reference to it is relatively rare, incidental, and only of 'historical' relevance. It is true that much of what the TaNaKh recounts takes place outside of the Land, but this is almost always because the Israelites/Jews are on their way to or from it. The Qur'an, by contrast, mentions the Holy Land in passing, never dwelling on the Land itself, with the exception of one, controversial passage, to which we shall return shortly.

Third, while the Qur'an offers believers an eternal message, it is assumed to be shaped by events and concerns related to the prophet Muhammad and his career. In fact, a genre of Islamic literature entitled *asbab al-nuzul* or 'occasions of revelation' explains often in great detail the particular events in the Prophet's career that purport to be the occasion of the revelation of each verse. The two main peoples with whom the Prophet had significant and formative interactions—interactions that triggered revelations—were the pagan Arabs of Mecca and the Jews of Medina. It is important to stress that relations with the Jews could dictate the content of revelation, initially in ways that perhaps sought to attract Jews to the Qur'an's message through stressing parallels, and later—as the relationship between Muhammad and the Jews soured—in ways that defined Islam in contradistinction to the Jewish religion. Two examples of this latter phenomenon are said to date from the year 624 CE, roughly two years after Muhammad emigrated from Mecca to Medina.

In the first example, Muslim tradition explains that Muhammad had seen the Jews of Medina fasting on Yom Kippur, 'He asked them: "What is this?" They said, "This is a good day, this is the day when Allah saved the Children of Israel from their enemy and Moses fasted on this day." He said, "We are closer to Moses than you." So he fasted on the day and told the people to fast.' In 624, however, the obligation to fast on Yom Kippur was abrogated by a qur'anic verse that told Muslims to fast instead during the month of Ramadan (Qur'an 2:183–5).

An ornately decorated Qur'an.

> O you who have believed, decreed upon you is fasting as it was decreed upon those before you so that you may become righteous...The month of Ramadan [is the month] in which was revealed the Qur'an, a guidance for the people and clear proofs of guidance and as the criterion [between right and wrong]. So whoever sights [the new moon of] the month, let him fast it; and whoever is ill or on a journey—then an equal number of other days. Allah intends for you ease and does not intend for you hardship and [wants] for you to complete the period to glorify Allah for that [to] which He has guided you; and perhaps you will be grateful.

In the second example, the 'direction of prayer' (*qibla*) was transferred from Jerusalem to Mecca, for which the verse Q. 2:144 was revealed:

> We have certainly seen the turning of your face, [O Muhammad], toward the heaven, and We will surely turn you to a *qibla* with which you will be pleased. So turn your face toward al-Masjid al-Haram [in Mecca]. And wherever you [believers] are, turn your faces toward it [in prayer]. Indeed, those who have been given the Scripture well know that it is the truth from their Lord. And Allah is not unaware of what they do.

In other words, during the early years of Islam, Muslims fasted not on Ramadan but on Yom Kippur, and faced Jerusalem rather than Mecca during their prayers. Interestingly, the Holy Land in this case *does* feature in Islamic Scripture, but the trend described is one of *de*sanctification rather than the familiar stress on the Holy Land's centrality to religion, captured in the TaNaKh and New Testament.

Common to both of these examples is the fact that our understanding of the relevant verses is dependent on the Islamic tradition. For while there is a near consensus amongst Muslim (and western) authorities that the original direction of prayer in Islam was Jerusalem, and that the original fast day in Islam was Yom Kippur, the qur'anic verses themselves only hint at this and the gaps are necessarily filled by exegetes. Perhaps the most famous qur'anic passage assumed to be dealing with the Holy Land, the verses concerning the Prophet's 'Night Journey', are also dependent for their content and context on the details supplied by the Muslim exegetical tradition. Qur'an 17 begins with the following verse:

> Exalted is He who took His Servant by night from al-Masjid al-Haram ('the Haram prayer place') to al-Masjid al-Aqsa ('the remotest prayer place'), whose surroundings We have blessed, to show him of Our signs. Indeed, He is the Hearing, the Seeing.

What is God telling us here? We are not told who His 'servant' is, nor what (or where) the 'Masjid al-Haram' and 'Masjid al-Aqsa' are. As before, Islamic tradition fills in the gaps. Most interpretations—both ancient and modern—assert that it refers to a Night Journey undertaken by Muhammad from the mosque in Mecca (the 'Haram' Mosque) to a mosque in Jerusalem (the 'remotest' mosque). Not all would agree. Some ancient exegetes held that the 'remotest' mosque was elsewhere in Arabia. The qur'anic scholar Uri Rubin has convincingly shown that these exegetes were reflecting politically motivated 'Shi'ite' traditions that sought to downplay the region of Greater Syria where the despised Umayyad dynasty (r. 661–750) were based. The majority view,

Rubin shows, was that the remotest mosque was indeed in Jerusalem. The fact that this mosque is in 'surroundings' that God has 'blessed' lends support to the identification, as the Holy Land is often described as 'blessed', and the fact that the following seven verses deal with the Jews and their Temple seems to clinch the argument in favour of Jerusalem. But, Rubin explains, it was a New, Heavenly Jerusalem, and the Night Flight was a vision of the sort found in the biblical book of Ezekiel, and in the non-canonical books of Enoch.

The precise meaning of this verse, and particularly the location of the 'remotest' mosque, has deceptively wide-ranging implications: if it is determined that this mosque is indeed in Jerusalem then it would be perhaps the only reference to Jerusalem in the Qur'an, but a reference nonetheless. In a viral clip on youtube.com, an Israeli scholar of Arabic engaged in a heated debate with a journalist from the Al-Jazeera network, in which the former insisted that Jerusalem does not appear in the Qur'an. The journalist was insistent that it does and was visibly shaken by the audacity and confidence of his interviewee on the issue. Does Jerusalem appear in the Islamic Scripture or not?

To answer the question we must return to another, equally pivotal question—one that we first raised when considering the TaNaKh: What *is* Scripture? We have considered this question above, with reference to the Judeo-Christian scriptures and the place of books such as the Book of Jubilees within them. That is a question of 'canon' (or of what pieces does the scriptural puzzle consist?). Qur'an 17:1 begs a different question: assuming that the books, chapters, and verses of the canon are agreed upon (as they are in the case of the Qur'an), who decides the meaning of Scripture's very words? Just as 'Zion' is taken to mean 'Jerusalem', Islamic tradition takes 'the remotest Mosque' to refer to a place in Jerusalem. External, modern-scholarly approaches to such questions differ from internal, traditional ones. We are thus left to accept that there is no consensus concerning the boundaries of Scripture and its meaning. That the same can be said of the boundaries of the Holy Land itself is clearest from the case of Islamic conceptions of the Holy Land, to which we will now turn.

While Qur'an 17 is thought to depict Muhammad's journey from Mecca to Jerusalem, Muslim tradition itself was moving in the opposite direction. As stated, the Qur'an reflects events in the life of its Prophet and the latter's career did not take place in Canaan but in the Arabian region of the Hijaz, a region that includes with it the holy cities of Mecca and Medina. Modern scholars have demonstrated that Judeo-Christian traditions concerning the 'Holy Land', and even biblical history itself, were translated to this Arabian region. The biblical verses that refer to the Temple as God's 'house' (e.g. Isa. 56:7) are mirrored in the qur'anic and early Islamic phrase 'God's house', with reference to Islam's most sacred shrine, the Ka'ba in Mecca (e.g. Qur'an 2:125). The Jewish pilgrimage festival centred on the Temple, the Hag, is similarly echoed in, and paralleled by, the Muslim pilgrimage to Mecca, the Hajj. The Temple's foundation stone (*eben shetiyyah*) and traditions associated with it are identified in Islamic traditions about the Ka'ba's black stone, and the list continues. Unsurprisingly, in light of this, F. E. Peter's book on Mecca is called *Mecca: A Literary History of the Muslim Holy Land.*

It is not simply that Mecca comes to play in Islam the role that Jerusalem played in Jewish and Christian cultures, or that the Hijaz replaced the biblical Holy Land, but that entire biblical episodes were lifted from their Canaanite context and transferred to Arabia in Islamic tradition. Rubin has demonstrated, for instance, that the 'stations' on the pilgrimage to Mecca are connected in Islam with Moses, or with Adam and Eve, using popular etymologies to establish these links (the mountain of 'Arafa', a station on the route, is derived from the Arabic root meaning 'to know', and thereby connected with Adam and Eve coming to 'know' each other there). Even the Judeo-Christian traditions about a spiritualized or eschatological Holy Land are transferred to Arabia: the well-known Muslim scholar Hasan al-Basri (d. 728) described the Hijaz as '[a region that] guards over the rivers and trees and which will be the location of the gardens on the Day of Resurrection'.

This free-flow of Holy Land materials, between Judeo-Christian and Islamic traditions, and between the biblical Holy Land and the Islamic one, was always likely to lead to confusion or attempts to harmonize the inconsistencies or discrepancies that such inter-cultural borrowings created. One particularly notable example of this is Kamal Salibi's [in]famous 1985 book *The Bible Came from Arabia*, in which he argued that the

A traditional Qur'an lesson.

place names in the TaNaKh actually refer to places in south-west Arabia and were subsequently reinterpreted by Jews in the second century BCE to refer to sites in the Holy Land. Although his theory was almost universally rejected the book might still serve to highlight the muddle that ensued from the biblicization of the Hijaz.

We have seen that Muslim Scripture and its associated Tradition deals extensively with the Holy Land—it is simply a different, Arabian Holy Land with which it deals. Scholars such as Harry Munt and Stephen Shoemaker have argued that this focus on a different yet equal Holy Land was a conscious attempt on the part of Muslims to carve out for themselves an Abrahamic identity in contra-distinction to the Judeo-Christian ones that dominated in the region. We have also seen that Muslim Scripture never quite lets go of the biblical Land of Canaan, to which it also refers, both for 'historical' interest and, possibly, with regards to Muhammad's Night Flight thereto. But here, too, we are reminded that for all of Jerusalem's holiness, Mecca surpasses it, as we are told in the Qur'an itself: 'Indeed, the first House [of worship] established for mankind was that at "Bakkah"—blessed and a guidance for the world' (Qur'an 3:96). If, as many exegetes hold, 'Bakkah' is a synonym for 'Mecca' then already in the Qur'an Mecca's precedence over other holy cities is stressed. The superiority of Mecca over Jerusalem was compounded by a long list of sayings attributed to the Prophet himself, and to the earliest (and most prestigious) generation of Muslims. According to one such saying ('hadith'), a man by the name of Abu Dharr asked Muhammad 'Which mosque was established first?' to which the prophet replied 'al-Masjid al-Haram [in Mecca]'. When asked which was second, he replied 'al-Masjid al-Aqsa [in Jerusalem]'. In a similar vein, a genre dedicated to the 'Merits of Jerusalem' developed in Islamic literature, focusing on the city's holiness and other attributes. Running through this corpus is the assumption—occasionally made explicit—that Mecca is nonetheless pre-eminent, and that much of what makes Jerusalem special is quite how close it gets to Mecca. A lone exception to this is the unique place Jerusalem, and the Holy Land more generally, holds in Islamic eschatological literature. For all that the Qur'an urges its audience to repent in preparation for the impending Day of Judgement, the details of this End-of-Time scenario are provided only sparsely and it would appear that the gaps were filled in later Islamic Tradition through fruitful recourse to Jewish and Christian eschatological materials.

Conclusions

In the late 630s the second caliph of [Sunni] Islam, 'Umar I ibn al-Khattab (r. 634–644) conquered the Holy Land for Islamic forces. He is said to have been accompanied to Jerusalem by a Jew who guided him to the Temple Mount and advised him on his next moves there. The Jews who had been banished from the Land under the previous, Byzantine rulers, were allowed to return, and the Temple Mount was cleared of the refuse that the previous rulers had allowed to accumulate as an unmistakable reminder that Jewish aspirations in the Land would amount to nothing. Some two decades later, the Muslim ruler Mu'awiya ibn Abi Sufyan (r. 661–680) is said to have undergone his enthronement ceremony in Jerusalem: 'He sat down on Golgotha, he prayed there, and he went down to the tomb of the blessed Mary to pray in it.' A subsequent ruler, 'Abd al-Malik ibn Marwan (r. 685–705), named his son Sulayman ('Solomon') and built one of the most striking Islamic monuments in history, the Dome of the Rock, on the Temple Mount. Unsurprisingly, a contemporaneous Jewish text interpreted the rise of Islam in Messianic terms.

What is curious about all this is that for all that the Qur'an and its associated Tradition chose to focus on Mecca, and in significant ways thereby downgraded the importance of Jerusalem and the Holy Land, it is Islam in its first century that seemed to meet Judeo-Christian scriptural expectations about the Holy Land. Scripture and the Holy Land could thus intertwine in unexpected ways, with fluid conceptions of both scripture and of the Holy Land itself contributing to a flexibility in the three religious traditions that is, lamentably, rarely in evidence nowadays.

FURTHER READING

Chapter 1: The Birth of Israel

ARCHAEOLOGY OF THE SOUTHERN LEVANT IN THE 2ND MILLENNIUM BCE: INTRODUCTORY BOOKS

Ben-Tor, A. (ed.), *The Archaeology of Ancient Israel* (New Haven, 1992) (papers by Aharon Kempinski, Rivka Gonen, and Amihai Mazar).

Levy, T. E. (ed.), *The Archaeology of Society in the Holy Land* (London, 1995) (papers by David Ilan, Shlomo Bunimovitz, Lawrence Stager, and Israel Finkelstein).

Mazar, A., *Archaeology of the Land of the Bible, 10,000–586 BCE* (New York, 1990) (chapters 6–8).

Steiner, M. L., and A. E. Killebrew (eds), *The Oxford Handbook of Archaeology of the Levant, c.8000–332 BCE* (Oxford, 2014) (chapters 30 [Cohen], 31 [Bourke], 36 [Panitz-Cohen], 37 [Fischer], 41 [Gilboa], 42 [Herr]).

THE HISTORICITY OF THE BIBLE, WITH A FOCUS ON THE PATRIARCHS, THE EXODUS AND THE CONQUEST

Dever, W. G., *What Did the Biblical Writers Know, and When Did They Know It?* (Grand Rapids, 2001).

Finkelstein, I., and A. Mazar (ed. B. B. Schmidt), *The Quest for Historical Israel: Debating Archaeology and the History of Early Israel* (Atlanta, 2007).

Finkelstein, I., and N. A. Silberman, *The Bible Unearthed: Archaeology's New Vision of Ancient Israel and the Origin of its Sacred Text* (New York, 2001).

Frerichs, E. S., and L. H. Leski (eds), *Exodus: The Egyptian Evidence* (Winona Lake, 1997).

Friedman, R. E., *Who Wrote the Bible?* (New York, 1987).

Halpern, B., 'Eye Witness Testimony: Parts of the Exodus Written Within Living Memory of the Event', *Biblical Archaeology Review* 29/5 (2003): 50–7.

Hoffmeier, J. K., *Israel in Egypt: The Evidence for the Authenticity of the Exodus Tradition* (New York and Oxford, 1996).

Hoffmeier, J. K., *Ancient Israel in Sinai: The Evidence for the Authenticity of the Wilderness Tradition* (New York and Oxford, 2005).

Kitchen, K. A., *On the Reliability of the Old Testament* (Grand Rapids, 2003).

Levy, T. E., T. Schneider, and W. H. C. Propp (eds), *Israel's Exodus in Transdisciplinary Perspective: Text, Archaeology, Culture, and Geoscience* (Springer, 2015).

Millard, A. R., 'How Reliable is Exodus?', *Biblical Archaeology Review* 26/4 (2000): 50–7.

Na'aman, N., 'The Exodus Story: Between Historical Memory and Historiographical Composition', *Journal of Ancient Near Eastern Religions* 11 (2011): 39–69.

Provan, I., V. P. Long, and T. Longman, *A Biblical History of Israel* (Louisville, 2003).

Redford, D. B., *Egypt, Canaan and Israel in Ancient Times* (Princeton, 1992).

Rendsburg, G., 'The Date of the Exodus and the Conquest/Settlement: The Case for the 1100's', *Vetus Testamentum* 42 (1992): 510–27.

Thompson, T. L., *The Historicity of the Patriarchal Narratives, The Quest for Historical Abraham* (Berlin and New York, 1974).

Van Seters, J., *Abraham in History and Tradition* (New Haven and London, 1975).

ETHNIC GROUPS IN THE IRON AGE I: ISRAELITES, PHILISTINES, AND CANAANITES (WITH A FOCUS ON THE EMERGENCE OF ISRAEL)

Ben-Shlomo, D., *Philistine Iconography: A Wealth of Style and Symbolism* (Fribourg, 2010).

Bloch-Smith, E., 'Israelite Ethnicity in Iron I: Archaeology Preserves What is Remembered and What is Forgotten in Israel's History', *Journal of Biblical Literature* 122 (2003): 401–25.

Bunimovitz, S., 'Socio-Political Transformations in the Central Hill Country in the Late Bronze–Iron I Transition', in I. Finkelstein and N. Na'aman (eds), *From Nomadism to Monarchy* (Jerusalem, 1994), pp. 179–202.

Bunimovitz, S., and Z. Lederman, 'Canaanite Resistance: The Philistines and Beth-Shemesh—A Case Study from Iron Age I', *Bulletin of the American Schools of Oriental Research* 364 (2011): 37–51.

Davies, P. R., *In Search of Ancient Israel: A Study in Biblical Origins* (Sheffield, 1992).

Dever, W. G., *Who Were the Israelites and Where Did They Come From?* (Grand Rapids, 2003).

Dothan, T., *The Philistines and Their Material Culture* (New Haven, 1982).

Faust, A., *Israel's Ethnogenesis: Settlement, Interaction, Expansion and Resistance* (London, 2006).

Faust, A., 'The Emergence of Iron Age Israel: On Origins and Habitus', in T. E. Levy, T. Schneider, and W. H. C. Propp (eds), *Israel's Exodus in Transdisciplinary Perspective: Text, Archaeology, Culture and Geoscience* (Springer, 2015), pp. 467–82.

Faust, A., and H. Katz, 'Philistines, Israelites and Canaanites in the Southern Trough Valley During the Iron Age I', *Egypt and the Levant* 21 (2011): 231–47.

Faust, A., and J. Lev Tov, 'The Constitution of Philistine Identity: Ethnic Dynamics in 12th–10th Centuries Philistia', *Oxford Journal of Archaeology* 30 (2011): 13–31.

Finkelstein, I., *The Archaeology of the Period of Settlement and Judges* (Jerusalem, 1988).

Finkelstein, I., and N. Na'aman (eds), *From Nomadism to Monarchy* (Jerusalem, 1994).

Killebrew, A. E., *Biblical Peoples and Ethnicity: An Archaeological Study of Egyptians, Canaanites, Philistines and Early Israel 1300–1100 BCE* (Atlanta, 2005).

Killebrew, A. E., and G. Lehmann (eds), *The Philistines and Other 'Sea Peoples' in Text and Archaeology* (Atlanta, 2013).

Levy, T. E., and A. F. C. Holl, 'Migrations, Ethnogenesis, and Settlement Dynamics: Israelites in Iron Age Canaan and Shuwa-Arabs in the Chad Basin', *Journal of Anthropological Archaeology* 21 (2002): 83–118.

Levy, T. E., R. B. Adams, and A. Muniz, 'Archaeology and the Shasu Nomads: Recent Excavations in the Jabal Himdat Firdan, Jordan', in R. E. Friedman and W. H. C. Propp (eds), *Le-David Maskil: A Birthday Tribute to David Noel Freedman* (Winona Lake, 2004), pp. 63–89.

Na'aman, N., 'The "Conquest of Canaan" in the Book of Joshua and in History', in N. Na'aman and I. Finkelstein (eds), *From Nomadism to Monarchy* (Jerusalem, 1994), pp. 218–81.

Rainey, A. F., 'Israel in Merenptah's Inscription and Reliefs', *Israel Exploration Journal* 51 (2001): 57–75.

Stager, L. E., 'Merenptah, Israel and Sea Peoples: New Light on an Old Relief', *Eretz Israel* 18 (1995): 56*–64*.

Stager, L. E., 'Forging an Identity: the Emergence of Ancient Israel', in M. D. Coogan (ed.), *The Oxford History of the Biblical World* (New York and Oxford, 1998), pp. 123–75.

Yasur-Landau, A., *The Philistines and Aegean Migration at the End of the Late Bronze Age* (Cambridge, 2010).

Chapter 2: Iron Age: Tribes to Monarchy

For further information and references to primary and secondary sources on individual points, see:

Grabbe, L. L., *Ancient Israel: What Do We Know and How Do We Know It?* (London/New York, 2007).

General bibliography

Fritz, V., and P. R. Davies (eds), *The Origins of the Ancient Israelite States* (Sheffield, 1996).

Grabbe, L. L. (ed.), *Israel in Transition: From Late Bronze II to Iron IIA (c.1250–850 BCE): Volume 1 The Archaeology* (London/New York, 2008).

Grabbe, L. L. (ed.), *Israel in Transition: From Late Bronze II to Iron IIA (c.1250–850 BCE): Volume 2 The Text* (London/New York, 2010).

Handy, L. K. (ed.), *The Age of Solomon: Scholarship at the Turn of the Millennium* (Leiden, 1997).

Killebrew, A. E., and G. Lehmann (eds), *The Philistines and Other 'Sea Peoples' in Text and Archaeology* (Atlanta, GA, 2013).

Liverani, M., *Israel's History and the History of Israel* (translated by C. Peri and P. R. Davies; London, 2005).

Mazar, A. (ed.), *Studies in the Archaeology of the Iron Age in Israel and Jordan* (Sheffield, 2001).

Reich, R., *Excavating the City of David: Where Jerusalem's History Began* (Jerusalem, 2011).

Stavrakopoulou, F., and J. Barton (eds), *Religious Diversity in Ancient Israel and Judah* (London/New York, 2010).

Steiner, M. L., *Excavations of Kathleen M. Kenyon in Jerusalem 1961–1967, vol. III, The Settlement in the Bronze and Iron Ages* (Sheffield, 2001).

Thompson, T. L., with the collaboration of S. K. Jayyusi (ed.), *Jerusalem in Ancient History and Tradition* (London/New York, 2003).

Vaughn, A. G., and A. E. Killebrew (eds), *Jerusalem in Bible and Archaeology: The First Temple Period* (Atlanta, 2003).

Chapter 3: Israel and Judah, *c.*931–587 BCE

Ahituv, S., *Echoes from the Past: Hebrew and Cognate Inscriptions from the Biblical Period* (Jerusalem, 2008).

Arnold, B. T., and R. S. Hess, *Ancient Israel's History: An Introduction to Issues and Sources* (Grand Rapids, 2014).

Arnold, B. T., and H. G. M. Williamson (eds), *Dictionary of the Old Testament: Historical Books* (Downers Grove, IL, 2005).

Cogan, M., *The Raging Torrent: Historical Inscriptions from Assyria and Babylonia Relating to Ancient Israel* (Jerusalem, 2008).

Coogan, M. D., *The Oxford History of the Biblical World* (New York and Oxford, 1998).

Davies, P. R., *Memories of Ancient Israel: An Introduction to Biblical History—Ancient and Modern* (Louisville, 2008).

Dever, W. G., *What Did the Biblical Writers Know and When Did They Know It? What Archaeology Can Tell Us about the Reality of Ancient Israel* (Grand Rapids, 2001).

Finkelstein, I., and A. Mazar (ed. B. B. Schmidt), *The Quest for the Historical Israel: Debating Archaeology and the History of Early Israel* (Atlanta, 2007).

Grabbe, L. L. (ed.), *Good Kings and Bad Kings: The Kingdom of Judah in the Seventh Century* BCE (London, 2005).

Grabbe L. L. (ed.), *Ahab Agonistes: The Rise and Fall of the Omri Dynasty* (London, 2007).

Kuhrt, A., *The Ancient Near East, c.3000–330* BCE (London, 1995).

Lemaire, A., and B. Halpern (eds), *The Books of Kings: Sources, Composition, Historiography and Reception* (Leiden/Boston, 2010).

Miller, J. M., and J. H. Hayes, *A History of Ancient Israel and Judah* (2nd edn, Louisville, 2006).

Moore, M. B., and B. E. Kelle, *Biblical History and Israel's Past: The Changing Study of the Bible and History* (Grand Rapids, 2011).

Shanks, H. (ed.), *Ancient Israel: From Abraham to the Roman Destruction of the Temple* (3rd edn, Washington, 2010).

Stern, E., *Archaeology of the Land of the Bible, II: The Assyrian, Babylonian, and Persian Periods (732–332* BCE.*)* (New York, 2001).

Williamson, H. G. M. (ed.), *Understanding the History of Ancient Israel* (Oxford, 2007).

Chapter 4: Babylonian Exile and Restoration, 587–325 BCE

Barstad, H. M., *The Myth of the Empty Land: A Study in the History and Archaeology of Judah During the 'Exilic' Period* (Oslo, 1996).

Bedford, P. R., *Temple Restoration in Early Achaemenid Judah* (Leiden, 2001).

Blenkinsopp, J., *Judaism: The First Phase. The Place of Ezra and Nehemiah in the Origins of Judaism* (Grand Rapids, 2009).

Briant, P., *From Cyrus to Alexander: A History of the Persian Empire* (Winona Lake, IN, 2002).

Faust, A., *Judah in the Neo-Babylonian Period: The Archaeology of Desolation* (Atlanta, 2012).

Gerstenberger, E. S., *Israel in the Persian Period: The Fifth and Fourth Centuries* B.C.E. (Atlanta, 2011).

Grabbe, L. L., *A History of the Jews and Judaism in the Second Temple Period, 1: Yehud: A History of the Persian Province of Judah* (London, 2004).

Japhet, S., *From the Rivers of Babylon to the Highlands of Judah: Collected Studies on the Restoration Period* (Winona Lake, IN, 2006).

Knoppers, G. N., *Jews and Samaritans: The Origins and History of Their Early Relations* (Oxford, 2013).

Kuhrt, A., *The Ancient Near East, c.3000–330* BC (London, 1995), pp. 589–701.

Lipschits, O., *The Fall and Rise of Jerusalem: Judah under Babylonian Rule* (Winona Lake, IN, 2005).

Lipschits, O., and J. Blenkinsopp (eds), *Judah and the Judeans in the Neo-Babylonian Period* (Winona Lake, IN, 2003).

Magen, Y., *Mount Gerizim Excavations, Volume 2: A Temple City* (Jerusalem, 2008).

Middlemas, J., *The Templeless Age: The History, Literature, and Theology of the 'Exile'* (Louisville, 2007).

Southwood, K. E., *Ethnicity and the Mixed Marriage Crisis in Ezra 9–10: An Anthropological Approach* (Oxford, 2012).

Stern, E., *Material Culture of the Land of the Bible in the Persian Period 538–332* BC (Warminster, 1982).

Stökl, J., and C. Waerzeggers (eds), *Exile and Return: The Babylonian Context* (Berlin, 2015).

Watts, J. W. (ed.), *Persia and Torah: The Theory of Imperial Authorization of the Pentateuch* (Atlanta, 2001).

Williamson, H. G. M., *Studies in Persian Period History and Historiography* (Tübingen, 2004).

Chapter 5: The Hellenistic and Roman Era

General overviews

Meyers, E. M., and M. A. Chancey, *Alexander to Constantine: Archaeology of the Land of the Bible* (New Haven, 2012).

Schürer, E., *The History of the Jewish People in the Age of Jesus Christ.* Vol. 1. Rev. and ed. G. Vermes and F. Millar (Edinburgh, 1973).

Schwartz, S., *Imperialism and Jewish Society, 300 BCE. to 640 CE* (Princeton, 2001).

Seeman, C., and A. K. Marshak, 'Jewish History from Alexander to Hadrian', in J. J. Collins and D. C. Harlow (eds), *Early Judaism: A Comprehensive Overview* (Grand Rapids, MI, 2012), pp. 30–69 (= Collins and Harlow, eds, *The Eerdmans Dictionary of Early Judaism* [Grand Rapids, MI, 2010], pp. 25–55).

The Hellenistic period

Bickerman, E. J., *The God of the Maccabees: Studies on the Meaning and Origin of the Maccabean Revolt* (Leiden, 1979).

Bickerman, E. J., *The Jews in the Greek Age* (Cambridge, MA, 1988).

Hengel, M., *Judaism and Hellenism: Studies in their Encounter in Palestine during the Early Hellenistic Period.* 2 vols (Philadelphia, 1974).

Honigman, S., *Tales of High Priests and Taxes: The Books of the Maccabees and the Judean Rebellion against Antiochus IV* (Oakland, CA, 2014).

Regev, E., *The Hasmoneans: Ideology, Archaeology, Identity* (Göttingen, 2013).

Sievers, J., *The Hasmoneans and Their Supporters: From Mattathias to the Death of John Hyrcanus I* (Atlanta, 1990).

The Roman period

Berlin, A. M., and J. A. Overman, *The First Jewish Revolt: Archaeology, History, and Ideology* (London, 2002).

Goodman, M., *The Ruling Class of Judea: The Origins of the Jewish Revolt AD 66–70* (Cambridge, 1987).

Hengel, M., *The Zealots: Investigations into the Jewish Freedom Movement in the Period from Herod I until 70 A.D.* (Edinburgh, 1989).

Horbury, W., *Jewish War under Trajan and Hadrian* (Cambridge, 2014).

Marshak, A. K., *The Many Faces of Herod the Great* (Grand Rapids, 2015).

McLaren, J. S., *Turbulent Times? Josephus and Scholarship on Judaea in the First Century CE* (Sheffield, 1998).

Richardson, P. W., *Herod: King of the Jews and Friend of the Romans* (Columbia, SC, 1996).

Literature

Collins, J. J., *Jewish Wisdom in the Hellenistic Age* (Louisville, KY, 1997).

Collins, J. J., *The Apocalyptic Imagination* (3rd edn, Grand Rapids, MI, 2016).

Nickelsburg, G. W. E., *Jewish Literature Between the Bible and the Mishnah* (2nd edn, Minneapolis, 2005).

Schürer, E., *The History of the Jewish People in the Age of Jesus Christ.* Vol. III.1. Rev. and ed. G. Vermes, F. Millar, and M. Goodman (Edinburgh, 1986).

Stone, M. E. (ed.), *Jewish Writings of the Second Temple Period* (Philadelphia, 1984).

Religious life and institutions

Collins, J. J., *The Scepter and the Star: Messianism in Light of the Dead Sea Scrolls.* (2nd edn, Grand Rapids, MI, 2010).

Levine, L. I., *Jerusalem: Portrait of the City in the Second Temple Period (538 BCE.–70 CE.)* (Philadelphia, 2002).

Levine, L. I., *The Ancient Synagogue: The First Thousand Years* (New Haven, 2005).

Sanders, E. P., *Judaism: Practice and Belief. 63 BCE–66 CE* (Philadelphia, 1992).

Safrai, S., and M. Stern (eds), *The Jewish People in the First Century: Historical Geography, Political History, Social, Cultural and Religious Life and Institutions.* Vol. 2 (Assen, 1976).

Sects and sectarianism

Baumgarten, A. I., *The Flourishing of Jewish Sects in the Maccabean Era: An Interpretation* (Leiden, 1997).

Collins, J. J., *Beyond the Qumran Community. The Sectarian Movement of the Dead Sea Scrolls* (Grand Rapids, MI, 2010).

Lim, T. H., and J. J. Collins (eds), *The Oxford Handbook of the Dead Sea Scrolls* (Oxford, 2010).

Saldarini, A. J., *Pharisees, Scribes, and Sadducees* (Wilmington, DE, 1988).

Stemberger, G., *The Jewish Contemporaries of Jesus: Pharisees, Sadducees, Essenes* (Minneapolis, 1995).

Chapter 6: A Christian Holy Land, 284–638 CE

Avi-Yonah, M., *The Jews of Palestine: a Political History from the Bar Kokhba War to the Arab Conquest* (New York, 1976).

Baldovin, J., *The Urban Character of Christian Worship: the Origins, Development and Meaning of Stational Liturgy* (Rome, 1987).

Ben-Ami, D., Y. Tchekhanovets, and G. Bijovsky, 'New Archaeological and Numismatic Evidence for the Persian Destruction of Jerusalem in 614 CE', *Israel Exploration Journal* 60 (2010): 204–21.

Binns, J., *Ascetics and Ambassadors of Christ: the Monasteries of Palestine 314–631* (Oxford, 1994).

Bitton-Ashkelony, B., *Encountering the Sacred: the Debate on Christian Pilgrimage in Late Antiquity* (Berkeley/Los Angeles/London, 2005).

Chryssavgis, J., 'The Road from Egypt to Palestine: the Sayings of the Desert Fathers: Destination and Destiny', *ARAM* 15 (2003): 97–108.

Di Segni, L., 'The Samaritans in Roman-Byzantine Palestine: Some Misapprehensions', in H. Lapin (ed.), *Religious and Ethnic Communities in Later Roman Palestine* (College Park, 1998), pp. 51–66.

Di Segni, L., and Y. Tsafrir, 'The Ethnic Composition of Jerusalem's Population in the Byzantine Period (312–638 CE)', *Liber Annuus* 6 (2012): 405–54.

Drijvers, J., 'The Conversion of Aelia Capitolina to Christianity in the Fourth Century', in A. Papaconstantinou, N. McLynn, and D. Schwartz (eds), *Conversion in Late Antiquity: Christianity, Islam, and Beyond* (Farnham, 2015), pp. 283–97.

Gutfeld, O., 'The Urban Layout of Byzantine-Period Jerusalem', in K. Galor and G. Avni (eds), *Unearthing Jerusalem: 150 years of Archaeological Research in the Holy City* (Winona Lake, 2011), pp. 327–50.

Hirschfeld, Y., *The Judean Desert Monasteries in the Byzantine Period* (New Haven, 1992).

Hunt, E., *Holy Land Pilgrimage in the Later Roman Empire, AD 312–460* (Oxford, 1982).

Hunt, E., 'Constantine and Jerusalem', *Journal of Ecclesiastical History* 48 (1997): 405–24.

Irshai, O., 'The Jerusalem Bishopric and the Jews in the Fourth Century: History and Eschatology', in L. Levine (ed.), *Jerusalem: its Sanctity and Centrality to Judaism, Christianity, and Islam* (New York, 1999), pp. 204–20.

Kingsley, S., *Shipwreck Archaeology of the Holy Land: Processes and Parameters* (London, 2004).

Klein, K., 'Do Good in thy Good Pleasure unto Zion: the Patronage of Aelia Eudokia in Jerusalem', *Wiener Jahrbuch für Kunstgeschichte* 60–61 (2011–12), 85–95.

Leyerle, B., 'Landscape as Cartography in Early Christian Pilgrimage Narratives', *Journal of the American Academy of Religions* 64 (1996): 119–43.

Markus, R., 'How on Earth could Places become Holy? Origins of the Christian Idea of Holy Places', *Journal of Early Christian Studies* 2 (1994): 257–71.

Patrich, J., *Sabas, Leader of Palestinian Monasticism: a Comparative Study in Eastern Monasticism, Fourth to Seventh Centuries* (Washington, 1995).

Perrone, L., 'Christian Holy Land Pilgrimage in an Age of Dogmatic Conflict: Popular Religion and Confessional Affiliation in Byzantine Palestine (fifth to seventh centuries)', *Proche Orient Chrétien* 48 (1998): 5–37.

Perrone, L., 'Byzantine Monasticism in Gaza and in the Judaean Desert: a Comparison of their Spiritual Traditions', *Proche Orient Chrétien* 62 (2012): 6–22.

Piccirillo, M. 'Early Christianity in Jerusalem', in Z. Kafafi and R. Schick (eds), *Jerusalem before Islam* (Oxford, 2008), pp. 189–99.

Rubin, Z., 'The See of Caesarea in Conflict with Jerusalem from Nicaea (325) to Chalcedon (451)', in A. Raban, and K. Holum (eds), *Caesarea Maritima: a Retrospective after Two Millennia* (Leiden/Boston, 1996), pp. 559–74.

Schick, R. 'Jerusalem in the Byzantine Period', in Z. Kafafi and R. Schick (eds), *Jerusalem before Islam*, (Oxford, 2008), pp. 169–88.

Steppa, J.-E., ([2]2005), *John Rufus and the World Vision of anti-Chalcedonian Culture* (Piscataway, NJ, 2005).

Tsafrir, Y., 'Procopius and the Nea Church in Jerusalem', *Antiquité tardive* 8 (2000): 149–64.

Walker, P., *Holy City, Holy Places? Christian Attitudes to Jerusalem and the Holy Land in the Fourth Century* (Oxford, 1990).

Weksler-Bdolah, Sh., 'The Fortifications of Jerusalem in the Byzantine Period', *ARAM* 18–19 (2006–7): 85–112.

Chapter 7: The Coming of Islam

Avni, G., *The Byzantine-Islamic Transition in Palestine: An Archeological Approach* (Oxford, 2014).

Elad, A., *Medieval Jerusalem and Islamic Worship* (Leiden, 1995).

Gil, M., *A History of Palestine, 634–1099* (New York, 1992).

Grabar, O., *The Dome of the Rock* (Cambridge MA and London, 2006).

Griffith, S. H., *Arabic Christianity in the Monasteries of Ninth-Century Palestine* (Aldershot & Brookfield [VT], 1992).

Levy-Rubin, M., 'New Evidence Relating to the Process of Islamization in Palestine in the Early Muslim Period: the Case of Samaria', *Journal of the Economic and Social History of the Orient* 43/3 (2000): 257–76.

Levy-Rubin, M., 'Were the Jews Prohibited from Settling in Jerusalem following the Arab Conquest?: the Authenticity of al-Tabari's Jerusalem Surrender Agreement', *Jerusalem Studies in Arabic and Islam* 36 (2009): 63–82.

Levy-Rubin, M., 'Changes in the Settlement Pattern of Palestine Following the Arab Conquest', in K. G. Holum and H. Lapin (eds), *Shaping the Middle East: Jews, Christians, and Muslims in an Age of Transition 400–800 CE* (Bethesda MD, 2011), pp. 155–72.

Prawer, J., and H. Ben-Shammai (eds), *The History of Jerusalem: the Early Muslim Period 634–1099* (Jerusalem, 1996).

Raby J., and J. Johns, *Bayt al-Maqdis: Abd al-Malik's Jerusalem*, 2 vols (Oxford, 1992).

Chapter 8: The Holy Land in the Crusader and Ayyubid Periods, 1099–1250

PRIMARY SOURCES IN TRANSLATION

Albert of Aachen, *History of the Journey to Jerusalem*, ed. and trans. S. B. Edgington (Oxford, 2007).

Fulcher of Chartres, *A History of the Expedition to Jerusalem, 1095–1127*, trans. F. R. Ryan, ed. H. S. Fink (New York, 1973).

Gabrieli, F., *Arab Historians of the Crusades* (Berkeley and Los Angeles, 1984).

Ibn al-Athir, *al-Kāmil fi'l-tawārīkh. The Years 541–589/1146–1193: The Age of Nur al-Din and Saladin*, trans. D. S. Richards (Aldershot, 2006).

William of Tyre, *A History of Deeds Done Beyond the Sea*, trans. E. A. Babcock and A. C. Krey (New York, 1943).

SECONDARY SOURCES

Asbridge, T., *The Crusades: The War for the Holy Land* (New York and London, 2010).

Barber, M., *The New Knighthood: A History of the Order of the Temple* (Cambridge, 1994).

Cobb, Paul M., *The Race for Paradise: An Islamic History of the Crusades* (Oxford, 2014).

Eddé, A.-M., *Saladin*, trans. J. M. Todd (Cambridge, MA, 2011).

Hillenbrand, C., *The Crusades: Islamic Perspectives* (Edinburgh, 1999).

Madden, T., *Crusades: The Illustrated History* (Ann Arbor, 2004).

Nicholson, H., *The Knights Hospitaller* (Woodbridge, 2003).

Phillips, J., *Holy Warriors: A Modern History of the Crusades* (London, 2010).

Tyerman, C., *God's War: A New History of the Crusades* (London, 2007).

Chapter 9: The Holy Land from the Mamluk Sultanate to the Ottoman Empire, 1260–1799

Amitai-Preiss, R. *Mongols and Mamluks: The Mamluk-Īlkhānid War, 1260–1281* (Cambridge, 1995).

Amitai, R. 'The Mamluk Institution: 1000 Years of Military Slavery in the Islamic World', in P. Morgan and C. Brown (eds), *Arming Slaves: From Classical Times to the Modern Age* (New Haven CT, 2006), pp. 40–78.

Auld, S., R. Hillenbrand, and Y. Natshah (eds), *Ottoman Jerusalem: the Living City, 1517–1917* (Published on behalf of the British School of Archaeology in Jerusalem in cooperation with the Administration of Auqaf and Islamic Affairs, Jerusalem, Altajir World of Islam Trust, London, 2000), 2 vols.

Cohen, A., *Palestine in the 18th Century: Patterns of Government and Administration* (Jerusalem, 1973).

Cohen A., and B. Lewis, *Population and Revenue in the Towns of Palestine: Sixteenth Century* (Princeton, 1978).

Cyrtin-Silverman, K. *The Road Inns (khāns) of Bilād al-Shām* (Oxford, 2010).

Drory, J., 'Founding a New Mamlaka: Some Remarks Concerning Safed and the Organization of the Region in the Mamluk Period', in M. Winter and A. Levanoni (eds), *The Mamluks in Egyptian and Syrian Politics and Society* (Leiden and Boston, 2004), pp. 163–87.

Holt, P. M., 'The Sultan as an Ideal Ruler: Ayyubid and Mamluk Prototypes', in M. Kunt and C. Woodhead. (eds), *Suleyman the Magnificent and his Age* (London and New York, 1995), pp. 122–37.

Humphreys, R. S., *From Saladin to the Mongols* (Albany, 1977).

Hütteroth, W. D., and K. Abdulfattah, *Historical Geography of Palestine, Transjordan and Southern Syria in the late 16th [sixteenth] Century* (Erlangen, 1977).

Irwin, R., *The Middle East in the Middle Ages: The Early Mamluk Sultanate, 1250–1382* (London, 1986).

Lewis, B., 'Cities of Palestine during the Sixteenth Century: Based on Documents of the Ottoman Archive', *Jerusalem Studies of Eretz Israel* 2/5 (Jerusalem, 1955): 117–27.

Ma'oz, M. (ed.), *Studies on Palestine During the Ottoman Period* (Jerusalem, 1975).

Rabbat, N. O., *Mamluk History through Architecture: Monuments, Culture and Politics in Medieval Egypt and Syria* (London, New York, 2010).

Schur, N., *Napoleon in the Holy Land* (London, 1999).

Chapter 10: From Napoleon to Allenby: The Holy Land and the Wider Middle East

Aldridge, J., *Cairo: Biography of a City* (London, 1970).

Ansary, T., *Destiny Disrupted: A History of the World Through Islamic Eyes* (Philadelphia, 2009).

Bartlett, W., and J. Carne, *Syria, The Holy Land, Asia Minor, Etc* (London, 1836).

Chandler, David, *The Campaigns of Napoleon* (London, 1967).

Chenevix Trench, C., *Charley Gordon: An Eminent Victorian Reassessed* (London, 1978).

Churchill, W. S., *The Great War*, Vol. IV (London, 1933).

Gilbert, M., *Winston S. Churchill, Vol. IV, 1917–1922* (London, 1975).

Haywood, J. A., *Modern Arabic Literature 1800–1970* (New York, 1972).

Irwin, R., *The Lust of Knowing: The Orientalists and their Enemies* (London, 2006).

Kassir, S., *Beirut* (Berkeley, 2010).

Khalidi, W., *Before their Diaspora: A Photographic History of the Palestinians 1876–1948* (Washington DC, 2010).
Marcus, A. D., *Jerusalem 1913: The Origins of the Arab-Israeli Conflict* (New York, 2007).
Marshall-Cornwall, Sir J., *Napoleon as Military Commander* (London, 1967).
Porter, J. l., *Murray's Hand-Book for Travellers in Syria and Palestine* (London, 1892).
Rodenbeck, M., *Cairo: The City Victorious* (London, 1998).
Said, E., *Orientalism* (New York, 1979).
Salibi, K., *A House of Many Mansions: The History of Lebanon Reconsidered* (London, 1988).
Shlaim, A, *The Iron Wall: Israel and the Arab World* (London, 2000).
Vatikiotis, P. J., *The History of Egypt: From Muhammad to Sadat* (London, 1980).
Yammine, A., *Quatre Ans de Misere: Le Liban et La Syrie Pendant la Guerre* (Cairo, 1922).

Chapter 11: Pilgrimage

Ben-Arieh, Y., *Jerusalem in the 19th Century: the Old City* (Jerusalem, 1984).
Ben-Arieh, Y., *The Rediscovery of the Holy Land in the Nineteenth Century* (Jerusalem, 1979; revised edition, 2007).
Elad, A., *Medieval Jerusalem and Islamic Worship: Holy Places, Ceremonies, Pilgrimage* (Leiden, 1995).
France, J., 'The Destruction of Jerusalem and the First Crusade', *Journal of Ecclesiastical History*, 47 (1996): 1–17.
Frenkel, M., 'Pilgrimage and Charity in the Geniza Society', in A. Franklin et al. (eds), *Jews, Christians and Muslims in Medieval and Early Modern Times* (Leiden, 2014), pp. 59–66.
Hummel, R., and T. Hummel, *Patterns of the Sacred: English Protestant and Russian Orthodox Pilgrims of the Nineteenth Century* (London, 1995).
Hunt, J., *Four Paths to Jerusalem: Jewish, Christian, Muslim, and Secular Pilgrimages, 1000 BC to 2001 CE* (Jefferson NC, 2002).
Isphording, B., *Germans in Jerusalem, 1830–1914* (Jerusalem, 2009).
Jacobs, M., *Reorienting the East: Jewish Travelers to the Medieval Muslim World* (Philadelpia, 2014).
Kister, M. J., '"You Shall Only Set out for Three Mosques": a Study of an Early Tradition', *Le Muséon* 82 (1969): 173–96.
Larsen, T., 'Thomas Cook, Holy Land Pilgrims, and the Dawn of the Modern Tourist Industry', in Swanson (ed.), *The Holy Land*, 329–42.
Limor, O., 'Sharing Sacred Space: Holy Places in Jerusalem Between Christianity, Judaism, and Islam', in I. Shagrir et al. (eds), *In Laudem Hierosolymitani: Studies in Crusades and Medieval Culture in Honor of B. Z. Kedar* (Aldershot, 2007), pp. 219–31.
Morris, C., 'Memorials of the Holy Places and Blessings from the East: Devotion to Jerusalem before the Crusades', in Swanson (ed.), *The Holy Land*, pp. 90–109.
Meri, J., *The Cult of Saints among Muslims and Jews in Medieval Syria* (Oxford, 2002).
Meri, J., *A Lonely Wayfarer's Guide to Pilgrimage: 'Ali bin Abi Bakr al-Harawi's Kitab al-Isharat ila Ma'rifat al-Ziyarat* (Princeton, 2004).
Meri, J., 'The Cult of Saints and Pilgrimage', in A. Silverstein and G. Stroumsa (eds), *The Oxford Handbook of the Abrahamic Religions* (Oxford, 2015), pp. 499–517.
Pringle, D., *Pilgrimage to the Holy Land, 1187–1291* (Farnham, 2012).
Reiner, E., 'A Jewish Response to the Crusades: the Dispute over Sacred Places in the Holy Land', in A. Haverkamp (ed.), *Juden und Kristen zur Zeit der Kreuzzüge* (Sigmaringen, 1999), pp. 209–31.

Reiner, E., 'Traditions of Holy Places in Medieval Palestine: Oral versus Written', in R. Sarfati (ed.), *Offerings from Jerusalem: Portrayals of Holy Places by Jewish Artists* (Jerusalem, 2002), pp. 9–19.

Swanson, R. N. (ed.), *The Holy Land, Holy Lands and Christian History* (Woodbridge, 2000).

Walker, P., *The Weekend that Changed the World: The Mystery of Jerusalem's Empty Tomb* (London, 1999).

Weber, E., 'Sharing the Sites: Medieval Jewish Travellers to the Land of Israel', in R. Allen (ed.), *Eastward Bound: Travel and Travellers 1050–1550* (Manchester, 2004), pp. 35–51.

Wilkinson, J., *Jerusalem Pilgrims before the Crusades* (Warminster, 1977).

Wilkinson, J., et al., *Jerusalem Pilgrimage 1099–1185* (London, 1988).

Chapter 12: Sacred Spaces and Holy Places

Auld, S., and R. Hillenbrand, *Ottoman Jerusalem: The Living City: 1517–1917* (London, 2000).

Avner, U., 'Sacred Stones in the Desert', *Biblical Archaeology Review*, 27/3 (May/June 2001): 30–41.

Avner, U., 'Excarnation: Food for Vultures', *Biblical Archaeology Review*, 37/6 (November/December 2011): 40–9, 71.

Barkay, G., 'Mounds of Mystery: Where the Kings of Judah Were Lamented', *Biblical Archaeology Review* 29/3 (May/June 2003): 32–9, 66, 68.

Ben-Arieh, Y., *Jerusalem in the 19th Century: The Old City* (Jerusalem and New York, 1984).

Ben-Arieh, Y., *Jerusalem in the 19th Century: Emergence of the New City* (Jerusalem and New York, 1986).

Bloch-Smith, E., *Judahite Burial Practices and Beliefs about the Dead* (Sheffield, 1992).

Burgoyne, M. H., and D. S. Richards, *Mamluk Jerusalem: An Architectural Study* (London 1987).

Dever, W. G., *What Did the Biblical Writers Know and When Did They Know It?* (Grand Rapids MI, 2001).

Garfinkel, Y., and M. Mumcuoglu, 'Triglyphs and Recessed Doorframes on a Building Model from Khirbet Qeiyafa: New Light on Two Technical Terms in the Biblical Descriptions of Solomon's Palace and Temple', *Israel Exploration Journal* 63 (2013): 135–63.

Hawari, M., *Ayyubid Jerusalem (1187–1250): An Architectural and Archaeological Study* (Oxford, 2007).

Hawkins, R. K., *The Iron Age I Structure on Mt Ebal: Excavation and Interpretation* (Winona Lake IN, 2012).

Hess, R. S., *Israelite Religions: An Archaeological and Biblical Survey* (Grand Rapids MI, 2007).

Hillenbrand, R., and S. Auld (eds), *Ayyubid Jerusalem: The Holy City in Context 1187–1250* (London, 2009).

Hirschfeld, Y., *The Judean Desert Monasteries in the Byzantine Period* (New Haven CT and London, 1992).

Holladay, J. S. Jr, 'Religion in Israel and Judah under the Monarchy: An Explicitly Archaeological Approach', in P. D. Miller Jr, P. D. Hanson, and S. D. McBride (eds), *Ancient Israelite Religion: Essays in Honor of Frank Moore Cross* (Philadelphia PA, 1987), pp. 249–99.

Hurowitz, V. A., *I Have Built You an Exalted House: Temple Building in the Bible in Light of Mesopotamian and Northwest Semitic Writings* (Sheffield, 1992).

Israeli, Y., and D. Mevorach (eds), *Cradle of Christianity* (Jerusalem, 2000).

Johns, J. (ed.), *Bayt al-Maqdis: Jerusalem and Early Islam* (Oxford, 1999).

Levine, L. (ed.), *Ancient Synagogues Revealed* (Jerusalem, 1981).

Levy, T. E., 'Cult, Metallurgy and Rank Societies: Chalcolithic Period (ca. 4500–3500 BCE)', in T. E. Levy (ed.), *The Archaeology of Society in the Holy Land* (New York, 1995), pp. 226–44.

Magen, Y., 'Bells, Pendants, Snakes and Stones: A Samaritan Temple to the Lord on Mt. Gerizim', *Biblical Archaeology Review* 36/6 (November/December 2010): 26–35, 70.

Magness, J., *The Archaeology of Qumran and the Dead Sea Scrolls* (Grand Rapids MI, 2002).

Meshel, Z., *Kuntillet 'Ajrud (Ḥorvat Teman): An Iron Age II Religious Site on the Judah-Sinai Border* (Jerusalem, 2012).

Netzer, E., 'A Synagogue from the Hasmonean Period Recently Exposed in the Western Plain of Jericho', *Israel Exploration Journal* 49 (1999): 203–21.

Petersen, A., *A Gazetteer of Buildings in Muslim Palestine (Part 1)* (Oxford, 2001).

Pringle, D., *The Churches of the Crusader Kingdom of Jerusalem: A Corpus*, 4 vols (Cambridge, 1993–2009).

Raby, J., and J. Johns (eds), *Bayt al-Maqdis: 'Abd al-Malik's Jerusalem* (Oxford, 1992).

Ritmeyer, L., *The Quest: Revealing the Temple Mount in Jerusalem* (Jerusalem, 2006).

Stern, E. (ed.), *The New Encyclopedia of Archaeological Excavations in the Holy Land*, 5 vols (Jerusalem and Washington DC, 1993–2008).

Tsafrir, Y. (ed.), *Ancient Churches Revealed* (Jerusalem, 1993).

Ussishkin, D., 'The Sacred Area of Early Bronze Megiddo', *Bulletin of the American Schools of Oriental Research* 373 (2015): 69–104.

Zevit, Z., *A Study of Ancient Israelite Religions: A Parallactic Approach* (New York, 2001).

Chapter 13: Scripture and the Holy Land

Antrim, Z., *Routes and Realms: The Power of Place in the Early Islamic World* (Oxford and New York, 2012).

Brueggemann, W. *The Land: Place as Gift, Promise, and Challenge in Biblical Faith* (Philadelphia, 1977).

Davies, W. D., *The Gospel and the Land: Early Christianity and Jewish Territorial Doctrine* (Berkeley, 1974).

Janzen, W., 'Land', in D. N. Freedman (ed.), *The Anchor Bible Dictionary*, vol. 4 (New York, 1995), pp. 143–54.

Lightfoot, R. H., *Locality and Doctrine in the Gospels* (New York, 1937).

Lohmeyer, E., *Galiläa und Jerusalem* (Gottingen, 1936).

Minear, P., 'Holy People, Holy Land, Holy City: The Genesis and Genius of Christian Attitudes', *Interpretation* 37 (1983): 18–31.

Munt, H., 'No Two Religions: Non-Muslims in the Early Islamic Hijaz', *Bulletin of the School of Oriental and African Studies* 78/ii (2015): 249–69.

Peters, F. E., *Mecca: A Literary History of the Muslim Holy Land* (Princeton, 1994).

Rubin, U., 'Islamic Retellings of Biblical History', in Y. Tz. Langermann and J. Stern (eds), *Adaptions and Innovations: Studies on the Interaction between Jewish and Islamic Thought and Literature from the early Middle Ages to the late Twentieth Century, Dedicated to Professor Joel L. Kraemer* (Leuven, 2007), pp. 299–313.

Rubin, U., 'Between Arabia and the Holy Land: A Mecca-Jerusalem Axis of Sanctity', *Jerusalem Studies in Arabic and Islam* 34 (2008): 345–62. [Reprinted in: Rubin, U., *Muhammad the Prophet and Arabia*, Variorum Collected Studies Series, no. XI (Ashgate, 2011).]

Rubin, U., 'Muhammad's Night Journey (isra') to al-Masjid al-Aqsa: Aspects of the Earliest Origins of the Islamic Sanctity of Jerusalem', *al-Qantara* 29 (2008); 147–65. [Reprinted in: Rubin, U., *Muhammad the Prophet and Arabia*, Variorum Collected Studies Series, no. VII (Ashgate, 2011)].

Salibi, K., *The Bible Came From Arabia* (London, 1986).

Shoemaker, S., *The Death of a Prophet: The End of Muhammad's Life and the Beginnings of Islam* (Philadelphia, 2011), ch. 4.

Weinfeld, M., 'The Extent of the Promised Land: The Status of Transjordan', in G. Strecker (ed.), *Das Land Israel in biblischer Zeit* (Gottingen, 1983), pp. 59–75.

Wheeler, B. M., *Mecca and Eden: Ritual, Relics, and Territory in Islam* (Chicago, 2006).

INDEX

Page numbers in *italics* refer to illustrations and maps.

PICTURE ACKNOWLEDGEMENTS

akg-images 309; akg-images/Albatross/Duby Tal 247; akg-images/Gérard Degeorge 294; Istanbul Archaeological Museum/akg-images/Erich Lessing 78; akg-images/A.F. Kersting 172; akg-images/Erich Lessing 25, 64; akg-images/Jean-Louis Nou 302; akg-images/Pictures From History 241; akg-images/ullsteinbild 245; Nimrod Aronov/Albatross/Alamy Stock Photo 55; Duby Tal/Albatross/Alamy Stock Photo 15, 51, 122, 127, 248; Nir Alon/Alamy Stock Photo 108; Art Collection 2/Alamy Stock Photo 136; www.BibleLandPictures.com/Alamy Stock Photo 44, 71, 123, 142, 144, 151; The British Museum/World History Archive/Alamy Stock Photo 80; Chronicle/Alamy Stock Photo 238; Globuss Images/Alamy Stock Photo 254; Hemis/Alamy Stock Photo 139 (foot); imageBROKER/Alamy Stock Photo 320; Independent Picture Service/Alamy Stock Photo 138; Hanan Isachar/Alamy Stock Photo 24, 203, 322; The Israel Museum/World History Archive/Alamy Stock Photo 77; Moris Kushelevitch/Alamy Stock Photo 319; Barry Lewis/Alamy Stock Photo 370; Louvre, Paris/Peter Horree/Alamy Stock Photo 251; Musée d'Orsay, Paris/J.Enrique Molina/Alamy Stock Photo 273; Sérgio Nogueira/Alamy Stock Photo 157; Eitan Simanor/Alamy Stock Photo 291; RnDmS/Alamy Stock Photo 231; Walker Art Gallery, Liverpool/Archivart/Alamy Stock Photo 40; World History Archive/Alamy Stock Photo 367; © Badè Museum, Pacific School of Religion 88; www.BibleLandPictures.com/Zev Radovan 82, 295; BibleWalks.com 87, 109, 177, 237, 299; Bischöfliches Dom- und Diözesanmuseum Mainz (SENSUM Graphikbüro, Bernd Schermuly) 206; Biblioteca Medicea-Laurenziana, Florence, Italy/Mondadori Portfolio/Electa/Sergio Anelli/Bridgeman Images 101; Bibliothèque Nationale, Paris, France/Bridgeman Images 219; The Israel Museum, Jerusalem/Bridgeman Images 10, 12, 26, 83, 146; The Israel Museum, Jerusalem, photo: Yoram Lehmann/Bridgeman Images 41; Pictures from History/Bridgeman Images 93; Private Collection/Photo © Zev Radovan/Bridgeman Images 49, 54; © The Trustees of the British Museum 67, 70, 73, 79, 92, 95, 115; Brooklyn Museum, Charles Edwin Wilbour Fund, 54.50.34. CC-BY. Photo: Brooklyn Museum 105;

Cadbury Research Library: Special Collections, University of Birmingham: Mingana Collection, Ms. Christian Arabic 93, p. 3 192; Master and Fellows of Corpus Christi College, Cambridge 226; Courtesy of the Ben-Zvi Institute, Jerusalem. Photo: Ardon Bar Hama 196; Estate of Alistair Duncan 217; Israel Finkelstein 11, 20, 21; Emmanuele Contini/NurPhoto/Getty Images 360; De Agostini Picture Library/Biblioteca Ambrosiana/Getty Images 104; DEA/C. Sappa/De Agostini/Getty Images 214; Godong/UIG/Getty Images 364; Izzet Keribar/Getty Images 355; Richard T. Nowitz/Getty Images 359; Griffin Aerial Imaging, courtesy of the Tel 'Eton Expedition 16; Thomas B. Hall III 325; Richard S. Hess 330; Imperial War Museum. © IWM (Art.IWM ART 2443) 263; Courtesy of the Library of the Institute for Palestine Studies 271, 277; Photo: Clara Amit, courtesy of the Israel Antiquities Authority 166; iStock.com: 211, 236, 233, 292, 135 (top); Courtesy of the Library of Congress 242, 269, 275, 280, 303; Jürgen Liepe 13, 28; Courtesy of the Madaba Plains Project excavations at Tall al-`Umayri, Jordan. Artist: Rhonda Root © 2001: Professor Rhonda Root (Andrews University) 35; Mary Evans Picture Library 261, 279; Mauritshuis, The Hague. Photo: Margareta Svensson 53; Garo Nalbandian 316; National Library of Israel, Yahuda Ms.Ar.969, fol.3 191; Courtesy of the Oriental Institute of the University of Chicago 39, 59; © Denys Pringle 331, 332, 33, 336, 337, 344, 347; © The Ramat Raḥel Excavations, Institute of Archaeology, Tel Aviv University. Photo: Sky-View 96; © RMN-Grand Palais (musée du Louvre)/Mathieu Rabeau 66; Rehav Rubin 187; By permission of Saint Catherine's Monastery, Sinai, Egypt. Photo courtesy of Michigan-Princeton-Alexandria Expeditions to Mount Sinai 184; Photo © 2018 Scala, Florence 171, 176, 285; Sania Sharawi 265; Shutterstock.com 135 (foot), 139 (top), 161, 165, 307; Gianni Dagli Orti/REX/Shutterstock 228; De Agostini Picture Library/REX/Shutterstock 89; David Silverman, dpsimages.com 174; Sonia Halliday Photo Library 221, 313; Courtesy of the Studium Biblicum Franciscanum, Jerusalem 179; T.C. Ministry of Tourism, KUV AM, DOESIMM, and Directorate of Museum of Turkish and Islamic Arts 175; © UK Government Art Collection 267; Uppsala University Library, MS C 691, fol. 39v. 210; Geoff Wiggins 201.

Picture research by Sandra Assersohn